AFTERLIVES OF AFFECT

Afterlives
of Affect

SCIENCE, RELIGION, *and an*

EDGEWALKER'S SPIRIT

....

Matthew C. Watson

DUKE UNIVERSITY PRESS *Durham & London* 2020

Designed by Matthew Tauch
Typeset in Garamond Premier Pro by
WestchesterPublishingSer vices

Library of Congress Cataloging-in-Publication Data
Names: Watson, Matthew C., [date] author.
Title: Afterlives of affect : science, religion,
    and an edgewalker's spirit / Matthew
Watson.
Description: Durham : Duke University

    Press, 2020. | Includes bibliographical
    references and index.
Identifiers: LCCN 2019047961 (print)
LCCN 2019047962 (ebook)
ISBN 9781478007975 (hardcover)
ISBN 9781478008439 (paperback)
ISBN 9781478012078 (ebook)
Subjects: LCSH: Schele, Linda. |
    Anthropology—Philosophy. |
    Ethnology—Philosophy. |
    Anthropology—Methodology. |
    Ethnology—Methodology. | Ethnology—
    Religious aspects. | Anthropological
    ethics. | Anthropologists.
Classification: LCC GN33. W36 2020 (print) |
    LCC GN33 (ebook) | DDC 301.01—dc23
LC record available at https://lccn.loc.gov
    /2019047961
LC ebook record available at https://lccn.loc
    .gov/2019047962

COVER ART: Photograph of Linda Schele at the K'inal Winik
Maya Conference, Cleveland State University, 1988

Contents

....

Acknowledgments

....

I wrote this book on edgewalking across four places of residence and five academic positions. Most of it emerged during periods of deep uncertainty about my academic future. It long felt like a risk that I had no choice but to take. The research that formed its foundation developed through archival work on a distinct dissertation project and series of articles on the politics and ethics of Maya hieroglyphic decipherment, graciously supported by the National Science Foundation and the Wenner-Gren Foundation for Anthropological Research. What follows that project here is an ethnographic story of the aura, or socio-mystical allure, of one figure in the field of decipherment, the late Linda Schele. During a period of delicate social, geographical, and psychic balance, Schele's spectral figure drew me in, offering support. But Schele was more than a tightrope walker's spotter. Both artist and bricoleur, she refashioned the tightrope into a towrope, pulling me back into the world of hieroglyphic decipherment. There she equipped me with new technologies of balance, vision, and—most importantly—imagination. When the initial piece of writing for this project, reprinted here as the chapter "Animals," was published in the journal *Cultural Critique*, I dedicated it to Linda. And Linda Schele—as both person and world (or should I say cosmos?)—merits the first acknowledgment here. Thank you, Linda. I acknowledge you. I owe you more than I know. Our debts to the dead are infinite.

But I'm also indebted in finite, even practical, ways to the living. My education in anthropology at Grinnell College and the University of Florida was superb. At Grinnell, I became enchanted with questions of historical epistemology and ethnographic writing through close work with Katya Gibel Mevorach. Katya honed my composition and editing practices. Her mark on my scholarship has stuck. Jon Andelson was also an inspiring teacher of anthropological approaches to religion and cultural theory. The writing stage of this project was nourished by later engagements with fellow Grinnell alumni. Kate Herold, Allison Foley, and Gabe Rosenberg offered encouragement and willingness to consider protean ideas. I am particularly grateful to Gabe for inviting me to participate in a writing group where I shared an early chapter. He assured me that this weird project had a place, and this support became vital again when I later sought to secure a press.

My experiences at the University of Florida were vibrant—intellectually as well as socially. Susan D. Gillespie offered outstanding, detail-oriented, generatively critical mentorship. This early stage of the project also benefited by the support of generous faculty across departments, including Florence Babb, Brenda Chalfin, Mike Heckenberger, Stacey Langwick, Anthony Oliver-Smith, Peter Schmidt, Malini Johar Schueller, and V. Betty Smocovitis. I am grateful to Lizzy Hare for her long-standing, patient, and caring engagement with my work and with this manuscript. Julienne Obadia has been a vitalizing interlocutor. At UF, I also learned and benefited from diverse engagements with a wide range of friends and colleagues, including Ingrid (Newquist) Ahuja, Roberto Barrios, Scott Catey, Amy Cox Hall, Mike Degani, Jean Dennison, Joe Feldman, Lauren Fordyce, Heather Freiman, Ed González-Tennant, Rebecca Gorman, Rachel Harvey, Kiran Jayaram, Nick Kawa, Karen Pereira, Noelle Sullivan, Josh Toney, Erika (Roberts) Tremble, Bryan Tucker, Megan Teague Tucker, and Jeffrey Vadala.

Following this intensive graduate school experience, I spent six years in visiting positions across four institutions: George Mason University, North Carolina State University, Texas Tech University, and (for my initial year here) Mount Holyoke College. At George Mason, I appreciated the encouragement of Andy Bickford, Johanna Bockman, Lisa Breglia, Hugh Gusterson, Jeffrey Mantz, and Susan Trencher. The two years that followed at North Carolina State University allowed me the space to conceive this book project. Danielle Carr was an insightful and imaginative early reader. I also appreciated the care and encouragement of Raja Abillama, Troy Case, Michaela DeSoucey, A. J. Faas, Nora Haenn, Shea McManus, John Millhauser, Sasha Newell, and Tim Wallace. At Texas Tech, Mario Beruvides, Jaime Cantu, Bruce Clarke, Jen Dunn, Art Durband, Brett Houk, Esther Lee, and Chris Witmore offered thoughtful support.

In western Massachusetts and beyond, I am grateful to diverse friends and colleagues for aid, criticism, inspiration, and encouragement—direct and indirect—at different stages of this project (and this project's kith and kin): Alessandro Angelini, Ed Barnhart, Tom Boellstorff, Matei Candea, Dwight Carey, Amy Coddington, John Collins, Yagil Eliraz, Nora England,

Abou Farman, Mike Fortun, Lolmay Pedro García Matzar, Nora Gortcheva, Sherine Hamdy, Donna Haraway, John Hartigan, Stefan Helmreich, Alanna Hoyer-Leitzel, EJ Jetmore, Alissa Jordan, Rosemary Joyce, Carol Karasik, Peter Keeler, Eleana Kim, Anne Shaw Kingery, Eben Kirksey, Sarah Lynn Knowles, Eduardo Kohn, Roopa Krithivasan, Nicole Labruto, Andy Lass, Ada Link, Martino Lovato, Barb MacLeod, Tim Malacarne, Lynda Manning-Schwartz, William Mazzarella, Lisa Messeri, Julia Miller, Alfonso Morales, Moisés Morales Márquez, Diane Nelson, Morten Nielsen, Sandra Noble, Ruth Ozeki Lounsbury, Anand Pandian, Morten Axel Pedersen, Jason Pribilsky, Dan Rogers, Danilyn Rutherford, Dorion Sagan, Robert Samet, Michael Scanlon, Caterina Scaramelli, Nick Seaver, Allen Shelton, Sydney M. Silverstein, Kate Singer, Jamie Sisson, Spencer Smith, Marilyn Strathern, Eleanor Townsley, Nancy Troike, Ken Tucker, Walter Wakefield, Rick Warner, Caitlin Yoakum, and Marc Zender.

My time at Mount Holyoke College has been a true joy. Having attended Grinnell after growing up in the Wabash College community, I've long valued how liberal arts colleges light the dreams of unsteady funambulists. In the anthropology program at Mount Holyoke, I enjoy a remarkably thoughtful and caring group of colleagues: Elif Babül, Bill Girard, Liz Klarich, Lynn Morgan, Michelle Pietras, Joshua Roth, and Sabra Thorner. Debbora Battaglia, Kasey Clark, and Jack Gieseking each offered careful reads of full manuscript drafts. Debbora has been a particularly impassioned supporter. Thank you for the cosmic care, Debbora. Jack and Kasey each replied to my stories of epistolary intimacies with handwritten letters of their own. I cherish them.

This project transects ethnographic and archival research that I conducted, most intensively during 2007–8, in Guatemala, southern Mexico, and Austin. I am grateful to Mayanists (both amateur and professional), activists, and friends and family of Linda Schele who were willing to speak with me about her (and their) works and lives. David and Elaine Schele were particularly generous, allowing me into their home to review Linda Schele's correspondence and papers. This project is, among other things, an effort to affirm the kinds of fabulous worlds that more-than-charismatic leaders, like Linda, can tow us into. It would not have been possible without David and Elaine.

Working with Duke University Press to breathe book-life into a manuscript has been vitalizing. I'm grateful to Liz Ault for being willing to entertain a weird first book project. Her tactful editorial hand has shaped this into a better book. Stuart McLean and an anonymous reader offered substantive and gracious criticism and direction. I am particularly grateful to Stuart for helping me to imagine a more robustly fictional anthropology. The editorial team and production staff at Duke have been excellent. Thank you.

My time in New England has allowed me the privilege of greater proximity to my immediate family. My parents, Jamie and Dwight Watson, remain among my most careful and supportive readers. They have always encouraged me to imagine one step beyond. Evan and Emily Watson have nourished my edgewalk with familial care, music, and Plan Bee beer. Ellie Watson continues to remind me how permeable the border between reality and fantasy can be. I love you all.

Finally, my affective and intellectual life has become much livelier since it was joined by Li Cornfeld. Li's prescience, poetic imagination, and readerly sensitivity have vitalized my attention to magic of all kinds. My final chapter, here, is on Love. And the afterlife of Love is a life lived, in quarantine and beyond, with you. I admire you, Li.

The trouble with edgewalking is the brute, if cosmic, reality of gravity. I'm sure that, across these pages, I sometimes tumble off the edge. Perhaps it's presumptuous—moot?—to ask the reader to lend a hand in moments of disequilibrium. Whether you, reader, prefer to help steady this writer or see him err into air is your prerogative. Either way, I thank you for being here.

Edgewalking Affect

Imagine yourself walking onto the plaza at Palenque, a Maya archaeological site tucked into the northeastern corner of Chiapas. A crumbling palace, complete with a multistoried tower, sprawls before you. But as you approach the structure, your attention drifts to a steep limestone stairway on the right. Inscription-adorned columns front a temple at the stairway's apex. Pulling your gaze up and away, the sunstruck temple blurs into its mountain backdrop.[1]

Imperial traveler Frederick Catherwood drew Palenque's temples as architectural mountains: living, growing ruins in a struggle against lush tropical flora (figure Intro.1).[2] Palenque walks the edge between culture and nature. It's an architectural growth straddling the lowland plain that spreads from an oily Tabasco coast and the mountains that rise south and southwest toward the Guatemalan border. The site feels awesome, mysterious, a secret folded into the mountainside, among the sylvan homes of hiding jaguars and howling monkeys. Were you to venture into the highlands, toward the site of Toniná and the colonial city of San Cristóbal de las Casas, you'd feel the air cool and dampen. Oversize tropical leaves give way to aromatic pine forests, as cow pastures become coffee plantations.

Yet you have no itch to venture on, to leave Palenque on this quiet, warm afternoon in late December 1973. You unstrap your sandals and sink blistered feet into cool grass, pondering the ponderings of ancient Maya astronomer-priests. You're starting to feel the peace of their oh-so-unmodern lives. Idleness becomes ideal.

FIGURE INTRO.1 — Frederick Catherwood, *General View of Palenque*, 1844. Color lithograph.

But before the serenity sets in, a rustle of moving, muttering bodies distracts you from behind. They're not monkeys, exactly. The eager leader's a striking sight; she's adorned in several shades of denim, paired with a large hat and pair of glasses. You're sizing up the camera strapped to her side, as she calls out: "*Didja* see Venus? Come on! We're off to the tower!" The followers are an oddball assembly—old and young, plump and skinny, threadbare T-shirts brushing against designer safari jackets. They ramble toward the palace observatory, with no impulse to slow or clarify their odd sortie's aim. Your peace now disrupted, your curiosity piqued; there's no choice but to resandal and take flight toward the tower.

A few months later, that Venus-bound frontrunner, Linda Schele (1942–98), would circulate a letter recounting what came next. Then a young art instructor at the University of South Alabama, Schele was rediscovering herself through Palenque. The site seemed to generate a profound emotive and affective response. Palenque spirited Schele. And she wanted, above all else, to share her feelings of discovery, spiritual and scientific alike. She opens the letter with "dear colleagues [*sic*], friends, and friendly crazies" before drawing you into her orbit: "I have been germinating an idea on the tomb lid and the sarcophagus sides ever since Floyd, Masako, Moises, David Schele, and others witnessed the gift that Palenque gave to us to tell us we did good at the pmrp [First Palenque Round Table]."[3] Venus, incarnate in, as, or through Palenque, has offered you a gift.[4]

What might that planetary neighbor and god of love present to late twentieth-century scholars and travelers buzzing about ancient Maya ruins? How might climbing that tower offer a new vision of Palenque? It's a good place to start. After all, the structure's identification as a possible astronomical observatory—rather than merely a watchtower—owed to the presence of a Venus hieroglyph painted onto a landing.[5] Where did Schele's Venus lead?

> As we awatched [sic] the solstice sun set in conjunction with Venus, Jupiter, and high above Mars, the conjunction plunged literally into the top of the [Temple of the] Inscriptions on an angle that seemed to be perfect for the first run of the stairs to the tomb. It was [as] if the sun were being pushed into the underworld through Pacal's tomb by Venus.[6]

The remains of the seventh-century Palenque king, Pakal (formerly spelled Pacal), were deposited below that inscription-adorned temple in an elaborately carved sarcophagus. The sarcophagus lid may be the most widely known Palenque inscription. Its depiction of the descent of Pakal into the maw of the underworld is omnipresent in Palenque tourist kitsch today, long after the stairway to the tomb was closed to visitors.

You knew that you'd witnessed something extraordinary on that solstice afternoon. Schele's animation was evident. But it took a few months for her germinating idea to take solid root:

> When I was talking last Wed. to a group of Gillett's [Grillett Griffin's] friends at Princeton, the implications of that glorious night burst upon my mind and I realized that Palenque had given to us on that night the full interpretation of the tomb lid. I hope you have a good copy of the lid available because here it goes.[7]

The analysis that follows is a poignant if protean account of the astronomical referents of the sarcophagus's enigmatic inscriptions. Do you feel it? If you do, you're not alone. The final typewritten lines of Schele's correspondence express gratitude for the social conditions of this discovery: "Let me add another humble thanks to Betty Benson for letting me get near Floyd [Lounsbury] again. I sat there in awe watching him work." She switches to pen to sign her name and add a final reflection: "Linda (lost in the deserts of South Alabama)."[8]

FIGURE INTRO.2 —
Linda Schele, *Detail of
Maya Hieroglyphs from
Stela 12, Structure 40,
Yaxchilan.* Ink on Mylar
drafting film. DRAWING
(SCHELE NUMBER 6216)
© DAVID SCHELE,
COURTESY FOUNDATION
FOR THE ADVANCEMENT
OF MESOAMERICAN
STUDIES, INC.,
WWW.FAMSI.ORG.

Schele was finding her place in an emerging collective of anthropologists, art historians, and linguists who, in the 1970s, began to make major inroads into the lexical form and linguistic content of ancient Maya inscriptions (figure Intro.2).[9] After a century and a half (or more) of failed efforts to deduce the structure and sense of Maya glyphs, this small group of scholars began to transform these meaning-averse objects into legible modernist "texts."[10] Their originary "*aha* moments" crescendoed into a sustained declaration of unitary originality. Ancient Maya inscriptions were no longer incomprehensible rebus writing comprised of esoteric, nongrammatical astrological content, as some earlier scholars had maintained.[11] The heavens still mattered. But the sky became a limit, tool, and visual form facilitating linguistic knowledge production, rather than signifying a recession into speculation on ancient priestly ideation. Glyphs were fully linguistic signs, not unlike what you're reading right now. The move was nothing less than a self-styled paradigm shift.[12]

With a few minor exceptions, writing on this transformation has been internal to the epigraphers' community. This book makes a different kind of sense, an ethnographic sense, out of their world. Between 2006 and 2008, I completed ethnographic and archival research in three major sites of epigraphic knowledge production and public engagement: Austin, Texas; Palenque, Mexico; and Antigua, Guatemala.[13] In Austin, I participated in a public workshop on decipherment that's happened annually since 1977. I also worked with Schele's extensive research-oriented correspondence. She has shape-shifted into the central figure—both guide and trickster—of this project. Three and a half decades after that solstice afternoon, I spent a summer and change hanging out at Palenque, talking to guides, tourists, and a smattering of amateur Mayanists and expatriates drawn to the site's romantic, trippy allure. The allure is indebted—though not, exactly, for its trippiness—to Schele. And, in Antigua, I interviewed Maya activists who'd learned about the ancient writing system from Schele and her colleagues. They drew on this linguistic and historical resource to strengthen indigenous solidarities across linguistic barriers that starkly divide Guatemalan speakers of Mayan languages.[14]

The ethnographic story that followed this fieldwork offered a sustained critique of decipherment as a public and postcolonial science. Anthropologists have shown that the sciences are in and of culture.[15] Sciences are systems that assemble texts, objects, memories, and bodies into ways of thinking, feeling, imagining, and ordering that we call "knowledge" and, sometimes, "power." And they innovate technologies that transform how we relate, produce, reproduce, and destroy: microchips, medicines, data, bombs, and so on.[16] I have attended to epigraphy as a site of scientific visualization, as a science that produced and depended on committed publics, and as a historical resource with complex political implications for speakers of Mayan languages. I parsed the complicated relationship between Maya archaeologists and epigraphers, who imagine abstract forms such as "history" and "context" in quite disparate and sometimes contradictory ways. As an anthropologist of science, I'd taken my work as showing that Schele and her colleagues were complex, idiosyncratic humans like the rest of us. In narrow terms, their decipherments seemed solid. In broad terms, they seemed to reproduce a range of colonial assumptions about language, text, and history.[17] By attending both to the material practices of workshop pedagogy and to the rather unconsidered Eurocentric ideology of language and text in play, I raised some epigraphers' hackles.

This project, nonetheless, takes off in another direction, traces a different line of flight, or opens a distinct sphere of exchange.[18] Once I surfaced from my initial immersion into the glyphers' social and epistemic world, I began

FIGURE INTRO.4 —
Peter Mathews and Linda
Schele, 1973 Round Table.
IMAGE FROM *CRACKING
THE MAYA CODE*.

to reread Schele's letters and rethink the field's sensibilities. On returning to the digitized archive, I was struck, again and again, by Schele's joy in decipherment, the feel of Palenque's spirit bursting into Schele's active, curious mind. Rereading led me toward a more empathetic understanding of her effusive imagination. Many of her scholarly peers, and certainly the succeeding generation of epigraphers, have sought to domesticate and control her excessive elation. But I came to feel, as a deeper, intuitive truth, the joy that Schele channeled as she built a committed public of amateur epigraphers, lovers of the ancient Maya.

EXTRAORDINARY AFFECTS

This is a book about extraordinary affects at an intersection of cultural, historical, and scientific research.[19] Its core image or motif is the break from everyday knowledge production. Such breaks imbued a rather banal space of historical research with an aura of joyous revelation. The break from the everyday that emerges most vividly here is Schele's visual encounter with the nighttime sky, a series of imaginative experiments that cultivated, in Schele, a profound understanding of—and attachment to—a reconstructed ancient Maya cosmology or astrology. The book itself breaks from science studies frames and follows such moments of constellational exploration into fields of animating, affective effusion. Altogether, *Afterlives of Affect* takes decipherment as a site of late twentieth-century discovery that embraced, and even propagated, a zestful, contagious high-modern enthusiasm. This amounts to an experimental ethnography that tiptoes at times toward ficto-criticism and takes anthropology itself as the science of the extraordinary or the alien. I warn you here, at the outset, that this is quite unlike narratives of discovery offered by those involved in hieroglyphic decipherment. It won't reaffirm the triumphant rhetoric that has framed dominant stories of how scholars turned inscribed stones, pots, and codices into lively, voiced texts. It turns this triumphalism—and the experiences that animated it—into a site for considering the affect of discovery, as an expression of excess that blurs domains including science, history, art, and religion.

Discovery, viewed critically, appears blissfully naive, a feeling predicated on a failure to grasp the historically situated, social, and contingent character of all claims to knowledge. It is this deflationist pessimism that I *experiment against* here. I value feminist critiques of the scientific gaze's "abstract masculinity" as a form coconstructed with a demure, resistant, sexualized

Nature.[20] But I want something more. I want to feel the contagious effervescence of discovery, as an exceptional, vitalizing encounter, and even as a cosmic revelation: the stars coming into line. I want to feel this through the traces of Linda Schele, as a spiritual figure who helped to popularize a new image of the ancient Maya, an image that enlivened her followers, an image that calls us to rediscover discovery. Blinded by the flash of discovery, I offer this extraordinary affect as a site for opening up *an excitable anthropology*. An excitable anthropology struggles against the field's deflationist, pessimistic, and nihilistic impulses.[21] It's a glowing semantic oversaturation of human liveliness and postliveliness that has no time for anthropology's gloomy, gothic deflation of worlds, its tendency to dispense with excitement through whatever critical sensibility's du jour.

So, this is less a descriptive treatise on or about than the trace of an experiment in becoming inspired by a lively responsiveness. I have reinscribed—and, hence, transformed—this economy of affect as I've worked to inhabit it. Ethnographic moods and methods dictate that such an experiment should follow from shared experience, immersion into a world that predicates its subsequent textual reduction. My ethical, aesthetic, and practical obligation, then, is to evoke—virtually, through the mediation of texts—a site that overflowed, at times, with an ebullient genius. I do so as an ally of the archaeologists. I was trained in archaeology but have since wandered off. From this meandering position, I construct an image of decipherment, in an intricate guise, as an erotic, artistic science, rather than a dusty hermetic and hermeneutical bookishness. This image evokes Schele's attachment to the experience of discovery, the sudden flash of insight that transformed semantically opaque inscriptions into legible, sensible signs.[22]

By traversing edges between science, religion, history, and art, Schele energized diverse followers to take up hieroglyphic studies. A contemporary and colleague of Carl Sagan, she embodied and popularized the extraordinary affect of discovery-bound, cosmic revelation. The story here honors her edgewalking, her spiritual science. Decipherment was an organically structuralist science that took on, through Schele's personage, a spiritual dimension. The 1970s–80s struggles between structuralism and competing theoretical perspectives—particularly Marxism—that played out broadly in the US and French academies also flared at times in this corner of Maya studies. But I have worked to reanimate this science with a difference, to spirit it into other conversations, other ways of feeling and reflecting. This is a story, then, not of Schele alone (as person or figure), but of the passionate optimism of late twentieth-century modernism. It is a story of "systems of attitudes" and "structures of feeling" that animated structuralism and interpretive anthropology,[23] twentieth-century language-obsessed methods and epistemologies that shared the hopeful sense that interpretation could be endlessly deepened, that knowledge might be progressively accrued, that "the sky's the limit."

This amounts to a future-oriented memorialization tracking a realm of inspired attachments to a hyperreal ancient Maya world.[24] It takes Maya studies as a site for considering how historical and cultural inquiry generates affective and semiotic attachments that belie dominant cultural and ideological distinctions between science and religion.[25] I am interested in showing how a historical moment fans imaginative methods at the edge of self and other, past and present, knowledge and belief. Positioned against the fears of the Cold War and the prevalent paranoias of twentieth-century critical theory, the book shapes a virtualized Schele into a complex being—and a complex of beings both human and not—engaged in historical knowledge production through a science of decoding that is at once spiritual, scientific, and aesthetic.[26] In Schele's care, this science became a quasi-spiritualist sacralization of an indigenous past. Schele emerges here not simply as a charismatic authority, let alone a naive appropriator of indigenous culture, but as the mediator, the anima, the breath or soul of ancient Maya lords re-membered through structuralist ordering practices and revoiced for the 1970s and 1980s.[27] Decipherment, in an experimental, affect-oriented reading, comes to exemplify a moment of optimistic modernism that breathed the possibility of spiritual imagination into an ever-more-alienated and seemingly secular world.[28]

I am accompanying or supplementing Schele as a formful being who generated a more capacious cosmos than she could have anticipated.[29] My responsibility is to cast off critical inhibitions in order to inhabit this time-bending cosmic ecology. But this isn't just a matter of ethnographic inhabitation and description; my hope is to transmit Schele's cosmos into a dreamy *beyond*, transforming her "edgewalking"—Schele's word—into an anthropological provocation to live well with the dead, and a theo-anthropological experiment that refuses, obdurately, to cede its claim to scientificity. Through waxing and waning attention to one popular scholar, *Afterlives of Affect* speaks nearby Schele's decipherment as a system that irreverently ignored the borders dividing aesthetics, science, and religion.[30]

As an ethnographic technique, "speaking *nearby*"—Trinh T. Minh-ha's phrase—may fail the anthropological obligation to speak *of* decipherment—as an ecology of cultural, religious, and scientific practices—in its own terms.[31] But speaking nearby introduces an array of other obligations, including the obligation to render ethnographic accounts that exceed close and careful reportage hinged to interpretive or critical elaboration. Ethnography can navigate between evocation and interpretation, becoming a space of experimental makings and a literary technology for sociocultural critique.[32] Ethnography can partake of and transmit worldly—or supraworldly, cosmic—fantasies, affects, and forms of magic.

Ethnographers have long fixated on the excessive, the magical, the mysterious, and the sublime. Along these lines, James Clifford has tracked ethnography's weave with 1920s French surrealism.[33] Marcel Mauss's fixation on exotic forms of magic and exchange tangled with Georges Bataille's erotics, an affirmation of transgression and excess, and a dalliance with death.[34] Bataille's ethnological surrealism drew him to an image of Mexico, and, particularly, to an aesthetic valorization of human sacrifice among the Aztecs. Such surrealist—or hyperrealist—narratives constructed indigenous Mesoamerica as a critical alterity exceeding and destabilizing "Western" norms of rationality and order; and it remained such in Schele's constructions. Mauss's and Bataille's romanticism left a lasting imprint on works of French and US philosophy and philosophical anthropology. A Maussian attention to the dialectics of exchange and personhood helped refine the critical projects of Claude Lévi-Strauss and Jacques Derrida, just as Bataille's excess-oriented Nietzschean vision helped propel the neovitalist experiments of Michel Foucault, Gilles Deleuze, and followers such as Trinh and Clifford in literary theory and anthropology. The tension—both epistemological and aesthetic—between dialectical critique and affective affirmation remains in anthropology today, and it has come to pervade the theoretical substratum of this book.[35]

The analysis here tracks the limits of dialectical frames through attention to affectively saturated scenes of discovery that break from conventional images of knowledge production, including images generated by both scientists and science studies critics. Along these lines, I have found Walter Benjamin's concept of the "dialectical image" particularly generative.[36] Consider these passages from Benjamin:

> It's not that what is past casts its light on what is present, or what is present its light on what is past; rather, image is that wherein what has been comes together in a flash with the now to form a constellation. In other words, image is dialectics at a standstill. For while the relation of the present to the past is a purely temporal, continuous one, the relation of what-has-been to the now is dialectical: it is not progression

but image, suddenly emergent.—Only dialectical images are genuine images (that is, not archaic); and the place where one encounters them is language.[37]

> Where thought comes to a standstill in a constellation saturated with tensions, there appears the dialectical image. It is the caesura in the movement of thought. Its positioning, of course, is in no way arbitrary. In a word, it is to be sought at the point where the tension between the dialectical oppositions is the greatest. The dialectical image . . . is identical to the historical object; it justifies blasting the latter out of the continuum of history's course.[38]

The dialectical image, then, appears as a bind suspending the processual, temporal movement of history and thought. Maybe it's the historical object becoming fugitive, freeing itself from systemic capture by the machine of dialectical movement. It resonates, then, with Fred Moten's construction of improvisation in jazz.[39] Improvisation becomes an escape from the dialectical structure of performance, a break from any conceit of structure, save the conceit that demarcates the limits of improvisation, articulating a difference between play that conforms, to some extent at least, to an established—even inscribed—musical structure and play that liberates itself from the confines or expectations of such structures. Improvisation jams structure, just as "image is dialectics at a standstill," jamming the history-machine's gears.

Affect theory, I suggest, lends the dialectical image with metaphysical form. It takes shape as the improvisational jam of historical process. It amounts to a sensitive and sensible appeal to a language of antiteleological and antidialectical becoming.[40] The magic of science studies scholars' affirmations of worldly objects as agential or active beings amounts to their elevation to the status of dialectical images. It's likely no coincidence that the kinds of objects that have activated affirmationist thinkers' *breaks* from dialectical-historical reasoning are often *scientific* objects, both facts and epistemic things proclaimed by scientist-spokespersons to be timeless, atemporal.

The emergence of these epistemic things breaks the processual movement of science as science-in-action. The gene is such a dialectical image, as is the Classic Maya king Pakal. They are actors or forms rendered knowable and consequential through scientific processes of dialectical reasoning; they emerge from such processes, but, subsequently, take shape as ahistorical beings, facts no longer constrained by the contingencies and uncertainties of the worldly process of scientists doing scientific things, building scientific systems. They may be *surprises*; the surprise, as the deconstructive moment of unsettling encounter with the unknown, the deconstructive encounter that calls us into provisional realizations that we no longer know ourselves, that we have never really known ourselves; the dialectical image arrives as a surprise.[41] The discovery—or *aha* moment—is such a surprise, what Jacques Derrida calls the *arrivant*.[42]

This book seeks to gift the reader a field of discovery—Maya hieroglyphic decipherment, or epigraphy—as a field of dialectical images that broke from historical reasoning in a manner demonstrative, even indicative, of a late twentieth-century, high-modernist epistemic confidence and optimistic joy. It's a story of epigraphic discoveries as surprising breaks from processes of historical reasoning. I've taken up moments in which a historical-dialectical mode of reasoning—typically implicit among the epigraphers and archaeologists discussed here—gives way to a being or form that seems to generate unusually heightened feelings. This deeply Euroamerican set of beliefs and feelings—the feelings and beliefs that we call Maya epigraphy—entailed a constitutive alternation between historical reasoning, reasoning that could be conceived within a dialectical language, and moments of imaginative, affectively saturated escape.

At its stylistic surface, this remains a work of experimental anthropological theory. I respond to Anand Pandian and Stuart McLean's incitement to modes of ethnographic curiosity and craft that treat "writing as a practice immanent to the world, rather than as a detached reflection upon the world."[43] They continue: "Imagine ways of writing that might put ourselves more deeply at risk than what we have tried till now. What could such experiments look like, and what, if anything, might they achieve?"[44] The experiment here aspires toward immersion into a historical dreamworld that hinged on a joyous affect, if not an "apparatus of *jouissance*."[45] It leans at times toward a US southern regional affect that weaves the ordinary's excess into a textured, textual exuberance layered with despair, as exemplified by the poignant ethnographic evocations of Kathleen Stewart and Allen Shelton.[46] But the ruination at work in ancient Maya studies is a more dispersed worlding, with diverse bodies, spirits, and letters crossing the Rio Grande, assembling in sites such as Austin and Palenque. These spirits congeal into beings that inhabit and animate ruins that may evoke liveliness more than plight.

Affect-oriented literary ethnographers such as Stewart and Shelton offer us spirited and spiriting works of prose.[47] Stewart's *Ordinary Affects* sets aside

heavy-handed theoretical exposition in favor of a kind of auratic suggestion. In vignette after vignette, she develops a work of exquisite, if at times
discomfiting, evocation. *Ordinary Affects* layers scenes of hope or despair,
marked periodically by the possibility of some experience or form of life
coalescing before giving way to tendrils of feeling and movement that either
dissipate the temporarily achieved social organism or leave us in a kind of
impasse. We may find ourselves in impasses knowingly—an experience that
may lead to self-doubt or depression—or unknowingly, which Lauren Berlant
captures with the poignant phrase "cruel optimism."[48] Such ethnographic
poiesis immerses readers into both fluxes and structures of feeling in the
contemporary United States, as we endeavor to imagine more peaceable,
just, and flourishing futures, a real challenge in the present. Stewart has
turned America—and I use that troubling noun deliberately—into an assemblage of ethnographic fragments. But if any affect-oriented or fictocritical
work captures unstable Schele-esque American dreamworlds, it's Shelton's
Where the North Sea Touches Alabama.[49] Shelton's book tumbles through
mourning into dream after dream of excessively layered southern pasts. A
bulldozer-operator unearths a nineteenth-century coffin on the Shelton
family's Alabama property, and Shelton begins to inhabit the fantasy—the
knowledge—that it contained the corpse of his friend Patrik Keim, a decay
artist whose figure resists exorcism. Dreams within fantasies within dreams
within landscapes within fantasies within love.

Schele won't be easy to exorcise either. One book surely isn't enough to
pull it off. Her knotty roots haven't yet succumbed to the rot that turns us
into soil. And colonial soil is quite sticky. I don't think that decipherment
can be cleansed with finality of what sociologist Aníbal Quijano termed the
"coloniality of power."[50] Historical narratives wind through colonial and
capitalist productions of race and culture, as objects of knowledge, fantasy
(never innocent), and political control.[51] Reconstructions of ancient Maya
elites' inscriptions as writing do more than celebrate indigenous ingenuity.
They reconstitute the traces of past actors for present ends, including tourism
industries' capitalist ends and states' nationalist ends.[52] Failure to perceive
epigraphy's imbrications in morphologies of capitalist exploitation often
reads, to me, as naive complicity. The cosmological accounts that I take up
here involved epigraphers' arrogation of authority to characterize the inner
lives of precolonial indigenous persons. Ancient names, scenes, and figures,
like the ceramic pots on which they were painted, are commodifiable forms.
They are historical-aesthetic objects simulated and circulated through tourist

economies and patrimonial projects that strategically instrumentalize and profit from an aestheticized indigeneity shorn of its decolonial politics.[53]

"Maya," after all, is an extrinsic, translinguistic, transstate colonial and post-colonial ethnonym that disciplines, represses, and extracts value from hetero-geneous collectives, reduced to "culture(s)" or, even worse, "population(s)."[54] In the wake of these discursive-political mechanisms of repression, we should remember that the coloniality of power contains and, in some ways, scripts its social-metaphysical inverse, the power of decoloniality.[55] Tracing the po-litical, cultural, and religious functions of terms such as "Maya culture" and "Maya hieroglyphs" with ethnographic nuance helps to reconstitute them as resources for decolonial struggle. This struggle may involve indigenous activists' and allies' efforts to resituate and resignify such terms of colonial discourse or—in what we might term an "ethno-pessimist" frame—to an-nihilate them in the service of liberating ensouled but indigenized bodies.[56] Such political struggles, of course, have their own complex, highly debated histories within fields of Maya—including pan-Maya—activism.[57]

In spaces of such (de)colonial tension, experimental ethnography com-prises an allied field of aesthetic interventions that strategically opt to suspend methods of critique in order to become differently attuned to our objects, allowing their magic to transform us (which does not mean internalizing their ideologies). Here I background the sometimes-paranoid tools of criti-cal theory to take up a (mostly) affirmative effort to speak nearby Schele, in her world of 1970s–1980s optimism.[58] I won't pummel you with too much biographical detail. Instead, I'll offer an opportunity to feel with Schele's effort to feel the ancient Maya as an unsettling of present predicaments, colonial and otherwise. This unsettling certainly doesn't mean that Schele's historical practices were not deeply implicated in settler colonial states that have long constructed the Maya as an object of both colonial repression and imperial fantasy.[59] But it does mean that even cultural systems as parochial as Maya studies—a field long predicated on romanticizing the "closed corporate community"—may offer us vital concepts to think our way across the divide between science and religion.[60] If you edgewalk with us, be willing to fall.

EPI-BIOGRAPHY

In an interview that served as the basis of a short documentary about her contributions to Maya hieroglyphic decipherment, Schele labeled herself an "edgewalker." As I have here, the filmmakers took up the term in their title:

Edgewalker: A Conversation with Linda Schele.[61] Released the year after her death, the material for the documentary appears to be a single interview with Schele, conducted after she was diagnosed with pancreatic cancer. The producers make prominent, if not exactly probing, use of the edgewalker concept; they mobilize the term in the title and open with Schele's self-description as such. A discussion of the film serves the dual purpose of providing biographical background on Schele and cutting to the core of this book's thematic claim, that science and religion—as heterogeneous bodies of knowledge and affective modes of becoming—synthesize (though not without risk or remainder) in sites of historical and cultural knowledge production. The biography-oriented film amounts to an effectively crafted story that textures a thoroughly American subject. Its similarity to other sources that dip into Schele's biographical being, such as archaeologist Michael Coe's *Breaking the Maya Code*, suggest that it's a coherent public self-fashioning of Schele's making.[62]

Linda Dean Schele (née Richmond) was born October 30, 1942, in Nashville, Tennessee. As Coe recounts, with a few of Schele's words, she grew up a Tennessee "redneck."[63] Her father had been a farmer and, in the film, she describes her mother as hailing from a "hillbilly" Tennessee family.[64] Throughout her life, Schele spoke with a marked Tennessee drawl. She describes her parents as hard workers with limited education who achieved incremental socioeconomic success after the Great Depression and Second World War. Her mom worked as a commercial artist in advertising and her dad became a salesman, starting his own business in the early 1960s. They had two children: Linda and Thomas. The documentary draws the viewer through family photos of Schele's childhood as she describes how they achieved "upper-middle-class" status. Linda attended Litton High School, where she played basketball, before leaving suburban Nashville for the University of Cincinnati.

In college Linda "fell in love" with the world of academia. Initially conforming to her parents' desire that she undertake a sufficiently vocational track, she began her college career as an advertising major. After a year, she switched to fine arts, but agreed to take a BS degree in education to help ensure her employability. Betraying the habits of speech that proved alluring to some of Schele's public followers, she remarks, "I always liked the BS part of that." And a young professor introduced her to English literature, an experience that Linda called "a rare, unreproducible, intellectual journey into magic."[65] She opted to pursue literature at the next level, enrolling in an MA program at the University of Connecticut. But the experience was disappointing; Linda used the phrase "nitpicking bullshit" to describe her year in Connecticut.

Graduate work in literary studies seemed to cast aside the big themes of Western thought and the "joy of reading great works" for critical analyses of minutiae.[66] So Linda left the graduate program and worked for a year at Boston's Electric Boat Corporation.[67] There she was a piping draftsman for atomic submarines: "After a year of that, I truly did not want to work." In lieu of employment, she returned to the University of Cincinnati and to painting. Back in Ohio, she adopted her instructor's "philosophy of the happy accident." As Michael Coe has summarized, it went like this:

> (1) know your craft very, very well; (2) get your first mark on paper or canvas; (3) go on from there, "keeping yourself in an alpha state, so that when a happy accident happens, you are prepared to follow it wherever it will lead you." "That's what I do when I do research," Linda says. "I just set out a very large sort of vacuum-cleaner, trying to pattern all of the data I can, without any predisposition of what is going to come, and then let the damn stuff pattern on me, and I start following the patterns wherever they lead me."[68]

Little did Schele anticipate that she would spend the second half of her life offering vital contributions to a scholarly field oriented almost exclusively to minutiae. Especially during the early years of decipherment, the field's epistemic form entailed producing incremental readings of discrete hieroglyphic sign elements. But what makes Schele worthy of close treatment is not a diligent attentiveness to the narrow, intricate, everyday work of decipherment. It is, instead, this will-to-joy, this desire to follow the happy accidents wherever they lead. Decipherment, for her, involved an ongoing, if irregular, series of small discoveries. Rather than seeing hieroglyphic studies as a chore or a bore, she seems to have regarded it as an opportunity for continuous worldly discovery. She lent this dimension of discovery with profound, perhaps inflated, importance. She did so in part by recognizing and rectifying the everyday banality of decipherment, weaving particular emergent readings into the grand historical narratives of ancient Maya lords' lives.[69]

But before Schele turned to Maya studies, she completed her MFA in art in 1968. Concerned that her husband, David Schele, would be drafted and sent to Vietnam, Linda took the first job offered to her, a teaching position at the University of South Alabama. Early in their time in Alabama, the couple decided to take advantage of their proximity to and connections in Mexico.

David knew architects who were collaborating with scholars on a project at the Maya site of Chichén Itzá. Linda states that they had a last-minute itinerary and route change that led them to the site of Palenque. Having stopped in the city of Villahermosa, the couple visited an archaeological and zoological park, La Venta, where they met an "exiled" Salvadoran who encouraged them to seek out, in Palenque, the tour guide, amateur Mayanist, and entrepreneur Moises Morales. With Schele unable to pronounce the Spanish name *Moises*, the Salvadoran apparently implored them, "Just ask for Moses." On arriving in Palenque, they toured about before encountering this legendary Moses while walking out of the site. Linda and David stayed in Palenque for twelve days. Moises introduced Linda to the Mayanist art historian Merle Greene Robertson. Schele was taken with the site and the people who gravitated to it. So she began to learn from Robertson, an experience that would set the stage for her subsequent public and not-so-public collaborations with a smattering of Mayanist scholars and amateurs.

Schele's attachment to Palenque was no temporary romantic fling (as Moises, who witnessed the constant flow of enamored visitors, assumed it would be). They returned that summer; Robertson was building her house— named Na Chan-Bahlum—in Palenque. Schele began to reconstruct herself and her career in close dialogue, often over drinks, with Robertson and the archaeological ceramics expert Robert Rands. She describes this as a "sort of *magic* time in Palenque."[70] The site, Schele says, "hit me so hard." Through Palenque, Schele came to feel herself a deeply animated and empowered being. She had cast aside literary criticism to embrace the joys of visual art. But here, in this encounter with a place formed by rulers and artists of the first millennium of the current era, Schele came to realize that she might offer the world more than her surrealist paintings.

At the time, Schele regularly taught a broad survey course on the introduction to art, a course that presented art out of context or, as she says, in a nonchronological, nonhistorical framework. After two years of teaching the course, she apparently had begun to question what it would feel like to inhabit a society where art, *rather than science*, was understood as the central cultural practice and mechanism of social cohesion. In Palenque's stucco-adorned temples, she saw—she *imagined*—this world with art at its core. And there were serious questions to ask about what some of that stucco and stone signified. She tried to learn it from the masters, reading Sir J. Eric S. Thompson's *Maya Hieroglyphs without Tears*. But she found herself frustrated to the point of crying through it.[71]

In late December 1973, Robertson put on a public workshop, the first (of many) Palenque Round Tables, or Mesa Redondas.[72] There Schele met a student of archaeology, Peter Mathews, and an eminent linguistic anthropologist and Yale professor, Floyd Lounsbury. In *Breaking the Maya Code*, Coe revels in Schele's contrast with the archaeological aristocracy:

> The minute I met Linda Schele at the Palenque conference, I thought, "Here's somebody who would have never made the Carnegie 'Club'": with shirttails hanging over her faded jeans, her then-chubby face wreathed in smiles, her salty Southern speech, her ribald sense of humor, she would have horrified Eric Thompson, Harry Pollock, and the rest of the Carnegie crowd.[73]

In 1924, archaeologists funded by the Carnegie Institution of Washington began an extensive excavation and reconstruction of Chichén Itzá.[74] Linda was no Carnegie, no snobby scholar. She was no Sir J. Eric S. Thompson. But the trip, and the site of Palenque in particular, drew her into the ancient Maya world and its profession. So, while Linda "would have never made the Carnegie 'Club,'"[75] she also would have never made the ancient Maya the Maya we know today without it.

Linda emerged from that meeting as an interloper unburdened by academic dogma stumbling, Venus-bound, into a series of profound discoveries. She was an outsider with a keen aesthetic eye who teamed up with Mathews and Lounsbury to upend the Carnegie Club's doctrinaire interpretation of Maya glyphs as abstract symbols and rebus writing that didn't amount to a fully grammatical script. Together they determined the broad outline of the Palenque dynastic sequence, making sense of inscriptions that conveyed major dynasts' names and dates (figures Intro.4 and Intro.5). The Round Table entailed sessions in the morning and evening, leaving the afternoon for the participants to head up to the site, where they could examine the enigmatic hieroglyphic inscriptions directly. Although Linda characterizes this experience as the "scarediest [*sic*] time," she also emphasizes that Lounsbury and Coe went out of their way to welcome her into a fold populated by moneyed elites and still tasting of antiquarianism. Schele would have to make a decision. As she puts it, "There came a point around 1974 or 1975 . . . I just sat there and realized that I had a choice to make . . . and it included this built-in prohibition against betraying the art. . . . Did I want to be teaching painting as a mediocre painter at a third-level university in the outbacks of the United States, or did I want to be a world-famous Mayanist?"[76]

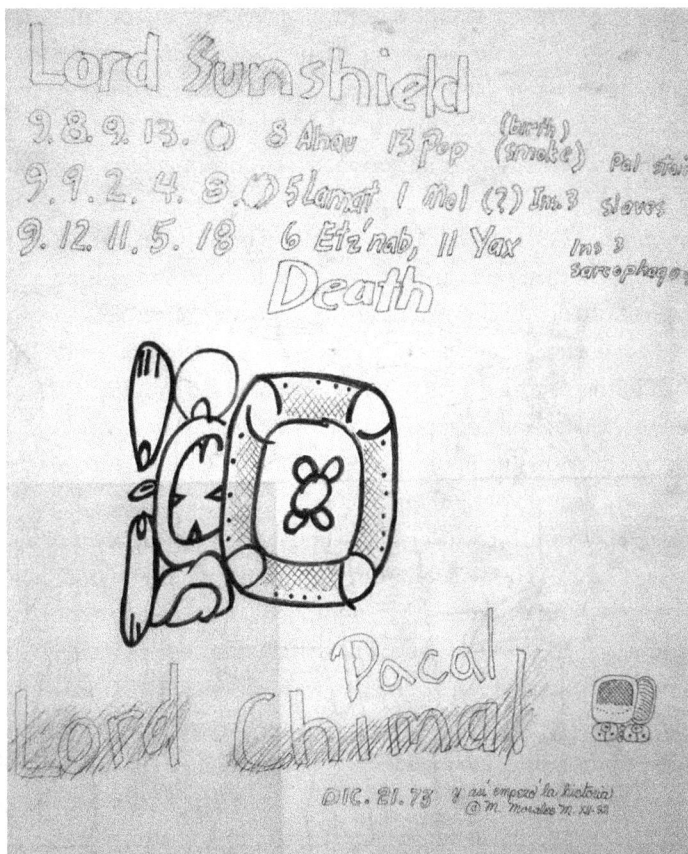

FIGURE INTRO.5 — Poster presenting the decipherment of *Pacal* (later changed to *Pakal*), hung on the wall at the first Palenque Round Table meeting. ACCESS TO THE POSTERS FOR THE PURPOSE OF REPRODUCTION WAS PROVIDED BY ALFONSO MORALES.

So, it happened that, in 1980, an artist who couldn't speak a Mayan language completed (after three rushed years) a PhD in Latin American Studies at the University of Texas (UT)–Austin, with an award-winning dissertation titled "Maya Glyphs: The Verbs."[77] Before writing the thesis, Schele had already begun to offer public workshops on hieroglyphic analysis at UT-Austin. The pedagogical method developed for the workshops cultivated awareness of aesthetic patterns in inscriptions that reflect underlying grammar, namely sentence structure and some elements of syntax. Schele had begun to play an integral role in the continuous, slow, and laborious project of hieroglyphic decipherment. She worked in close collaboration with Mathews and Lounsbury, and, despite serious limitations to her understanding of Mayan languages, she helped train the next generation of Mayanist epigraphers, including the MacArthur "Genius Grant" recipient David Stuart. Perhaps most importantly, she continued to put on annual glyph workshops at UT-Austin, and, late in her career, taught the basics of decipherment to speakers of Mayan languages in Guatemala and Yucatán.[78] At the height of their popularity in the 1980s, hundreds of aspiring-amateur epigraphers attended Schele's UT-Austin workshops. Over the course of her career, Schele increasingly became a part of the intellectual establishment that had initially seemed alien to her. Why, then, did she and her followers stick with the edgewalker trope? In what ways did she maintain a balancing act? Schele offers us an opportunity to speculate about what edgework (to twist Wendy Brown's phrase) might entail.[79]

Here I seek to inhabit Schele's edgy world with an ethnographic difference. I partake of Schele's cosmic sublime by tracking her rhetoric of decipherment from the muck and muddle of the tropospheric plane of terran cobecoming into a stratospheric sublime, a floating-off that ultimately entangles Schele with fellow high-modernist apollonian travelers, including Carl Sagan and David Bowie. "Troposphere," which designates the atmospheric stratum that we Earth-bound beings inhabit, derives from the same Greek root that offers us "trope," language's escape into the figurative. "Trope" can also designate ancient Greek skepticism, musical notations guiding chants of the Torah, verses sung in Christian services, and the sun's apparent and seemingly deceitful change of course at the solstice.[80] I am encouraging a self-aware, rather weird (or tropospheric), and consistently self-critical elaboration of—and escape from—the ethnographic dialectic. I'm advocating for Linda Schele as a trickster guide calling us to follow her rabbit-footsteps, inspiring us to better inhabit an interspecies, interspiritual troposphere.

STRUCTURE

Chapter 1, "Sacrilege," takes form as an experimental series of layered, intersecting vignettes. Reading Schele's archive alongside Maya ethnography, archaeology, and critical theory, the chapter moves through intertwined evocations of sacrilege, the life/death boundary, Maya spirit companionship, and sorcery. By bringing Schele's professional correspondence into conversation with Mayanist ethnography, I begin to rethink Schele's artistic and epigraphic method as a mystical practice of engaging the dead. I also introduce the corollary problem of Schele's role as a sustaining spiritual presence mediated through her traces—writing, images, and memories—in the contemporary world.

Chapter 2, "Animals," follows by developing how the contemporary privileging of life, or *bios*, in cultural anthropology, science studies, and Continental philosophy risks substituting biocentrism for anthropocentrism, thus reifying "life" in the effort to undo it. I open up a sympathetic critique of anthropologists' efforts to extend the field's subject or object of knowledge beyond the human. This critique takes shape through descriptions of my ethnographic encounters with David Schele and with animal art in the margins of Linda's letters. The chapter attends carefully to Schele's rich engagements with other beings (including Maya hieroglyphs, animal spirit companions, ancient Maya scribes, and her scholarly collaborators). It shows how Schele navigated boundaries between life and death, present and past, human and animal, writing and art, scholar and amateur, science and religion, and rationality and irrationality.

Chapter 3, "Cosmos," explores personal and intellectual attachments among seven researchers: Dorion Sagan, Carl Sagan, Linda Schele, Ilya Prigogine, Isabelle Stengers, Lynn Margulis, and me. I evoke how their circuitous connections conditioned distinctive forms of knowledge production that eschewed clear classification as art history, philosophy, or physical and biological science. The chapter follows how such pathways of personal and cosmological experience animate historical and scientific knowledge claims and blur the line that demarcates the spiritual and the scientific. In particular, it suggests that science and cosmology tend to converge when we attempt to address and cope with the unthinkable nature of death (and, by implication, the form of history). Thus, the problem of human finitude in the face of the vast temporal and spatial expanses of the cosmos should encourage both humility and openness in knowledge production.

We turn, then, from the sky back to the earth in chapter 4, "Bones." Here I bring Schele's encounters with the ancient Maya dead into engagement with explorations of finitude and mortality in the writing of novelist Ruth Ozeki and the bone paintings of Georgia O'Keeffe. Ozeki is the daughter of Schele's close collaborator and correspondent, linguistic anthropologist Floyd Lounsbury. Drawing inspiration from Ozeki in responding to G. W. F. Hegel's famous claim that "Spirit is a bone,"[81] the chapter traces how writerly and artistic creativity offset finitude and mortality. Here I develop the claim that Schele's approach to decipherment was an artistic and spiritual means to live with and beyond death and that she increasingly incorporated Maya cosmological practices into this process against the religious-cultural backdrop of US Protestantism.

Chapter 5 takes Schele as a site for rethinking "genius." In its US reception, the notion of a culture's spirit or genius carries resonances of nineteenth-century Romanticism and even spiritualism. Spiritualism took communication with the dead, often through mediums or "spirit guides," as a central practice. Examining Schele's historical praxis as a form of Romantic spirit mediation, the chapter critically assesses the popular image of the genius. I continue to elaborate how Schele's neospiritualism involved rendering Maya cosmological doxa intelligible within the implicitly Protestant frames of US public life. Examining Schele's specific experiences of creative historical imagination, the chapter reinvigorates a spiritual sense of "genius" as a being or medium capable of breathing life into the words of the dead. Here I press explicitly against institutionalized academic assumptions that systems of historical knowledge require "secular" framings or foundations and suggest that they may be suited to neospiritualism.

The final chapter, "Love," circles an exemplary piece of "fan mail" sent to Schele. Treating Schele as a subject of adoration—an exemplary *amateur*, or lover—the chapter works through "love" in ethical and religious terms as a minimal expression of collective, common world-making. I take up love as a powerful resource for rethinking historical knowledge production as a spiritual and scientific pursuit. Both chapter 5 and chapter 6 develop these themes in close dialogue with an off-kilter reading of Lévi-Strauss's early conception of the "floating signifier."[82] Lévi-Strauss appreciated the decipherers' affinity for structural methods. And here I read Schele's structuralist inclinations as a convergent form and force with her latent Christianity. Ultimately, I take the joy of decipherment as an imperative to consider forms of both erotic and agapic love, as generative reanimations of a past that's never fully and finally past. Schele's cosmically oriented spirit guides me into a suggestive consideration of anthropology itself as a theological and spiritual project.

This book, then, amounts to a person-centered experimental ethnography.[83] Part of this experiment entails traversing between fact and fabulation, a well-trodden, if still vertigo-inducing, edge for anthropology.[84] Such edge-walking, as Schele knew well, doesn't absolve an author from the responsibility to care well for both facts and forms. But the care that I put into this writing has required me to re-form and trans-form a vision of Schele's spirit. It's an edgewalk with different kinds of entries and exits for different kinds of readers. These portals may correspond to different voices that emerge within the text; one is more evocative, and the other more analytical. I hope that you'll enjoy the spiritual and scientific wonder of this world, in steps both surefooted and precarious.

Chapter One

....

Sacrilege

SACRILEGE I

Standing in David and Elaine's dining room, doing my damnedest not to impose unduly, I photographed 2,300 pages of Linda's private documents. I flipped hastily through the papers, deciding on the fly which to digitize.

... *Dear Merle; tables of dynastic calculations; Kimbell Art Museum, Fort Worth Texas; dear collegues [sic], friends, and friendly crazies* ...

Time and again, looking up to stretch my neck, I peered beyond into a living room adorned with bright paintings. Linda's biomorphic surrealism. I resisted the urge to slip surreptitiously around the table with my camera, align its lens with the framed shapes, and shoot away.

... *Dear Floyd; William Morrow & Company; Lévi-Strauss; Yale; Nancy on Lookout Mountain; Dear Palencophiles* ...

Every couple of hours, or so, I completed my work with a set of catalogued documents. I returned the pages to the archival box and carried it to the dim office at the rear of the house, where David sat silently at his desk. In the back corner, I ascended the stepladder, heaved the box onto the shelf, and retrieved the next few years of correspondence. During the initial sidelong encounters with David, I briefly mentioned notable letters or posed half-considered questions, asserting my reality in the form of nervous small talk. I seem to recall the exchanges fading to numbers—"1980 to 1982"—before dissipating altogether.

. . . Dear Fellow Crazies; Dumbarton Oaks; Carl Sagan; postcards from Skyline Farm; a tempest in a teapot from the Sanger Clinic; Dear Dr. Schele . . .

I wanted to inquire about the paintings. Were they all Linda's, including the portrait of the Maya woman? Did she stop after becoming a Mayanist? And, of course, Could I photograph them? But I didn't summon the necessary bit of courage. The stillborn question induced psychic stagnation; it mossed up my head.

. . . Dear Peter; the National Center for Atmospheric Research High Altitude Observatory; Brown; Alabama; Jared Diamond; Querida Linda . . .

While guiding me to his late spouse's letters, David advised that they dated only to 1974. They hadn't retained documents from the era before Linda began to transform our understanding of the ancient Maya. Or, less likely, he'd chosen not to share them. Unfazed (at that point, at least), I lost myself in the traces of her last two decades, poring over piles of technical glyph-talk interspersed with private contracts, recommendations, letters of adoration, even an anonymous poison-penned missive defaming someone I know.

But not the paintings. Sacrilege.

Sacrilege.

. . . Dear David; Dumbarton Oaks; North Austin Hieroglyphic Hunches (and North Austin Half-Baked Glyphic Possibilities); Dear Dr. Kubler . . .

THIS ISN'T A BIOGRAPHY

On January 20, 1989, Frank Freidel wrote his son, who lived out west in Dallas, from his Harvard Department of History office.[1] Frank began: "I've been so energetic in suggesting ways that you and Linda Schele can improve your ms. [manuscript] that I'm a bit concerned that I have not said enough, from the standpoint of someone totally out of your field and discipline, about its basic strength." The tone reveals both the presidential biographer's populism and the aging father's tenderness. The book's structure is clear, with well-focused chapters effectively summed-up. "I never lost sight of your major themes and findings," he said.[2] Frank's colleague, archaeologist Gordon Willey, had recently shared some comments concerning Linda Schele and David Freidel's doings. Such kind words from the graying Harvard professoriate.

This book, the one that you're reading, aspires to be an American book, and not a biography. Gilles Deleuze and Félix Guattari thought American books were different. "America is a special case," they said.[3] "*Leaves of Grass*," they said. The West, in particular, with its wild thoughts, lines, and bodies, "with its Indians without ancestry, its shifting and displaced frontiers . . . America reversed the directions: it put its Orient in the West, as if it were precisely in America that the earth came full circle; its West is the edge of the East. . . . The American singer Patti Smith sings the bible of the American dentist: Don't go for the root, follow the canal."[4]

I'll follow the canal, all right, but I can't go for all that, for people without history right there smack in middle—"it is always in the middle"[5]—without filiation, without descent.

This punk piece isn't a biography; it ain't your father's biography.[6] But the "Indians" find their ancestors in the end.

ELAINE MARKSON LITERARY AGENCY, INC.

In June 1989 a literary agent sent a reply to Linda.[7] The letter began: "I am very intrigued by the Startrek novel and hope you will print it out (ah the new world—remember carbon copies??) [*sic*]."

The New World, the Americas, then up to the stars. From the looks of it, Linda was angling for a film or TV series to complement the book. She signed a contract in September, less than a month before the Wall fell; "the earth came full circle."[8] The novel wasn't realized, I guess. Not in that world. But, with *Star Trek*, according to Linda,

> what you have is a kind of bubble of reality that people go into and come out of. They write novels about it, they go to movies about it, they debate over the Internet about it, they use it metaphorically to try and cope with their own lives. And when they go into that bubble they accept the rules of the reality, both positive and negative. A lot of people say it's not real but that's not the question, because when you go into that universe you accept its rules. Part of the joy is being able to go into that world, accept its rules, play its game and then come out again. That's what I do with the Maya. I accept everything I find in their world as real.[9]

Let me repeat this point: "A lot of people say it's not real but that's not the question." And this one: "That's what I do with the Maya. I accept everything I find in their world as real." Isn't this akin to ethnographer Michael Taussig's stubborn refusal to let fiction and nonfiction come unstuck?

We destroy only as creators, says Nietzsche. What he means is that by analysis we build and rebuild, in ever so particular a manner, culture itself. And nowhere will this be more pertinent than in anthropology—the study of culture. But what is also meant is the blurring of fiction and nonfiction, beginning with the recognition and appraisal that this distinction is itself fictional and necessary. That too is a Nervous System, the endorsement of the real as the really made up.[10]

This book, the one that you're reading, is a bubble of reality, a made-up world about the worlds that Linda makes up and that make Linda up.

But there's a step here that neither Schele nor Taussig seems keen to endorse. "Materials and Methods." The worlds that Linda makes up, that the ancient Maya make up, that *Star Trek* speculators make up, that ethnographers make up, and that rabbits, cats, and limestone blocks make up are made, by different means, of different matters.

They're not made mainly of digitized images of paper and carbon copy traces of epistolary intimacies, like this one.

ELIMINATION (A THESIS)

The writer John Berger takes us to task for eliminating the dead.[11] The word *eliminate* descends from the Latin *ēlīmināre*, "to thrust out of doors," "to expel."[12] There's time and timelessness, he teaches, a core of the living surrounded by the dead. Those expelled are timeless, but not tranquil: "Having lived, the dead can never be inert."[13] Religions, he thinks, concern themselves with transactions across the *limen*, the threshold, the door between life and death: "The mystifications of religion are the result of trying to systematically produce such exchanges." We are, apparently, failing more than ever. "A uniquely modern form of egotism has broken [our] inter-dependence" with the dead. This has led to "disastrous results for the living, who now think of the dead as *eliminated*."[14]

To eliminate, then, also means to ignore or set aside as irrelevant. It's used formally in this sense by philosophers enamored with cognitive science.[15] They're called "eliminativists" (God save us). They distrust categories of experience and affect—belief, desire, perhaps pain. Life itself might even be subject to elimination. Eugene Thacker points out that "the trials and tribulations (mostly tragic) of 'life' as a philosophical concept readily lend themselves to the eliminativist approach."[16] Is life biological?

Theological? Something else altogether? If we try to brass-tack it, forget the canals, and follow life down to the root, we find molecules or information, but not answers: "Either everything is alive or nothing is alive; either everything is pulsating flux and flow, auto-affecting and self-transforming, or everything is silence, stillness, and the enigmatic, vacuous hum of nothingness."[17]

That's dark. As an anthropologist, I was trained to resist going eliminative.

Might Berger be hasty in treating the dead as outcasts of the secular world's "uniquely modern form of egotism"?[18] Bruno Latour argues that we've never been modern—that we've never strictly segregated nature from culture.[19] Today's scientific rites amount to modes of mystification; spirit genes descend from one generation to the next. As Berger says, the dead are a timeless reservoir of memory. But do they really surround us? What if the dead are the core of the living, and not vice versa? The dead live in, with, and through us; as memories, yes, and also as artifacts, letters, paintings, genes, and spirits.

"Having lived, the dead can never be inert."[20]

Might it be egotistical to presume ourselves the living? In the end, no matter what we think, or what the writer might think we think, we've never been modern and we've never exiled the dead.

We *are* the dead; the late Linda Schele is alive.

SCIENCE AND TECHNOLOGY STUDIES

Gillett Griffin wrote in quasi-calligraphic longhand. The script's pleasurable to read. Even comforting. A lively contrast to the aseptic typewritten standard. His letters *f, g,* and *y* swoop down to collide with words below.

A 1984 note breaks from his typical reflections on Mesoamerican art to put forth a scientific hypothesis: "I came up with this idea for the carving of Xochipala bowls—and thought of you."[21] A sketch to the left depicts a muscular loinclothed man, hair held back by a headband. With both hands he leverages a dowel into a piece of stone spinning on a potter's wheel. At the foot of the apparatus, three rabbits run in place, putting the wheel in motion. Linda loved rabbits; the rabbit would become her Maya coessence, her animal spirit companion.[22]

It's a risky occupation for the man (and probably for the rabbits too). Obsidian safety glasses shield his eyes from errant shards of stone.

Among speakers of Mayan languages today, one word for "person" is *vinik*. Late sixteenth-century speakers of Tzotzil Mayan used *vinik* to designate humans, animals, and sometimes even the dead.[23] Living persons, animal persons, dead persons.

Vinik also means the number 20. The 260-day Maya calendar is divided into thirteen months of twenty days. Each day is associated with a specific personality type. One's birthday comes with a categorical destiny; destiny is a Maya theory of personality or personhood. There are, then, twenty categories or classes of persons. Members of one class are predisposed to become scholars; another class, thieves. Ethnographer John Monaghan informs us that

> as one counts through the twenty day signs, one counts through all possible social identities, all possible physical combinations, all possible temperaments, and a full range of lucky and unlucky personal contingencies. While some might say that the most salient aspect of our humanity is our capacity for rational thought, in Mesoamerica, it appears to be the possession of a destiny, which makes humanity, in this tradition, not so much rational as "twenty."[24]

Monaghan proceeds to suggest that ancient Maya calendars may have been "social charters" rather than "divinatory devices" (as earlier scholars had argued).[25] Social order was cosmically ordained and inscribed in the calendar. Maya society wasn't composed of freely associating individuals. Their ritual practices and economic exchanges were guided by cosmic forces. Persons were partial. They were 5 percent whole.

Birth follows the dictates of destiny, of being and time, which equates in Mesoamerican cosmologies to "a universal life force that is substantively, spatially, and temporally continuous."[26] Destiny endows persons with specific corporeal and spiritual qualities: "Extending the Kaqchikel [Mayan] expression, destiny is all about giving being a face."[27]

FACE-TO-FACE

A face. The body acquires a form as it acquires a face. What, then, might we do with Deleuze and Guattari's affirmation of humans' defacialized destiny? They tell us that "if human beings have a destiny, it is . . . to escape the face, to dismantle the face and facializations."[28] They desire a mode of becoming that eludes the face as an organizing and identifying feature of collective recognition and identification. This entails not a return to the status of animality, but a becoming-other. Indeed, they advocate here "quite spiritual and special becomings-animal."[29] Deleuze and Guattari must never have faced a Maya face, a face that embodied destiny, a face that registered relational multiplicity and evaded the inscription of bodily territory with the individualist ideology that they laboriously distain. A face that was partial already. Later they even say that "'primitives' may have the most human of heads, the most beautiful and most spiritual, but they have no face and need none."[30] *Ah*, well, then, this is surely a special sense of "face." "The face is not universal," they say. "It is not even that of the white man; it is White Man himself, with his broad white cheeks and the black hole of his eyes. The face is Christ."[31]

Did Linda have a face? Did she have a face early in her life, when she was "taken by the romance and idealism of entering the world of Methodist missionaries"?[32] Did she have a face during her disenchanted middle years, or later, when she came around to Maya spiritual existence? Could Deleuze and Guattari have affirmed this strange spiritual transformation, the temporal conjuncture between ancient Mayas' mode of becoming-animal and an artist's?

Did Schele have a face while comatose on her deathbed when her husband David had her initiated into the Orthodox Church?

> Father Bob decided to give Linda the church name Sister Scholastica, after Saint Scholastica, the twin sister of Saint Benedict. Together these two saints are credited with establishing the monastic movement in Europe, which is largely responsible for preserving learning during the Dark Ages, an endeavor that corresponded to Linda's effort to restore to the modern Maya a sense of their ancestors' history and written language.[33]

Linda faced and refaced the ancient Maya, offering the "Indians" ancestors, bringing the ancient into the fold. But does Linda have a face today? A multiplicity of faces? Have I defaced her? Or will I do so by zooming in too close, exposing pores both clean and dirty?

I remember a shrine for Linda in the Scheles' house. Perhaps in the front hallway, beside the living room. Drawings, photos, a Maya cross, *veladora* candles . . .

The ancient Maya often buried the deceased beneath their floors. Archaeologist Michael Coe even described Maya centers as "necropolises" for religious "cults of the dead."[34] But burying or curating human remains in and around the house may have served quite practical purposes. Descendants used bones to establish rights to land.[35]

By curating bodies of the dead, kin cohabiting Maya houses also curated their souls.[36] If ethnographic literature is any aid,[37] the ancient Maya may have believed that each person had an eternal soul destined for a descendant's body.[38] Souls may have been linked to names, which recur in lists of kings at sites like Palenque. Not only were ancient Maya persons partial; they also each possessed a "vital essence" previously embodied by a series of ancestors.[39] The reallocation of a soul has been termed *k'ex*, the same word used to designate the transfer of power to new community title-holders.[40] Living *with* the ancestors means living *as* the ancestors, names and all.

So we need not treat ancient Maya houses as cultish haunts of the necrotic. Instead, we might conceive Maya death as a soul movement that temporarily ticks up an otherworld's population before the soul's reincarnated once more. Archaeologist Susan Gillespie even suggests that souls and names were household property.[41] She would like us to

> see the dwelling as the place where the corporeal and noncorporeal elements of humans intertwined in an unending cycle of death and renewal; hence, it was equally associated with regeneration and immortality. The physical house is better understood as a locus for the enactment of claims to group continuity through the curation, transformation, and renewal of that group's material and immaterial property. It was thus a place of life.[42]

Let's dwell in the Schele house as uninvited guests. "The physical house," Gillespie says, "was . . . a place of life."

Yes, yes. "Having lived, the dead can never be inert."[43]

Ethnographer Evon Vogt recounts that each of the eight thousand Tzotzil Mayas living in Zinacantán in the late 1960s possessed an "animal spirit companion":

> Each person and his animal spirit companion share the same soul. Thus, when the ancestral gods install a soul in the embryo of a Zinacanteco, they simultaneously install the same soul in the embryo of an animal. Similarly, the moment a Zinacanteco baby is born, a supernatural jaguar, coyote, ocelot, or other animal is born. Throughout life, whatever happens of note to the Zinacanteco happens to his animal spirit companion, and vice versa.[44]

The companions lived in supernatural corrals in a mountain east of town center: Bankilal Muk'ta Vits (Senior Large Mountain). Ancestral gods cared for the spirits there. During the daytime, the gods would transform spirits into domestic animals and set them free to graze beyond. But if a spirit's human counterpart violated a community rule—fighting with kin, refusing to pay taxes, and so on—trouble was in order for the spirit companion: "Anything that stirs up the wrath of the ancestral gods against a particular Zinacanteco can lead quickly and directly to punishment by causing the person to experience some form of soul-loss, or, in more serious cases, by having his animal spirit companion turned outside its corral to wander alone and uncared for in the woods."[45]

If your animal spirit companion's set free to wander alone in the woods, you'll become quite sick. You'll need a shaman to preside over an elaborate curing ceremony.[46] At the literal height of the ceremony, on the summit of Senior Large Mountain, you'll provide the gods with a black chicken on a pine-needle-covered plate. Before the trek, you'll drink a cupful of this *pullus sacer*'s blood; the shaman will drain it for you from the neck before sewing the bird back up. Your offering to the ancestral gods is a *k'esholil*, which is to say a *k'ex*, a replacement, a substitute for your soul. You'd better hope they accept it.

PROFESSOR OF PHYSIOLOGY

He signed the letter simply and sloppily: "Jared." Red pen. No signed surname. The typing below has the details: "Jared M. Diamond, Professor of Physiology."[47]

Diamond was a prestigious Tanner Lecturer at the University of Utah in 1992, when his first popular book, *The Third Chimpanzee*, hit shelves in the United States.[48] Schele took part in a Utah panel with Diamond, discussing the topic "Why (Some) Civilizations Fall and Rise." "Your contributions and talk were terrific," Diamond wrote, "just as I was sure that they would be."

Five years later the physiologist published the Pulitzer Prize–winning *Guns, Germs, and Steel* and became, inadvertently perhaps, a public spokesperson for anthropology.[49] Two years after that I encountered anthropology through Diamond when I read his books in a first-year tutorial, or freshman seminar, at Grinnell College.

In 1992, when Diamond wrote Linda, he was working on *Guns, Germs, and Steel*. All flattery aside, he asked about good accounts of the Spanish conquest in Mesoamerica.

Schele may have replied to Diamond's proto-email ARPANET address, included below his red signature. She too was a technophile and early email adopter. Her archive begins to dwindle that year, 1992: the Columbian quincentennial, on the eve of NAFTA, the eve of masked Maya rebels—with guns, without leaders, names, or faces—rising from the Lacandón jungle to reconquer Mesoamerica.

TO PUT IT ALL SUCCINCTLY

"To put it all succinctly," Vogt summarized, "I am glad that I admitted you to my Freshman Seminar on the Maya in the autumn of 1964 and have been glowing with pride in your accomplishments ever since."[50]

Vogt wrote these words in a letter to David Freidel, closed-copied to Linda, three decades after admitting his colleague Frank's son into his Harvard tutorial. Freidel and Schele had dedicated their popular-press book, *Maya Cosmos*, to Vogt, the ethnographer.[51] Vogt shared that

> the volume sparkles with new ideas about the general themes of Maya cosmology, many of which will undoubtedly be controversial to Mayanists and Mesoamericanists, and some of which may not prove to be valid as they are subject to further empirical examination. But, I, for one, feel strongly that our field needs scholars who are way out in terms of novel conceptions and new and felicitous ways of expressing familiar conceptions. I am reminded of

the manner in which the ideas of Levi-Strauss shook up the field of mythology and became endlessly controversial, but, in the long run, served to significantly stimulate the development of structural interpretations of culture.

The French mythmaker himself, Claude Lévi-Strauss, shared Vogt's praise, at least with respect to Linda's book *The Blood of Kings*.[52] The month of his seventy-eighth birthday, November 1986, Lévi-Strauss wrote Linda from his Laboratory of Social Anthropology at the Collège de France in Paris:

> Dear Professor Schele,
>
> Your very kind letter dated September 7 only reached me a few days ago. Thanking you for it gives me an opportunity to express once again my admiration for the amazing results you and your colleagues have achieved in the field of Mayan studies. It is often said that I disregard history. Nothing can be more wrong. Historians and structural analysts both strive after the same end: to discover some kind of order behind facts which are given piecemeal. This order can be hidden in the past, or it may lie in the present though at a deeper level. The two approaches are complementary, and nothing demonstrates it better than your work which combines so successfully history and structural analysis. With congratulations and regards, please believe me
>
> Yours sincerely,
>
> *Claude Lévi-Strauss*[53]

YOUTH OR INEXPERIENCE OR EXCESSIVE ENTHUSIASM

French men live, on average, about seventy-eight years. Claude outlasted most, making it more than a century: 1908 to 2009.

Classic Maya kings lived, on average, to about fifty-four. Maya commoners, who tended to die by their third decade, would have considered rulers' lives unthinkably long.[54] And some rulers were Maya Methuselahs, making it to their sixties or seventies.

In 1952, Mexican archaeologist Alberto Ruz Lhuillier discovered one such ruler's remains in an elaborate sarcophagus below Palenque's Temple of the Inscriptions. Physical anthropologists working with Ruz estimated that the king died at age forty or fifty.[55] Ruz claimed that glyphs on the tomb supported this conclusion. His reading confirmed that the man died a few months shy of forty.[56]

This interpretation of Palenque's stone and bone stood solidly for two decades. Then, in 1973, at a workshop down the road from the site, Schele and Peter Mathews deciphered a list of dynasts.[57] The oldest at death was the temple crypt's denizen, whose name they read as Pacal (now spelled Pakal). Linda and Peter's Pakal survived for eighty years, outliving today's average Frenchman.

The upstarts' claims displeased Ruz and fellow Mexican archaeologists. Mathews and Schele made no mention of the osteological estimate. They didn't bother to refute it. So Ruz arranged a skeletal reanalysis, and it confirmed his team's first claim.[58] Whatever the hieroglyphs say, or whatever you say they say, the king died at forty.

Ruz lacked patience for Mathews and Schele: "I believe that their youth or inexperience or excessive enthusiasm has led them to stray from the more reliable, more rigorous, more scientific path."[59]

Was Pakal forty at death? Or eighty? The controversy pitted archaeological science against new techniques of glyphic interpretation, and Mexican scholarship against US American. Some sidestepped the squabble, guessing that the bones weren't Pakal's at all,[60] or that the inscriptions were propaganda.[61]

Others addressed it directly. In the late 1990s, Mexican scholars put together another reanalysis. Enlisting well-known bioarchaeologist Jane Buikstra, they went at the bones once more. Buikstra had been prepared to deal one last blow to the epigraphers' readings.[62] But scientific techniques change, and results change with them: "This revisit of the Pakal remains in 1999 should convincingly resolve the age controversy. Our results point to an advanced age at death consistent with the record in the inscriptions, but not with the earlier bioarchaeological estimates."[63]

Neither Schele nor Ruz heard the news. Not in this world, at least. Ruz died in '79 and Schele in '98. Ruz, seventy-three at death, was buried on the plaza before Pakal's temple. The man who discovered Pakal now rests beside him.

On the Temple of the Inscriptions sarcophagus lid, Pakal is depicted descending the axis mundi, the tree of life, Yax Che,' the first tree, the ceiba, or the maize plant crossed by a bicephalic snake (figure 1.1). His descent traverses what the Maya called "the road of awe," the passage into the otherworld, Xibalba, the Milky Way.

A bejeweled bird perches over Pakal's journey on the sarcophagus lid. It's Itzam-Yeh, the avian avatar of the Maya god who placed the third and final hearthstone in the center at the moment of cosmic creation. The god's name derives from the term *itz*, a spiritual substance that gives form to the potent liquids of Maya bodies and lives: sweat, blood, milk, semen, tears, tree sap, candle wax, and the water that fills sacred sinkholes, or cenotes, in Yucatán. Linda called itz "cosmic ooze, the magical stuff of the universe."[64]

The king's flesh sublimated into goo and then dust, returning to what Freud called the "quiescence of the inorganic world."[65] His itz oozed to Xibalba, but maintained worldly contact through a molded mortar snake linking the tomb vault and the temple floor above.[66]

Souls vaporize. Or they become miasmatic. "The living," Nietzsche said, "is only a form of what is dead."[67]

METHODOLOGY

With respect to Linda's "philosophy of the happy accident," Coe editorializes: "Not Floyd's—or Tania's—methodology by a long shot, but it has led to truly important results."[68]

Tania was Tatiana Proskouriakoff, a Soviet-born, Pennsylvania-raised Mayanist art and architecture expert. Tania had trained to be an architect at Penn State in the late 1920s, before joining a University of Pennsylvania field project at the site of Piedras Negras in 1936.[69] Proskouriakoff developed what Coe calls her "methodology" in a series of articles published in the early 1960s.[70] By associating patterns of dates in architectural inscriptions with the lives of Classic Maya rulers, Tania challenged the Carnegie consensus that Maya glyphs lacked historical content. As archaeologist Rosemary Joyce puts it, "These few pages literally changed the basic premise of Maya scholarship. Maya monuments, Proskouriakoff demonstrated, far from presenting only gods and priests, record the deeds of human beings and form the basis for a Maya history."[71] Linda and company relied heavily on Tania's "historical

FIGURE 1.1 — The central motif on the lid of Pakal's sarcophagus in the Temple of the Inscriptions at Palenque. The classic period king descends the tree of life toward Xibalba. DRAWING COURTESY OF SUSAN D. GILLESPIE.

approach" to develop their decipherment of Palenque's dynastic lineage and then to "crack the code."

In early 1977, Linda completed a draft of a paper on grammatical expressions designating events of dynastic accession.[72] In a letter "to the Group," her inner circle of colleagues, Linda mentioned that she was sending the manuscript to Proskouriakoff "with trepidation."[73]

Tania's late-January reply, typed on stationery from Harvard's Peabody Museum of Archaeology and Ethnology, begins with the salutation "Dear Linda (if I may)."[74] The first paragraph reveals why Schele felt hesitant to send Proskouriakoff the paper:

> I have been critical of <u>some</u> of your conclusions, as well as some of your drawings (e.g. the omission of a stairway to the Temple of the Cross), and some of your vocabulary (e.g. a "monolithic" stairway?), but I have never criticized your ethics—only your manners. You have deeply hurt the feelings of Alberto Ruz, who is a fine archaeologist, and my friend of long standing, but if you are ready to mend fences, I will meet you half-way.

Proskouriakoff proceeds to signal her support for linguistic decipherment, qualified by her admitted ignorance of Mayan languages and attendant reluctance to participate in the developments. The well-mannered correspondent tactfully makes no mention of Linda's linguistic ignorance.

So why the trepidation? Did Linda fear that her method—to "let the damn stuff pattern on me"—might not meet Tania's standards of rigor?[75] On this note, Proskouriakoff appends a brief postscript, a fine example of what her biographer deemed "Tania's dry sense of humor":[76] "I will read your paper as soon as I can, but on 'methodology'—no comment. Never use it myself—it interferes with my thinking."

ART AND SCIENCE

Schele hadn't set out to change the field of ancient Maya studies. And she certainly wasn't trained to do so. She contrasts her position—and the positions of other amateurs that she brought into the field—with that of elite students at the center of Maya studies, those trained by Coe or Willey at Yale or Harvard.

While teaching her introduction to art at the University of South Alabama, Schele began to consider how a society with art at its center might look. "*Ya* know," Linda says, "I don't care what artists say and how they protest, in our world we rely on science as the tool that we use to investigate reality and to create materialized symbolic representations of how we understand reality. We use art to pursue other things. And I knew that there had to be societies in the world where art was that primary tool rather than what we call science."[77]

Linda's phrasing is seductive. She seems to hold what we call art and science at arm's length. Yet she desires a world where art substitutes for science, where art posits and answers questions about reality. And look how Linda defines science: "the tool . . . to investigate reality and to create materialized symbolic representations of how we understand reality."[78] Like many of us who study science as a cultural process and product,[79] Linda defines science as a creative act of giving material form to symbols held to describe a reality external to human consciousness. This, arguably, takes science as a form of art.

But Linda wasn't in the business of defining science. She was, it seems, in the business of discovering and constructing a world with art at its core. Linda's initial entry into the site of Palenque must have been a hallucinatory experience: "When I walked into Palenque I saw what I had anticipated and I saw that kind of dream materialized into a real place."[80] Linda set out in haste to discover the voices captured in the traces of that ancient Maya city and to articulate them anew in the present. When she found the art world she'd imagined, Linda became—it seems—something of a scientist, a spokesperson for the past.[81] To repeat one of Linda's stock phrases, she set out to "turn [Palenque] into a historical place."[82] This meant, for Linda, deducing the details of dynasts' names and lives.

Like Ruz and others since,[83] I've wondered how Linda and company could sincerely believe that telling the stories of a few kings and queens—after decades of intensive archaeological research—amounted to the inaugural conferral of history upon the ancient Maya. I've wondered how they could identify so fervently with these political elite. Did Linda, in discovering a few details of a few rulers' lives, imagine that she was reviving a vibrant artists' utopia, a place where scientific reductionism and political utility didn't smother the human spirit?

When we met in that painting-adorned living room in 2007, David Schele described how, by the mid-1970s, Linda and her peers had grown frustrated with the lack of US public interest in avant-garde, experimental art. Linda moved to Maya studies to construct or discover a truly imaginative space, a cosmos with creation at its heart. In the process, Linda became a scientist like no other.

In 1998 a former student, Andrea Stone, organized a conference panel to honor Schele and her work. That January Schele promised Stone, "I'll be there if I can."[84] Linda died of pancreatic cancer on April 18. She didn't live to be honored that December in Philadelphia.

As the conference crowd settled, ethnographer Duncan Earle lit copal incense to signal the ceremonial importance of the matter at hand. Copal smoke snaked to the rafters as Elin Danien, a participant in Linda's public workshops on Maya glyphs, stepped to the podium. When Danien began to discuss Linda, Stone recounts, "the microphone taped to the podium slipped and made a loud boom. Elin turned her eyes heavenward and said, 'Sorry, Linda.' The crowd let out a great roar, and I knew that Linda had kept up her end of the bargain; she *was* there."[85]

More than two decades before this spirit revival, Schele and Mathews sent a letter from Palenque to Proskouriakoff and fellow art historian Heinrich Berlin.[86] The note, typed by Linda and written in a reserved and formal voice, begins by sharing, "We have been discussing for several years the idea of organizing a Festschrift to commemorate the contribution that both of you have made to the study of the Maya."

Schele and Mathews hoped to solicit Proskouriakoff and Berlin's approval for the festschrift, an edited volume to commemorate their career contributions to the field. They write,

> We know from personal experience that both of you prefer not to participate in large organized events, and we suspect that your natural reaction to this proposal will be to refuse. However, both of us, in agreement with the rest of the world, believe that both of you have been the dominant and most productive minds in hieroglyphic studies for the last thirty years. Our debt to you and our dependence on your work cannot be too strongly emphasized. We feel strongly that to organize a Festschrift in your honor is a necessary and extremely important thing for us to do. We hope that you will understand our feelings and the respect that motivates our actions.

They were right. Berlin and Proskouriakoff rebuffed the request. "As you correctly anticipated, my reply is a definite NO," Berlin wrote.[87] "As far as I am concerned, such Festschriften in reality are heaping insult upon injury."

Berlin considered such volumes "certifications of senility" delivered delightfully by generations of successors.

It's easy to account for Berlin's and Schele's divergent replies to their heirs' proposals. After all, the latter knew her death was imminent. Why protest finitude? The conference session was no preemptive funeral. But this point of contrast doesn't capture the full extent of the difference. From that panel emerged a festschrift like no other.[88] Yes, *Heart of Creation: The Mesoamerican World and the Legacy of Linda Schele* celebrates Linda as a scholar and person. But it doesn't require laborious effort to situate the scholar, to show how her ideas arose from flesh and blood. Linda's students and colleagues followed her tracks, but couldn't catch her.

Linda *was* there when Danien took to the podium. I mean that in all seriousness. It's an anthropological fact. And in June 1998, a month after her death, Linda was at a celebration of her friend Gillett Griffin's seventieth birthday. A colleague saw her there, in the flesh of her coessence, her animal spirit companion: "Many of Linda's friends were there. Standing under a huge tent placed on the grass between university buildings, I looked over and saw, near a building at the end, a rabbit hopping along the lawn. It stopped, looked toward the tent, and then went on."[89]

They couldn't catch Linda. I can't either.

SACRILEGE II

Sacrum legere, the root of *sacrilege*, means "to purloin sacred objects." The word is used aptly by those who criticize archaeological excavations of burials. For example, Pawnee scholar and activist James Riding In says, "We saw [archaeologists'] professional activities as sacrilege and destructive, while they professed a legal and scientific right to study Indian remains and burial goods."[90] Disturbing graves, it seems, causes Pawnee spirits to become restless. Wandering spirits are trouble. They "often beset the living with psychological and health problems."[91]

The Maya have their share of wandering spirits, coessences set free to roam the woods, the mountains, *el monte*. But it's not clear whether ancient Maya subjects would have shared Pawnee sentiments concerning the sacred status of graves. Ancient Maya burial practices pose problems for archaeologists today: "Many Maya tombs were reentered and also reused, housing multiple bodies in differing states of articulation, so these graves cannot easily signify the status and identity of a single individual at a fixed point in time follow-ing immediately after death."[92] Tombs don't always contain who or what you expect. Sometimes they even show up empty, suggesting their status as mere temporary sites for processing corpses.

Of course, some cases of tomb reentry may well have served wicked ends. In the 1960s, ethnographer Benson Saler identified the act of tampering with human remains as a technique of malevolent magic performed by speakers of K'iche' Mayan in highland Guatemala. As an example, Saler relates that a local drunk removed bones from a *ladina* woman's grave to rebury on an indigenous woman's property.[93] The motivation for this attempted act of contagious magic—cut short by police intervention—was to render the in-digenous woman so witless that she'd sell the land at bargain price.[94] In this case, which unfolded during Saler's stay, the villagers debated the perennial question of whether the subject was a true sorcerer or "merely a drunk who had been carried away by rum or cupidity."[95]

As Saler relates,

> A genuine as contrasted to a spurious sorcerer, apparently, is one who seriously and soberly performs a magical act against another human being. The commonest of such acts are doll burial, the exhumation and reburial of human remains, the burial of other objects (e.g., photo-graphs, nail clippings, hair, or a piece of the clothing of the individual against whom the action is directed), prayers recited over copal fires or burning, black candles, and incantations delivered in the cemetery. In all cases, the act is believed to be potentially most effective if per-formed at night.

As far as I can tell, few archaeologists are true sorcerers. And it's hard to know whether the ancient Maya who reopened royal tombs did so in order to complete secondary burial practices, to satisfy their own archaeological curiosity, to indulge their cupidity, or to attempt sorcery—whether seriously or spuriously.

If anyone's a sorcerer or perpetrator of sacrilege here, it isn't likely Linda. Is it me? After all, I dig through her letters, exhuming statements from one document to rebury in another.

Chapter Two

....

Animals

Life oozes. Life oozes off tongues and fingertips, sticking to screens that feed us. Life itself. We eat it up.[1]

We anthropologists have long obsessed with the human as a form of life. In 1851, Robert Gordon Latham carved out a chasm between history and anthropology, those two means of studying "Man." The inheritors of Herodotus were to study "Man's Civil history."[2] The rest of us were charged with the rather impure science of "Man's Natural history," or "the study of Man as an animal."[3] Latham's anthropology was the branch of zoology that treated the specificities of Man the species. He put it this way: "Anthropology deals *with Man as compared with the lower animals.*"[4]

Latham had much to offer the few, curious higher-animal specimens of the Victorian era who sought self-knowledge on pan-specific scale. But his trans-specific comparative impulse, his considerations of Man vis-à-vis monkey, apparently discomfited readers in the age of the penny press: "Anthropology deals too much with such matters as these to be popular. Unless the subject be handled with excessive delicacy, there is something revolting to fastidious minds in the cool contemplation of the *differentiae* of the Zoologist 'Who shows a Newton as he shows an ape.'"[5]

Despite the pathology of our revolting fastidiousness—that is, our evolving empiricism—anthropology has not yet succumbed to selective pressures leading to extinction. We live on despite the best efforts of predatory politicians and university administrators wreaking environmental havoc on the habitats of the liberal arts and sciences. Specters of *Scopes*?

Through such trials of strength, anthropology's life endures. As does its fascination *with* life, with Man as a *form* of life, and an *animal* form at that. In his oft-repeated definition of culture, Clifford Geertz pegged Man as an animal before declaring his unique entanglement in those confounding "webs of significance."[6] While, for this reader at least, the cadence of Geertz's phrasing retains allure, his metaphor proves odd, even a bit clumsy: "Man is an animal suspended in webs of significance he himself has spun. I take culture to be those webs."[7]

Consider the trope for a moment. The sovereign signifier is a venomous, predatory arachnid.[8] Geertz's Man is an arthropod.[9] Well, either that or a mythic monster, a chimerical hybrid.

Are we spiders? Spider-Men? Spiders spin threads of silk from abdominal glands, composing webs that their arachnologist companions divide into different architectural types.[10] There are two-dimensional orb webs composed of radiating circular threads supported by a matrix of silky segments spun from the center. Then there are three-dimensional tangle-webs or cobwebs woven by black widows and their kin in the *Theridiidae* family. These are spun in a more rhizomatic fashion, lines of flight extending from a central dragline and plateauing in all directions.[11]

Long before Romans invented the English foot, this octopod used its body as a measuring device to construct architecture that is at once its home and its devious technology of entrapment.

In the masculinist fantasy of Cold War–era anthropology, Richard Lee and Irven DeVore declared "Man the Hunter"![12] Here we find his ancestor, "Spider the Trapper"! The web awaits . . .

In October 2008, the *Telegraph* ran two stories featuring photographs of giant Australian spiders eating finches trapped in their webs.[13] The Australian Reptile Park's head spider keeper, Joel Shakespeare, identified them as golden orb weavers. The article clarifies:

> Greg Czechura from Queensland Museum said cases of the Golden Orb Weaver eating small birds were "well known but rare."
> "It builds a very strong web," he said.[14]

A very strong web. In 2002, researchers affiliated with Nexia Biotechnologies and the US Army published an article in *Science* describing their insertion of orb web–weaving spiders' dragline silk genes into bovine mammary and baby hamster kidney cell lines suspended in aqueous solutions.[15] They synthesized water-insoluble fibers with a strength comparable to "native" draglines. The synthetic draglines are "three times as tough as aramid fibers and five times stronger by weight than steel."[16] The authors suggest that the material could be used in microsurgery and as a substitute for nylon.

A popular science article covering the development in the *Independent* ran under the headline "A Spider's Web That Could Catch an F-16."[17] The author explains, "Scientists made synthetic spider silk that is five times stronger than steel yet soft enough to be woven into a bulletproof vest." A very strong web, indeed. Charlotte saved Wilbur first, the rest of us second.[18]

Microsurgery. Military technology. Know your audience. The web's a risky tool, materializing biopolitics' duality. Spiders spin both sticky and nonsticky threads. And they're not immune to their own technologies of entrapment.[19] A wrong step could leave them stuck. The octopods must take care to avoid being ensnared in their own designs.

Mustn't we all?[20]

Anthropos as *arthropoda*. With tongue in cheek, linguistic anthropologist Michael Silverstein calls Geertzian interpretive anthropology "symbols-and-meaningism."[21] Perhaps we should rechristen it "*arthro*pology." Would that bring us back to—as the philosophers say—"the things themselves"?[22] I'd like to see symbols and meaning catch an F-16. I guess the golden orb weaver's web is stronger than Geertz's metaphor. Does that thought indulge a category mistake or perform a queer comparison?[23] I don't know.

Geertz probably didn't intend his metaphor to be taken either so seriously or so playfully. But I wouldn't put it past him.

Anyway, enough spin.

HAUNTING I: LINDA'S RABBITS

A letter written to Floyd, Peter, and Dave on October 14, 1978 (figure 2.1), concludes:

> Well, think about it. I shall expect to be shot down in glorious flames in the near future. (!!!!You've got to admit I'm tossing around the linguistic jargon with much more abandon after my summer cram course with the Hopkins!!!!****¢¢¢¢%%%%$$##@@____++++).
> Well, if I am to have room for a rabbit drawing I have to stop now. I am looking forward to getting the tear-sheets on the astronomy article and so is the class.[24]

I have been working on the 'flat!-cycle'phrase also. I think I'm going
to have trouble with your suggestions for a reading, Floyd. We both accept
the ka part of it and neither of us can make the wa make sense. It is the
T126 prefix that is going to give us trouble. I know you believe it should be
read hi or ih. I don't know your set of evidence,but there is some you are
going to have to disprove to get a reading of hi. T126 is the prefix in the
wife glyph. It should have a reading of a there to give atan . And I have found
another substitution that favors a. Look at D11 on the TFC. This glyph, T228.
168:518:130,   appears in the name phrase of Lady Beastie. Since it does not
appear consistantly with her name, it is a title of some sort. A very similar
title appears throughout the Maya corpus, especially in Peter's Early Classic
lintels of Yaxchilan. Look up the list under T518 in Thompson's Catalog. In
almost every case, the title glyph includes T126 as the prefix. On the TFC
the prefix is T228, the turtle beak, which we know to be a. Furthermore
when the T518 title appears in verbal form (TI 3: E3 and H2), it appears
without either T126 or 228. The verbal form is inflected with T130:116,
Barbara's wan. If she is correct about the wan inflection, the verbal form must
be a positional verb, which is expected with an accession expression. However,
the fact that T168:518 can appear as an inflected verb for accession, suggests
that when it appears in nominal form as a title, it ought to have an article.
Ah is the expected article. Well, think about it. I shall expect to be
shot down it glorious flames in the near future. (!!!!You've got to admit I'm
tossing around the linguistic jargon with much more abandon after my summer
cram course with the Hopkins!!!!****¢¢¢¢※※$$##@@___++++).

     Well, if I am to have room for a rabbit drawing I have to stop now. I am looking
forward to getting the tear-sheets on the astronomy article and so is the class.

FIGURE 2.1 — Linda Schele to Floyd Lounsbury, Peter Mathews, and Dave
Kelley, October 14, 1978, p. 4. PHOTO BY THE AUTHOR.

One of the bipedal rabbits sketched below has rigged a rope through a ring affixed to the top of the fourth percentage sign in the childish dash of exclamatory symbols. She tightly grasps the rope, which seems to suspend a large stone hieroglyphic sign element above her coworker's head.[25]

Don't suspect foul play. The cottontail is collaborating with a dozen industrious conspecifics. They're assembling a Maya hieroglyph, piece by piece. Two workers march lockstep toward the center while suspending a crescent-shaped stone from a crossbeam propped on their shoulders. Another appears to be heaving a stone sphere as if it were a shot put. By all appearances the rabbits' assembly is proceeding according to design.

That is, all appearances but one. Each worker-rabbit handles either a crescent or a sphere. These crescents and spheres—circles, really—complement one another. Two crescents facing the same direction interspaced by one or more circles comprise a distinct Maya sign (figure 2.2). Hieroglyph experts today generally interpret this sign as a syllable pronounced *ya* that may perform the grammatical function of marking root words, particularly those that begin with vowels, as possessives.[26] For example, the logographic sign *ak'ab* means "night." Prefixed with the *ya* sign, it's read *y-ak'ab* and signifies "his, her, or its night."

This reading was not yet established in 1978, when Linda wrote this letter to Floyd, Peter, and Dave. Linda acknowledged in the letter that Floyd, the linguist of the bunch, read the sign phonetically as *hi* or *ih*. Linda diverged from her elder pen pal, speculating that it might be a substitute for the phoneme *a* (pronounced *ah*), an agentive prefix associating individuals with places or qualities. *Naab'* means "water," and *a naab'*, "he or she of water."

Given this context, the rabbits' actions begin to seem more psychotic than industrious. They affix *a* after *a* after *a* onto a zoomorphic main sign, probably another rabbit. They keep coming with more *a*'s. There's no end in sight. Their protean sculpture isn't really legible at all.

Linda stopped—she *had* to stop—with space for nine more lines on the fourth page of that letter. Nine lines—I counted. In lieu of those lines, Floyd, Peter, and Dave stared at this scene of bestial chaos. Maybe they stared slack-jawed as I did thirty years later. What did Floyd, Peter, and Dave make of this mess? Linda was a brilliant artist. She could hand-draw intricate hieroglyphic signs from memory on cue.

By Linda's standards, it's a sloppy sketch, perhaps little more than a min-ute's distraction. But in that minute, that distraction, and that sketch, Linda said all that was needed. Floyd, Peter, and Dave knew that Linda identified with rabbits. In an early contribution to the field, Linda identified signs as literal and metaphorical rabbits.[27] She read a glyph that included a rabbit-sign as the succession of a Maya lord, an act expressed metaphorically, she suggested, as "'rabbiting' or as 'following the footprints of the ancestors.'"[28] Here, the by-no-means-parsimonious and by-no-means-necessarily-true interpretation that makes me its mouthpiece screams that this work of art depicts Linda, Floyd, Peter, Dave, et alia. Linda was a brilliant collaborator. Is Linda that zoomorphic main sign, that rabbit in the middle? Through glyphic tracks and traces, her *Leporidae* family succeeded, followed, or "rab-bited" the ancestors.[29] The sketch has to show the labor of collaboration and the tedium of decipherment.[30]

"Decipherment"—*yuck*! I've never liked that metaphor much. Maya hi-eroglyphs aren't ciphers. They're not codes. They're complex aesthetic forms and material objects with no unified mode of signification. Their reduction to modernist texts has come at significant cost. But I should disclose my secret suspicion that Linda knew it all along. Linda's like those Balinese peasants who didn't need Geertz to figure out what their cockfights were all about.[31] They knew it already. Well-selected informants typically do. She knew that the typewriter couldn't fully capture either what hieroglyphs meant or what it meant to interpret them. And I've come to love this sketch, and others like it, for revealing Linda's discomfort with the modernist assumption that texts are texts and images, images, and ne'er the twain shall meet.[32]

In the *Popol Vuh*, a K'iche' Maya cosmogony, the gods' inaugural at-tempts to create human beings fail, and result instead in the ancestors of today's animals.[33] In their third attempt, the gods create monkeys, animals often depicted centuries earlier as scribes on Classic Maya ceramic vessels (figure 2.3). These Classic monkeys were, perhaps, the spirit companions or coessences of the scribes themselves.[34] In other words, in a manner quite

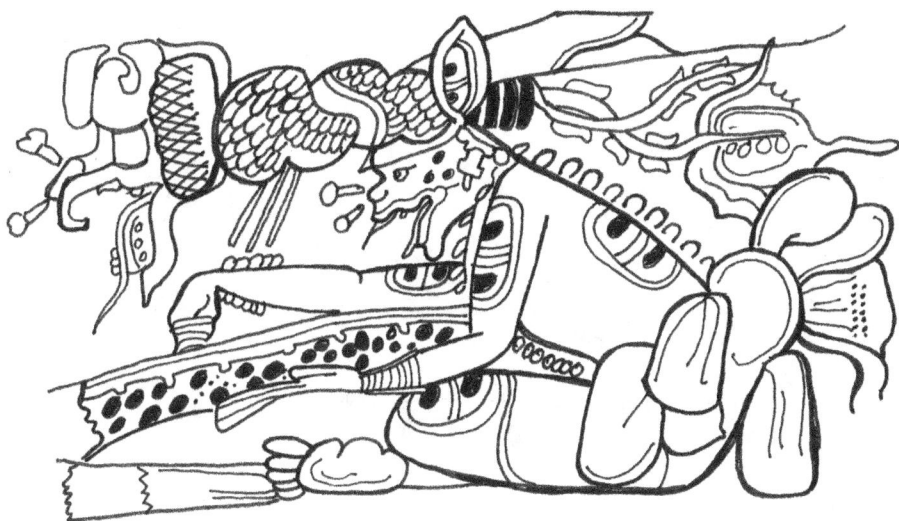

FIGURE 2.3 — Linda Schele, *A Monkey Scribe Depicted on a Classic Period Ceramic Vessel*. Ink on Mylar drafting film. The monkey scribe is painting in a bark-paper book and wearing a Phaeton headdress adorned with a water lily blossom.
DRAWING (SCHELE NUMBER 3530) © DAVID SCHELE, COURTESY FOUNDATION FOR THE ADVANCEMENT OF MESOAMERICAN STUDIES, INC., WWW.FAMSI.ORG.

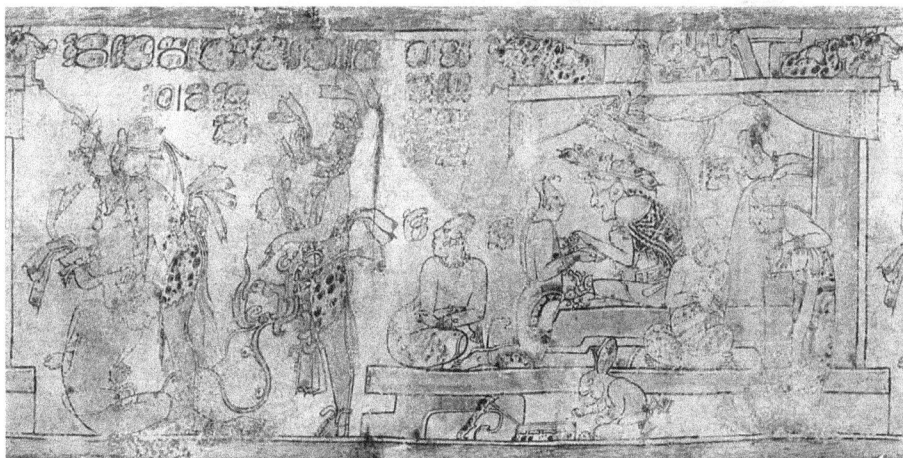

FIGURE 2.4 — Rollout photograph of the Princeton Vase (K511). PHOTOGRAPHY BY JUSTIN KERR.

FIGURE 2.5 — Linda Schele, line drawing of the rabbit scribe depicted on the Princeton Vase (figure 2.4). Ink on Mylar drafting film. DRAWING (SCHELE NUMBER 3539) © DAVID SCHELE, COURTESY FOUNDATION FOR THE ADVANCEMENT OF MESOAMERICAN STUDIES, INC., WWW.FAMSI.ORG.

revolting to fastidious minds indeed, the scribes were, at once, human and monkey. But there's also an odd pot, the Princeton Vase, that diverges from this celebration of monkey-scribe consubstantiality by depicting a scribe as a rabbit (figures 2.4 and 2.5).[35] Peter used this rabbit-scribe as his letterhead for a while.

Unlike Peter (I think), Linda *was* a rabbit. At the very least, she was a rabbit when the world weighed down and the path seemed unclear. She was a rabbit in those evening moments of reflection when her day's labor felt like heaving giant stones into a pile that just screamed *a, a, a!* We can all sympathize.

But get me straight. I'm not saying that Linda's rabbit drawings were a romantic diversion or escape, let alone an orientalist appropriation of indigenous ontology,[36] even if they were.[37] And I'm not saying that Linda's rabbit drawings were like the Balinese cockfights that Geertz famously deciphered as "a Balinese reading of Balinese experience; a story they tell themselves about themselves,"[38] even if they were that too. As critical and interpretive stances de jure, these readings seem too clean. They just don't stick. Maybe I need to resist reading all together. Against the grain of my socialization as a historicist and contextualist trained to read contingency at every turn, I have to take the rabbit as a being that has persisted transhistorically, a paradigm (as the structuralists say), a constant (as a mathematician might), inhabiting ancient Maya worlds as it inhabits the present.

Surrounded by fellow Trekkies and *Doctor Who* fans in the weird world of Maya studies in 1980s Austin, Linda became a time-traveler. Linda's rabbits were transtemporalizing technologies. Like (some) other animal icons that accompany Maya hieroglyphic texts, rabbits were—conceivably, at least—known knowns in a maelstrom of semiotic madness. In this sense, then, animal figures provide a passageway between past and present, a tunnel through which the ancient becomes manifest again. Caves in the depths of the jungle and on coastal plateaus are portals to the Maya otherworld.[39] Schele and David Freidel titled the first chapter of one of their popular-press books "Time Travel in the Jungle."[40] Like, or as, that oddball ancient Maya scribe, Linda didn't just imagine herself as a rabbit. She burrowed down and became one.[41]

In correspondence with Linda, the Princeton University Art Museum curator Gillett Griffin frequently drew her as a rabbit or rabbit scribe (figure 2.6). It was his favorite.[42] Like Linda and like some of the Floyds, Peters, and Daves, Gillett seemed to imagine hieroglyphic interpretation as a mimetic and occasionally transformational act.[43] In discerning the sense and reference of hieroglyphic texts, Linda imitated ancient Maya lords or scribes. In the "*aha* moment" of deciphering a sign, she *became* one. I've sometimes suspected that this quasi-mysticism, this science fiction, spawned a species of scientism. Considering oneself the first in a millennium to read and understand a hieroglyphic text can do that. It's an elementary form of religious life, and a powerful one at that.[44] And religion is one of the main institutions producing social facts. Linda believed that hieroglyphs were a window directly into ancient minds. And decipherment was a "rite of transformation" that accorded the ancient Maya status as real, present beings.[45]

If the Maya were really real, the Mayanists, as both priests and participants in this rite of passage, this *becoming-Maya*, were really surreal. An *Archaeology* magazine article on photographer Justin Kerr describes the heady times that surrounded an important exhibition on ancient Maya ritual like this:

> When "The Blood of Kings" finally opened . . . it was a smash. The show and its catalogue—featuring Lady Xoc on its cover—explored Maya art, texts, and iconography through the lens of art history for the first time. It was an archaeological, aesthetic, and intellectual triumph. "After the opening, we were all so high," says Kerr. "This was the greatest Maya show that had ever been put on." At a private museum reception, giddy in their gowns and tuxedos, some of the curators and their colleagues marked the event with an ancient ceremony. "David Freidel, a Mayanist at Southern Methodist University, had brought a bowl and a bunch of obsidian and some paper, and we actually sat

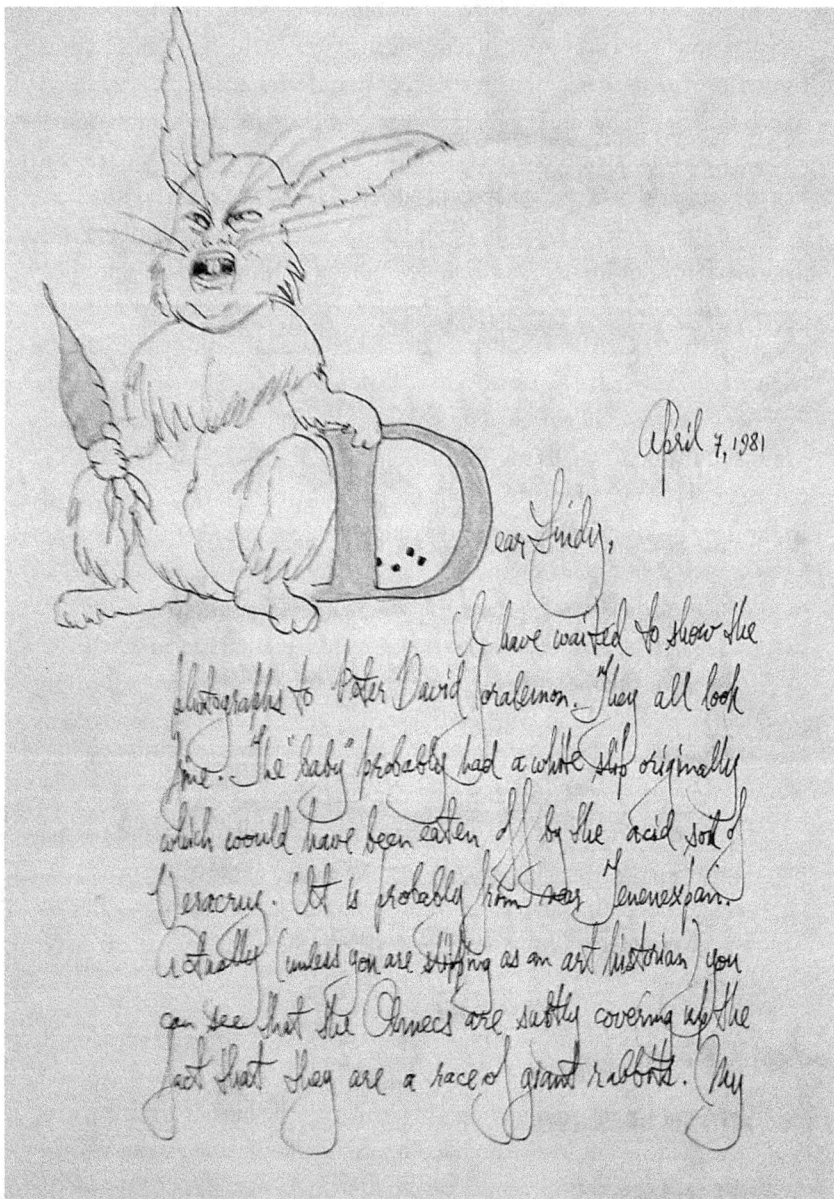

April 7, 1981

Dear Lindy,

I have waited to show the photographs to Peter David [Joralemon]. They all look fine. The "baby" probably had a white slip originally which would have been eaten off by the acid soil of Veracruz. It is probably from way Tenenexpan. Actually (unless you are stiffing as an art historian) you can see that the Olmecs are subtly covering up the fact that they are a race of giant rabbits. My

FIGURE 2.6 — Gillett Griffin to Linda Schele, April 7, 1981, p. 1. PHOTO BY THE AUTHOR.

around that table and we let blood, because that's what Lady Xoc on the lintel is doing! We were crazy!" Kerr says, laughing.[46]

Linda was crazy. Linda was a rabbit. Linda was Maya. And Linda was a genius, classically so. In an interview recorded for the documentary film *Cracking the Maya Code*, Gillett Griffin shared this assessment:

> Linda had a wonderfully bawdy sense of humor. . . . She was lots of fun and I didn't realize that this woman was one of the most brilliant people I will ever have met, and I have told people again and again that I'm the only surviving friend of Albert Einstein. But as far as I'm concerned, Linda had the more remarkable mind of the two. Einstein was a dreamer. Linda was also a dreamer. But she made the dreams a reality. She was really an extraordinary person that way.[47]

This passage didn't make the cut for the film. Too grandiose, perhaps. But Gillett's right. She was.

LIFE ACTUALLY

Life is a privileged conceptual tool and object of inquiry in cultural anthropology and critical theory today. To put my cards on the table, I think this privilege unfounded. In this respect I differ from thinkers like Latham and Geertz. As good anthropologists, these cats thought human life something particularly special. They indulged speculations that the human was not an animal like any other. The anthropologists' human emerged as a semiotic, sapient, political, tool-making monster of an animal. An exceptional life-form. This premise, perhaps, is now on the rocks. But the broader commitment to *life* as something that humans share with a special class of biotic beings appears firmly entrenched in our modes of thought. This commitment to life, this neovitalism or biocentrism, is the problem that I take on here, arguing that anthropology's turn from the human hasn't gone far enough.

But I shouldn't run ahead of myself. Slowly now. Let's take the turn.

Once anthropology's founding premise, human exceptionalism may now fall forlorn. Anthropology seems, again, to have come undone. *Logos*, the word, hangs insecurely affixed to *anthropos*, the human. Anthropologists—or so they go on calling themselves—study mushrooms, meerkats, honeybees, insects (writ large), plants, and microbial cultures.[48] Balinese monkeys get a mention.[49] There's an awkward dance going on here. Lacking choreography, we grope for a manageably noncontradictory term to denote this crowd's disavowal of, or at least discomfort with, the science of the naked ape. Terms include "the species turn," "animal anthropology," "the anthropology of life," "multispecies ethnography," and "zooethnography."[50] The sentiments behind these efforts vary, of course. But they share the point that the human's much more than human.

The lapsed Catholic, lapsed biologist, and—some say—lapsed Marxist feminist Donna Haraway, who would famously "rather be a cyborg than a goddess," is a high priest here.[51] We're multispecies organisms all the way down. We impinge on other living beings. They impinge on us. We host them while they parasitize us, and vice versa.[52] And what counts as "us" and "them" in these rhizomatic, sometimes-symbiogenetic cobwebs remains an open question.[53] The human organism itself entails and requires a mess of microscopic bacterial bodies. Donna puts it this way:

> I love the fact that human genomes can be found in only about 10 percent of all the cells that occupy the mundane space I call my body; the other 90 percent of the cells are filled with the genomes of bacteria, fungi, protists, and such, some of which play in a symphony necessary to my being alive at all, and some of which are hitching a ride and doing the rest of me, of us, no harm.[54]

Their bodies, ourselves.

Summing up some of these trends, Eben Kirksey and Stefan Helmreich write, "Multispecies ethnography . . . encourages us to ask, ethnographically, what happens when *Homo sapiens* and its interspecies, multispecies, and quasi-species familiars, burrow into the biology that animates the anthropos?"[55]

There's a lot going on here. On the one hand, the multispecifics, as we might call them, insistently retain some sense of ethnography. They tend to defend cultural anthropology's celebration of encounters across difference that give rise to *deep hanging out*, sustained dwelling with beings composing other worlds.[56] The bounded field sites pronounced passé in the 1990s are even back on the table.[57] Perhaps the multispecifics' challenge remains the problem of translation, rendering other worlds into compelling literary accounts, simmering descriptions until they thicken.[58] A word of caution: we should avoid emulating our forensic anthropologist friends and resist the urge to boil Geertz or Haraway down to the bone.

Or perhaps we *should* indulge that act of ethnographic emulation, following along as our forensic messmates macerate their specimens. Forensic anthropologists make bodies intelligible, legible, and legally actionable by doing away with them, suspending them in aqueous solutions at a constant temperature that enables anaerobic microbes to feast until they're full.[59] The scientists enlist millions of these putrefying microorganismic actors in their careful production of scientific and legal facts. Together they deflesh bodies, liquefying life but sparing bare bones, endoskeletal us. Maceration leaves us with disarticulated piles of mostly inorganic matter that tells stories about the past to the osteological literates.

Life oozes off the bone. And this is precisely my point. Arguments against human exceptionalism run aground when they substitute biocentrism for anthropocentrism. Now, if these were our only options, I'd take biocentrism any day. I'm happy extending the field of the social to other animal—that is, animate—that is, breathing and soulful—beings. But why stop there? What argument compels us to empathize for biotic (or biotic and cyborgian) enti-ties while ignoring the endless stream of "nonliving" (and nontechnological) things that comprise the cosmos?[60] Is this delimited extension of empathy even possible? The boundary between life and nonlife isn't clear. Biotic sys-tems entail and require nonbiotic components. You have inorganic bones. Your "life"—if we must go on calling it that—depends on your "nonlife." As categories, life and *bios* have their limits, their margins, their brackets, their constitutive exteriorities (to be deconstructive about it [which is inadvisable these days (it seems)]).

Life is slippery. Dorion Sagan puts it this way: "Ultimately the category of life may obscure our view of natural processes in their cosmic setting. 'Life' is integrally and eternally connected to the 'nonliving' universe from whence it derives. Earth is no more a rock with some life on it than you are a skeleton infested with cells."[61] Sagan conceives life—both yours and Gaia's—in thermodynamic terms. Bucking the presumption of a contradic-tion between the evolution of life and the second law of thermodynamics, he points out that organisms persist as heat-producing beings. Our bodies may appear orderly, but they are, in fact, entropic entities, rechargeable batteries dissimulating disorder as heat.

The warmth of the human touch is the universe falling apart. How dystopian!

Life is contingent. Stefan Helmreich argues that "life forms and forms of life inform, transform, and deform one another."[62] We can read "forms of life" here, in Ludwig Wittgenstein's sense, as the conditions that render our interactions and communications collectively intelligible.[63] Geertz, of course, called forms of life "webs of significance."[64] In his rich ethnographic accounts, Helmreich follows scientists to that great beyond at the bottom of the deep blue sea.[65] There life finds itself categorically and ontologically caught, like the finch suspended in the golden orb weaver's web, entangled and uncertain of its fate. The spider hovers menacingly. Will this meal be its last? Will we chow down on life, feed on our own metaphysical substrate? The web's no dialectic. There's no synthesis to be found.

True to her name, the black widow blends appetites.[66] She consummates first, consumes second.

So do ethnographers. Animals, beware.

Beware of skeletons infested with cells. Beware of empirical eyes.

HAUNTING II: LINDA'S SPIRITS

One after the other, they each asked, "Did you know Linda?" The question put my inner monologue on the defensive (*I* was the ethnographer. Wasn't *I* supposed to be asking the questions?).

"No, no I didn't," I'd confess embarrassedly. Linda died in 1998, two years before I enrolled in an anthropology course for the first time. But somehow this seemed like a poor excuse. I *should* have known Linda. Not because it was possible, but because Linda was an architect of the impossible.

To be honest with myself (and with you as well, since you're here), I learned of Linda for the first time in fall 2005. It was a meeting with my dissertation adviser. Susan was saying "Linda-*this*" and "Linda-*that*," and I was thinking nervously that I really ought to figure out who this Einstein sans surname was.

So I read *A Forest of Kings* and *Maya Cosmos*, coauthored tomes published by Harper for an audience of scholars and enthusiasts.[67] Schele was no Conrad, and no John Lloyd Stephens. The professional writer Joy Parker got a line as the third author of *Maya Cosmos*. But some of the truest passages in that book are Linda's personal accounts of discovery, the series of "*aha* moments" which led her to argue that Maya mythology, past and present, narrates the cyclical movement of their constellations. In recounting this discovery in *Maya Cosmos*, Schele tends to identify the objects of hieroglyphic and astronomical study as the agents of knowledge production themselves:

> Letting this remarkable record of their minds and hearts speak to us has been one of the most exhilarating experiences of our lives.[68]

The key to the unfolding of Creation was given to David Freidel.[69]

The sky opened up before us in all the glory it could steal from the electric streetlights.[70]

I saw something else that I think I was supposed to see.[71]

Later it occurred to me that the mother-fathers [mythological beings from the Maya creation texts] had conspired to get me there exactly when I was supposed to be [to see the constellations as the Maya saw them in the eighth century].[72]

Linda's science—and science it was—was a metaphysical journey tracking ancestors' footsteps down the "road of awe." She tripped into the spiritual otherworld, Xibalba, the Milky Way. For a reader of science studies like me, the author's displacement of agency onto scientific objects leaps off the page. Nature speaks for itself; scientists, like rabbits, are cultureless portals. But in *Maya Cosmos* these passages work a little differently. They redeem *wonder*, maybe even *magic*, as integral to scientific discovery.[73]

My road of awe has led a different direction. One evening in July 2007 it took me for the first time to a home in Austin's hilly suburbs. I was meeting with David, Linda's spouse until her death. David's a different kind of architect, an architect of buildings. He greeted me at the door in chorus with a loudly squawking parrot, making it all the easier to make the familiar strange and the strange familiar. The exotic, at last! My ethnographic field notes make no mention of rabbits. Then again, rabbits don't squawk at awkward guests, and my empirical eyes were not yet calibrated to their importance. I did note that the house was packed with books, Mesoamericana, and quite a few of Linda's vivid paintings, composed in a style that she described as "biomorphic surrealism."[74] *Far out, man!*

When I asked how Linda's art shaped her hieroglyphic acuity, David pointed to one of those paintings and challenged me to make sense of it. The sprawling shades of red were Greek to me. An abstraction of an animal's skull, he explained. Linda had a highly cultivated sense of form, of morphology, and she was keen at moving in either direction, from the real to the surreal or vice versa. Take a peek at a Maya text or two. They're columns of rounded squares: iconic heads and hands of humans and animal others interspersed with lines and dots and dashes and hatches, all the shapes known to "Man" and more. A master semiotician in the etymological sense, Linda diagnosed hieroglyphs' symptoms, their key signs.[75]

From the real to the surreal or vice versa. She stripped the signs all the way down to the bone, that inorganic core, that rabbit that endures. What *is* decipherment if it isn't maceration? What *is* decipherment if it isn't conjuring?

From the real to the surreal or vice versa. Linda was spirited, in every sense. And communing ethnographically with one David or another may amount to a kind of conjuring, reconjuring a conjurer.

> There are more things in heaven and earth, Horatio,
> Than are dreamt of in your philosophy.[76]

More things in heaven and earth, indeed, things like shamans and spirit companions. *Maya Cosmos* boasts the subtitle *Three Thousand Years on the Shaman's Path*. The road of awe led to a Maya culture stripped of its historicity and power to transform. She stripped it all the way down to the bone, the spirit, the *geist*, the cosmological kernel of transtemporal Mayanness.

Ethnographer one minute, provocateur the next, I raised the point to David. Three millennia of cultural continuity among speakers of disparate languages who didn't and still don't consider themselves a unified group seemed like a pretty bold position.

Linda, David affirmed, "could have argued either way." She "could turn on a dime."

Right, of course. Spiders spin both sticky and nonsticky threads. And they're not immune to their own technologies of entrapment. A wrong step could leave them stuck. The octopods must take care to avoid being ensnared in their own designs.[77]

"So why'd she have it *that* way," Goliath pressed.

"To stick her finger in someone's eye," David replied. Right, of course. Epigrapher one minute, provocateur the next.

You get my point, I think. Ethnographers are edgewalkers balanced between imitating the other and becoming her.

Edgewalker. In the documentary film by that name, Linda describes herself like this:

> There are people who are centralists and there are people who walk on the edge. And I think it's the edgewalkers that continually push the box, and push the shape at the edge. And I think they're the people that make fields change.
>
> I have always deliberately chosen to be an edgewalker, knowing that my work is going to be wrong. Because I'm putting out new ideas, and so forth. But I also change the nature of the field and change its directions and get other people to take on different kinds of questions— that I would never be able to do if I was a centralist. And beyond that, I'm not a trained academic. I'm a trained painter. How can a trained

painter compete with people from Yale and Harvard in the play job of holding the center? The only place where we have a chance to exist as leaders is on the edge. That's why the amateurs come in and kick the box.[78]

An *amateur*—the term taken through French from the Latin *amare*—is a lover. You have to really love something to do it well enough to be wrong. And it helps to have companions, a term which derives, as Haraway reminds us, from the Latin *cum panis*, "with bread."[79] Linda, generous in spirit and substance, broke bread with Floyd, Peter, and Dave, and of course with David too. Not to mention the rabbit.

Down the rabbit hole once more, I guess. It haunts me. At best the drawing's a spectral rabbit, but I still can't outrun it. Am I wrong? Is the animal ethnography's end point, or is it just a point of passage on the road to an alien anthropology beyond?[80] Do rabbits like us have the patience required to slow down and "follow the footprints of the ancestors"?[81]

Though I love etymologies, I try not to give much credence to them. They're not very ethnographic. But it would be negligent not to mention that "animal" derives from the classical Latin *anima*, meaning "air, breath, life, soul, spirit."[82] We animals are all haunted. *Anima* is the irrational side of the soul. It's opposed to *animus*, the rational side, the mind and will. Burrowing into this etymology might help animal anthropology take on a soul like Linda's (figure 2.7).

To deny that death marks an absolute rupture with life—as I have to—is, of course, classically irrational. The loss of breath, secular Cartesians imagine, extinguishes the soul along with the society of cells, those monads that stick to our bones.[83]

I doubt that my irrationalism would fly among the Classic Maya either, whose term for soul was *ik'*, meaning the breath of life. The *ik'* sign takes the shape of a capital *T*, the shape of windows in palace walls at the site of Palenque, windows that let in the cosmic breath.[84]

The breath of spirits led Linda down the road of awe to Palenque:

> I'm an alcoholic and when I was in the hospital for thirty days to confront my problem, the counselors said the solution had to be a spiritual one. As an academic, this is a problem. But as I walked through Palenque, I felt a strong sense of the spiritual. That allowed me to find resources to cope with the problem.[85]

Walking with the shadow of death, Linda found her *pharmakon*, her drug that's both poison and cure.[86] Her addiction to spirits like scotch opened the

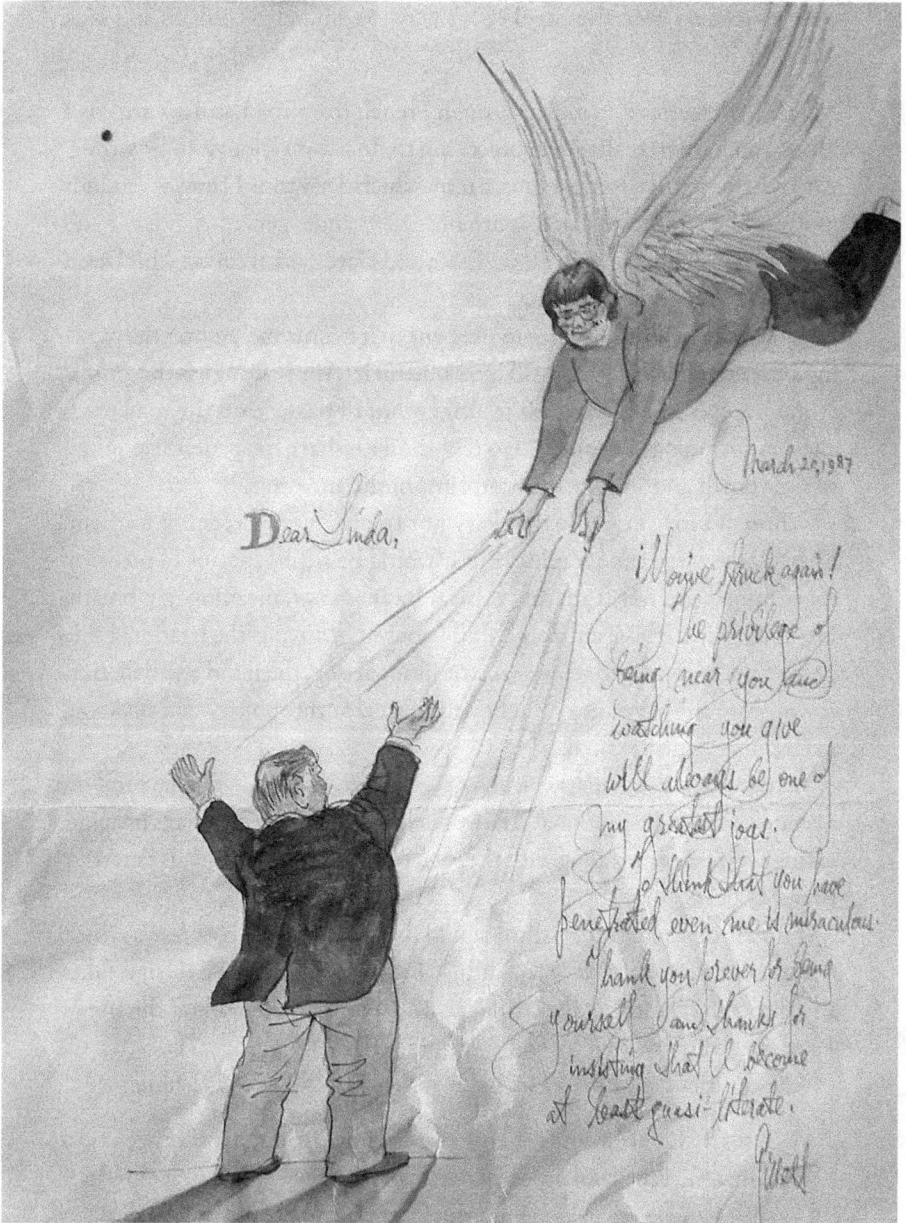

FIGURE 2.7 — Gillett Griffin to Linda Schele, March 20, 1987. PHOTO BY
THE AUTHOR.

path toward spirit companionship. Ghosts burrowed into Linda's biology. So she broke bread with *ánimas palencanas*.

In his book *Specters of Marx*, Jacques Derrida says,

> There has never been a scholar who really, and as a scholar, deals with ghosts. A traditional scholar does not believe in ghosts—nor in all that could be called the virtual space of spectrality. There has never been a scholar who, as such, does not believe in the sharp distinction between the real and the unreal, the actual and the inactual, the living and the non-living, being and non-being.[87]

Jacques seems, at times, to have thought himself that scholar. Did Jacques secretly believe in a sharp distinction between the amateur and the scholar? Maybe he needed a bit more love.

Or maybe a bit less. The acolytes of this master of the margin lined up out the door at Yale. It's hard to "compete with people from Yale and Harvard in the play job of holding the center."[88]

In a documentary film on his work, Derrida jokes that that he read very few books, but read them very well.[89] Jacques would have done better by reading a bit more ethnography, a bit more science, a bit more Marx, and maybe a bit of Linda as well.[90] Claude Lévi-Strauss, who read Linda and wrote to her, outlived his critic Derrida. *I mean . . .* Claude outlived Jacques, *so to speak*.

No—let's defer this thought. I'm speaking ill of the dead, disturbing skulls in the graveyard. Sprawling shades of red.

Linda's cells rebelled and her life oozed down the road of awe to the great beyond on April 18, 1998.[91] Stricken with pancreatic cancer at fifty-five, she knew it would happen. She said, "Somewhere on Lake Atitlan they're going to bury me and plant a fruit tree over me. And that's a very Maya thing to do."[92]

So, Linda, Linda, listen:

> Rest, rest, perturbèd spirit. So gentlemen
> With all my love I do commend me to you,
> And what so poor a man as Hamlet is
> May do t'express his love and friending to you,
> God willing shall not lack. Let us go in together,
> And still your fingers on your lips I pray.—
> The time is out of joint: O cursèd spite,
> That ever I was born to set it right.—
> Nay come, let's go together.[93]

Ethnographers' informants have long struggled to find the "right" answer to each question posed by the strange strangers who strangely show up at the door or hover hauntingly beyond the palace walls.[94]

I've learned one answer here. The next time I'm asked, "Did you know Linda?," I'll reply, "Yes, yes I did."

Chapter Three

....

Cosmos

DORION SAGAN

"I'm following you, Dorion!" I called from behind as he hurried down the hallway toward the auditorium.

Dorion's head swiveled and his gaze met mine. His eyes seemed glassy, lost in space. Did he recognize me in this second encounter? Dorion's the kind that knows too little and too much about you.

His plenary lecture mere minutes away, Dorion stopped and words spilled out, unrestrained: "My mom had a stroke. She's in the hospital. We're waiting to hear."

His lecture proved unthinkable, divine.

* * *

To be *plenary* is to be "full, complete, or perfect; not deficient in any element or respect; absolute."[1] A conference's plenary session pretends to assemble all attendees, all participants in a unified ritual act. The plenary, then, evokes what we might call a *planetary event*.[2] The plenary has planetary aspiration, ambition. The planetary event entails a plenary consciousness, a collectivity that exceeds. A plenary talk delimits and affirms the conferential cosmos, assembling the audience into one room, obligating us to rub shoulders with those whom we otherwise might not see, might not care to see. The plenary amounts to a singularity, a totalizing form like the potlatch of the northwestern Pacific coast, that classic event of events for Americanist anthropology, that event that may reveal the more troubling face of the gift: debt, indebting, rendering dependency, the Dionysian giver's constitution of an ambit of control.[3]

But neither the potlatch nor Sagan's plenary escapes history and worldliness. What anthropologists know as the potlatch is a complicated historical effect of the colonial restructuring of indigenous social orders. The image of the potlatch that anthropologists today reproduce is a settler image of an institution enabling Kwakwaka'wakw people to grapple with the shifting cultural experiences and power dynamics of colonial encounter and rule. As Joe Masco recounts, "The expanding ritualism [of the second half of the nineteenth century] played an essential role in a ritual calculus for restoring the souls of the dead and represents a vigorous Kwakwaka'wakw attempt to overcome the social and spiritual consequences of the colonial situation through traditional religious understandings."[4]

Potlatch practices reflect a Kwakwaka'wakw cosmology that attributes souls to all beings while holding that the quantity of cosmic souls remains finite. Souls, which people may lose or steal, must be carefully protected, requiring regenerative ritual as a moral practice: "The Kwakwaka'wakw's preservation of inherited names was but one aspect of the intricate ritual calculus for restoring the souls of the dead to their initial positions within the cosmic scheme."[5] The potlatch should not be tokenized as a model or paradigm of and for anthropological thought on ritual (though the extent to which such a tokenized image has offered the paradigmatic model for anthropological constructions of Maya and other indigenous cosmologies is a history-of-science question worth asking).[6] The intensification of the potlatch followed an 1862 epidemic that cost Kwakwaka'wakw people 70 percent of their population.[7] Its cultural function and historical rise to prominence, then, are not trivial matters. I do, however, want to think nearby this form in considering plenary events such as Dorion's lecture as modes of divination, conferential interventions into the cosmic order, gifts that serve the end of soul maintenance.[8] Perhaps the potlatch is a more *honest* expression of ritual-cosmological care for worldly souls than an academic conference.

My literary method in this chapter centers the experimental evocation of partial connectedness; I call it "six degrees of Carl Sagan." Inscribing "partial connections" exceeds the insistence on a primacy of relations, or a partibility of the self; it's a technique of soul maintenance in a finite and vulnerable world.[9] Schele achieved status as an ensouling public spokesperson by maintaining an array of social and epistemic attachments that extended far beyond the community of Mayanist scholars and amateurs. This chapter evokes how these attachments across ostensible epistemic, aesthetic, and spiritual differences vitalized the public science of Maya epigraphy.[10] By re-visioning decipherment as a heterodox, never-pure science, I begin to substantiate my suggestion that conventional framings of historical discovery and its ritual exposition—Dorion's, Linda's, ours—too readily assume an impermeable boundary between secular and spiritual knowledges.[11] My edgewalk here amounts to an experiment in revealing this ostensible boundary as a fantasy that—in the service of producing more richly artistic sciences—we might better do without.

Dorion's talk ensouled passionately. He prefaced the plenary by sharing that his mother—the important evolutionary biologist and radical thinker Lynn Margulis—had suffered a medical emergency inducing a comatose state. His plenary talk, then, conveyed a kind of critical feeling—the feeling of being *in crisis*. It felt, to me, like an honest, touching exposition, a structured speech event animated by a desire to protect the fullness or completeness of his family, his integral, intimate, and intellectual attachment to kin. The force of this event may have been intensified by the secular religiosity that Sagan's kin, particularly his father Carl, assertively promoted. Whether we're in a personal crisis, such as Dorion's, or a cultural crisis, such as the Kwakwaka'wakw's, we may summon the collectivizing power of ritual to mend holes rending our experiences of being and becoming. So, Dorion's plenary was indeed a plenarist engagement, a making-full of the world that resists nihilistic impulses.[12] It was a calling into a crowd of modest listeners,[13] an interpellation insisting that we do the soulful work of maintaining forms of academic life and afterlife: reading well, thinking well, speaking sometimes to a few, and sometimes to as many as possible, and doing so as a moral commitment that attends our cosmo-spiritual companionship.[14]

Crisis can induce a collective will, a praying-if-not-exactly-praying-together, that serves both the classic Durkheimian end of reproducing the social order and a more ephemeral end, irreducible to such social realism—even, perhaps, the version promoted by the sociological kin-network's gift to anthropology: Marcel Mauss.[15] As Reinhart Koselleck and Janet Roitman have each unpacked, the terms *crisis* and *critique* share a common root, with ramifying implications. Roitman offers a compelling summary of Koselleck's historiographic work on the subject:

Koselleck provides an illustration of the temporalization of history, or the emergence of "history" as a temporal category. He attributes the emergence of the category of history as a temporality to the concomitant displacement of the term "crisis," arguing that, by the end of the eighteenth century, crisis is the basis for the claim that one can judge history by means of a diagnosis of time.[16]

Crisis, then, becomes an operative category for a historical consciousness through which critical events organize memory into a temporally structured and temporally structuring collective sensibility, fantasy, or trauma.

Roitman, further, reads crisis as an incursion of the transcendent that undoes the everyday. It is "a transcendental placeholder because it is a means for signifying contingency; it is a term that allegedly allows one to think the 'otherwise.'"[17] Crisis, then, generates a surplus of temporal imaginaries, including counterfactual pasts and futures formed through extraordinary affects. Critical events such as discoveries and medical crises rend the affective order. But they do so in different ways. Historical (or, for that matter, microbiological, astronomical, etc.) discovery introduces novel forms, beings, or concepts into modalities of collective sensing and feeling, our communities or cultural systems. Naming and narrating beings such as Pakal enacts a critical realignment, the making of an "otherwise" history, a different story, a new resource for sensing the past.[18] The extraordinary affects of history and science tend toward this kind of introductory ethos; they are more additive than subtractive, aspiring more toward plenarism than nihilism. Extraordinary events, such as discoveries, bring new—or relationally transformed—actors into social collectives or worlds. In this sense, science, including Dorion's staged discovery, is a making-full of the world that struggles against finitude—his mother's finitude, but not only. Decipherment, as an extraordinary feat, or a structured-and-structuring series of small feats, has generated a buzzing *affirmative otherwise*, a past knowable through forms that resemble, perhaps, the narrative-driven, conflict-oriented, emplotted modern novel. Epigraphic discovery, as a reworlding of the ancient Maya, promotes an ideology of history trafficking in an image of knowledge production as the act of progressively naming and storying Maya elites. As we now know them, these elites pervasively recorded the crises that they endured and affected.

Epigraphy, then, has facilitated—through linguistic analysis—the critical reconstruction of contemporary images of the ancient Maya world, a world rift with its own crises. History becomes a body of organized facts, eventing actors that induce, structure, or respond to critical events. This mode of populating the past may differ fundamentally from the other kind of critical interruption at hand here, the crisis that Dorion experienced that December day, the prospect of his mother's death. The extraordinary affect attending the coming death of one's close kin may hue toward pessimism, even nihilism. The affirmative otherwise that Dorion offered was the possibility that we might commune together, working toward the re-ensouling maintenance of a world where each of us experiences microcosmic crises, crises that evoke ultimate forms of crisis, the ultimate, eventual undoing of the cosmos itself. Dorion embraced and adopted a plenarist sensibility against that eventuality, a hope within or against tragedy, a being-together that exceeded maternal citation, an articulation of his biologist-mother's social being that incorporated an audience of modest-enough listeners into a multispecies muddle, the world called "Lynn Margulis."[19]

Perhaps Schele's mode of populating her followers' historical consciousness with ancient Maya beings differed fundamentally from Sagan's effort to channel his mother's soul. But reflection on the latter helps to put Schele's plenarist tendencies into high relief. She promoted the epigraphic vision of an ancient Maya world by populating that world with distinctive, named persons and personalities. This suggests a biopolitical sensibility, a fixation on the individual as a unit for measures of the population.[20] In its transhistorical and transcultural projection, this fixation didn't attend adequately to the reality that people conceive personhood in quite different ways. One might even ask, here, whether Schele's and the epigraphers' plenarist desires, their desires to name and populate the past, reveal the flip side of a Carl Saganesque cosmic neomysticism. Just as Dorion's father called his viewers and readers to encounter the cosmic sublime as an act of wondrous scale-expanding science, Schele directed her followers' vision to the cosmically ordained order of very particular people at very particular times. To rescale our being as a minuscule, specific cosmic accident was, also, to call us into a kind of humanist affinity, a liberal attachment to all people in all times and places. The unrelenting optimism of this modernist sensibility insists that if "the ancient Maya" constructed a world with art at its center, we can too.

Maybe decipherment's plenarist affirmation of an otherworld *should* call us to into critical reworldings, including new modes of artistic-cum-political becoming. Did it make the weird world of Austin—during the long civil rights movement, during and after the Vietnam War—feel a little more intimate, structured, sensible, and collectively caring, let alone *just*? If so, for whom? Maybe decipherment, its recent practitioners' elitism and disengagement from basic theoretical and historiographic questions aside, entailed something of a reparative project.[21] At least it did for Linda and her followers—Austinite or not. And maybe, for now, that's enough.

And maybe history and science thought otherwise—including the astronomical gaze, including the impassioned plenary—can amount to reworlding soul maintenance, to critical realignment, to repair.

CARL SAGAN

I read *Broca's Brain* as a child, I think.[22] At eleven, twelve, twelve and a half. I hardly remember.

The penultimate chapter's titled "Gott and the Turtles." It drowns our conceits in the unthinkable expanse of the cosmos.

Sagan repeats an old story:

> A Western traveler encountering an Oriental philosopher asks him to describe the nature of the world:
> "It is a great ball resting on the flat back of the world turtle."
> "Ah yes, but what does the world turtle stand on?"
> "On the back of a still larger turtle."
> "Yes, but what does he stand on?"
> "A very perceptive question. But it's no use, mister; it's turtles all the way down."
> We now know that we live on a tiny dust mote in an immense and humbling universe. The gods, if they exist, no longer intervene daily in human affairs. We do not live in an anthropocentric universe. And the nature, origin and fate of the cosmos seem to be mysteries far more profound than they were perceived to be by our remote ancestors.[23]

"We now know." Sagan repeats the phrase again and again. A refrain.

The refrain punctuates Sagan's Gifford Lectures on Natural Theology, presented at the University of Glasgow in 1985. Sagan knew that "Kant . . . knew about objects that were then called nebulae. It was not clear whether they were within our Milky Way or beyond—we now know, of course, most of them are beyond. Some of the nebulae were again flattened systems made, we now know, of stars."[24]

Gifford Lecturers are an elite bunch. The social anthropologist James Frazer; the physicists Werner Heisenberg and Niels Bohr; the philosophers Alfred North Whitehead, Hannah Arendt, and William James. James published his Gifford Lectures as *The Varieties of Religious Experience*.[25] Years after Sagan's death, Ann Druyan edited and published her astronomer-husband's lectures. It's titled *The Varieties of Scientific Experience: A Personal View of the Search for God*.[26] In her introduction Druyan lets us know that "Carl admired James's definition of religion as a 'feeling of being at home in the Universe,' quoting it at the conclusion of *Pale Blue Dot*, his vision of the human future in space."[27]

Sagan felt at home on this pale blue dot, this tiny dust mote. He didn't fear the great cosmic sneeze. Most of us are more fragile.

Sagan sought to change the climate from religious to scientific experience. A simple substitution. A secular switcheroo. Prostrate yourself now before the immensity of the cosmos.

But the substitution might not be so simple. Becoming open to the surprises of other worlds means accepting that your world, however immense and humbling, might have limits too.

Is this why Sagan invokes non-Western cosmologies again and again? Does this explain why he takes that "Oriental" account of endless turtling as an affirmation of his own cosmic vision? Sagan opens the glossy book *Cosmos*, an adjunct of his TV series by that name, with a quote from the colonial K'iche' Maya book of cosmogenesis, the *Popol Vuh*:

> The first men to be created and formed were called the Sorcerer of Fatal Laughter, the Sorcerer of Night, Unkempt, and the Black Sorcerer. . . . They were endowed with intelligence, they succeeded in knowing all that there is in the world. When they looked, instantly they saw all that is around them, and they contemplated in turn the arc of heaven and the round face of the earth. . . . [Then the Creator said]: "They know all . . . what shall we do with them now? Let their sight reach only to that which is near; let them see only a little of the face of the earth! . . . Are they not by nature simple creatures of our own making? Must they also be gods?"[28]

The chapter is titled "The Shores of the Cosmic Ocean." Sagan was a speck of sand on the shore. He was at home in the universe. His toothy smile and salt-and-pepper hair beamed into the living rooms of a half billion people. He was at home on those curved glass screens. For Dorion, too much so:

> I guess my problem with him boiled down to this: just as talking familially to the masses about the beauty of the cosmos on the Tonight Show with Johnny Carson made him a father figure to millions, so his air of unassailable authority, 1950s-style paternalism, and intellectual

arrogance made him emotionally distant as a father. He was that same television guest in his own living room, only he was now also the host. If I, his eldest son, was a privileged member of his audience, I was still, well, a member of his audience. Sometimes one felt more like a camera than a family member.[29]

Browsing Carl in the library one day, I noticed that he had a shelf-mate named Miriam Sagan. I assumed it was coincidence, that she was no relation. But it turns out that the author of *Map of the Lost* is a distant cousin of Carl's.[30] I pinched a line above from her first poem there: "At eleven, twelve, twelve and a half."[31] "Relatives," as Marilyn Strathern points out, "are always a surprise."[32]

* * *

The planet is a totality rendered thinkable through a view not from nowhere, but from particularly located spheres in space. Planet Earth becomes conceivable as a speck of dust if we share with Carl Sagan the magic "dialectical image" of Earth as the blue planet, the image of Earth from a space that's no more "outer" than "inner," a space that doesn't offer any privileged, central stargazing standpoint.[33] Only by depriviledging the human can Carl Sagan feel at home in the universe. One might, writing in a cynical mood, suggest that Carl Sagan's paradoxically cosmic being entailed and required alienation, even from his most proximate kin. Carl Sagan's plenary consciousness promoted a unified ecological, material vision of the cosmos writ large. But what's the cost of this scientific worldview? Does this plenary consciousness come in exchange for a planetary consciousness that privileges our ecological and material entanglement with collectives of "living" (and "nonliving") beings located in particular places, such as the precarious turtling that we call "Earth"?

Maybe the introduction of the turtle and turtling here puts Schele's rabbiting into sculptural relief. Were I compelled to pick a side, I'd take the hare over the tortoise every time. This isn't just because I've known a caring, thoughtful, loving hare or two. To "hare" is also to harry, to worry, to harass; to frighten, to scare. I wish not to hare you into a frightful escape, a flight from scientific materialism, or even from what Wilfrid Sellars and Ray Brassier have called the "scientific image" of the human.[34] I'm telling a less-scary, not-so-nihilistic story about cosmic (non)life. I tell this story as a settler descended of settlers who violently settled "the Americas" or, as some Native writers and activists call the continent, "Turtle Island."[35] Like Stephen

Hawking and Clifford Geertz, Carl Sagan told a version of that contact zone of a turtle tale.[36] His version traffics in a plenary modernism; he seems to assume that receiving the same sound waves, hearing the same sounds, amounts, *presto change-o*, to listening to the same ideas.[37] Just as ancient Maya orators stood atop the Temple of the Inscriptions, pronouncing their dynastic truths, Linda Schele stood on stage at UT-Austin, and Carl Sagan ported through TV tubes in corners of living rooms damn near everywhere. But there's a stark difference between the Maya dynasts and their latter-day saints. We know—we now know—that Schele's and Sagan's speech acts reflect a modernist ideology of language and rationality, a notion that truths stated clearly will not just be heard, but understood and internalized.[38] They worked to brass-tack their strange intuitions, precepts, and concepts into an image that might inaugurate a kind of collective sense. For Sagan, this was a collective sense of human particularity set against the sublime cosmic infinity of space. For Schele, this was a collective sense that ancient Maya lives were like all lives, that ancient Maya writing was like our writing, that we might be able to communicate not only with the darkest corners of the cosmos, but with that more mysterious, numinous alterity, the past. Schele populated the world with a litter of ancient Maya beings. *Litter: confusion, clutter, mess; brood, progeny; trash, refuse, debris, rubbish.*

This messy modernism's plenary consciousness may take shape, then, in gatherings, assemblies that make it possible for a clutter to think-feel together, to touch each other, rubbing shoulders and straining toward the same auditory waves, turning confusion into common knowledge.[39] Achieving plenary/progeny consciousness through collective witnessing-listening requires partaking of, and reproducing, a ruinous rationality, a modernist conceit of communication as the transferal of neutral, alienable ideas from one subject to another.[40] I can't but tell a different kind of story, a story of partial connection, a story of epistolary and epistemic attachments that do not—cannot—desire, let alone presume, finality or totality; brooding-attachments-becoming-ruins. It's a story of cobecoming that seeks to free us of the image of human science as a nonpoetic, nonerotic endeavor, an endeavor that thinks the human as the phenotypic effect of a primary form such as genetic code. It's a story of science as a litter of brooding progeny who refuse rubbish.[41]

So, I wish not to hare—as in frighten or scare—you. Let alone to harass you. But I do think that we need to be hared—as in worried—out of the turtle's shell. I make my alliance, a noninnocent alliance, with the hare here not just because Linda did; my noninnocence is not her insensitive appropriation. We should take it up, rather, because Linda, read queerly (read fully), wished to hare her followers out of staid and mistaken truths. This staid and mistaken truth wasn't the gene with all of its biopolitical bluster, or rationality with its presumption of speech's neutrality,[42] but the simple mistaken image of the ancient Maya as unsophisticated spiritualists. There is, then, some arsenic-irony laced into the paint of my portraiture here. Dialectical images, including hieroglyphs and the images of those who make them, host contagion. Do I inscribe the decipherers in the form of those purportedly unsophisticated spiritualists that they dispossessed of their Eden? Is this a dialectic or an eternal return?

The image poisons the dialectic, our assumptions about the dialectic, as a movement of consciousness or history.[43] The floating signifier can become a hollowed-out sign: the commodity, the hieroglyph, the gene.[44] Desire it however you wish. Narrate it however you wish. You could write a fractal story, a story about a dialectical image that takes the form of that dialectical image. But you'll need to harry the writing, worry the readers.[45] You'll have to worry them into considering the exclusions of their dialectic. To fill in the hollowed-out sign or object is to receive the gift. It's also to incorporate—to allow our bodies to reform around the shape of the spirit or *geist*. To take the ghost, joyfully or not, into the body machine. Science can be a generative, surprising encounter with the unknown, a jaunt into the epistemic open.[46] Scientists build apparatuses for internalizing the world (though it's not a fractal internalization, per se, as their internalizations entail chains of mediation, deformation).[47] Science, as a collective, machinic feeling-into-the-cosmos, undoes us.

In their reflection "'Otherwise Anthropology' Otherwise," Debbora Battaglia and Rafael Antunes Almeida urge anthropologists to take up a "transfigurative" ethnographic praxis that machines mutual, reciprocal "apparatuses of welcoming,"[48] opening ethnography to experimentation that articulates situated modes of becoming into sites of diplomatic, cosmo-political, value-constituting exchange.[49] They call the idea-machine that machines their machine the *onto-dispositif*. The onto-dispositif feels into relations of mutual touch through "heterogeneous *exchange protensions*." Examples of heterogeneous exchange protensions include Mars rovers, bioart sculptures, and ET/UFO believers' experiments on us terrans. Such formful beings generate more than ethnographic and technological sensibilities; they stage modes of sensory exchange and, hence, change. This protensive grappling might reorient us to what Trinh T. Minh-ha calls the "nearby."[50] It might offer what Sara Ahmed calls a "queer phenomenology" of the nearby, with orienting entailments that recursively undo any fantasy of consciousness that projects the self into a relationless void of (outer) space.[51] *Lift off or buzz off?*

Such a protensive phenomenology, if you'll forgive my channeling of the recombinant voice, shouldn't simply trash the shell-machine-protected spirit-tortoise inner space to brood with the hare that hares it. *Brood: family, progeny; worry, mope, agonize, dwell on.*

The semiotic/somatic flesh of the turtle, in its biospiritual fullness, matters too (it must be saved). It's just that sometimes the truth-bound turtle is too slow and brooding. Its undistractable, ploddingly linear emplotment propels the tortoise across the finish line first. But the rabbit's encounterful competition—even if it's only more encounterful in her dreams—will have felt more by the plot's *fin*. Here, then, is the meta-irony of the tale of tortoise and hare, in the form of its abstract-but-meaningful popular reception. The tortoise finishes the race, victoriously, with one story; the hare's late arrival matters little because the hare's a deprogrammer, a deprogrammatic protension that exchanges the race's oppositional, dialectical movement for a capacious internalization of worldly surprises (the hare as affect theory's trickster figure).[52] This chapter is an apparatus for welcoming loser hares. The meta-irony is that the hare loses by winning otherwise, by feeling more, and better, in the process. The hare's here, after all. What does Derrida call her?—the *arrivant*?[53]

"She'll only win," you may protest, "at the cost of a reflective inner self, a considered consciousness." But your agony dwells in philosophical exhaust: the exhaustion of endless philosophical counterclaims; or the toxic black-smoke by-product of sparked fuel ("epistemology," "psychology"). The insistence on a coherent inner consciousness is a modern industrial waste product. Boil out the toxins; turn coherent self-reflection into a tasty soup for hairy companions, a litter of prodigious progeny. The hare may well be "ether, quintessence."[54] But she has a lively inner space too: a recombinant internalization of a multiplicity of forms, achieved through a frenzied anticritical rush of feelings with(in) the morphology of that experiential form that we touch-feel as the world. After all, you have to fill that body-without-organs up with *something*.[55] Nourish yourself. Listen to Linda. *Read like a rabbit.* Touch and see like a rabbit. Fix your gaze on alien others in trans-species encounters that would make a denuded Derrida blush;[56] catch their eye, sizing them up, learning them, feeling them out before fleeing in a fugitive *poof*: the cotton puff transfigures into occlusive, white smoke. The specular becomes spectral, leaving us to speculate (i.e., science). The hare's a dissipative ontology.

Maybe otherwise anthropology read otherwise might consider the possibility of being other-wise or otherly wise, taking up another kind of wisdom. Or another kind of wise-cracking. The hare cracks wise, troping circles around the tortoise. Could cracking wise become a dissipative onto-dispositif that machines open singularizing plenary ontologies? Such punnery may amount to strategic catachreses evoking the tendency of anthropology's ontological discourse to cohere into a closed plenary consciousness. Plenary consciousness isn't only closed; it's an enclosure, an insistence on the boundedness of thought, gathering us into a plenarist collective, a consciousness that fences us into modes of proprietary (im)propriety that we call things like "the academy," "the Department of Anthropology," and "*HAU: A Journal of Ethnographic Theory*." A recombinatory aesthetics reigns within the dominant plenarist anthropology of becoming, a force(ful) field that we call things like "desire," "affect," "becoming," "culture," "the gift."

My intention isn't to counter totalizing modes of disci-plenary enclosure. Though Brassier's tortoise of a nihilistic metaphysics could offer an escape here; nihilism, classically speaking, is the doctor's cure for plenarist totalization.[57] Instead, I want to make light of disciplinarity, to crack it (up) so that rays of light might shine through. It can be hard to find disinfectant sunshine in a post-Enlightenment world. Even the gene portends a plenarist totality; it so easily—"evilly," I just misspoke, catachrestically, while reading this passage out loud—becomes a selfish monadic microcosmos enclosing us from within. The gene and its spokespersons dictate that we prefix each and every noun with that living etymon, *bio-*. And the ontologists and the affectologists (like me?), like the biopoliticians (be they critical or naive), all hue to a plenarist feeling, because it feels good to rub shoulders with our clutch; it feels good to feel like *maybe, just maybe* we all might hear the same thing, feel the same thing. Can you see this dialectical image stereoscopically? Do you feel me?

It feels good (to some) to say that everything is a flux of becoming, a dynamic flow, an affective formation; it hares the subtractive function of critique with a plenarist metaphysical coherency. Vitalist, including Spinozist and Deleuzian, ontologies feel good because they, at once, affirm a kind of dynamic becoming-other and prescribe for us a common, rather stable and coherent language for naming this multitudinous wave.[58] But to "contain multitudes" is also to *contain* multitudes,[59] to enclose the contradictions, to refuse them an emanative form that cracks our bodies-without-organs, including the canon. *Cite Deleuze. Cite Deleuze.* Deleuzian flirtation with accelerationism is a losing position.[60] Maybe theory writ large is a losing position; theory as an insistence on the plenarist containment and enclosure of thought; it's an ordering, often tenuous, of thought, being, and becoming, a nonreciprocal capture that deflates extraordinary affects, including those of discovery. But to cite Deleuze (and Guattari) might be an act of deflating, defacing them, as a sacrilegious refusal to heed their functionalist prescription, their enclosing insistence that students read their book, *Anti-Oedipus*, best because they read it as a "little non-signifying machine"; they use it like a hammer.[61] Books, mind you, can also be technologies of enclosure. *Shut it!*

This is getting hairy. I'm jumping out of my privilege, off the privy-ledge, and into the muck, the negative, the waste, the shit. Shit.[62] As Deleuze, sounding more like an exchange theorist than he might like, puts it, "A book is a little cog in a much more complicated external machinery. Writing is one flow among others, with no special place in relation to the others, that comes into relations of current, countercurrent, and eddy with other flows—flows of shit, sperm, words, action, eroticism, money, politics, and so on."[63] To regard the ancient Maya as cultural sophisticates on account of their highly pictorial writing system is to take writing as a civilizational achievement, to enclose the Maya in the project of expansion that gave geographical form to the entwined, consequential historical fantasies that we call capitalism and the Enlightenment.[64] Maybe a more careful and even caring act of Maya historicization might look to their shit, what archaeologists have called "paleofeces" or "coprolites." That takes us down to earth, a dark earth, a fecund *terra preta*.[65] What if we weighted tales of excretory infrastructure, rather than that star dust we call "writing," when glorifying and attaching to pasts? The triumph of reading ancient Maya writing is by now, after all, a well-digested past, a past past.

To polish the sacralized history of Maya lords, whether inhabiting—like the hare—dreamstate alterities, or vying for political control, is to forget that history is full of shit (such forgetting can be called "ideology"). Our waste becomes earth, as our bodies do (redundant?). Pakal's death-scene, in the sarcophagus lid inscription, draws us into the maw of the underworld, figured as serpent, an entry into the jaws of a being that will digest and shit "him" out. So, what do we make of the fact that Pakal's entombment is figured as descent down a tree or cornstalk into the body of a legless creature that might stalk fertilized fields of corn, beans, and vegetables and, if threatened, sink its fangs into your legs? The serpent, mind you, is no friend of hare or tortoise. The apparent darkness of this scene—in an enclosure beneath Palenque's Temple of the Inscriptions—finds its curious counterpoint in the skyband that edges the edge of the sarcophagus lid.

What if this skyband signifies that the sarcophagus itself amounts to an exchange protension? Entombment opens a sphere of exchange between this world and that of the dead.[66] Exchange with the dead, here, also entails cosmological change, transformation. This may be a recognition of finitude in the wake of the cosmic expanse of space, but it may also be a calling to the otherworlds that one sees and imagines while standing on the Temple of the Inscription's platform. In the film *The Fountain*, the passage into the otherworld, Xibalba, takes the form of a movement through the Milky Way into a psychocosmic beyond, death as the Fountain of Youth.[67]

But what sensory exchange is possible in this site of cultural response and responsiveness to Pakal's death? What kind of welcoming apparatus is a skyhacking hare?

LINDA SCHELE

Her most popular book was *Maya Cosmos: Three Thousand Years on the Shaman's Path*.[68] In late 1986, seven years before it appeared, Carl Sagan wrote her.[69] He likely dictated the unsolicited letter to a secretary in the Laboratory for Planetary Studies at Cornell's Center for Radiophysics and Space Research:

> Dear Dr. Schele:
>
> I had the pleasure of seeing your "The Blood of Kings" Exhibition in Cleveland last week and wanted to tell you how impressed I was both artistically and with regard to the major advances being made in understanding Mayan life and ritual. I wanted to pass on to you one suggestion: Is it not now time to publish an edition of the Popol Vuh with Mayan illustrations.
>
> With every good wish,
>
> Cordially,
>
> *Carl Sagan*
>
> CS/EY
> CC: DR. MARY MILLER

In 1985, ethnographer Dennis Tedlock published a lightly illustrated edition of the *Popol Vuh* through Simon and Schuster.[70] The mass-market edition appeared the next year, the year *Blood of Kings* hit exhibition halls, the year Sagan wrote to Schele.

Maybe Schele alerted Sagan to this development when she replied—according to the stamp on Sagan's letter—on November 17, 1986. Maybe she passed along a copy of Tedlock's edition. I don't know. All I know about that letter can be found in Carl's reply:

17 DECEMBER 1986

Dear Professor Schele:

Many thanks for your kind letter. I'm curious about the number 142 nonillion. Could I trouble you to tell me in what context this number appears, and also, for clarity, how this number is written in the usual exponential notation (for example, 142×10^{30})?

With many thanks,

Cordially,

Carl Sagan

CS/EY[71]

One hundred forty-two nonillion! Sagan's credited with popularizing the term *billion* (which pales by comparison). In 1980, when his thirteen-part TV series *Cosmos: A Personal Voyage* aired on PBS, there were about 4.5 billion people on Earth. Of those 4.5 billion, ten were billionaires. So, in 1980, a time when there were billions of us and a few of us with billions of dollars, the handsome starry-eyed cosmic witness implored viewers to think bigger than ever. Sagan's catchphrase became "billions and billions." He later denied having said it on the series, attributing the phrase to Johnny Carson's mop-headed caricature: "I never said 'billions and billions.' For one thing, it's too imprecise. How many billions are 'billions and billions?' A few billion? Twenty billion? A hundred billion? 'Billions and billions' is pretty vague."[72]

Linda's number, 142 nonillion, is much more precise. Did Carl really not know it? One nonillion is written as a one followed by thirty zeros. So, he got the exponential notation right: 142×10^{30}. Was Linda ribbing Carl with this figure? Was Carl kidding back?

Like Carl, Linda was larger than life. So the immensity of Sagan's cosmos, the 10 billion trillion stars, didn't cow her. She one-upped 'im.

During my interview with David Schele, he recalled Linda's friendship with Carl (it was the first I'd heard of it). At Carl's invitation, she'd presented a lecture on cultural concepts of the universe to an audience at NASA's Jet Propulsion Laboratory in Los Angeles. The flyer deposited in Linda's letters bills the event as a "Blue Ribbon Panel" on "Exploration of Neighboring Planetary Systems (ExNPS)."

I'd like to think that Linda took the opportunity to share her experience attending a Maya ceremony, the Festival of Games, in Chamula, Mexico, in 1992. There, while blending in with precultural monkeys battling the Sun-Christ for cosmic control, she began to test her hypothesis that Maya cosmology narrated the movement of their constellations. The final confirmation of her hypothesis came six months later while Schele stood in a pitch-black vegetable field in the Mexican state of Quintana Roo:

> The scorpion blazed away in the south next to the rattlesnake in Sagittarius, and below them the Milky Way spread outward in the form of the buttress roots of the tree. To the north, I saw the great Bird diving toward the horizon as it had at Chamula half a year earlier, but this time it was surrounded by the sparkling light of a billion stars. In the center of the sky above our heads, we saw the dark cleft that the Maya read as the head of the crocodile. The tree, the scorpion, the crocodile, the bird—all of the images I had seen on computer screens, on the pages of astronomy books, and in the pictures created by the ancient Maya, were there. And they were so much bigger than I had imagined for I had grown used to seeing them at the scale of a page I held in my hand. It truly was the Path of Awe painted with all the brilliance the Itz'at of the Sky had originally given it.[73]

Prostrate yourself now before the immensity of the cosmos.

When I asked David to share Linda's take on the ownership of ideas produced collaboratively, he said, "Linda would have been adamantly opposed to the ownership of ideas. She hardly ever spoke in terms of 'I think that . . .' It was always, 'Now we think . . .'"

Right. Now we think . . . We now know . . . A refrain.

* * *

Classic Maya mythology stories the spark of cosmic creation as an image appearing. Schele and Khristaan D. Villela read a stela from the Maya site of Quiriguá as narrating the originary moment as the Maya date (4 Ahaw 8 Kumk'u) followed by a seemingly innocuous phrase: "appearance or manifestation of an image."[74] The glyphs' scribe contoured the image as a triad of stones placed by distinct gods across three locations: a house, an "Earth-Town," and water, possibly ocean. Taken together, this image comprises, in the epigraphers' readings, a cosmic hearth; Maya hearths, they attest, are triangularly three-stoned. Schele and Villela, though, proceed to present another image of the cosmogenetic image, one in which a "double-headed turtle . . . cracks open for the rebirth of the Maize God."[75] The cosmic beauty of these readings is how Schele and company describe the intricate correspondence between Classic Maya imagery and the movement of the stars, gathered into inferred ancient Maya constellations. The narrative of joyful sky-staring discovery is less pronounced here than in *Maya Cosmos*, but it glows nonetheless:

> On August 13 . . . at sunset, the World Tree arched overhead, but by the time the sky became dark enough to see the Milky Way, it had turned into the crocodile tree, and by 10 P.M., the Big Dipper, known as the bird *Itzam-Ye* or Twelve-Macaw in the Popol Vuh, had fallen almost entirely and the tree had begun to change into the canoe. By 2 A.M. the canoe stretched across the sky from east to west and with it came the turtle and hearth in Orion and the Peccaries in Gemini. By 4 P.M. [*sic*], the hearth and the turtle were half way up toward the zenith, and by dawn they were high in the sky just east of the zenith point. In 1000 B.C. they were exactly at zenith. As the text says, the gods painted the images of creation on the sky. As dawn broke, a stone-wielding Chak . . . , like those worn hanging from the belt of Chan-Bahlam on the outer panel of the Temple of the Cross, cracked open the turtle shell with his lightning stone, so that the Hero Twins could water their father the Maize God into life again.[76]

Schele and Villela are hacking together a forceful and compelling narrative of cosmogenesis. The story assembles images of architectural inscriptions from Quiriguá, Palenque, and Copán with bone inscriptions from Tikal and painted scenes sourcing to ceramic vessels and the Paris Codex. Across these diversely mediated and multiply mattered images, Schele and Villela find scenes that narrate the movement of the Milky Way on key Maya dates. The Maya story of creation—we are to understand—is recorded in celestial cycles. No, it's not simply recorded. The gods painted creation on, or *as*, the sky. The astrological movements depict the following: the emergence of the Three Stones of Creation; the rise, sometimes out of a cracked or cleft turtle carapace, of the "World Tree," First Father or the Maize God, or the "Crocodile Tree," which may be crossed by an ecliptic snake, and harried by a scorpion and a great bird, Itzam-Yeh; the rotation of the World Tree leading to its transformation into a Cosmic Monster, or the sky canoe propelled by Paddlers and containing First Father; the sinking of the canoe and the descent of First Father into the place of Creation. This summarizes, as succinctly as I can, the grand-historical synthesis of Maya cosmogenesis postulated by Schele and her colleagues. For them it was, effectively, the symbolic "key" to understanding a great deal of Maya imagery and belief. They use this intricate elaboration of cosmic movements to decode the imagery of Maya inscriptions such as the Palenque Palace Tablet, the central tablet in the Temple of the Foliated Cross, and Pakal's sarcophagus lid (figures 3.1 and 3.2).

Schele and Villela proceed to convey, following Dennis Tedlock, that the Yucatec Maya concept of "waking up" or "dawning" also comprised cosmogenesis, the creation of the world; and the related K'iche' term from the *Popol Vuh* associates world creation with whitening and dawning.[77] Dawning, for the ancient Maya, appears to have offered a regular, cyclical reenactment of cosmic creation: "So just as the inscriptions say, the image of the First Three Stones and the turtle come to the zenith at dawn so that the creator of humankind and the universe can be reborn after his defeat by the Lords of Xibalba."[78]

Would it be wrong to read this reading of ancient Maya readings of ancient Maya skies as a deeply modernist, hopeful exchange, an exchange crafted around a wakeful clarity of cosmic vision offered in the extraordinary moment of a cosmic coming-together, a turtle-shell-cracking vision of cosmic order and sensibility? But what, then, would be the exchange protension? Here it isn't simply—say—the telescope, or one's cyborg-eyes turned skyward. The exchange isn't exactly with the sky, as either finitely orderable or infinitely sublime object of knowledge. What Schele "now knows"—what we now know—is that *the sky itself* is the protensive mediator that draws epigraphic, art historical, and anthropological inquiry into engagement with the past. What fascinates me is not only the structural correspondence between constellational movements and Maya iconography, but also how the cosmos itself—viewed on particular dates and times from particular latitudes—becomes a protensive technology that wakes us into the richness of past worlds. This is neither a banal reduction nor a romantic affirmation of archaeoastronomical techniques. It is an insistence that the deep-structural constant, or underlying paradigmatic structure, of Maya epigraphic inquiry

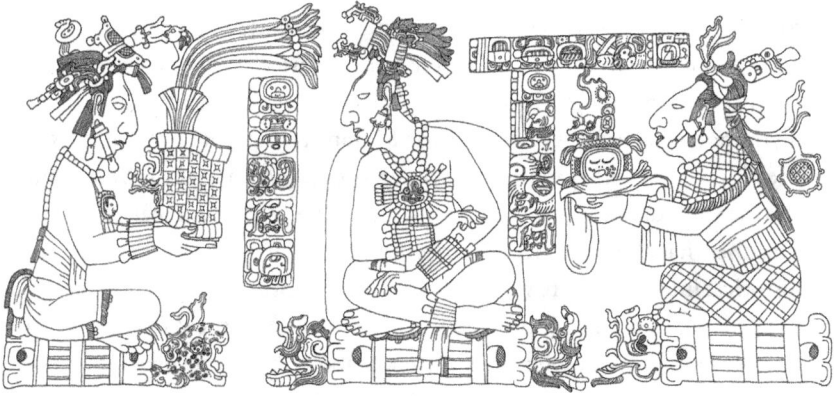

FIGURE 3.1 — Linda Schele, *Palenque Palace Tablet Detail of Figures*. Ink on Mylar drafting film. DRAWING © DAVID SCHELE. IMAGE COURTESY OF THE LOS ANGELES COUNTY MUSEUM OF ART.

FIGURE 3.2 — Linda Schele, *Interior Panel from the Palenque Temple of the Foliated Cross*. Ink on Mylar drafting film. DRAWING © DAVID SCHELE. IMAGE COURTESY OF THE LOS ANGELES COUNTY MUSEUM OF ART.

took form, during this era, as the constellations themselves.[79] It is an effort to understand the excess of a decipherment that has proceeded from narrow semantic inference to a totalizing transhistorical cosmological system.

My phenomenological queering of Mayanists' decoding of ancient Maya mythopoesis passes, then, *through* the Mayanists' incorporation of the sky itself.[80] The Mayanists must draw the sky—that form at once most distant and most proximate—into their cosmic laboratory. They must scale the sky in a manner that allows its incorporation into their structuralist technology of historical inference. Here we see the visible sky's entire moving image incorporated into the exchange protension. On the one hand, the sky gives rise to a brutally literal structuralist set of inferences about the direct correspondence of ancient Maya concepts of cosmogenesis and imagery dating from vastly different historical eras, running the gamut from pre-Maya "Olmec" imagery at sites dating to around 1000 BCE to late twentieth-century Chamula cosmology. On the other hand, this incorporation of the cosmic beyond, *which may well be the originary image, the waking flash of cosmogenesis,* is an incorporation into the embodied, experiential being of Linda Schele herself, a truly extraordinary affect. Perhaps Schele becomes Pakal descending the world-tree, passing down Xibalba Be, the Road of Awe, into the cosmic otherworld. Or, perhaps, she becomes First Father growing out of the cracked turtle's carapace, nourished by the Hero Twins. Either way, Schele becomes the axis mundi, the cosmic passage into an otherworld through the protensive incorporation of a "social drama" inscribed into a sacralized transhistorical sky.[81] The incorporation of the sacred sky into Schele's person also entails the dissolution of Schele into the protension, and the dissolution of the protension into the field of being/becoming that we call relationality, affect, God, cosmos.

Writing on the search for extraterrestrial intelligence (SETI), Stefan Helmreich offers that "extraterrestrial communications, many SETI scientists believed, would copycat our own; aliens would tune into the same channels as earth scientists. Dedicated radio astronomy hams, they would be happy to join in a spaced-out signal-to-noise jam session."[82] Unlike these sky "listeners," radiophysicists with whom Carl Sagan may have cavorted, Schele converted the sky itself into a communicative channel, a protension that joined present with "alien" past. She came to know the sky as a cosmic writing-pad, where narrowly meaningful messages might pass from ancient to present. We now know that Schele's colonial hare descended into Turtle Island's cracked carapace; as she passed the hams, maybe she jammed them.

The fourth poem in *Map of the Lost* is "Ben-Hur."[83] It takes us to the Palace of the Governors in Miriam Sagan's home, Santa Fe. We find Lew Wallace perched in a window, penning his carefully researched tale of Roman betrayal and conversion. Wallace's wife writes to implore the governor

> To draw the shade, the curtain,
> As he bends to the light of the oil lamp.
> Every ruffian and bandit he has subdued
> Might ride past, circling from the end
> Of the Santa Fe Trail
> And in vendetta, shoot him through the head.
> Pull the curtain closed, she pleads.[84]

Certain in his sovereignty as governor and author, he ignores her. Perhaps he leaves the envelopes sealed, piled by his desk. He fears no bullet through the window, no falling roof tile, no traitorous servant's swift act of defenestration.

Wallace reinscribed the crucifixion in the dim New Mexico Palace. But he wrote most of *Ben-Hur: A Tale of the Christ* before venturing west to the territories.[85] The bulk of the 1880 book took form not far from my childhood home in Crawfordsville, Indiana. In 1895, in the midst of *Ben-Hur*'s long run as the best-selling US novel, Wallace began a new construction project in eastern Crawfordsville: an eclectic copper-domed brick study on a foundation of Carnegie steel. As Wallace broke ground for the study, construction ended on a Queen Anne one block away. There, a century later, I spent my childhood.

Not too long ago, an elementary school friend took on a public archaeology project on the grounds of the Lew Wallace Study.[86] She excavated a reflecting pool. I wasn't there. I was in Florida, reading Linda's letters, reading Bruno Latour and Isabelle Stengers.

Perhaps they were measuring and mapping the reflecting pool as I pored over a document sent on October 30, 1989, from Linda to William Morrow and Company.[87] Linda supplied the publisher with a list of well-known supporters who might pen gracious quotations for the dust jacket of *A Forest of Kings*, a book coauthored with friend David Freidel.[88] Seventh on the list, well below Octavio Paz and Carl Sagan, appeared Ilya Prigogine, a Nobel laureate chemist who spent part of each year at Linda's home institution,

UT-Austin. Linda advised: "If you send him the galleys, he may simply ignore them, but a comment from him would carry a lot of weight in the world of science."

I don't know how the world of science received *A Forest of Kings*, and I don't know whether these words on the back cover made a difference:

> For the first time, I had the feeling of discovering the human dimension of the Maya civilizations. . . . A remarkable contribution to human history.—I. Prigogine, Nobel Laureate

It's easy to side, sometimes, with the ruffian or bandit who careens off the Santa Fe Trail to take a shot at the governor, at Lew or at Linda. It's hard to dig a reflecting pool, to stay home, to contribute to human history, to build a copper-domed study on a foundation of Carnegie steel. It's hard to care about the neighbors. It's so deeply un-American.

Sagan's "Ben-Hur" concludes,

> These restless so-called citizens of empire
> Believe some new spirit walks with them day and night
> As to the unseen gods, the governor thinks
> Maybe they are right.[89]

* * *

The critic in me gets stuck on Prigogine's twice-employed adjective *human*. Discovering the "human dimension" of "Maya civilization" contributes, remarkably, to "human history." We bandits, for a stretch now, have been eager to prefix negating or transforming morphemes to the nominal, and ism-ed, form of that word: antihumanism, nonhumanism, posthumanism. The image of the human that ism-ed frameworks challenge might be well captured by Leonardo da Vinci's *Vitruvian Man*, that aesthetic figure of Enlightenment reason and proper, able-bodied human proportionality.[90] It seems a fitting image to align with Prigogine's construction of *A Forest of Kings*, as Prigogine himself captured something of the idealized Renaissance subject, the kind of figure who tracks effortlessly between realist aesthetics and mind-bending science. But the ruffians will go on pointing out that such framings and phrasings deny the humanity of the ancient Maya, in the act of claiming to recuperate it. What dimension of the so-called "Maya civilizations" previously lacked humanity? Such a framing effectively denies humanity to contemporary speakers of Mayan languages; it is brutally complicit with colonial constructions of "the Maya" that glorify an ancient past, while they ignore present pain—and beauty. But it's hardly surprising today that a Belgian chemist needed two white US Americans to humanize the Maya for him. "The Maya," as such, have been an object of colonial fantasy for at least two centuries; such statements iterate an established imperial practice of extending "history" to subalternized groups as an act that secures colonizers' power to determine who does or doesn't belong in their story of "human history."[91]

But what strikes me here is the proximity of *feeling* and *discovering*. *The feeling of discovering*. It animates my hopefully-not-too-paranoid suspicion that the historical content of books like *A Forest of Kings* matters less to many readers than the heightened, animated feelings that they contagiously convey. It enriches my feeling that Freidel and Schele were engaged in a kind of literary magic, a magic less like Dorion's sleight of hand than Mauss's and Lévi-Strauss's shared insistence that language itself harbors an affective, magical capacity.[92] The truth claims of Schele's books—and our books— matter, but only to the extent that they successfully cultivate animatedness, the feeling that something new or strange is in the air. It may help if the form or object of that novelty is the magic trace of an ancient body, stela, or temple.

Maybe the heightened feeling of partaking in or virtually witnessing a discovery of the sort that Schele was inclined to convey approaches—along affective lines—what Prigogine and philosopher Isabelle Stengers characterize as a far-from-equilibrium thermodynamic system, a system where material processes seem to reverse the entropic descent into disorder, giving rise to "dissipative structures" that appear more orderly than the systemic states that precede them.[93] Perhaps Prigogine thought *A Forest of Kings* was one such dissipative structure in the history of science: "The history of science is far from being a linear unfolding that corresponds to a series of successive approximations toward some intrinsic truth. It is full of contradictions, of unexpected turning points."[94] Prigogine and Stengers's book was an ambitious collaborative effort by chemist and philosopher to edgewalk or transgress the boundary delimiting the "two cultures."[95]

It makes sense that Prigogine wanted to walk alongside the spirits reanimated by Mayanists' pens: "We now know that far from equilibrium, new types of structures may originate spontaneously."[96]

We now know. We know Pakal, and Kan-Balam, and the Maize God. We see them in the reflecting pool in Wallace's walled-in property, that fractal form that mirrors the cosmos from within. There rises Schele-as-the-Maize-God out of the Chak-cracked-turtle-shell. A centering cosmic force, a magnetic, auratic exchange protension.[97] The feeling of discovering promises to be contagious; the feeling of discovering is relentless insistence upon our basic, mimetic capacity. But who knows what kinds of spirit-structures or unseen gods originate here? And who knows what contagions they carry?

ILYA PRIGOGINE

Before traveling to Cleveland, the exhibition *The Blood of Kings* debuted in May 1986 at the Kimbell Art Museum in Fort Worth, Texas.[98] The previous September, David Freidel accepted Schele's invitation to participate in a symposium accompanying the event. Writing to Schele at her UT-Austin post, Freidel, a professor at Southern Methodist University, asserted, "It is a special pleasure to witness this celebration in Texas, the coming of a new intellectual heartland in our field."[99]

The Ilya Prigogine Center for Studies in Statistical Mechanics and Complex Systems stood at UT-Austin, the capital of the emerging ancient Maya studies world. As *The Blood of Kings* debuted, Prigogine's career was at its apex. In 1977 he received the Nobel Prize in Chemistry for his work on nonequilibrium thermodynamics. Two years later Prigogine and Stengers published their popular integration of scientific and philosophical thought, *La nouvelle alliance*. It was translated into English in 1984 as *Order out of Chaos: Man's New Dialogue with Nature*.[100] The original French title referenced the authors' ambitions to develop a thermodynamic systems–inspired theory of temporal becoming that would renew the deserted dialogue between scientific and cultural thought.

The book received more French praise than American, but Prigogine and Stengers found one strong supporter in the heartland of ancient Maya studies. Having described his anticipated exhibition talk as "the most important lecture I have ever given—or am likely to give in the future," Freidel's September 1985 letter proceeded to align knowledge of ancient Maya politics and social order produced through hieroglyphic decipherment with developments in thermodynamics theory:

> I anticipate that Saturday will be cathartic following on Mike's [Michael Coe's] Friday inauguration, and that Sunday will hence be completion of the initial vision and opening the way to the future.

Whatever else I do, I will presume that the audience has absorbed the demonstration that we can do what we say we are doing [inferring political structures and practices from hieroglyphic decipherments] and will look to the implications for general theory and method in human evolution. This paradigm, exemplary case, may be based in privileged information [elite Maya inscriptions]; but it speaks to the advent of civilized life and challenges historians of the phenomenon to search out the parallel dynamics. The timebound law of Human evolution, to follow Prigogine's concept of context, is culture itself. Rather than being the prison of the scientific mind in its quest for Reality, it is a prism of determinate structure which, when comprehended, reveals that Reality in its most vital form. Unveiling the Maya Truth, we see the human Truth behind it. I suspect the Maya would have approved of this show and symposium, especially if the conversation gets a little bloody at the end.[101]

If Prigogine had at least one reader in the ancient Maya studies world, the reverse was also true. Prigogine's hobbyist fascination with ancient art may have cultivated his willingness to theorize science as an open system enmeshed in broader cultural processes. Prigogine and Stengers close their first chapter with these words:

Each great period of science has led to some model of nature. For classical science it was the clock; for nineteenth-century science, the period of the Industrial Revolution, it was an engine running down. What will be the symbol for us? What we have in mind may perhaps be expressed best by a reference to sculpture, from Indian or pre-Columbian art to our time. In some of the most beautiful manifestations of sculpture, be it in the dancing Shiva or in the miniature temples of Guerrero, there appears very clearly the search for a junction between stillness and motion, time arrested and time passing. We believe that this confrontation will give our period its uniqueness.[102]

In January 1989 Prigogine wrote Schele to inquire about images on an ancient Maya vase that he intended to purchase on the antiquities market.[103] He enclosed two photographs of the vase, and likened its images to Japanese and Chinese art. Prigogine had done his homework, but failed to find any similar "zoomorphic monsters" in Schele and Mary Miller's impressive exhibition catalog, *The Blood of Kings*.[104]

I wonder whether Schele replied with those monsters' names, giving vital form to that Maya reality, evoking the "junction between stillness and motion, time arrested and time passing."[105]

* * *

And the anthropologist in me wonders whether *La nouvelle alliance* was, in the end, particularly *nouvelle*. The book does, indeed, employ thermodynamic frames to grapple with complexity and emergent properties. But constructing such an *alliance* between scientific and humanistic thinking—even one rooted in ecological and systems approaches—was hardly a novelty. Alfred Kroeber purportedly characterized anthropology as the "most humanistic of the sciences and the most scientific of the humanities." It strikes me that such a formulation might be too generous to the sciences and the humanities. Anthropology is a ritually reproduced sacralization of a social order that fixates, again and again, on referentially overflowing, overdetermined signs: culture, kinship, ecology, gender, and so on. What might make anthropology distinctive is that it refuses a priori relegation to the status of a humanistic or scientific pursuit, let alone that dastardly—dangerous, even—US chimera, the social sciences. We may need a reminder that, after World War II, prominent anthropologists increasingly turned toward systems-based and ecological thinking to make sense out of the complex encounter between "nature" and "culture," encapsulated, perhaps, by the anthropological fixation on kinship (including incest, that Oedipal fantasy). Systems theorists have long advocated for modes of "ecological" thinking that attend to being as a complex imbroglio that can't be parsed, quickly and easily, into nature and culture.[106]

Whatever Freidel, writing this letter in what seems to be a rather mystic mood, might have intended by Prigogine's "timebound law of Human evolution," the idea that culture might be a "prism of determinate structure" refracts our anthropological vision. It may call to an Americanist vision born, in part, of Franz Boas's early psychophysical work on the optical properties of water.[107] But here, in place of aqueous cultural immersion, we witness Freidel holding his breath before diving into a sanguinary symposium. I wish that his prism were a bit more refractory, a cubist contortion of realist forms that committed itself to the richness of particularity, the frank reality that inferring a human truth from Maya facts indulges a cardinal anthropological sin, generalizing from the particular. In the prismatic and fractal hall of mirrors that we call—because we don't quite know what else to call it—the human experience, forms such as culture, species, and time seem like truths to read athwart and tell slant.[108] And what of this skew-whiff fantasy that the Maya "would have approved" of *The Blood of Kings* exhibition and symposium? You need not have worried, David. Even the zoomorphic monsters approved.

ISABELLE STENGERS

Bruno Latour opens his forward to Isabelle Stengers's *Power and Invention* by posing and answering a series of clever questions about the Belgian philosopher of science.[109] The second reads,

> Would you say that she is the philosophical right hand of the Nobel Prize winner for chemistry Ilya Prigogine?
>
> Yes, since she wrote several books with him—and yet she has spent the rest of her life trying to escape from the mass of lunatics attracted to this "new alliance" between science and culture that they both created.[110]

Stengers surely spends her waking life absconding from the multitude of David Freidels mobbing the streets of Brussels. And this book adds one more lunatic to the tally.

The term *lunatic* derives from the Latin *lūna*, meaning "moon." To be a lunatic, classically, is to be "affected with the kind of insanity that was supposed to have recurring periods dependent on the changes of the moon."[111] Was Lew Wallace, writing by the light of the oil lamp, a lunatic? How about the stargazing Linda Schele, reading the Maya cosmos in the heavens of Quintana Roo?

Given her apparent aversion to moon-blinded madmen, Stengers's absorption in Deleuze's philosophy seems odd. Deleuze and Guattari exalt the figure of the mad (if not madness itself), finding philosophical stimulation in the schizophrenic. "Schizophrenia is like love," they say.[112] "The schizophrenic is the universal producer."[113] Deleuze and Guattari denounce neurotics. But code-scrambling "schizos" they love; they call their work schizoanalysis.

Stengers, it seems, is quite taken with Deleuze's figure of the idiot, a close relative of the schizophrenic:

Deleuze's idiot, borrowed from Dostoevsky and turned into a conceptual character, is the one who always slows the others down, who resists the consensual way in which the situation is presented and in which emergencies mobilize thought or action. This is not because the presentation would be false or because emergencies are believed to be lies, but because "there is something more important." Don't ask him why; the idiot will neither reply nor discuss the issue. The idiot is a presence or, as Whitehead would have put it, produces an interstice. There is no point in asking him, "What is more important?" for he does not know. But his role is not to produce abysmal perplexity, not to create the famous Hegelian night, when every cow is black. We know, knowledge there is, but the idiot demands that we slow down, that we don't consider ourselves authorized to believe we possess the meaning of what we know.[114]

T-h-e . . . i-d-i-o-t . . . s-l-o-w-s . . . u-s . . . d-o-w-n . . . The idiot proffers no final solution. He knows not what his knowledge means. Knowledge isn't the endgame. Might the phrase "we now know," then, become an incitement to curiosity? Instead of closing the conversation, "we now know" calls us to discern what our knowledge means or—better—what it does, how it makes this world—or another—a more peaceful place to dwell.

Perhaps it's apt that Stengers terms her political, scientific, and philosophical program "cosmopolitics."[115] Stengers's "cosmos" doesn't designate the unthinkable expanses of space above and below that field in Quintana Roo. Stengers wrenches the cosmos agape, splicing it with a politics that aspires toward radical democracy, openness to whatever arrives, an effort to build better worlds at all scales.

But if Carl Sagan and Linda Schele seem to have closed the cosmos too quickly, let us not, in turn, judge them with haste. Standing in that Quintana Roo field with heart thumping, staring breathlessly at scorpions, world-trees, birds, crocodiles, and a billion stars, Linda was a tiny dust mote, and a lunatic building a slightly better world.

* * *

One might even suggest that Stengers, in her throwaway reference to "the famous Hegelian night," closes the cosmos a bit quickly, judges with too much haste. Given Stengers's and Latour's shared aversion to Hegel, one might presume that the latter advocated immediate trust of perception that leads one to believe that dusk actually blackened the ungulates. But, by slowing down a bit, we might come to recognize this passage from the preface of Hegel's *Phenomenology of Spirit* as what it was: a criticism of Schelling's claim for absolute knowledge emanating from the immediacy of our perception and corollary intuition.[116] It is Hegel who implies that his friend Schelling needs to slow down, needs to consider the possibility that the world might be a bit more confounding than it appears.

Schele was no Schelling. Her reading of the Quintana Roo cosmos had some complex conditions and predicates. Her *aha* moment, here, was characterized not by *absolute* immediacy but, rather, by a conditional and predicated immediacy. Here's structuralism's rub. The narrative sense of a text, its immediate meaning, is secondary, epiphenomenal, perhaps even ephemeral. Accessing the underlying form or structure of the text requires an apparatus, a protension for perceiving—and hence entering into exchange relations with—an obscured, generative matrix of cultural ideations given paradigmatic primacy. The deep structure of ancient Maya cosmology does not simply reveal itself to observers. Such revelation requires a cosmically expansive material-semiotic technology.

Schele's allure, for me at least, emanates from her profound capacity to build such technologies, such apparatuses. Structuralism's foundational material culture—the tools of Lévi-Strauss's cut-and-paste method—can be inferred without much trouble.[117] Each syntactical unit in a narrative— each syntagm—requires its own note card.[118] They can, then, be rearranged in order to pass, always provisionally, from a text's apparent structure and meaning to its "deeper," more fundamental sense. But the passage from surface to depth isn't so direct. Meaning reads itself into us athwart, slant, queer, wibbly-wobbly, skew-whiff. (Above my office desk is a poster of the Tablet of the Ninety-Six Glyphs, drawn by Linda and generously gifted to me by Maya Meetings administrator Michael Scanlon. I'm tempted to tilt it, to turn it askew.) It's not, simply, that we don't know what our knowledge means. More fundamentally, we may be unaware of our knowledge's epistemic structure. Cosmopolitics, as Latour and Stengers each formulate it, insists that we slow down to consider more carefully the composition of our systematizing arrangements.[119] Cosmopolitics is a prescriptive footnote to structuralism's fundamental conceptual innovations. It is a technique for composing modes of living-and-becoming-together that are sensitive to their own provisionality and exclusions.[120] But maybe the cosmo-aesthetic moment of revelation tells a different kind of story about how to make knowledges and how to make worlds. Maybe the democratic project of slow science might require a little inspiration, a moment of revelation, a cosmic suspension of self that enables the past to speak through you, to interpellate you from within: *aha!*

LYNN MARGULIS

Isabelle Stengers spliced politics into the cosmos as Lynn Margulis spliced genesis into symbiosis. "Symbiosis" is bio-speak for playing well together. Microbial symbionts hang out in your gut, aiding digestion of the world beyond. You need them as they need you. It turns out that microbes, and some "higher" organisms as well, acquire and incorporate sets of genes from members of other species that they consume or dwell with. Writing with Dorion, Margulis describes slugs that ate and incorporated the genes of green algae; their descendants became photosynthetic; now for nutrition they don't eat—they sunbathe.[121] Margulis claims that the immense contemporary variation in species reflects a history of organisms acquiring each other's genomes. This flies in the face of evolutionary biologists' basic Darwinian tenet, the claim that speciation results from genetic mutations affecting sexual selection through time.[122]

Donna Haraway takes symbiogenesis as life turtling away: "Yoking together all the way down is what sym-bio-genesis means."[123] Haraway even tries to transfect Margulis with the chaotic open systems of Deleuze and Guattari, that pair of idiot philosophers who espouse "a different kind of 'turtles all the way down,' figuring relentless otherness knotted into never fully bounded or fully self-referential entities."[124] "A different kind of 'turtles all the way down'"; the symbiogenesis of poetry and science; *Map of the Lost* leans against *Conversations with Carl Sagan*.

Am I after a different kind of turtling here? Am I after tight couplings and potent transfections that lead to unexpected kin? The offspring of these couplings become cosmic progenitors, cosmogenitors in the play of genesis and genetics, the endless turtling that makes symbionts of the varieties of religious and scientific experience. Like William James and Carl Sagan, I desire to feel at home in the universe.

Dorion's eyes welled up that November day with the tender vulnerability that comes of realizing that one might be alone in the universe, lost in space. The day before, Dorion and I had discussed spirits. He didn't think much of them. If I'm after genesis and cosmogenesis, then I may as well take up the lunatic task of spiritual regenesis, the task of writing the dead. Lynn Margulis died of a hemorrhagic stroke on November 22, 2011. Lynn's daughter, Jennifer Margulis, recounts that her mom desired to be cremated:

> She didn't want hoop-la. The no nonsense of cremation appealed to her, I think.
>
> We chose an urn made out of pink Himalayan rock salt to put my mother's ashes in. My brothers and I agreed on it right away. Every rock salt urn is unique. It was natural but it had pizzazz, just like my mom. We know she would've liked it.[125]

It's hard to imagine liking your urn, the cosmic abode of your earthly form. And perhaps Dorion still doesn't believe in spirits. I think I understand. But below Jennifer's comments appears a photo of Lynn, looking natural with pizzazz and standing next to a sign that reads "Sabemos tan poco." Jennifer doesn't translate the Spanish phrase. It means, "We know so little." The photo's legible, perhaps, as a classic expression of scientific modesty. We know so little of this immense and humbling universe.

But might there be another reading? Might the photo be a way to say that genes are spirits too?

* * *

Dorion opened his plenary lecture, later published in *Cosmic Apprentice: Dispatches from the Edges of Science*, with a quotation from the physicist Richard Feynman: "This universe just goes on, with its edge as unknown as the bottom of the bottomless sea . . . just as mysterious, just as awe inspiring, and just as incomplete as the poetic pictures that came before. But see that the imagination of nature is far, far greater than the imagination of man. No one who did not have some inkling of this through observation could ever have imagined such a marvel as nature is."[126] The universe, Dorion wants us to know, keeps calling him back.

Is it possible to imagine an imagination without the cosmos, however provisionally and contingently known, in place as its foundation or necessary condition? Whether or not the cosmos is finite, we humans—and our multispecies kin—certainly are. We'll all follow Lynn Margulis and Linda Schele down the road of awe; as particular organisms, we cannot simply will ourselves into dissipative structuration, reversing the entropic movement of heat across barriers, the undoing and unbecoming of the human as a site of self-knowledge and organismic sociality. We age. All the same, it is a bit silly for Feynman to insist on the imagination of "nature" exceeding that of "man." This particular human imagination, after all, allows for the projection of something called imagination onto something called nature. This human imagination may also allow for that mind-bending, death-transcending beauty and horror of a fantasy called transhumanism.[127] Human finitude comes with some neat features, including the cosmic sublime, that religious fact we call infinity, which these days tends to call itself God.

Anthropology, after all, is a science of symbiogenesis. Dorion, then, as a cosmic edgewalker, a Lindaesque amateur tuned in to the edge of science, is an honorary anthropologist, an anthropologist by practice if not training.[128] Dorion's dispatches, including the dispatches with or on his mother Lynn, traffic in a sense that we, as life-forms, incorporate one another, or, better, ensoul one another. If "life" has any sense whatsoever, if I'm to write it confidently without the scare quotes, it must designate an intricate weave of being and becoming, the reality of the social as the symbiogenetic. Human life may also denote a kind of metacognitive and metalinguistic capacity, the fact that we think about how we think, and speak about how we speak. Thinking about thought and speaking about speech enable us to have a profoundly reflective capacity, and, hence, a responsive attachment to others, including the indexically displaced traces of others that we call memory, including memories of the dead.

Life turtles away, dissipating, winning the race to cosmic dissolution and the ultimate alterity, whether hares like Lynn and Linda are ready or not. And we go on storying the world. Here is Geertz's version of the turtle tale:

> There is an Indian story—at least I heard it as an Indian story—about an Englishman who, having been told that the world rested on a platform which rested on the back of an elephant which rested in turn on the back of a turtle, asked (perhaps he was an ethnographer; it is the way they behave), what did the turtle rest on? Another turtle. And that turtle? "Ah, Sahib, after that it is turtles all the way down."[129]

So, for Geertz, a high-modernist, a subject deeply committed to the sense and interpretability of cultural worlds, the turtle story was not about the sublimity of a cosmos that recedes beyond comprehension. Geertz, like Lévi-Strauss and Schele, seems to evoke a rather numinous sense of the sublime, a sense that reality recedes to a horizon within us, and that interpretation is an endless voyage toward that horizon. This may well be a Kantian dream, a dream of the lovely and cruel marriage of rationality and empiricism.

The edge between the biogenetic and the spiritual is fine, a razor's edge. Few have enough balance to avoid splitting themselves into two. Avoiding ruin requires rich attachments, nourishment from all sides, including spotters' affirmations that our funambulist act is, ultimately, a magic trick, sleight of hand, sleight of foot, a slight against any insistence on the great divide between the cultural and the natural, an acknowledgment that, instead, we are supported by webs—some of them fractally recursive Indra's nets—that ramify wildly, neither trees nor rhizomes, entangling and supporting ever more as our thought and writing becomes riskier, wilder, lost in *el monte*, in the heath.[130] But if we manage to secure ourselves to thinkers and doers as adept and capacious as Dorion, Lynn, and Linda, we'll edgewalk quite capably, receiving others' dispatches well, casting out responsive responses in turn.

Edgewalking is the alien anthropological science of mutual care and responsiveness, forms of attachment that, as Geertz might affirm, run deep.

Chapter Four

Bones

A few days before Thanksgiving 2014, I visited the Georgia O'Keeffe Museum in Santa Fe, New Mexico. A small exhibition hall was cleared to frame museum attendees' experiences with a short film on O'Keeffe's life.[1] In 1929, just months before the crash, O'Keeffe, a native Wisconsinite living in New York, discovered her "spiritual home" in northern New Mexico. Scoping the desert-scape, the Gene Hackman–narrated documentary opens, a bit ominously, "This is O'Keeffe country."[2] In 1934, O'Keeffe began to spend every summer and fall at Ghost Ranch, her home north of Santa Fe. A decade and a half later, after the death of her artist husband, Alfred Stieglitz, O'Keeffe would remain. The amber and burnt orange desert hues vitalized O'Keeffe; New York's sylvan verdancy bored her.

The film is eager to construct O'Keeffe as a creature of sand and bone. We learn that she "became an iconic, mythic figure, the loner in the desert."[3] Many of her paintings from the desert years zoom in on the sun-bleached skulls and long bones of deer, cows, horses, and other beasts (figure 4.1). The historian of American art Wanda Corn has noted that the first New York exhibition to include selections of O'Keeffe's bone paintings confounded reviewers familiar with her earlier flowers and cityscapes. Corn says, "One critic wrote a very little review, but he . . . didn't even mention the bone paintings as if he couldn't find a vocabulary that would put femaleness and bones together in some inherent way."[4] I'd like to think that the spiritual renaissance of O'Keeffe's New Mexican setting enabled her to put to rest all those overbearing Freudian readings of her floral motifs.

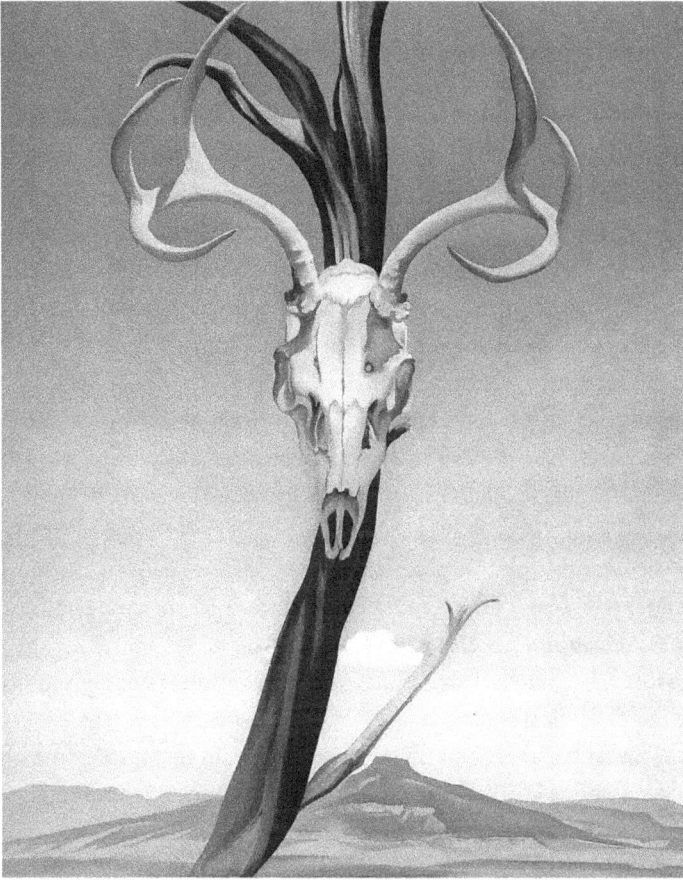

FIGURE 4.1 — Georgia O'Keeffe, *Deer's Skull with Pedernal*, 1936. Oil on canvas.

Though here I admit to being reminded of a more recent psychoanalytical thinker's tendency to dally, instead, with bones. The Slovenian philosopher and psychoanalyst Slavoj Žižek turns now and again to a classic line by Hegel: "The Spirit is a bone."[5] The phrase pops off the page of Hegel's *Phenomenology of Spirit* in a critical analysis of phrenology, or the effort to infer intelligence from bone morphology.[6] It appears as a wry and dismissive summation of phrenologists' reductions of mind to matter. For Hegel, *geist*, or Spirit, as consciousness, passes through and takes the form of matter only to surpass it, transforming into actualized self-consciousness. This synthesis gives rise to a substantive ethical subject who is capable of understanding that freedom isn't constrained by the determinants of matter or society. Freedom emerges, instead, as the dialectical effect of the individual's constitutive encounters with such forces. To be free, we must recognize our unfreedom. To achieve such categorical freedom, one's Spirit must traverse the inert, passive, deterministic material world. For a moment, at least, bone animates us; rigid mineralized tissue becomes Spirit itself.

Examining Žižek's writing on the topic, Fredric Jameson describes the "Spirit is a bone" passage as the "ultimate Hegelian paradox."[7] Pressing Hegel into the mold of his materialist successor, Jameson takes the phrase to mean that "Marxism is an economic rather than a political doctrine."[8] These eminent philosophers have spent ungodly quantities of paper and ink deciphering such Hegelian witticisms.

So I should simply ignore it. But somehow, in anthropology's osseous haunts, I can't. I have to bone up on the possibility that Spirit is a bone. After all, isn't the problem of anthropology, as Latour puts it, "how to get bones and divinities to fit together"?[9] This chapter's ethnographic method is to introduce this philosophical fragment into lives both collagenous and calcified. In the desert of O'Keeffe, we also encounter the intertwined spirits of Linda Schele and novelist Ruth Ozeki.

I suspect that Schele, Ozeki, and O'Keeffe wouldn't need a philosopher's toolkit of dialectical sublation and psychoanalytical scrutiny to understand that the Spirit is a bone. So I invite you to entertain this suspicion with me, to follow along as I follow these three artists' encounters with bones, not as inert and passive objects or simply signs of death, but as vibrant, even vital matter.[10]

RUTH OZEKI

In her essay "The Art of Losing: On Writing, Dying, and Mom," Ozeki describes how she reconciled with her estranged mother through the detour of her grandmother's death.[11] Ruth's mother, Masako, was a second-generation Japanese American whose parents had returned to Japan after her father's internment in Santa Fe during World War II. When her mother died, at ninety-three, outside Tokyo, Masako called on Ruth to attend the funeral in her stead. Masako was aging and unwell; a bad leg would prevent her from participating in the Buddhist ceremony. So, Ruth traveled to Tokyo, where her aunt showed her the urn containing her grandmother's remains. Ozeki describes what followed with these words:

She went to the kitchen and brought back a small Tupperware container and a pair of wooden chopsticks, the disposable kind that you get with take-out sushi. I watched as she lined the Tupperware with one of my grandmother's fancy handkerchiefs, opened the urn, and started poking around inside with the tips of her chopsticks like she was trying to fish a pickle from a jar.[12]

Ruth's aunt identified three bones as she removed them to the Tupperware. Ruth wasn't familiar at the time with this memorial custom, *hone wake*, "dividing the bones." But she was charged with passing the bones, in turn, to her mother. After returning to the States, Ruth delayed this duty, leaving the bones shelved. Although her mother assumed they'd made the voyage, the bones' status was left unspoken.

The fragmented remains exercised unexpected power. They called Ozeki to explore her family's past, to face her heritage and escape her life-grown-dreary: "This might seem strange," she says, "but . . . it felt like . . . I had a mandate from my dead Japanese grandparents to engage with the world creatively."[13] Masako had a habit of identifying Ruth with her grandfather, a poet and photographer. The bones imbued this transgenerational equation with cultural generativity. Ruth's mandate to create spawned a documentary film that presents her experiences honoring this familial duty: *Halving the Bones*.[14] The film, Ruth says, "gave us the excuse to spend time together, and get to know each other again, and learn to talk about the important matters of life and death."[15] Ruth even arranged for Masako to move to the remote British Columbia island where she lived with her husband. There Ruth cared for Masako as Alzheimer's took control. Or, really, as Ruth makes clear, they comforted and cared for *each other* as the elder died. The film, the bones, opened a return to familial love.

This was a new experience for Ruth. Such an opening hadn't been available when her father died six years earlier, in 1998. As with her mother, Ruth witnessed her father's decline and death. She says,

> When my dad died, I was angry because he was angry and despairing. He did not want to die. He wasn't ready. I was in charge of his health care, but I couldn't do a damn thing to prevent or forestall this utterly unthinkable and unacceptably terminal outcome. I was mad at him for his lack of readiness and I was furious at myself for my impotence and lack of compassion. After he died, I couldn't think of him without a lot of pain and anger and confusion and despair, and a sense of having

failed him. I couldn't look at his picture without feeling my insides twist. I wanted to look away. And I did. I remember I drank a lot, too, in order to get through it. I took his death very personally.[16]

Coping with loss emerges here as an isolating problem. But if you're lucky, if the circumstances are right, there's the outward turn of poiesis: making, creating, writing. Ruth tells us that, "If creativity is a way of offsetting or coping with loss, then perhaps writing—our written language—exists on account of, or to account for, our mortality. If we were not able to count our days and to foresee our termination, then why would we bother to write things down?"[17]

Ruth's phrasing calls my response. Her father, Floyd Lounsbury, had an intimate, if professional, relation with both writing and death. Lounsbury was a professor at Yale and an accomplished anthropological linguist. He established the framework for analyses of Iroquoian languages and innovated the use of linguistic methods in analyzing kinship systems in the 1950s and 1960s. In the next and final stage of his career, Lounsbury turned to Maya hieroglyphic decipherment and close collaboration with Schele. Though Ruth doesn't mention it, her dad devoted a good deal of his career to deducing structural regularities of a language written by dead, *long*-dead human beings.

Maybe there's a subtext to that speculation that written language exists to account for mortality. In an essay on her mother, she's speaking of her father, and in her father's Mayanist terms, "to count our days and to foresee our termination." The ancient Maya celebrated cosmological and historical *counts* they accounted for *terminations*, rulers' ossifications. They developed a complex calendrical system, an interlocking pair of "day counts" and a linear "long count" retrojected to a starting date in the mythological past. Maya calendrical cycles entailed and prescribed patterns of significant events to ensure that ill fortune wouldn't befall the community.[18] The past became the present's backbone, the future's charter.

But this risks reducing Ozeki's claim to a rote trope. Maybe her father comes up only in passing because his presence invites such academicism. Look at how Ozeki describes the Yale anthropology faculty, circa 1969, in her wonderful, "somewhat autobiographical" short story "The Anthropologists' Kids." She says,

> They were tall white guys with stooped shoulders and sunburned necks that they protected from the rays with folded kerchiefs. Their skin, turned leathery from years in the field, had the crosshatched texture of plucked chickens. Their thin, sand-colored hair was matted with

sweat, and it stuck to their high receding foreheads when they took off their pith helmets. Some of them worked for the CIA.

I'm just kidding. They didn't wear pith helmets, at least not at home.[19]

Ruth's pith is almost too much to handle. But she's right about the CIA. Lounsbury and company worked closely with some admitted Cold War spies, including archaeologist Michael Coe.[20]

All the "tall white guys with stooped shoulders" married Asian women. In her description of the story, Ozeki says of their offspring,

> We called ourselves "half" (in Japanese, "hafu"), and thusly described, I must have felt somewhat diminished, divided, and estranged from myself. I clearly recall feeling as though one half of me was always studying the other, which I suppose it was. As a half-Asian, half-Anthropologist kid, I was genetically predisposed to ethnographic introspection— although the same is true for many writers.[21]

Ruth's autoethnographic sensibilities shine in *Halving the Bones*. Credited as Ruth Ozeki Lounsbury, she opens the documentary with a discussion of her name: "My name is Ruth, but I don't like it. . . . My mother chose it. . . . But Japanese people cannot pronounce *r*'s and *h*'s." And the Japanese pronunciation of "Ruth" means "She is not home."[22]

Ruth's documentary grapples in wrenching terms with experiences of dislocation from her family's ancestral home and from her mother. Highly sensitive to conventions of documentary filmmaking, Ruth also seeds dislocation, and attendant discomfort, into the narrative itself. She casts her mother, Masako, in terms that challenge the stereotyped delicate, shy Japanese woman. Ruth's Masako is "tough," "pragmatic," and "always straightforward about bodily functions."[23] We meet Masako, in historical or faux-historical footage, as she brushes her teeth and combs her hair in a kitchen. We meet Ruth at her mother's breast.

Ruth's great-grandfather, fond of geography, decided that his son and daughter would live beyond the island empire of Japan. He sent her grandmother to Hawaii, and arranged a marriage with another Japanese immigrant, an amateur botanical scientist and photographer. Ruth says, "He catalogued exotica and was drawn by twisted forms in nature. . . . People say I'm like him."[24]

Ruth tells this story with the aid of her grandmother Matsue's autobiography and footage that her grandfather took in Hawaii. Home movies, she says, of their time there. "This is my grandmother when she was young, whose bones I now keep in my closet." And, later: "Bones are tissue. They grow and change and die with a body. She was old when she died. The bones I have are hers but they're not the same as the ones she had there."[25]

In Hawaii, Ruth says, her grandfather wrote three poems a day. And she reads us three. Matsue colored her husband's photographs and took some of her own. Ruth wants desperately to understand the sense of place that Matsue felt during her Hawaii years. She wants to feel it so badly that she risks becoming an unreliable narrator. You see, Ruth lies to us, to her viewers, about the footage and the autobiography. Neither, as it turns out, is real.

To talk of bone and mothers is to talk of truth and memory. When we meet Masako, we quickly hear her say, "I don't think you can talk about accuracy in memory."[26] But if we can't trust Ruth, our storyteller, can we trust her mother, this story of her mother? Matsue, the mother's mother, left Hawaii abruptly to return to Tokyo in search of treatment for what she thought was—or perhaps simply told her husband was—a tumor. This tumor, as it turned out, was really a fetus on its way to becoming Masako.

And Ruth's mother lets us know, "I'm Masako. . . . I am not a tumor."[27]

But Ruth isn't so sure: "My mom, the tumor."[28] It was a family story, the kind that's repeated again and again, the kind that keeps families alive.

Ruth heard, and no doubt told, that story in her early years in Connecticut. There, as she taught herself photography, Ruth felt occupied by Japanese heritage. In turn, Ruth and her mother became metastatic vectors in New Haven. She says,

> Cancer invades a body. Mine was different from everyone else's in Connecticut, and it was obviously because of mom. Her genes in my body had prevailed. So you see it was this Eurocentric and primitive understanding of history and genetics that left me susceptible to a metaphoric confusion about my mother's origins. She'd started life as a tumor, and, cancerous, she'd spread. I was her offspring and hardly benign.[29]

Metaphors can be as hard to excise as tumors, and they can be just as deadly.

In the film's climactic scene, Ruth passes the bones, in a tea canister, to her mother (figures 4.2 and 4.3). There's no mistaking this for anything but surgery, and it's just as hard to watch. Spying the bones, Masako says, "Aren't they beautiful. They're colored! They're colored. . . . It's as if they were painted!"[30]

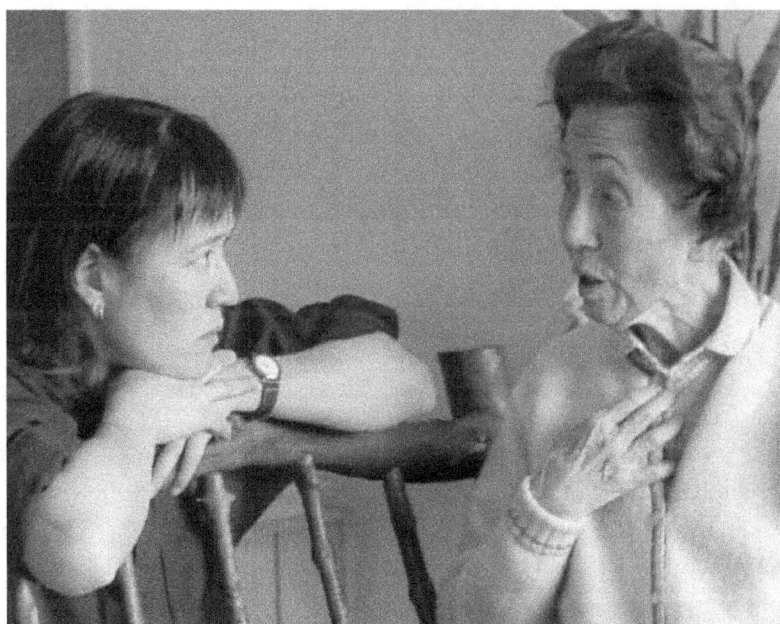

FIGURES 4.2 and 4.3 — Stills from Ruth Ozeki's *Halving the Bones*. ORIGINALLY
PUBLISHED IN OZEKI'S ESSAY "THE ART OF LOSING."

Reconstructing a hazy memory of her grandmother's wishes for the osseous traces, Ruth asks Masako to join her in a journey to Hawaii to discard the bones. Masako, pragmatic and present-minded as could be, defers the task, asking to retain them until her own death. She charges Ruth with casting both her bones and her mother's into the central Pacific surf.

We see no more of Masako. We don't learn that her mind went first, her bones second. We don't learn that they moved together to British Columbia. We don't learn how or when she died. Instead, we see Ruth setting up a camera on a cliff in Hawaii before propelling bone and ash into wind.

By all measures, this should be the end of *Halving the Bones*. But in a film on her mother, she's thinking of her father, and in her father's terms. "Epilogue (a Lounsbury)."[31] Ruth, Ruth Ozeki Lounsbury, still had a bone to pick with Floyd. Stopping in Pearl Harbor on the way back from Hawaii, surprised by the throng of *Japanese* tourists, Ruth spies a Lounsbury inscribed into stone: "T. W. Lounsbury." She asks,

> Is that a relative of Dad's? This was a disturbing discovery. In my search to come to terms with my mother and her past, I'd neglected my father's side of the family entirely. First of all, this business about being named "Ruth." I know I sort of blamed my mom for it, but it really wasn't her fault at all. My dad's family came from upstate New York, so naturally he was a big Yankee's fan. And the truth of the matter is that when I was born the big consolation for me not being a boy was that he got to name me Ruth. You know, after the Babe. He wanted me to be an all-American kid.[32]

"An all-American kid," *huh? Ya* know? Maybe Floyd got one.

LINDA SCHELE

In 1968, Schele submitted a thesis for a master of fine arts degree to the University of Cincinnati. Her project was a painting titled *Mira, Omicron Ceti* (figure 4.4). The copy deposited in the university library includes a photograph of the painting, six photographs of a deer skull, and a page and a half of commentary that mainly documents her artistic technique.[33] Schele says nothing of how the deer skull inspired the painting's forms. It depicts the object from varied angles and distances. Although some viewers may see skulls, the painting's contiguous, overlapping shapes elude final identification.

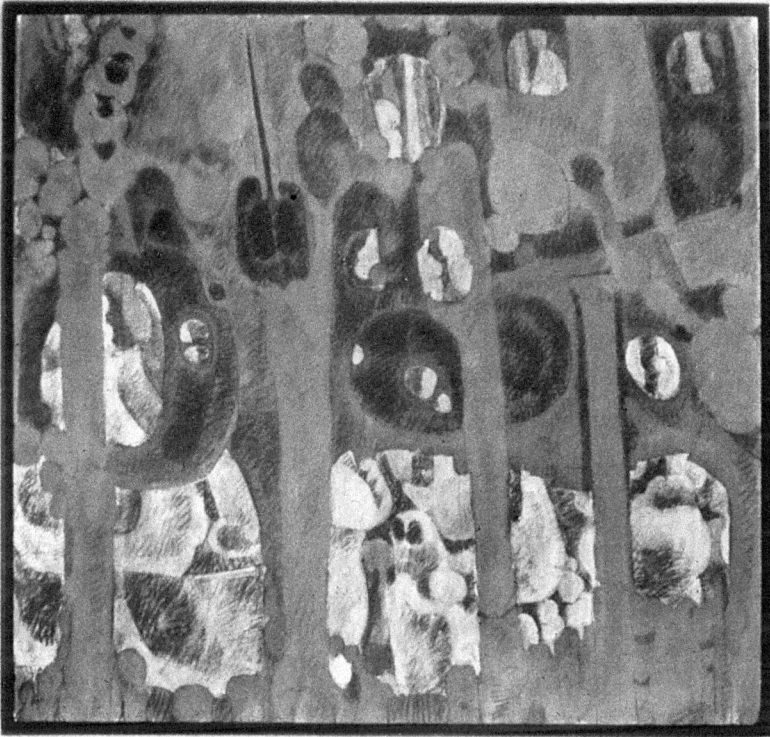

FIGURE 4.4 — Painting by Linda Schele. *Mira, Omicron Ceti*, 1968. Acrylic and charcoal on canvas. ORIGINALLY PUBLISHED IN SCHELE'S MFA THESIS, "MIRA, OMICRON CETI."

The form is alien, and Schele's commentary clarifies the terms of this alienness. She says,

> The title "Mira, Omicron Ceti" is a witness of my philosophies about and expectations for the painting. I wish the viewer to feel as if he is partaking of a liveable alien world perhaps as will be experienced eventually in interstellar travel. I wish him to be drawn in and through the painting and to feel himself adjust in scale to it. As a result of these feelings, I chose a name derived from the stars.

Mira, Omicron Ceti, at fifty-six by sixty-two inches, provides passage into an otherworld, an imagined corner of the cosmos. My eyes gravitate to the bones again and again, as if crashing against an ocean floor. I want to say that it's not a pretty painting. Mucky, oceanic features disrupt my efforts to discern its focal point. A shape in the top left quadrant looks like a skate plunging through a deep brown sea. Four vertical columns rise like stalagmites, marking the viewer's spatial distance from that mess of bones, that osteological cache, that cosmic sign of life's remainder.

But Schele's commentary resists my cold, melancholic tone. She concludes it with a quotation from a star atlas intended to clarify her choice to name the painting after a binary star system in the constellation of Cetus. The system comprises a pulsating giant named Mira A and its low-mass companion, Mira B. But Schele seems more drawn to the Latin name, Mira, meaning "wonderful."

So the painting's a romantic evocation of wonder, the artistic sublime reframed for the era of Apollo. Schele likely would have regarded such a reading as pretentious. But I also have good reason to suspect that Linda, at twenty-five years old in 1968, may have omitted a source of inspiration for her painting in the commentary. Schele was a devoted Trekkie. And a May 1967 episode of *Star Trek* depicts a uss *Enterprise* visit to the planet of Omicron Ceti III. There the arch-logical Spock is reunited with Leila Kalomi, a Hawaii-born botanist who'd pursued him romantically six years earlier on Earth. Those advances had failed. But, on Omicron Ceti, Kalomi had discovered spore-emitting flowering pod plants that, at once, protect colonists from radioactive rays and lull them into a state of peaceful bliss.[34] Kalomi draws on her botanical knowledge to succeed in seducing Spock. She tours him to a field of Omicron pods, where he's overtaken by flower power and expresses his true love for Leila. But when Captain Kirk finds out, he'll have none of it. After determining that violent anger functions to counteract the pod spore's psychoactive effects, he induces rage in Spock and reestablishes the ship's technocratic reign.

I think this story hangs behind the painting. Schele found an alien world in the morphology of that deer skull, and filled its cracks and crevices with the spirit of—dare I say it, corny as could be—*love.*

But Schele's love for paint as the primary medium of her spirit's expression ran shallow enough that, two years later, she was enticed away from studio art by the renowned romantic powers of an alien archaeological site in southern Mexico, Palenque. There Schele met Montana-born artist Merle Greene Robertson, who'd set up shop as the resident art historian and was working to photograph and produce rubbings of the site's extensive and elaborate stone architectural inscriptions. By apprenticing with Robertson, Schele began to establish herself as a knowledgeable contributor to the site's art history. Her breakout moment came in late 1973, in Palenque, at the first Round Table, hosted by Robertson and local tour guide Moises Morales. Her encounter with Mathews and Lounsbury led, once again, to the first compelling decipherment of Palenque's dynastic sequence. This innovation helped to establish the argument that Maya inscriptions contained clear historical information in a fully fledged, grammatical writing system.

Two months after the meeting, on February 13, 1974, Floyd wrote Linda for the first time.[35] In the letter, Lounsbury thanks Schele for sending her analysis of the Palenque dynastic sequence coauthored with Mathews. He writes, "The Palenque meeting was a truly great experience. And what wonderful people (including, and especially, you)! I hope we can all get together again." In residence at Harvard's Dumbarton Oaks museum in Washington, DC, Floyd conveyed support for Linda applying to join him. He closes the letter by conveying that "Masako sends her regards, and Ruth would too if she were here and knew I was writing."

I must admit that I'd read that letter many times before I looked up Ruth. I'd known Masako as Floyd's wife; he mentioned her often enough in such closing passages. But "Ruth" was just one more moniker in an archive packed with known and unknown names. Schele must have met Masako and Ruth at the Round Table. Ruth, then Ruth Lounsbury, would have been seventeen years old. Did she witness Schele's magisterial, or at least dramatic, presentation of their discovery? If so, what did Ruth make of that discovery?

Her father made much of it. But it's hard to tell from his letters alone. They couldn't differ more starkly from Schele's lively, loving, sometimes manic, sometimes rambling, artifacts of discovery. One early letter from Floyd begins,

> Dear Colleagues:
>
> Herewith I offer you what I guess I should call my "imaginative interpretation" of the latter part of the Inscription of the Temple of the Cross.[36]

I doubt that Linda ever spoke or wrote the word *herewith*. Just compare that opening with the next archived letter, this one written by Linda:

MARCH 24, 1974 AND THEREAFTER

> dear collegues [*sic*], friends, and friendly crazies:
>
> I'm typing this letter as an experiment to see if I can do it. My typewritter [*sic*] and technique have a problem.[37]

Linda doesn't let on about what the problem with the typewriter *is*. The letter, strewn with typos and scribbled-out words, wanders into cosmic revelations about Palenque.[38]

Such letters, as artifacts of Linda's life, often convey her intemperate, hallucinatory approach to research. Glyphic encounters could be *indulgences* for Linda, sites of intensity that inspired vividly imagined trips into the past. Linda's well-known popular writing can exude a divinatory quality. This style marks her contributions to *Maya Cosmos*.[39] Schele asks readers to virtually witness her revelations about ancient Maya astrology through accounts of generative quasi-ethnographic contact with contemporary Maya subjects in highland Chiapas. It's not quite interstellar travel. But it deftly overlays a long-standing US colonial construction of Mexico with the kind of spiritual science voiced by Carl Sagan. Schele teetered on the edge between scientific structuralism and the cosmic sublime, embodying just enough rationality and just enough mysticism to constitute a public of thousands of amateur epigraphers. The most devoted, the "glyphers," attended her annual workshops on ancient Maya writing at UT-Austin. The "glyphers" came back year after year, developing into a community of amateur epigraphers.

I think it's fair to say that Linda's interpretive labor and public engagement produced what Georges Bataille, in his theory of the general economy, called "excess."[40] By "excess," Bataille meant forms of profit or energy that can't be reassimilated into a system of production. As anthropologists beginning with Marcel Mauss have noted, such excess is expressed and dissipated through rituals.[41] In Linda's case, ritual dissipation of excess pervaded her professional life. It took form in intimate spaces of collaboration, such as the periodic, closed workshops at Dumbarton Oaks attended by Schele, Mathews, Lounsbury, Coe, and a few others. It took more public form in the UT-Austin workshops. There Linda made her vividly imagined trips into ancient Maya worlds into public sites of spectacle and collective becoming.[42]

In reading Linda's letters and speaking with those who knew her, one gets the sense that none of these sites of collaborative or public engagement exhausted her. Even the workshops, where she stood on stage for eight or ten hours a day conducting ritual dispensations of surplus knowledge, didn't sap her spiritual energy. In ethnographic interviews that I conducted in 2008, devoted workshop participants described ritual evening retreats to Linda's home, where they watched *Star Trek* and *Dr. Who*. But Linda, everyone knows, sat in one corner or another, carrying on in hushed tones about this glyph and that dynast.

The mythos of Linda folds her excesses into a vigorous exuberance retained beyond youth. A thoroughly American subject, she had little patience for elders, Floyd perhaps excepted. In having to deal with them, she could at times be timid. Linda's most carefully scripted letters are those addressed to older scholars such as Heinrich Berlin and Tatiana Proskouriakoff.

The case of Pakal's bones was particularly difficult. Was he forty years old at death, as Alberto Ruz Lhullier's team claimed? Or was he eighty, as Schele and Mathews's decipherment attested? Linda et alia had argued that the bones lied.[43] And they were probably right. But, boneheaded a paranoiac as I can be, I don't fully trust the glyphers' reglyphing either.[44]

Who's to decide, after all, where bone ends and writing or Spirit begins?

There's no better case than Maya writing. Not only do images of bone show up regularly in and around texts related and unrelated to death, bone itself was an occasional medium of inscription. Look, for example, at the incised human bones from Tikal's Temple I. They depict a dead or dying king flanked in a canoe by animal companions. In *The Blood of Kings*, Schele and Miller describe the scene in these terms: "The trip, a swift passage across the waters of this world under the guidance of the gods . . . is a metaphor for life. When the canoe of life sinks, the passengers drop beneath the surface of the water to enter Xibalba."[45] What a twisted form this is—a scene of death inscribed into a body's remainder.

What might Hegel's phrenologist make of this? For that matter, what would a forensic anthropologist? "The bones don't lie and they don't forget. And they're hard to cross-examine."[46] That's a poem—I think—by the late forensic anthropologist Clyde Snow. Snow—what a name! Bone can be white as fresh flurries. In his mad-hatter book on the history of color, Michael Taussig mentions bone only rarely.[47] What does come up is African ivory, that white-hot European fetish.

We bony beings tell our share of white lies. Ruth's lies are white. They're as white as the anthropologist Bronislaw Malinowski's unsoiled colonial garb, which draws attention where attention belongs in his staged fieldwork photographs. Taussig says, "He glows like Kurtz's ivory skull in *Heart of Darkness*. Light has chosen to condense itself into this lone figure, like sunlight focused through a magnifying glass onto a bright, burning spot."[48]

What vexes me most about Taussig's exceptionally frustrating book on color is that it's written in black-and-white. Even the photographs are reduced to grayscale. I can't forgive Taussig for this. I can't forgive him as I now forgive Linda for her line drawings that render inscribed stones and painted pots in the same bicolor palette. At the UT-Austin workshop on hieroglyphic writing in 2008, I asked an instructor whether colored pigments applied to stone inscriptions ever changed glyph elements' meanings. He didn't know.

And as far as I can tell, no one's really asking that question. But mustn't we? The midwesterner in me thinks of the recent crisis at the Corn Palace, that South Dakotan monument to maize as a "total social fact."[49] The palace royals readorn the building's facade every year with topical cob murals. The drought of summer 2012 left them four colors short. Does the reduction of Maya writing to bare-bone black-and-white text also leave us short?[50] Does it leave us with corny political melodrama? Or does it turn those images into what Taussig, elsewhere, calls "agribusiness writing"?[51] What *is* the Corn Palace if not an argument against agribusiness in its most antipoetic forms, those of feed corn and corn syrup? Doesn't the Corn Palace conceal a secret for midwesterners, the kind of secret that James Scott calls a "hidden transcript," a sly subtext that subverts the dominant narrative?[52] The story here is one of vibrant corn kernels reduced through genetic modification and evolutionary selection governed by profit motive to washed-out yellows and, of course, whites. As an Indiana kid I thought Dekalb® was a process, not a patented seed line. I was confused by peers, middle-school boys who'd say things like, "I'm working *dekalb* this summer." The World's Only Corn Palace, which I'd wager is also the Midwest's only *palace*, is a twelve-decade-long offensive against Monsanto and its ilk. We midwesterners prefer our struggles kind and subtle.

In his book on Maya peasants, Frank Cancian notes that corn farmers sometimes use a bone to split the ear from its husk.[53] The peasants of Zinacantán don't nail corn to their buildings. They turn it, instead, into tortillas and beer. It's fair to guess that their ancestors at Palenque didn't cob the walls either. But they did paint their temples, using toxic cinnabar powder for its distinctive vermillion hue. That powder billowed out of the sarcophagus of a Palenque noblewoman, probably Pakal's wife, who was affixed by her discoverers with a metonymic nickname, "The Red Queen."[54]

In inscriptions at Palenque's rival city, Toniná, Pakal's son Kan-Balam is named "Bone-Spirit Companion." (Here we have quite a different sense of "bone-spirit" from that found in English, where the term refers to a crude ammoniacal liquor by-product that results from carbonizing animal bones to produce a charcoal pigment called "bone-black.")[55]

For a time, this Bone-Spirit presided over Palenque. And here I should alert you that the Mayan name for Palenque was *baak*, meaning, of course, bone. The name Palenque, the Castilian term for *palisade*, may actually be a corruption of the Nahuatl term *palaanka*, "decay, putrescence."[56] Palenque's three name glyphs may all refer to bones. It was the city of bones in the west, where the sun, moon, and cyclic gods go to die. In 1968, Tzeltal Maya informants in highland Chiapas described a place called *palenka ch'en*, whose true name was *ak'obana*, derived from a term for ossuary buildings like Pakal's.

The archaeologists trowel on, slowly decalcifying the place. Only occasionally do they pay bones to the spirit world. Ruz offered his as tribute. He is buried on the plaza before Pakal's temple.

Linda died of pancreatic cancer in April 1998. Floyd followed her a month later. Linda profoundly transformed Palenque. A ceiba tree commemorates her there. But they wouldn't let her bones in. She was cremated and laid to rest, with Maya rituals, on the shores of Guatemala's Lake Atitlán.

GEORGIA O'KEEFFE

In a chapter simply titled "Savages" in his book *Excesses*, the philosopher Alphonso Lingis draws attention, in disturbing detail, to ritual Maya body modifications: flattening the forehead and drawing out the baby's brow; piercing ears, noses, and lips to insert beads or chains or rings; tooth filing and inlaying; clitoridectomy and circumcision; penis tattoos and bone or stone inserted into the glans.[57] He goes on, before insisting that, "What we are dealing with is inscription. Where writing, graphics, is not inscription on clay tablets, bark, or papyrus, but in flesh and blood, and also where it is not historical, narrative. Where it is not significant, not a matter of marks whose role is to signify, to efface themselves before the meaning, or ideality, or logos. For here the signs count: they *hurt*."[58]

Could Maya hieroglyphs, then, if they count at all, become legible as the futile excision of bodily pain? Were glyphs surgery? Was glyphic writing a therapeutic effort to make pain legible? Monumental inscriptions may have been conceived as material externalizations of Maya souls. Do their aesthetic indulgences reveal the ultimate irreducibility of pain and trauma to sense and language? Maybe the Spirit is a bone inserted into the glans, giving rise to textual germination.

But enough with these phallic philosophers.

Let's end this chapter where we began, in New Mexico with—or, at least, nearby—O'Keeffe. When I visited her museum, its guest exhibit featured the work of Mexican artist and anthropologist Miguel Covarrubias. He's well known for drawing Harlem Renaissance–era New York, that time and place when anthropologists, mostly white but some black, mixed quite freely with artists and writers. His images adorned the pages of the *New Yorker*, *Vogue*, and *Vanity Fair*. It's said that Covarrubias lent flesh and dignity to caricature as an expressive form. In so doing, he built not only on the Mexican modernism of friends, including Rivera and Kahlo, but also on the stark lines and billowing shapes of Maya buildings and Olmec head sculptures.[59]

Covarrubias's wife, Rosa, a dancer, convinced the oil baron and arts patron Nelson Rockefeller to fund the excavation and reconstruction of Palenque. Without Rosa's support, Ruz might not have discovered the bones of Pakal.[60]

In his 1937 ethnography, *Island of Bali*, Covarrubias blurs background and foreground in a color-laden description of island inhabitants. He says,

> No other race gives the impression of living in such close touch with nature, creates such a complete feeling of harmony between the people and the surroundings. The slender Balinese bodies are as much a part of the landscape as the palms and the breadfruit trees, and their smooth skins have the same tone as the earth and as the brown rivers where they bathe; a general colour scheme of greens, greys, and ochres, relieved here and there by bright-coloured sashes and tropical flowers. The Balinese belong in their environment in the same way that a humming-bird or an orchid belongs in a Central American jungle, or a steel-worker belongs in the grime of Pittsburgh.[61]

In 1929, before leaving for Bali, Covarrubias met O'Keeffe at the Taos home of the wealthy arts patron Mabel Dodge Luhan. Luhan moved there a decade earlier to found a literary colony with her husband and the anthropologist Elsie Clews Parsons. Luhan was a consummate and controversial host. D. H. Lawrence wrote about his unpleasant time there. Luhan shot back with a memoir on the author's stay: *Lorenzo in Taos*.[62]

* * *

The actor Dennis Hopper
bought the Luhan home.
He died of prostate cancer,
metastasized to bone.

The Spirit is a bone, but
not a snow-white bone.
A painted bone, a carved
bone, a weathered bone,

a tool. Ink, ash. A bone of
greens, greys, and ochres.
A bone weakened by cocaine,
cracked by cancer.[63]

That's a poem—I think—about Hopper and Hegel, Ozeki and O'Keeffe.
Above all, which is to say synthetically, about Linda. I struggle to stick with
O'Keeffe's Transcendentalist—or transhumanist—association of bones with
vitality. Bones are life and death; geist is and is not a bone. I'm not committed, either ontologically or anthropologically, to life itself. But I am committed to creativity, to writing as a technological means both to cope with death
and to endure it. This, I hope, is a feeling (which may be all I aspire to here)
shared by the artist subjects of my chapter. Let me be plain, antipoetic. The
opposition of spirit and matter requires no dialectics to resolve for women
who make art and history out of bones.

Putting femaleness and bone together requires courage, not dialectics
or psychoanalysis. I learned that from Georgia, who said, "It takes courage
to be a painter. I always felt I walked on the edge of a knife. . . . I might fall
off on either side but I'd walk it again. So what if you do fall off?"[64] And I
learned it from Linda, who said, "There are people who are centralists and
there are people who walk on the edge. And I think it's the edgewalkers that
continually push the box, and push the shape at the edge. And I think they're
the people that make fields change. I have always deliberately chosen to be
an edgewalker, knowing that my work is going to be wrong."[65]

Do the formalities of dialectical analysis teach us anything that isn't already apparent in Schele's willingness, an anthropological willingness, to
be wrong? Hegel's bone, the phrenologist's skull, marks the limits of signification, the necessary failure that gives rise to the possibility of an ethical
subject. The bone's a remnant of the dialectical circle, a form that resists

subjectification. It's an ivory-keyed improvisation; it's the constellational flare of a pulsing dialectical image.[66]

The synthesis of bone and spirit, nature and culture always leaves a residue, a remainder, a twisted form, a poem. Somewhere between glowing white animal bone and bone-black pigment, Spirit is born.

Chapter Five

Genius

Peers' and colleagues' postmortem reflections memorialized Schele as, at once, an antiacademic and a genius. I've mentioned one such passage already. Princeton art museum curator Gillett Griffin compared Schele to Einstein, and gave her the intellectual edge. Claiming status as Einstein's sole surviving friend, Griffin characterizes Schele as possessing a "more remarkable mind" than this classic embodiment of genius, and he clarifies that Schele excelled by turning dreams into reality.[1] Schele's student Andrea Stone attributed her "unique brand of genius" to a "strategy of 'total conquest' over a subject."[2] By the early 1980s, Schele's letters reveal that she considered this "strategy" both blessing and curse. Her close attention to the architectural art of Palenque led to exciting historical inferences concerning that site counterweighted by a lingering self-doubt about her knowledge of Maya history writ large.

Anthony Aveni lines up Schele's genius with her "showboat personality," her boldness, and her charismatic efforts as a popularizer.[3] He attributes all of these characteristics to "an incredibly infectious enthusiasm."[4] Aveni seems to draw on a patriarchal and sexist distinction between the (male) scholar as knowledge's producer and the (female) teacher as its mere distributor. The concluding passage in his homage both celebrates Schele and reminds us that she was a woman among men: "Linda's was an unorthodox sort of behavior for the scholar (especially the epigrapher), who is generally stereo-typed to live a lonely life among the stacks with laptop in tow. I believe this ineradicable capacity to reach out is one hallmark of the truly great teacher."[5] Schele's "behavior" apparently departed from scholarly conventions in her commitment to public engagement; this commitment made her a marked subject, an anomalous form of life among the (ostensibly) high-minded, socially averse world of scholars.

Aveni proceeds to recount an anecdote about an inquiry that he sent to Schele concerning use of one of her drawings. He concludes by reconstructing her reply, as he remembers it: "Dear Tony, Of course you may have my permission to reproduce any of my drawings for publication anytime and anywhere. Sincerely, Linda." He describes this comment as "like no other in my thirty-five years of publishing."[6] Schele deviated from the conservative norms of Aveni's territorial community of scholars. She reads here not simply as a teacher, but as the figure of a generous mother. References to Schele's bowl cut, her Levi's, her plaid shirts, and her vests seem to queer and masculinize her body, and they affirm the ambiguity—indeed, the edginess—of her subject position. The woman with power, creativity, and genius escapes a femme figuration. Linda's genius, it seems, was in tension—generative tension, I think—with her gender.

There's a series of photographs of Linda Schele and her protégé David Stuart sitting outdoors on the steps of Washington, DC's Dumbarton Oaks, a research library and museum managed by Harvard University. One of these photos shows up in the documentary *Cracking the Maya Code*, and another adorns Dumbarton Oaks' webpage dedicated to Stuart and his post–high school residency at that institution in 1983–84.[7] Stuart received his "Genius" grant while in residence at Dumbarton Oaks. On the museum's webpage, the photograph is dated 1985 and attributed to David's father, George Stuart, a *National Geographic* archaeologist and photographer (figure 5.1). David would have been nineteen or twenty, but he appears younger, fresh-faced, dressed in jeans and a long-sleeved denim shirt with dual breast pockets and sleeves rolled up past his elbows. Stuart's youthful appearance is intensified by the images' washed-out hue.

When the photograph from this series appeared during the prerelease screening of the documentary film *Cracking the Maya Code* at the Maya Meetings in 2008, it occasioned a restrained tittering among some audience members. A genius—you see—comes into this world as a full-fledged adult. Pretending that they had any kind of childhood, that they could engage in anything less-than-serious invites a kind-of-comical incredulity.

But there's no sign of play in these photos, even if Stuart could pass for thirteen or fourteen years old. In the image on the Dumbarton Oaks site, he appears inquisitive, sitting with a three-ring binder open on his lap, eyes

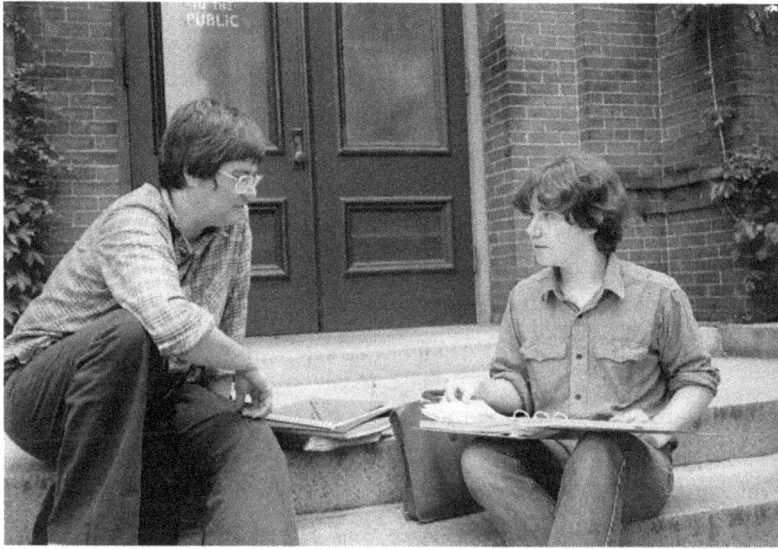

FIGURE 5.1 — Linda Schele and David Stuart, Dumbarton Oaks, 1985.
PHOTO BY GEORGE STUART.

pointed up toward Linda with lips parted slightly, as if the photograph caught him midsentence. He's the focal point of the father's photo, and one can easily imagine that neither Linda nor David realized they'd been caught in the act.

But Stuart's sight line redirects mine. His Levi's getup holds my attention briefly before passing it to his coconspirator. Here, as elsewhere, Schele performs a distinctive female masculinity.[8] In light-colored jeans, a hatched plaid shirt, and large-lensed glasses, she leans toward Stuart, gaze directed at his binder. Seated on a higher step, with right elbow firmly lodged onto knee, Schele commands authority. The clothing belies the aesthetic dimension of the research in progress; alongside Stuart's apparel, it suggests an effort to redress epistemic authority in working-class clothes that chafe against the ivy-clad wall in the background. On the steps between the decipherers appears a stack of files, topped by a bound document that looks to be the "Notebook for the Maya Hieroglyphic Workshop at Texas" from the 1980 session.[9] A light-colored leather briefcase leans between Stuart and the step, and Schele's legs partially obscure what may be a black bag, possibly a backpack.

The door behind her profile reads "TO THE PUBLIC." The photograph's frame cuts off the majuscule inscription's opening line, but it must be "CLOSED."

The image constructs Schele as a teacher as well as a gatekeeper. In the photo from this series that appeared in *Cracking the Maya Code*, Stuart eyes the lens as Schele's gaze remains fixed on the kid. She's ushering him into decipherment, tethering him, radioing out the assuring voice of ground control as Stuart not-so-tepidly tin-cans into space:

> Take your protein pills and put your helmet on
> Ground control to Major Tom
> Commencing countdown engines on
> Check ignition and may God's love be with you.[10]

The workshop notebook intertextually blasts us through the playful cosmic classrooms of the UT-Austin workshops.[11] Here, in the orbit of Dumbarton Oaks, she puts a prospective fellow genius to the test. The text that complements and gives sense to this interpolated iconography quotes a letter from Schele to Elizabeth Boone, Dumbarton Oaks' director of Pre-Columbian Studies. It recounts Schele's initial encounter with Stuart, in Palenque some seven or eight years earlier:

> When [the Stuart family] arrived, I was suffering from an injured foot and did not particularly wish to deal with a twelve year old enthusiast for glyphs so I sent him out to the back porch of Merle Robertson's house with a drawing of the Tablet of the Sun text and said "Come back kid when you've figured out what it says." To my amazement, to the utter astonishment of the Palenque community, and to his mother's knowing grin, that twelve year old came back in twenty-four hours with a complete reading of the text, and it only took a few judicious questions from me to generate his understanding.[12]

Schele's commentary seems to signal an increasing democratization of expertise within the field of Maya epigraphy. Here we have an encounter where the emerging woman genius skeptically puts an adolescent—a middle school "enthusiast"—to the test. Stuart not only passes the test; he signals his rise as another genius-in-the-making. The story of this corner of Maya studies, then, hinges on tropes of unconventional genius. David Stuart's status as one of few preeminent power-wielding epigraphers would normalize as he aged. But Schele's genius seemed to remain marked, unconventional (as if genius were ever conventional).

I suspect that this sense of incongruity, the non-fit between Schele and genius, had to do with more than an artist's desire to resist the stuffy conventionalities of academia or Maya studies (conventionalities reinstituted, in many ways, by Stuart and his peers). As I suggest in the previous chapter, the incongruity, non-fit, or confusion had as much to do with Schele being a woman, as it had to do with Schele being an artist. A passage in Margaret Atwood's book of essays *Negotiating with the Dead* raises this question—the disjunction of gender and genius—in reading an A. M. Klein poem that laments (male) poets' felt experiences of obscurity. On Klein's anguish, Atwood comments, "This psychic wound appears to be suffered largely by men. Women writers weren't included in the Romantic roll-call; in fact, the word 'genius' and the word 'woman' just don't really fit together in our language, because the kind of eccentricity expected of male 'geniuses' would simply result in the label 'crazy,' should it be practiced by a woman."[13] Schele may have suffered, but she refused to suffer the psychic wound of obscurity. She turned the ancient Maya world into the means—the raw materials—for her art. Although Aveni may reveal some subtextual reservations, he and others did, after her death at least, recognize Schele as a *woman genius*. To be both woman and genius, here, was a precarious edgewalk.

Atwood doesn't take the time to note that this tension between woman and genius runs much deeper than the nineteenth-century characterization of smart, eccentric women as "hysterics."[14] The Latin term *genius* designated the "male spirit of a family, existing in the head of the family and subsequently in the divine or spiritual part of each individual."[15] The base of this noun was the verb *gignere*, to beget, from which "genital" also derives. The genius was the man whose spirit animates his progeny, defining their "natural appetites" and inspiring their talents. More generally, a genius could be a demon or spiritual being. The French cognate *génie* can mean a patron saint in addition to a spirit conferred on a person at birth. Its phonetic similarity to the Arabic *jinn* led the French translators of *One Thousand and One Nights* to use the term to designate those supernatural figures of Islamic mythology. Hence the English genie. The German *Genius* can be more sociological than religious. It was generalized from a person's good or evil attendant spirit to the spirit of an era or a language. And, as *Genie*, it can refer to the personification of an immaterial quality in art or to an "exceptionally talented person." Though the term's aesthetic and Romantic sense references an artist's distinctive originality, it's weighed down by association with the Latin *ingenium*, the root of "engineer." In French, *génie* can refer to engineering, originally the construction of military defenses.[16]

It seems that there's some etymological precedent for casting the genius as the antischolar, or, to use that word more routinely subject to derision, the anti*academic*. Unlike the academic, alone in the stacks, the genius needs no recourse to knowledge produced and inscribed by others. At the dawn of Romanticism, the English term *genius* became opposed to *talent*. In light of its French industrial sense, this opposition may evoke—for anthropologists, at least—Lévi-Strauss's well-known distinction between the engineer and the bricoleur.[17] The engineer's scientific thought is genius; it produces its means and ends from whole cloth. The mythical thought of the bricoleur, on the other hand, is mere talent. The bricoleur works with ratty hand-me-downs, stitching new signifieds to old signifiers.

Consider a bit more closely how Stone characterizes Schele's "native brilliance." She says, "[Schele's] strategy of 'total conquest' over a subject meant that her work remained relatively focused, at least in the first decade of her career. This was not the case with most other scholars of Maya art, who often worked from published sources and handily jumped from site to site."[18] Stone and Aveni commonly suggest that Schele avoided published sources—scholarly hand-me-downs—in favor of a formal method. Close, sustained attention to the minutiae of Palenque's inscriptions led to sudden discoveries, as intricate art became legible text. But rhetorically constructing such transformation as "total conquest" is also senselessly insensitive to Schele. It's an act of epistemic violence against Maya peoples on Stone's part. Characterizing decipherment along these lines perpetuates the colonial *reducción* of Maya populations and Mayan languages—in its subordination of Maya aesthetic forms that elude and elide Eurocentric logocentrism—to the master narratives of Western art and writing.[19] I want Schele's legacy— her "mythistory"—to run free.[20]

After Lévi-Strauss rewilded thought, we're no longer supposed to believe in the engineer, the conqueror of language, the figure of originality.[21] Derrida, in his formative reading of Lévi-Strauss, models the objection in his characteristically clever way:

> A subject who supposedly would be the absolute origin of his own discourse and supposedly would construct it "out of nothing," "out of whole cloth," would be the creator of the verb, the verb itself. The notion of the engineer who supposedly breaks with all forms of *bricolage* is therefore a theological idea; and since Lévi-Strauss tells us elsewhere that *bricolage* is mythopoetic, the odds are that the engineer is a myth produced by the *bricoleur*. As soon as we cease to believe in such an engineer and in a discourse which breaks with the received discourse, and as soon as we admit that every finite discourse is bound by a cer-

tain *bricolage* and that the engineer and the scientist are also species of *bricoleurs*, then the very idea of *bricolage* is menaced and the difference in which it took on its meaning breaks down.[22]

Despite his incredulity toward Derridean deconstruction,[23] Latour has offered an empirical demonstration of this point. He followed real-life engineers around and proved them to be mere bricoleurs like the rest of us.[24]

But this book has suspended such disbelief in order to take seriously the Mayanist bricoleurs' myth of an engineered decipherment, and the joy that it induces. In this state of antiparanoid suspension, I want to have my critique and eat it too.[25] My method for doing so is mythocritical; I give my words and spirit over to the theological God-idea of the engineer, Schele as the engineer, the whole-cloth creator. In so doing, I find myself facing a person who was not talented, who was not book-smart, who cared little for stacks and less for theoretical argumentation. Join me here to find a being who wasn't a common bricoleur, a run-of-the-mill do-it-yourselfer, an academic like me and probably you. She was, rather, a true engineer, which is to say a genius, which is to say a *genie*, which is to say a spirit conferred onto a person, place, or institution at its birth. Is there any better candidate for the figure of the engineer—"the creator of the verb, the verb itself"—than this triumphant author of *Maya Glyphs: The Verbs*?[26]

So in case you haven't educed my point already, let me state it plainly. This book isn't about Linda Schele, Mayanist, or Linda Schele, Artist, or even Linda Schele as an ordinary being among beings. For Linda, *linda*, can mean beauty, and here, in language, we face the ineffable beauty of the scientific sublime. I warned you at the beginning that this isn't a biography, can't be a bio-graphy. But look at me trying to put the genie back in the bottle just as the question of the woman genius arises.

"Arises," as if it weren't of my own making. But is it?

In *Where the North Sea Touches Alabama*, Allen Shelton casts off the reliable narrator to inhabit a tragic soul-nourishing ethnographic antibiography of his artist friend Patrik Keim. He says:

> Even in the extreme forms of autoethnography or performative ficto-criticism, the narrator is a stable structure. Sometimes this narrator is the last piece of stability as even the grammar around that voice disintegrates. Patrik sent me a postcard with this phrase from Nietzsche: "I fear we do not get rid of God, because we still believe in grammar." I must be an atheist now.[27]

Allen, grieving in Patrik's wake, has to suspend his belief in grammar, in himself as purveyor of locutionary handholds securing our edgewalk. Allen's method is, simply, to fall off the edge. Inspired, I've tried to let go too. But Linda and Patrik, roughly contemporaneous nonrepresentational artists who both died in 1998, took different paths along the edge. Patrik's more unsettling, ruinous art wasn't Linda's hopeful spaced-out modernist cosmo-aesthetic, let alone her groovy Mayanism. Even with Derrida's help, I can't cop the courage needed to fall through her into abyssal nonbeing; the God-engineer's grammar-net catches hold, tangling me in the golden orb weaver's web.[28] I—a reliable enough narrator, I suppose—can't become an atheist yet.

You see, my friend Alanna, a mathematician and ingenious knight traversing the plains with her Sancho, sent me a postcard from the Corn Palace in Mitchell, South Dakota. "WE WERE EAR!" it declares. Alanna, in a cursive that belies her millennialism, adds: "I think this postcard says it all." Yes, we now know. Yes, but . . .

Yes, but the palace remains a crowning achievement of Mesoamerican seed-cyborg technology ported to Turtle Island's so-called Midwest.

Yes, but this passage in Derrida's *envois* dated June 5, 1977:

> Eros in the age of technical reproducibility. You know the old story of reproduction, with the dream of a ciphered language [*sic*]
>
> Want to write a grand history, a large encyclopedia of the post and of the cipher, but to write it ciphered still in order to dispatch it to you, taking all the precautions so that forever you are the only one to be able to decrypt it (to write it, then, and to sign), to recognize your name, the unique name I have given you, that you have let me give you, the entire strong-box of love supposing that my death is inscribed in it, or better that my body might be enclosed in it with your name on my skin, and that in any event my own or its survival or your own be limited to the life of—you.[29]

Yes, but Maya cosmology is a theory of destiny, of destination.[30] The road of awe. Yes, but Linda's destination, let alone mine, hasn't yet been dispatched, just as her letters haven't yet been deposited in the archive, UT-Austin's archive, to which they were promised, to which they are still destined. Yes, but Linda's letters weren't to me; my readings are perversions; yes, but as Derrida reminds, the postcard, naked to the world, never reaches its destination.[31]

I can't suspend my disbelief because of coincident discoveries—like the decipherment of the *way* glyph, the animal-spirit companion glyph—and because of plain old coincidences.[32] Having just inscribed Alanna's name, she—both the offspring of pastors and a genius postcarder—has now text-messaged me: "Spur of the moment overnight trip to Portland. Want me to bring you back anything? A lobster?"

Yes, I must accept your offer of a noninnocent gift portending crustaceous death, the hot-watery end of a being that some categorically disavow as a perverse abomination, an anomalous form of sacred dirt.[33]

Did Linda eat lobster? Rabbit? As Lévi-Strauss puts it, we are all cannibals![34]

* * *

Invocations of Schele's genius reconstruct her as innocent, as obsessed, as irreverent, as spiritual, as iconoclastic. They remind me of earlier affirmations offered in private correspondence to Schele by Carl Sagan and Claude Lévi-Strauss. I'm reminded, again, of how Lévi-Strauss wrote Schele to acknowledge the importance of her work for structural analysis. There he claims, "It is often said that I disregard history. Nothing can be more wrong. Historians and structural analysts both strive after the same end. . . . The two approaches are complementary, and nothing demonstrates it better than your work which combines so successfully history and structural analysis."[35] The exchange calls me to speculate about Schele's memorialization-as-genius in terms introduced by Lévi-Strauss some decades before he wrote that letter from his Parisian laboratory. I wish to hold here on a reading of Lévi-Strauss's *Introduction to the Work of Marcel Mauss*, inhabiting his conception of the "floating signifier" in a theo-anthropological mood. So I warn you that Schele occupies the margins for a few pages here; theoretical exposition edges her out. But I promise that she remains nearby, and even haunts my "nitpicking"—her word, remember?—theoretical detour. Before long—I promise—she'll edge back to near-center with another discovery.

Toward the conclusion of *Introduction to the Work of Marcel Mauss*, Lévi-Strauss rapidly moves from a discussion of the significance of *mana* and *hau* in the work of Mauss to a baroque analysis of the origin of language to a discussion of the relation between symbolism and scientific knowledge.[36] The concept that facilitates such rapid conceptual movement is mana, that paradigm of anthropological paradigms, that Polynesian term for sacred impersonal force.[37] In discussing scientific knowledge, Lévi-Strauss notes that "we appear to be far removed from *mana*, but in reality we are extremely close to it."[38] We are close to it because science as a centering intellectual, social, and moral edifice is not different in *kind* from the systematic symbolism of—say—Māori mythology. Both are intricate conceptual systems that make the world sensible. They differ only with respect to their methods of fixing each signifier to a discrete signified, closing the sign in on itself.

The language ideology operative within decipherment, as an expression of Saussurean linguistic science, rigidly insists on a coherent (and rather closed) pairing of a sign's form and its denotative meaning.[39] Decipherment proceeds from a subject's encounter with a field of inscribed signs to her inference of a sign's denotational meaning—its signified—to its transduction into the form of alternate signifiers in the target language of translation.[40] Epigraphers seem to assume that the lion's share of hieroglyphs entextualize signifiers with discrete, fixed, and inferable denotational senses. The collection of inferred signifieds amounts to Maya epigraphy's basic assemblage of facts.

But from an anthropological—even structuralist—perspective, are Maya glyphs predominantly closed signs, signifiers fixed in stone to their signifieds? After all, Lévi-Strauss insists that the symbolic domain of language has "from the start" contained signifiers—"signifier-totalities"—that elude efforts to fix them concretely to particular signifieds. Some words resist final semantic stabilization. They have a multitude of senses but lack firm denotative meanings. As Lévi-Strauss puts it, "There is always a non-equivalence or 'inadequation' between the two, a non-fit and overspill which divine understanding alone can soak up; this generates a signifier-surfeit relative to the signifieds to which it can be fitted."[41] We have a surplus of signification that we distribute as a "supplementary ration."[42] Organizing cultural concepts such as mana—or maybe *genius*, or *gender*?—have so much sense that they resist reduction to coherent signifieds. They're "floating signifiers" that mark the "disability of all finite [scientific] thought (but also the surety of all art, all poetry, every mythic and aesthetic invention)."[43] Rich in sense but poor in meaning, these terms unsettle scientistic desires to produce representations that mirror the world. More importantly, for Lévi-Strauss, they enable thought to persist in the face of the irreducible complexity of the world as it's given in experience. Floating signifiers shore up communication when speech seems to falter in its descriptive capacity. This supplementary role leads Lévi-Strauss to claim that a floating signifier is "a symbol in its pure state," "a *zero symbolic value*," a signifier that takes on any value needed to remedy discursive discontinuities and ensure a subject's linguistic, symbolic, and psychological persistence.[44]

The necessary-yet-destabilizing quality of the floating signifier's supplementary function became an integral problem for Derrida.[45] From a more semiotic perspective, it is a necessary condition for language itself, as a mode of symbolization that entails and requires the use of arbitrary signs. The arbitrary or conventional quality of all linguistic acts suggests that each and every symbol "floats"; though one might suggest that some come closer to "indexical" signification, signification through a semantic flow and transformation of sense across physical media, predicated on contiguity.[46] One might then extend the figurative language of "floating" by suggesting that symbols float at different altitudes, that they range in their semantic distance from a signified and its referent.

Here I wish to hold on to an element of Lévi-Strauss's introduction of the nonequivalence between signified and floating signifier that has received insufficient critical attention. This often-overlooked feature of Lévi-Strauss's conception of the floating signifier offers a rich point of entry into problems of historical and cultural knowledge. Namely, within this understanding of the human's linguistic condition, the human condition as linguistic, Lévi-Strauss conjures a godly presence.[47] At or through the empty, floating signifier, the signifier that can't quite close into a bounded sign, God rushes in. Again, Lévi-Strauss asserts that between the signified and the floating signifier there's "a non-fit and overspill which divine understanding alone can soak up."[48] The surfeit of the signifier exists because human language—as opposed to divine speech—suffers from the duality of the sign, the divide between signifier and signified. The human response to encountering a floating signifier is to attach it, provisionally, to a signified. The magic of human communication is its efficaciousness despite the divergent signifieds that speakers associate with an exchanged signifier. The coherency of communication is predicated on semantic gaps or lacunae. Divine understanding, on the other hand, is the flip side of divine speech. Divine understanding does not require the floating signifier, because it understands without the mediation of fallible utterances. Divine speech proves infallible, a transmission of meaning that cannot be misunderstood. The divine speech acts of Jewish and Christian theologies comprise true "performatives" that don't require supplementation by a floating signifier such as mana.

In the speech act theory of John L. Austin, a "performative" verb ostensibly differs from a "constative" verb in that it directly affects the world rather than simply describing it.[49] Austin maintains that all interlocutory speech acts, at the bare minimum, entail the performative effect of "informing." This construction of speech as a consequential form of action has been mobilized provocatively in anthropology, gender studies, and companionate fields.[50] That said, as Michelle Rosaldo effectively argued, Austin's speech act theory hinged on a particular Euro-American language ideology. This ideology presumes that language's main function is to convey straightforward and coherent "ideas" from one discrete subject to another.[51] Rosaldo's critique shows how speech act theory amounts, in the end, to a so-called "folk" theory of Western communication. Has the unwitting autoethnography of philosophers such as Austin and John Searle assumed a particular quasi-religious construction of pure, abstract performativity? Jewish and Christian doxa, from the opening passages of the Torah or Old Testament, offers a God who constitutes the cosmos by speaking it into being. "Performativity," then, may well be another word for "God," constructed here as the force of cosmic generativity.

In a surface reading of the structuralist view, unaided by a performative understanding of speech, the question of the floating signifier ostensibly remains within the domain of semantics. Cultural coherency and continuity persist because of the flex and flow of the floating signifier, which does not assimilate or "soak up" *all* meaning, but draws into itself sufficient presumably shared semantic content to facilitate communication. Although no speaker means precisely the same thing by "mana"—or, for that matter, "God"—some semantic overlap must exist for speech acts to be felicitous, or successful. This semantic overlap itself constitutes a provisional ground of reference, assuring that discursive exchange entails partial intelligibility. The floating signifier, then, remedies the disjuncture between subjects commonly participating in speech events (whether or not the interlocutors are aware of their cognitive-linguistic disjuncture). It might seem reasonable, then, to read Lévi-Strauss's valorization of the floating signifier as a rational and *secular* account of how communication functions, an account that need not appeal to "occasionalist" claims, such as the argument that divine forces guide human action or mediate human communication. The floating signifier emerges, in this fairly narrow semanticist reading, as a necessary, secular feature of language.

But it's not altogether clear that Lévi-Strauss's introduction of the floating signifier assumes a narrowly secular, antioccasionalist reading. Instead, he seems to be suggesting that signifiers such as mana and hau—anthropological untranslatables—function as catchalls, the ecological sinks of language. When an event proves incomprehensible, when a subject encounters the limits of her capacity to reduce the world to the finite and delineable terms of a cultural (mytho)logic, she ascribes it to the works of mana. Such an invocation of mana may appear simply as a reflection of the limits of secular rationality. From a linguistic perspective, this draws us back to the semanticist view.[52] But if one presses Lévi-Strauss into a more performative mold, as was Derrida's tendency, his invocations of mana (or, for that matter, God) begin to look like enactments of mana (or God). Speakers don't will a world (or a doxic, figural God as such) into being through the genie-like divine performativity of their speech acts. But, taken together, the performativity of collective will enacts a kind of God. The collective performativity of mana enacts or achieves mana. Mana emerges in discourse as a form and force that elicits relational response.

But such a view is certainly reducible to the social realism associated with Durkheim and, to a lesser extent, his nephew Mauss. Would explicit advocacy for the spiritual status of "culture" and "history" move us beyond the Durkheimian position that collective ritual practice and attendant speech sacralizes the social itself? Perhaps, as I believe, Mauss and Lévi-Strauss already surpassed this view through attention to the magical efficacy of language and the corollary introduction of a more relational construction of the human subject. This position was epitomized by the primacy of reciprocal obligations encapsulated in that tricky term *hau*, a Polynesian and Melanesian term reduced in its anthropological circulation to "the spirit of the gift."[53]

But the attention of subsequent anthropologists of religion has tended to focus far too restrictively on domains of cultural practice that look unequivocally like culturally dominant Western religions. The history of the anthropology of religion is often traced to nineteenth-century Classicists or Orientalists such as William Robertson Smith, read in complement to more ethnologically oriented scholars such as Edward Burnett Tylor and James Frazer. Such scholars—perhaps Tylor especially—complicated the reigning concepts of religion by constructing (or appropriating) more capacious categories, categories such as totemism and animism, that would valorize the practices of colonized subjects as fully "religious."[54]

This extension of "religion," as a domain of cultural practice or knowledge, nevertheless flowed through the capillaries of imperial power, as anthropologists since the nineteenth century have claimed to demonstrate the value and coherency of colonized cultures' belief systems in the act of subjecting such systems to the covering, controlling, and historically contingent category of "religion" (and its inverse image, "secularism").[55] The point of much anticolonial, postcolonial, and decolonial thinking has been to show how such moves subject colonized communities to institutions of Western control at the same time that they claim to speak for them in an affirmative or justice-oriented fashion. The point is not to fall back into critical denunciation of a mystified "power" but, instead, to suggest that this colonial project amounts to a form of epistemic comparativism that justifies—through anthropological categorization—the maintenance of "religion" as an isolable, narrow domain of practice and belief.

But what if we rejected this taxonomic domestication of "religion"? Such disavowal might allow us to slow down thought, and to consider, in light of Lévi-Strauss's *Introduction to the Work of Marcel Mauss*, how "religion" may better designate the forms of discursive experience that meet the limits of comprehension and thus turn to a floating signifier to soak up the spilled, disorderly nonmeaning, the referents or signifieds that appear, otherwise, inexplicable. And if this is the case, it's not simply a floating signifier such as "God" that functions as the supplement buttressing meaning and order, becoming a performative enactment of the infinite. "Culture" performs the same function. These floating signifiers are the engineer's voice voiced through us; and, as Derrida put it, "The notion of the engineer who supposedly breaks with all forms of *bricolage* is . . . a theological idea."[56]

The student of anthropology asks, "Why do the Maya regard the ceiba tree as the axis mundi?" The exasperated professor, short on time or patience, replies with an invocation of the divinatory sublime: "It's their culture."

The professor, of course, could—and sometimes does—offer historical genealogies and socio-symbolic contextualizations, tracing the associations that make the ceiba-as-axis-mundi a viable, consequential cultural belief and practice. But she couches the explanations, again and again—as I just have—as *cultural*. This overdetermined term is another way to invoke the infinite, particularly the infinite recess of meaninglessness—at least on the level of the symbolic—that characterizes the cosmos. Thus, the institution that constructs itself around the concept of culture—namely, anthropology—is, through and through, an appeal to the impossibility of secure or final truth-claims. Or, put differently, it is an admission of the finite and immanent status of our human capacity for comprehension. Efforts to define "culture" are like efforts to define "God" within Christian theology. "Culture" cohabits a rabbit hole with "God," "the infinite," and countless other lively signs. I suspect that we—and neighboring disciplines—would do little better with "ideology," "society," "history," "politics," "economy," "thought," "knowledge," or "being." Such floating signifiers play with the divine, even as we cover them with the vestments of secular scholarly seriousness.

I am asking for less seriousness, and more sincerity.

Beyond anthropology, one of the most prominent—and very *serious*—recent invocations of Lévi-Strauss's readings of Mauss's mana appears in Žižek's tour de force, *Less Than Nothing*.[57] A discussion of Lacan's engagement with constitutive absence leads Žižek to Lévi-Strauss's exposition of mana as a signifier with a zero function, and he quotes the commonly cited passage from *Introduction to the Work of Marcel Mauss* here at some length. But, in a symptomatic move, Žižek quickly and carelessly reduces Lévi-Strauss's concept to a positivist longing for adequation between language and world. In making this point, he quotes a passage that I reproduced above, the claim that mana "represent[s] nothing more or less than the *floating signifier* which is the disability of all finite thought."[58] Here Žižek rather problematically omits Lévi-Strauss's clarifying parenthetical: "(but also the surety of all art, all poetry, every mythic and aesthetic invention)."[59] Thus readers of Žižek are misled into believing that "the disability of all finite thought" signifies a longing for an isomorphic relation between word and world. Žižek acts like he's dressing Lévi-Strauss's idea up in the French materialist clothes of Althusser and Deleuze so as to salvage it from an ideological reproduction of brute "scientific positivism." He seems to regard Lévi-Strauss as reproducing an ideological distinction that holds science apart from the "'poetic' excess" of myth, art, or creativity.

But, in an earlier passage in the *Introduction to the Work of Marcel Mauss*, Lévi-Strauss has already subordinated the domain of the "real" to that of a receding deep-structural "language," which he, following Mauss, equates with both magic and exchange, and which he regards, suggestively, as integral to the human condition. Lévi-Strauss even offers, here, a rather protean "big bang" theory of language and cognition.[60] The human capacity for symbolic thought emerges in a flash with the first linguistic act: "Whatever may have been the moment and circumstances of its appearance in the ascent of animal life, language can only have arisen all at once. Things cannot have begun to signify gradually."[61] In Lévi-Strauss's baroque presentation, this act achieved an extraordinary performative effect: it brought the whole of language into being. A reading of *Introduction to the Work of Marcel Mauss* that accounts more generously for the origin—a *true* origin—of both "language" and the "floating signifier" reveals that Lévi-Strauss's effort to hold apart poetic excess and finite-scientific thought serves merely as a provisional rhetorical device. And if you read just beyond the passage quoted above by Žižek and by me, you'll find a remarkable valorization of the role of the floating signifier within *all human thought*, including scientific thought:

> I believe that notions of the *mana* type, however diverse they may be, and viewed in terms of their most general function (which, as we have seen, has not vanished from our mentality and our form of society) represent nothing more or less than the *floating signifier* which is the disability of all finite thought (but also the surety of all art, all poetry, every mythic and aesthetic invention), even though scientific knowledge is capable, if not of staunching it, at least of controlling it partially. Moreover, magical thinking offers other, different methods of channeling and containment, with different results, and all these methods can very well coexist.[62]

Žižek, then, has attributed a narrow "scientific positivism" to a thinker who presents magic and science as epistemic domains that may sometimes be at odds, but commonly manage to check the slipperiness of language, and that, ultimately, harbor a capacity to coexist peacefully. This is no straightforward positivist or scientistic longing. It strikes me, rather, as an ethnographic observation that implicitly owes as much to Malinowski's reflections on the complementarity of scientific, magical, and religious practices among the Trobrianders as it owes to Mauss's reflections on the cultural function of mana.[63] Read in these terms, then, Lévi-Strauss's floating signifier amounts to an anticipation of Isabelle Stengers's sense of "cosmopolitics," as the provisional, in-the-making coexistence of ostensibly contradictory claims about the world.[64]

Lévi-Strauss further justifies the integral role of the floating signifier to "all social phenomena": "In other words, accepting the inspiration of Mauss's precept that all social phenomena can be assimilated to language, I see in *mana, wakan, orenda,* and other notions of the same type, the conscious expression of a *semantic function*, whose role is to enable symbolic thinking to operate despite the contradiction inherent in it."[65] One may reasonably question Lévi-Strauss's perhaps overly semantic construction of language.[66] But within the confines of language-cum-the-social, Lévi-Strauss effectively shows himself to be a more faithful Hegelian than Žižek, his comrade-in-dialectics. In fact, if Žižek has any cause to mark up *Introduction to the Work of Marcel Mauss* as less than faithful, it arrives earlier, in a passage where Lévi-Strauss mobilizes Mauss's observation that Melanesians use the same words for the ostensible antitheses of buying/selling and lending/borrowing. On this point, Lévi-Strauss offers a striking commentary:

That is ample proof that the operations in question are far from "antithetical"; that they are just two modes of a selfsame reality. We do not need *hau* to make the synthesis, because the antithesis does not exist. The antithesis is a subjective illusion of ethnographers, and sometimes also of indigenous people who, when reasoning about themselves—as they quite often do—behave like ethnographers, or more precisely, like sociologists; that is, as colleagues with whom one may freely confer.[67]

In his narrow focus on the floating signifier, Žižek overlooks such passages. So he proceeds to err in claiming that, "Like the early Badiou and Althusser, he [Lévi-Strauss] excludes science from the dialectics of lack that generates the need for a suturing element."[68] Before introducing the floating signifier, Lévi-Strauss has already characterized dialectical thinking as a specific culturally and linguistically shaped modality of reason, a modality of reason accessible to both ethnographers and indigenized subjects who, here, become thoughtful, reflective autoethnographers.[69] This suggests the implicit current of anticoloniality that runs throughout Lévi-Strauss's oeuvre, in stark contrast to Žižek's overreliance on a universalized psychologizing dialectic that persistently misrecognizes itself, failing to see itself for what it is: unwitting, unreflective autoethnography.

Maybe the philosopher needs to return to the analyst's couch.

* * *

Among the most perplexing and difficult of hieroglyphic signs is the *way* glyph, now read as a subject's *nagual*, coessence, or animal spirit companion.[70] Schele didn't decipher this glyph. But she took up the decipherment with the kind of personal fervor and passionate attachment that made her a charismatic figure within the field. Schele's self-construction in the 1980s and 1990s drew on the Maya cosmology of those supposedly quintessential "closed corporate communities" of Highland Chiapas, Chamula and Zinacantán. Schele conceptualized her attachment to rabbits as a spirit companionship consistent with that of ancient Maya scribes who were increasingly conceptualized on the model of Highland Maya shamans.[71]

If the *way* glyph functioned as a complex organizing trope for the ancient Maya, maybe "genius" performed a comparable function for the collective of scholars and enthusiasts drawn to Schele. Perhaps close attention to "genius" may help us understand the cultural logic of decipherment, or even the logic of historical and cultural knowledge production more broadly. After all, didn't the mythology- and history-oriented Americanist anthropology to which Lévi-Strauss was so indebted conceive itself as the study of culture-as-genius, the "genius of a people"?[72]

In systematizing the Americanist corpus, Lévi-Strauss came to regard his own method as a mode of mythopoesis. The characterization of mythological analysis as mythopoetic construction is epistemologically consistent with Lévi-Strauss's introduction of the floating signifier as the ostensibly secular worldly substitute for divine mediation that ensures the enduring semantic functionality of language. It's not, however, the only solution. We could also appeal to the demonstrative function of scientific experimentation, including Schele's situated and experimental observations of the cosmic, astronomical order.

Talal Asad's reflections on the shifting status of sacred speech since the Reformation offer clarity at this juncture.[73] According to Asad, medieval Christianity fused the signifier and signified or the matter and meaning of biblical text. Receiving its message, and becoming inspired, involved devotional attention to the sensory feel of the text in both its material inscription and vocalization. Asad ascribes the movement away from such orthopraxic forms of textual engagement to higher biblical critics' introduction of arguments for the Bible's status as a body of myth. This mythologization of the text emerged as part of an ideology that ascribed to speech the status of a medium external to the real, a form that could both represent the world and mask or misrepresent it. This point presents an important early modern conjunction of biblical criticism, linguistics, and science. Here Asad quotes Michel de Certeau:

> The *experiment*, in the modern sense of the word was born with the deontologizing of language, to which the birth of a linguistics also corresponds. In Bacon and many others, the experiment stood opposite language as that which guaranteed and verified the latter. This split between a deictic language (it shows and/or organizes) and a referential experimentation (it escapes and/or guarantees) structures modern science, including "mystical science."[74]

In this light, Lévi-Strauss's reading of floating signifiers such as mana amounts to an alternative to the invocation of scientific experimentation as the social system that shores up the referential capacity of language.

This applies, of course, to cultural forms of life that achieve order through assiduous applications of their respective floating signifiers. But it applies equally to anthropology as a sustained and institutionalized metadiscourse that describes how those particular cultural signifiers organize—or even enact—their distinctive cultural forms of life. It is the role of anthropology not simply to affirm the inadequation and indeterminacy of reference in what many critics misunderstand as a "deconstructive" mode, but to trace how specific floating signifiers enable communities of human beings to persist without succumbing to the epistemological paralysis or even nihilism that may result from observations of the limits of intersubjective understanding. Given that anthropology doesn't exactly self-organize through experimental systems, it's reasonable to question whether the convergence of mythological analysis and mythopoesis is, in fact, anomalous.

Consider how powerful signifiers such as mana move from their native speech communities into those of the anthropologist. Perhaps anthropology's invocation and use of floating signifiers such as taboo, mana, hau, orenda, *kula*, and *baloma*—not to mention *way* and genius—marks a deontologization of language. Conceived as linguistic expressions of total social facts, these terms fill the void opened by the collective effort of modern science and metaphysics to cross out God.[75] If we follow Lévi-Strauss in believing that the gap between signifier and signified introduces a dangerous degree of malleability or play into communicative exchange, the affirmation of a complementary relation between deictic language and referential experimentation cannot amount to a sufficient condition for the maintenance of collective social life. The forms of witnessing and virtual witnessing that define Schele's experimental form of life may well solidify scientific inscriptions' social and pragmatic functions,[76] but their semantic function and signifying power remain subject to the constitutive rupture of the sign.[77] The epistemic cultures of science also depend on floating signifiers as supplements. The persistence of all cultures, including epistemic cultures, depends on constitutive supplements, culturally configured floating signifiers.

To paraphrase Lévi-Strauss, we seem to be far removed from Schele, but in fact we are very close to her. Hieroglyph experts have systematically worked to fix signifiers' entextualized forms to their Classic Maya denotations, to stabilize that zone of indistinction.[78] They succeeded in reducing the glyphs to a grammatical structure and a considerable body of semantic content.[79] But their efforts to stabilize the cosmological and religious referents of Classic Maya inscriptions have succumbed to periodic epistemic and interpretive impasses.[80] Such impasses mark the necessary, constitutive gaps between knowledge systems separated by a millennium.

Schele's escape from such impasses hinged on the appropriation of Maya cosmological concepts and the construction of circulable traces of revelatory scenes, the quintessential experience of the extraordinary affective-scientific break. One compelling example shows up in Schele's early correspondence, pre-dating the specific mode of romantic attachment to the ancient Maya that would later become integral to Schele's constitution of publics. Schele's mode of historical attachment appeals subtly to spiritual mediation, a remaking of the ancient that I come to describe with rising pitch, in the remainder of this book, as a form of *love*.

In January 1975, Schele wrote Lounsbury to develop some of her ideas about motifs concerning rodents or rabbits in Maya architectural inscriptions. The manuscript appears to be a working document comprised of ideas for her contributions to *The Mirror, the Rabbit, and the Bundle*, coauthored with Jeff Miller.[81] Schele had been engaging with Miller over a stela at the Maya site of Naranjo. The stela's central motif presents a forward-facing rabbit with what Mayanists at the time called "etz-nab-flint ears," ears marked by striations evocative of flaked flint. Schele recounts how the rabbit figure reminded her of Palenque glyphs, such as those in the Tablet of the Foliated Cross and the Tablet of the Slaves, that the collective of experts on the site denoted "rodent bone glyphs." With Miller, Schele had searched the "Vienna dictionary" for possible Maya terms designating "rabbit": "Conejo—thuul, balas thuul."[82] From the Vienna, they turned to the Motul dictionary to trace out the connotations of *thul ah,ub*: "seguir por el rastro (rastro is a trail made by animals in the forest, thus has the connotation of a path marked by the passage of something that has gone before)."[83] The Motul listings indicated that *thul* functioned in noun phrases with other morphemes: for example, "thul chuc, tah, te: asir or prender por el rastro o alcanzar o sacar por el rastro, asiendo o prendiendo, buscar de rastro." The suggestion here is that the Yucatec term for rabbit is metonymically linked to the trail that it produces. Schele was particularly drawn to the noun phrase *thul pach: seguir o ymitar*. As it turns out, *pach* had various ritual meanings related to cloth used in tribute as well as taking possession.

As Schele summarizes in the letter:

> Thul pach means to follow or imitate and thulah means "to follow a path made by something which has gone before you." Pachah means "to take possession, to adapt, to make appropriate, to award something, to select appropriately, to choose." The picture of the toothache glyphs fit primary meanings exactly. The picture is of a rabbit-Thul wrapped in an offering bundle because of the Yaxchilan and Bonampak bundles. In each case the bundle is offered by one figure to another and it is

specifically and carefully shown to have one kind of bundle tie and a special knot. The tie and knot are exactly those shown in the toothache glyph.[84]

From this evidence, Schele develops the argument that the rodent-bone glyph is a rabbit and the rabbit signifies accession to the status of dynastic lord. Thus she arrives at what, in *The Mirror, the Rabbit, and the Bundle*, becomes the argument for "rabbiting" as "following the footprints of the ancestors."

On the next page Schele tries to take apart the coincidence of the rabbit glyph and a lunar glyph. She explains:

> Before returning to the further explanation of the t'uul [i.e., *thul*] reading I would like to point out the behavior of the accession compounds of PN [the site of Piedras Negras]. We looked at all of the accession statements at PN and can say that the animal in the toothache glyph is usually not the rodent. At PN the concepts involved in t'uul are not as heavily involved as at Palenque. But very often we have the lunar glyph inserted within the bundle. In these cases I believe the reading should be pachan "to take possession." We could not figure out why the rabbit and moon could be interchangeable in some cases and why one or the other was not necessary. The [Palenque tablet of the] 96 glyph[s] lunar glyph with the rabbit sitting inside was the first hint. Why would a scribe insert a rabbit into a glyph reading culah when the element has no discernible function phonetically or morphemically? We got the answer when we went to the ruins on the 27th to watch the moon rise at sunset. I was standing in House 6 looking at the moon from where Pacal must have stood and I saw the answer—we even photographed it. Quite literally the rabbit is on the face of the moon. The Moon [*sic*] and the rabbit are quite literally the same thing. They may not be the same thing phonetically or morphemically, but visually and conceptually the rabbit is etched distinctly on the face of the moon. Wrap it up in a pach bundle and you have the accession compound at PN. I think that every Maya would have known that from his childhood and the two were intertwined visually and mythologically so much that a scribe in a fit of fantasy marked the verbal affix of a seating glyph at Palenque with the moon's constant companion, my beautiful friend, the rabbit.

The passage reveals Schele's early process or method in terms that illustrate her cognitive-epistemological disposition to decipherment. Given that she had little understanding of Mayan languages, Schele relied heavily on "visual and conceptual" cues as clues. Moreover, many of Schele's more technical accounts of deciphering signs oscillate, like this, between a kind of hermeneutical engagement with the corpus of decipherments and textual sources such as the "Vienna dictionary" and a more personal, embodied engagement with the places where glyphs were produced, particularly Palenque.

The movement from text to place and back tells a particular sort of story. The texts present a located or delimited research problem. Efforts to read passages such as that of the Tablet of the Ninety-Six Glyphs reach a provisional limit, a site of ignorance with respect to the syntactical and semantic referents of the narrative. Earlier scholars facing such a problem, such as Benjamin Lee Whorf or Yuri Knorosov, had no choice but to remain within the body of simulated inscriptions and the literature that works, hermeneutically, to interpret them. Their efforts amounted to a kind of hermeneutic extension of or addition to the existing literature.

Schele moves beyond such accounts not merely by virtue of more careful or intricate interpretative research. Rather, she stages an observational experiment: she goes to the site. Here she doesn't offer us a clear account of her motivation to undertake astronomical observation (to put it perhaps a bit too formally). She merely recounts that she found herself standing where Pakal would have stood (some thirteen hundred years earlier). From there she observes the rabbit on the face of the moon.[85] She and her colleagues, standing at night in the Palenque Palace, could feel and observe as Pakal felt and observed. Though Pakal was not the scribe who produced the Tablet of the Ninety-Six Glyphs or inscriptions that relate "accession" to rulership at the site of Piedras Negras, she invokes him as a being who, like "every Maya . . . from his childhood," would have seen the rabbit on the moon. Schele seems to infer that ancient Maya subjects would not have taken this as a happenstantial or arbitrary visual similarity. Rather, they would have seen the rabbit and the moon as "quite literally the same thing."

By putting herself in Pakal's shoes, Schele could make an astronomical observation that led to astrological, mythological, and historical inferences. This is an embodied, situated knowledge claim, and one that entails that Schele *edge* between text and place, positioning herself as the mediator or edgewalker who can resignify—even reanimate—a glyph by virtue of her experiential observations. "Being there" is not, then, just an extension of textual hermeneutics, as it sometimes seems in the work of Schele's anthropological contemporary, Clifford Geertz.[86] To be there is to partake of an ecology and astronomy that compels a mode of cosmological reasoning. To be there is to establish the conditions—at once scientific and spiritual—that open up a point of passage into the cognitive deliberations of Classic Maya scribes. To de-scribe this historical-psychological projection as a deliberation, though, seems to render it too formally. Schele has inferred a "fit of fantasy."

Could such astrological movement reflect a spiritualist sensibility rendered in secular terms? It strikes me that Schele makes no effort here to conceal the mystical conditions of her inference about the genius of the ancient Maya. Perhaps such a spiritual openness owes to the fact that the source is a piece of personal correspondence. Regardless, in Schele's historical construction, the scribe, as a proper Maya subject, would have associated the moon and the rabbit; he would have worked with a cognitive set that regarded moons and rabbits as—at least—associated. By emplacing the Maya signs in their landscape, Schele could begin to access the thought process behind particular acts of artistic and linguistic production.

In a sense, this is nothing but a humdrum moment of science in action, a typical account of archaeoastronomical fact production, not unlike accounts that lines the pages of Anthony Aveni's research.[87] But Schele's genius here is of a demonstrably spiritual sort. It's not simply a phenomenological movement away from mediated "text-artifacts" that resituates the glyphs within their worldly contexts, the Palenque landscape.[88] What's remarkable is how this worldly engagement folds into the envelope of glyphic-textual analysis. The key moment in Schele's method is neither fully epigraphic nor hermeneutic. She doesn't submit herself to the texts in order to be changed in a manner that enables her to subsequently read the texts with greater perspicacity.

Instead, she appeals to the necessity of emplacing the texts, resituating them within the contours of their landscape. The landscape does not comprise an empty space onto which any human meaning can be projected.[89] It is, rather, a particularly constrained and *spirited* place, a place characterized by historical pluripresence.[90] In order to surpass epistemic impasses—why this rodent or rabbit icon?—Schele had to partake of the genius of the place. She had to position herself within the landscape of Palenque in order to achieve the *revelation*—to reveal—that the rabbit and the moon were one and the same. This *emplacement* of hieroglyphic interpretation amounts to a chronotope that compresses time/history into a monumentalized, sacralized, patrimonialized, archaeologized place.[91] By standing where Pakal once stood, historical change becomes subordinated to the ever-repeating seasonal cycles of a place and its vantage point. In order to read the glyphs *as if they could be abstracted or alienated from their contexts of production and situation*,[92] Schele had to reembody the ancient Maya position, incorporating the moon itself into the "epi-ontology" that relationally and recursively constituted her.[93]

This geographically situated act of knowledge production sets up a culturally abstract, unsituated claim. The narrow claim about the rabbit on the moon does not pass, explicitly at least, through any body of evidence about Maya modes of belief or visuality. She may, of course, be drawing on such knowledge. But Schele is, at the same time, drawing on her own relationship to what she calls, in the romantic twist at the end of the passage, "my beautiful friend, the rabbit." By identifying with Pakal, vis-à-vis the presumed continuity of the Palenque landscape, she develops a form of scientific-historical vision that ostensibly allows her to see as an ancient scribe would have seen. What makes this example worthy of attention with respect to Schele is that the scribe sees something that Schele might want to see. He sees her "beautiful friend, the rabbit."

Through invocation of the moon-rabbit as a kind of astronomical constant, Schele effectively occludes both historical change and the cultural determinants of cognition. She flattens the diachronic and historical dimension into a spatially grounded synchrony. The assumed geospatial continuity, or belief that the site and the cosmos were effectively unchanged, enabled an observation about the present to function as a description of the past. By virtue of its occlusion of time and history, such affectively saturated "being there" becomes a spiritual mode of historical inference. Historical inference amounts to a spiritual practice by taking the imaginative form of historical transposition. There's a geographic and chronotopic movement at work here. Schele's experience allows her to observe as if she were an ancient Maya subject. And if the past is the sacred, becoming-ancient amounts to a religious enactment of pluripresence. She can project herself into the past through the being that is her "beautiful friend," a being that's becoming, if it hasn't already become, her *way*, her animal spirit companion.

This is probably not an unusual archaeological phenomenology. Archaeologists engaged in the process of excavating a site often indulge historical speculations, building an inferential discourse that contours the site's former inhabitants' lives. Many are dreamers like Schele. They harbor a kind of cosmological imagination and are taken with the allegories of science fiction. But there are two particularly significant points to make about Schele's turn here. The first concerns the logic of inference in play. As she witnesses the moon from a particular geographical location, Schele makes the considerable—

perhaps *absurd*—leap from her own contingent mode of experience and perception to that of the Maya. She articulates an opinion or belief that *every Maya* would have seen the rabbit as the moon and the moon as the rabbit. And she turns from this inference to "a scribe in a fit of fantasy." The fantasy here, of course, is *Schele's* fantasy. Schele must imagine herself *as* the lord or scribe. The reenactment of astrological perception elides the temporal gap between Schele and her object of knowledge. *This movement is characteristic of Schele's genius as a mystical engagement with the past.* Not only is Schele imagining herself here *as the scribe taken over by fantasy*; his fantastical act is to mark a seating or accession glyph with the moon's companion, the rabbit. The rabbit is not simply a rabbit. It is Schele's "beautiful friend." The rabbit is Schele. Schele is rabbit, scribe, and dynast. This ease of substitution, a romantic slipperiness, a becoming-floating-signifier, amounts to Schele's genius.

The chronotopic phenomenological imaginary at one corner of Schele's method helped to make her a compelling, charismatic figure within the field. At Round Table workshops in Palenque, participants would alternate between hearing presentations on developments in decipherment and trekking up the mountain road to the site itself. Such trips resituated inscriptions that had been mediated and re-mediated, cut out and abstracted from their material contexts. But such happenings couldn't resituate inscriptions in the *socio*material world of their initial production and ritual enactment. Instead, they constituted a new collective experience of place and a corollary historical imaginary. Maybe a better word than *imaginary* is Schele's term: *fantasy*.

The genius of decipherment, then, exceeded the colonial reduction of ancient Maya artifacts to texts legible in our reigning language ideology. Instead, it centered the production or reproduction of a collective fantasy. One term for this collective fantasy is "the Maya."

Schele drew Round Table workshop participants, Maya Meetings participants, and friends and colleagues into the fantasy of the Maya. And not just the fantasy of the Maya that has been constructed since the Maya came into being as an anthropological and linguistic object in the late nineteenth and early twentieth centuries. The fantasy of the Maya, the Maya-as-fantasy, that Schele performatively enacted with a range of perlocutionary effects (constituting a rapt audience and changing historical narratives) cannot be fully alienated from Schele as an embodied thinker, speaker, and writer. Standing in the Palenque Palace, Schele became what a structuralist might regard as a paradigmatic substitution *for* Pakal (opening up her own variety of mythocriticism through a metaphoric displacement). She performed a cultural function analogous to that of an ancient Maya lord standing in the same place.

As Schele narrates the semantic sensibility of a visual-cosmological landscape—or skyscape—that Pakal would have, as we say, naturalized, she produces a syntactical ordering of the world that enables her readers, or listeners, to use the figure of Schele to project themselves, fantastically, into the past and to imagine that they are seeing Pakal, rather than Linda.

But Linda had to get there first, and in this particular case, she got there with the aid of her friend the rabbit and her experience and perception of the moon. The rabbit emerges as a zoo-spiritual actor continuous in its morphology, as the moon maintains its status as an astro-spiritual actor that, in its iconic resemblance to the rabbit, conditions a transcultural continuity in the astrological reconstruction of an astronomical perceptual object. The rabbit and moon became beings that Schele and Pakal both knew, functioning as nonlinguistic but nevertheless semiotic transtemporal mediators. Her genius is to have given herself over to this pre- or nonlinguistic morphological continuity and iconic resemblance. She recognized—as a by-product, in part at least, of her biomorphic art—the paradigmatic resemblance between the trace of a rabbit/moon and the images of rabbits, which some scholars regarded as "rodents," in the inscriptions.

The inferences that she pressed off to colleagues in this letter were, in fact, somewhat dubious. The decipherment does not seem to have stood the test of time. But it doesn't matter. Facts can get in the way of what matters; and here what matters is method. The rabbit helped open Schele's spiritualist portal into the past, enabling her to become a mediator who reconstituted the ancient at the same time that she constituted a public of witnesses.

Wouldn't it be sensible to assert, then, that this spiritualist construction of the past deployed the rabbit as the floating signifier that shored up the possibility of transhistorical and transcultural communication? I have described the rabbit as a "known known in a maelstrom of semiotic madness."[94] But when pressed into the labored service of historical mediation, this "known known" gets pretty slippery. What Schele knew as a rabbit and the scribe knew as a rabbit weren't the same thing. But Schele had to give herself over to the rabbit anyway. The rabbit induced her subjective projection into the corpus of hieroglyphic inscriptions. It was a morphological inducement to aesthetic, historical, and linguistic speculation and imagination.

The rabbit, her beautiful friend, her spirit companion, was a palpable, lived, quite real fantasy.

Schele's fantasy of the Maya scribe seeing the rabbit in the moon is a projection of—or desire for—a shared affect. The scribe's fit of fantasy in inscribing the Tablet of the Ninety-Six Glyphs with a moon-rabbit is Schele's fit of fantasy as she sees that the moon itself is inscribed with a rabbit.

But this observation of paradigmatic substitution, predicated on morphological—or syntactic—commonality or repetition, does not amount exclusively to the fantasy of someone who may be misread here—ungenerously and inaccurately, I think—as a kind of New Age mystic. Such substitution is one of the core techniques of Lévi-Strauss's structuralism itself. In his exemplary reading of the Oedipus myth, a model for how to undertake structural analysis of mythology, Lévi-Strauss groups distinct narrative events and forms into pairs of binary oppositions, claiming that they are part and parcel of the same underlying structures within the text.[95] This ascription of structural repetition or parallelism enables us to descend, in however provisional a way, into the cultural unconscious that lends communicative actions with collective sense.

Schele's identification of the rabbit is a far less rigorous observation than Lévi-Strauss's laborious restructuration of mythological texts. Nevertheless, it entails a core structuralist assumption that would come to pervade both decipherment as an epistemic practice and the teaching of decipherment in social and pedagogical institutions such as workshops. Namely, the world, as perceived and cognized, is characterized by an underlying structural order that may be discerned through the identification of patterns.[96] For Lévi-Strauss, this was, quite reasonably, a necessary condition of human language and cognition. Human creativity entails a sense-making structuration of the cosmos, including, perhaps *especially*, the practice of taxonomic categorization. Consider Lévi-Strauss's poignant, if passing, criticism of Bronislaw Malinowski's insufficiently developed materialism in *The Savage Mind*. Against Malinowski's belief "that primitive peoples' interest in totemic plants and animals was inspired by nothing but the rumbling of their stomachs,"[97] as Lévi-Strauss pithily summarizes, he offers a brilliant ethnological summary of anthropological evidence for botanical classification around the world. As it happens, the conventional subjects of ethnographic study have more often sounded like botanists than like cash-crop producers. Persons, because they're persons, label the world. One might also say that labeling the world makes persons persons.

Mythology, then, amounts to the cognitive-cultural architecture through which people sense and make sense of the world. So, Lévi-Strauss claims that the human practice of categorization, the "science of the concrete," "meets intellectual requirements rather than or instead of satisfying needs."[98] Here he offers this example:

> The real question is not whether the touch of a woodpecker's beak does in fact cure toothache. It is rather whether there is a point of view from which a woodpecker's beak and a man's tooth can be seen as "going together" (the use of this congruity for therapeutic purposes being only one of its possible uses), and whether some initial order can be introduced into the universe by means of these initial groupings.[99]

Lévi-Strauss proceeds from this discussion of sympathetic magic—the use of a woodpecker's beak in medical treatment of a toothache because of their resemblance—directly to quoting and discussing a scientific taxonomist, who states, "All theoretical science is ordering and if, systematics [*sic*] is equated with ordering, then systematics is synonymous with theoretical science."[100] And he adds, "The thought we call primitive is founded on this demand for order."[101]

Science, then, from a structuralist point of view, amounts to an elaboration of the basic human inclination to order and make sense out of the world. This may appear to chafe against or contradict the more elaborate epistemological positions that sometimes motivate STS scholarship on scientific categorization.[102] It certainly *does not* contradict, a priori, the core idea in Latour's material semiotics that forms of scientific translation problematically betray the world through structural categorizations.[103] But it is at odds with the assumption that such acts of translational categorization are necessarily "reductive." When a botanist notes that the morphology of a leaf indicates that a tree should be categorized as an oak, she's not indulging a kind of epistemic violence against the world, as a processual flux of becoming. She is, instead, engaging in a necessary human impulse, a creative categorization of the world, a pre- or nonlinguistic awareness of iconic similarity meriting taxonomic categorization.[104]

Schele's genius was not linguistic. It was, instead, morphological, iconic, and taxonomic. She was a savvy participant in the science of the concrete. She partook of the genius of the ancient Maya and reconstructed it through a structuralist, mystical science. As Asad's critique of secularism indicates, Certeau identified both the experiment and linguistics as means to *deontologize* language. In her correspondence with colleagues, Schele periodically encounters the limits of her capacity to interpret the inscriptions in linguistic terms and finds herself needing to appeal to the linguistic expertise of colleagues such as Lounsbury. But she also compensated for such epistemic limitations by appealing to a situated experimentalism—archaeological phenomenology—that sought to reconstruct the relation between hieroglyphic signs and the sociomaterial environment of the ancient Maya. This experimentalism was a spiritual—and possibly deontological—system.

Especially early in her career, before her understanding of linguistics improved, such a phenomenological and imaginative engagement with the emplaced text-artifacts of the ancient Maya may have chafed against the more rigid modernist language ideology of colleagues such as Lounsbury, who implicitly constructed language as a body of knowledge and action separate from the material world. In the sentence previous to the Certeau passage quoted above, he offers that "in medieval ontology all treatment of language was in itself an experiment or a manipulation of the real."[105] Schele's contribution to the eminently modernist, structuralist reconstruction of the ancient Maya entailed drawing on the iconicity of inscriptions to reworld the texts in an experimental fashion. In some ways, today we have returned to the medieval position. At the very least, contemporary bodies of scholarship concerned with both performativity and language ideology readmit language as a real form and force in the world, rather than a separate and potentially illusory domain.

Linda, unlike some of her more by-the-books hermeneutic colleagues, upheld something close to that medieval ontology in which "all treatment of language was in itself an experiment or a manipulation of the real." Her sense of the real was more heady than hidebound. If Schele imagined reading glyphs as a mode of communing with the ancestors, ancestors who marked Palenque throne-accession glyphs with her "beautiful friend, the rabbit," can we really say that she upheld some stodgy secular construction of either history or text?

No, these texts and the places that emplace them, are clearly, at times at least, profoundly spiriting forces and landscapes. Schele's genius was not of a secular ontology. Schele's incursion into the Maya studies community and, through this community, into the ancient Maya world, amount to a *religious event*.

I am asking readers to follow the track of the rabbit (not just this rabbit; there are all kinds of others). And I'm saying that when we commune with rabbits, and do good anthropological work, we often find ourselves smack-dab in the middle of their ritual spaces.

So what I'm saying when I say that we should follow rabbits into the fire of rabbit ritual, rift with rabbit dogma, is that anthropology, as good historical science, is *spiritual* rather than—say—*ontological*. Anthropology is a religious post.[106]

Whether our writing is critical or reparative (or something else altogether) may not matter much. Maybe what matters is being willing, like Linda, to float into floating signifiers, like God or Genius, Pakal or Linda. And when we float off, maybe we'll come to accept that anthropology, love of culture, amounts to a series of spiritual questions.

In the meantime, let Linda rush in.

Chapter Six

....

Love

"Writers do not on the whole take kindly to theorists, rather as shamans do not always look with favour on anthropologists."[1] Or so says theorist Terry Eagleton.

But theorists, real theorists (which no one really wants to be anymore anyway, right?) must well be writers too. Maybe that's a backward way to say that theory is writing—or, maybe, that theory is Writing. But what's writing, anyway?

Ask a writer—say Cortázar—and he'll tell you that "everything is writing, that is to say, a fable. But what good can we get from the truth that pacifies an honest property owner? Our possible truth must be an *invention*, that is to say, scripture, literature, picture, sculpture, agriculture, pisciculture, all the tures in this world. Values, tures, sainthood, a ture, society, a ture, love, pure ture, beauty, a ture of tures."[2]

Love, pure ture. It's better in the original: *amor, pura tura*.

Cortázar's "honest property owner" pops out of nowhere. But we get it, I think. The *propietario honesto*, the humble operator of your neighborhood's corner store, is full of fables, even if he might be confounded by your simple truth that everything's writing, which is to say facts, which is to say structure, which is to say "love, pure ture, beauty, a ture of tures." Of course, if everything's writing, writing isn't anything in particular, is it?

Look at how anthropologist Michael Taussig demonizes anthropological inscriptions, including some of his own, as "agribusiness writing," before asking whether it's possible that anthropology's true magic emerges out of its reduction of magic to ostensibly banal functions such as solidarity promotion. He says, "I think of so-called shamans using sleight of hand to deal with malign spirits and sorcery. What we have generally done in anthropology is really pretty amazing in this regard, piggybacking on their magic and on their conjuring—their tricks—so as to come up with explanations that seem nonmagical and free of trickery."[3] So-called shamans, huh? The so-called anthropologist Claude Lévi-Strauss likewise suggests that mythological analysis amounts, in the end, to mythopoesis.[4] With all this myth and magic in play, how's one begin to divide the shamans from the anthropologists?

Maybe we should stick with the so-called writers. At least Cortázar gets right to the point: "society, a ture." Writing, agribusiness or otherwise, always reveals itself as a structure, a ture, like love and beauty, things no different in kind from scripture and agriculture. Oh, Cortázar, you damned anthropologist.

Antropología, una tura.

* * *

My anthropological romanticism sends me searching for love in all the wrong places. I feel like Horacio Oliveira, the protagonist of Cortázar's antinovel *Hopscotch*.[5] The book, at once a geo-psychic wandering and a slow attunement to the impossibility of conceiving—let alone reaching—a destination that isn't death or madness, opens with Horacio calling through the streets of Paris after his love, Lucía, using her nickname, La Maga. Look at this Oliveira character. Isn't he the antinovel's antiflaneur?—an Argentine in Paris who's lost his *maga*, his sorceress, his witch. He's later exiled, cast back to Buenos Aires after his arrest for a lewd rendezvous with a homeless woman. There Horacio finds himself working with old friends in a circus company that, naturally, acquires a mental asylum. He continuously mistakes his friend Talita for La Maga as the wall between asylum employee and resident slowly crumbles.

I'm arrested by Linda, or by her archive, or by Linda-as-archive. I can no longer tell the difference; I now know that I can't know how to delink fantasy from experience, myth from matters at hand; "I never had, and still do not have, the perception of feeling my personal identity. I appear to myself as the place where something is going on, but there is no 'I,' no 'me.' Each of us is a kind of crossroads where things happen. The crossroads is purely passive; something happens there."[6] Archival analysis, you must know, knows the self as a place, a crossroads, a post with its own incinerations, its own clever cryptograms and indeterminable, indecipherable gaps, gaps that make the *envois*, that series of love letters that we call life, incessantly maddening.[7]

My crossroads here is too busy to be imagined as passive; it feels more like Dwight Watson's cautious step into the ordered chaos of a Nanjing intersection:

> I must cross four vehicular lanes and two more reserved for bikes to reach the other side. It is not the four lanes flooded with cars that worries me (although I keep a watchful eye); it is the two broad lanes reserved for bicyclists, and bikers, the ubiquitous e-bikes, lithium and lead battery, mopeds and scooters that sneak up on you, that terrorise in silence, and their more aggressive motorized versions: gas motorcycles, 250cc choppers—the maximum cc allowed on the city streets of China. The electric, battery and combustibles join forces to present a clear and present danger to me and my pedestrian friends.[8]

The crossroads here are a cosmic panoply, not so pedestrian, with Schele crossing the threshold, edging into an ancient Maya causeway dense with traffic that transforms—*poof!*—into the road of awe, sending out astrological signs of all kinds, destinies-in-the-making, radiophysical messages, flashes of *pensée sauvage*, revelatory strokes of genius, and that functionless creativity that makes Maya inscriptions rendered as pic*tures* and sculp*tures* into grammatical texts.[9] A truth: the Maya, too, invented writing. Schele made that truth public by speaking it, charismatically, at an annual workshop, an intersection (or, better, a rest stop), a place to commune and fortify collective being.[10]

Decipherment can be storied down different lines or lanes; after all, it's an effect of intersecting mythologies with quite divergent proveniences. It can read as another painful chapter in the mythology of the Americas as Europe's colonial utopia. The Fountain of Youth or El Dorado is always just around the corner. Linda and her colleagues felt they struck gold by unearthing the grammatical structure of Classic Maya inscriptions in the 1970s. So who can fault them for the triumphalism that adorns popular books such as *Forest of Kings* and *Maya Cosmos*? As Taussig puts it, "If you don't know or can't feel the mythic power of gold and the fairy tales it has spawned circling around God and the Devil, then there is no hope for you."[11] "Gold" is one way to put it; "science" is another. Decipherment as El Dorado, as the golden city; with careers and "genius" grants on the line, I'm taking this more literally than you may think.

Horacio Oliveira's term for El Dorado is the "kibbutz of desire."[12] *El kibbutz del deseo* enters Oliveira's consciousness as the possibility of an event that ruptures the object- and language-littered experiential field, opening the subject to the sacred or the absolute, "la Gran Locura" (the Great Madness). After all, who really needs gold if you already have its mythology? Another word for the "kibbutz of desire" is, of course, La Maga, Oliveira's love, that witch Lucía.

I've thought a lot about what Linda Schele, my maga, would make of my thumbing through her letters, my pressing her traces into a spiritual cartography. I honestly don't know, can't know; maybe that's why I keep writing. And maybe it's not a very ethnographic thing to say, but I don't really care what some of Linda's followers, among her many devotees, think of this story. The feelings that I care about are those that we share in common, as followers—nay, lovers—at Linda's crossroads.

Love as what we share in common. Is it possible that shared sentiments and expressions of affirmation give rise not simply to public science through social technologies of witnessing that we understand all too well,[13] but also to a collective expression of love-*as*-the-commons?[14] The enthusiasts who attended Schele's annual workshops fell for her gritty and uncensored antiacademic style. The artist's entry into the painfully bourgeois, if sometimes eccentric, world of Maya studies was an *event*, and she knew it. What I'm saying here—at least what I'm flirting with—is that Schele's workshop, attended annually by hundreds of curious nonacademics who hung on her Tennessee drawl, amounted to a lively crossroads, or a kibbutz of desire.

* * *

I've never written about the amateurs' letters, the "fan mail."

I'm not sure why. They're not taboo. I guess they seemed banal. What an unanthropological thing to think.

Maybe I'm gullible. When I showed up to the UT-Austin Maya Meetings in 2008, lab notebook in hand, my efforts to interview long-term amateur epigraphers faltered. They met my approach with deferral. I was green; they were modest, or they were caught up in the flow of reunion. The ethnographer manages to be both boorish and a bore. What magic.

But the archive's aura provides the necessary, if unsettling, supplement. There's a letter to Linda from Joyce Livingston of Inverness, California, dated February 25, 1994.[15] Livingston's letter doesn't declare itself a piece of fan mail, as others do. But its fanaticism shows. She opens, "I have your 'Maya Cosmos' here beside me and it's a 'can't put down' book. Your excitement comes through—You know why I'm a Maya freak!" Might this amateur's response to Schele's work help us to estrange Linda's Mayanist estrangements without emptying them of magic and reducing them to sociological banalities? It turns out that Joyce Livingston sees herself in *Maya Cosmos*.[16] She sees herself because Schele narrates a trek they took together around the site of Tikal.[17] But what else does this amateur Mayanist see when she sees her name and story inscribed in *Maya Cosmos*? Is it possible that she sees herself here as a maker of Linda? Does she help make Linda into that lovely monster incessantly remaking the ancient Maya elites who sacrificed their political rivals in brutal performances of spiritual power?[18]

Livingston's affirmation and enjoyment seem to mirror Schele's. And we could think of this as a kind of mimesis; the audience of witnesses takes on the affective sensibilities of the monstrous prodigy. I wonder whether Joyce's joy, committed so faithfully—I hope—to the typed page is, in fact, a spiritual rechanneling of love, a countergift that barely knows itself as such and desires the purity of the giftless gift that a return prestation can only achieve, à la Derrida, from a position of total ignorance.[19]

After all, she doesn't *thank* Linda for giving her spectral presence within this masterful work of Mayanist art. She *corrects* Linda. She writes over the account in *Maya Cosmos*, recounting *her own* version, inserting a truer self into this remythologization of ancient mythology. She corrects Schele's story, a typical Linda-story about the discovery of a natural symbol, the movement from icon to referent as an act of decipherment, striking gold among the ruins. And here a Mayanist reader couldn't be less surprised that this natural symbol—this spiritual form—appears in the blooms of that most sacred and demonstrative Maya tree, the axis mundi, the ceiba. But Linda pulverizes the ceiba story. She tells it all wrong. Even screws up Livingston's profession. She's no "retired school teacher"; she's an artist, of course. An artist, which is to say, an explorer.

"Dr. Livingston, I . . ."

But, according to Joyce Livingston's 2010 obituary, she was more than an artist.[20] She was a nonconformer who became, or so it says, "a professional archaeological sketcher." Her son Dewey's quoted as saying, "Everything to her had an aesthetic."

But even if Livingston became a professional sketcher, she remained, no doubt, one of Linda's amateurs. I mean "amateur" in its etymological sense: a lover. The letter attests to the fact that Linda had many: "I was sorry to be only one of the 450-plus people at the Mesa Redonda who wanted to chat with you. Sometimes it must be hell to be a celebrity!"[21]

"I hope to see you again someday," Livingston says.[22] The eternal return of the amateurs, lovers of and through Linda. Lovers who climb to the top of Palenque's Temple of the Inscriptions in order to descend the slippery stairs into the musty inner sanctum, where the sarcophagus and bones of the seventh-century ruler Pakal persist as remains, remainders: "During the Mesa Redonda last June I had just re-read your account of Pacal's (Pakal's) burial ceremony, and was fortunate to be able to return to the tomb sans tourists. It was a moving experience—trying to visualize the ceremony."[23]

Am I wrong to insist that this effort to virtually witness an ancient Maya ritual can't be usefully reduced to rote critiques, to the pompous invocation of archaeological romanticism, or to STS's airpump-bursting, stony material-semiotic relationism?

Am I wrong to want to stay with troubled and troubling magic?[24] Am I wrong to insist that the artist here writes over Linda as an act of love, to insist that Linda *as Pakal* becomes her maga, her witch, as the past itself becomes our Sacred?

* * *

In an interview with Nicolas Truong, titled *In Praise of Love*, Alain Badiou describes the theater, or the theater company, as an "aesthetic expression of fraternity."[25] The invocation of company as community leads Badiou to the commons, and to the desire to reinvigorate a communist sensibility, a primary attachment to forms and objects that we hold in common. The theater company, of course, becomes legible as a site where a common text, a drama, is collectively enacted, animated, given new form and life.

I'm particularly caught here by Badiou's rapid movement from the theater as a common and communist art-form to love as an expression of the commons. Love becomes a valorization of subjects' cobecoming (or intrabecoming) through generative encounters. As Badiou puts it, "We can . . . say that love is communist . . . if one accepts . . . that the real subject of a love is the becoming of the couple and not the mere satisfaction of the individuals that are its component parts. Yet another possible definition of love: minimal communism!"[26]

Here love becomes, perhaps a bit too easily, a mode of resistance to liberal individualism. The excesses of the consuming subject are reinvested as affirmations not simply of the intersubjective, but of the supra-individual.

Love, the Sacred. But if such expressions evoke discrete conjugal pairings and households, as Badiou's slippage to a binary frame suggests, don't they reterritorialize and privatize the commons in its affective and political forms? Perhaps we should be especially wary of such tendencies in Badiou's work, given that he seems to reject the prospect of a politics of love. Asked if there's a "politics of love" along the lines of Derrida's *Politics of Friendship*, Badiou replies,

> I don't think that you can mix up love and politics. In my opinion, the "politics of love" is a meaningless expression. I think that when you begin to say "Love one another," that can lead to a kind of ethics, but not to any kind of politics. Principally because there are people in politics one doesn't love. . . . That's undeniable. Nobody can expect us to love them.[27]

We could nitpick Badiou's invocation of *parliamentary* politics here (that is, if he's not joking), or we could press his point into the service of a nimbler claim. Is it possible that what we term "love," as sustained affective exchange in the service of collective becoming, sublates the public/private distinction altogether?

The object of love becomes, not the lover, but love itself. One loves love through the mediation of a lover. A lover, thus, must be love's subject, never love's object. An immanent being cannot be loved. One can merely be a colover, a companion in love.

We could argue that such a (perhaps too-dialectical) conception redeems the prospect of love as a political project, rather than solely an ethical or social project. But I'd prefer to think that love-as-the-commons presents a prospect for coexistence irreducible to the political domain. Might love amount to an apolitical commons? If so, the meaninglessness of the "politics of love" arises not out of a feeling of disgust for slimy and sordid politicians, but out of a recalcitrant and perhaps naive—even cruel?—optimism for modes of nonagonistic collective worlding.[28]

For Badiou, the theater company, not the conjugal pairing, stages love. Love here takes as its locus a temporary material and aesthetic transformation of dramatic inscription into embodied action. Few theatrical productions result from the labor of an artistic dyad. Productions are emergent phenomena, scripted yet necessarily improvisational wholes irreducible to their *parts*. The love of the theater company is, thus, the social form, the social fact of a common (partial) love, a love of (partible) companionship, a living-and-eating (partially) together.

Schele's "staged discovery" was historical knowledge production as public science as performative action as a loving expression of the partible common world. History becomes a spiritual path; the past becomes (partitioned into) the Sacred. The difference between Schele's theater and ostensibly more conventional theater concerns *what* precisely was staged. She did not, of course, stage dramatic literature, though she no doubt sometimes verbalized Maya architectural inscriptions that originally functioned, in part, as scripts for performance.

Together with her company, her audience, her witnesses, Schele produced the past as a common world, a site of cohabitation. She was a charismatic authority as well as a spirit double, a being who lovingly reincarnated the ancient Maya, giving her body over to their scripts. As she elided or emptied the self, becoming a spiritual channel for ancient Maya beings, witnessing to their truths, her public-in-the-making committed itself to Schele as a present, immanent materialization of the ancient.

Perhaps love emerges here as a modality of and for apolitical worlding. Despite its tease at domesticity, love writes an expansive compass, promises an other-world, another world, the spiritual and cartographic promise of inhabiting differently, inhabiting with a difference, inhabiting difference. Love unsettles the exhaustive—and by now, *I pray*, nearly exhausted—appeal to the political in the social sciences and humanities. Love, freed of liberalism's cage-like emoting interiority (if you'll grant me that), becomes inhabitation beyond inhibitions, a being-there that can't account for or explain itself. Love is more capacious than desire. Desire desires production and reproduction, social and libidinal. Desire pines after a pleasurable note, a plateau, only to hold there, to feel the flux of becoming for a fleeting moment. I don't desire Linda; Linda, beauty, isn't desire.

Love is the commodious, endlessly expanding warmth and light of God. Love loves love.

So do we—you and I—give ourselves over to this love, this God?

Perhaps you're now thinking that my love, my word *love*, conceals an evangelical impulse (or perhaps you've been thinking such of this project from the beginning and have now found your final confirmation. "Aha! Now I've gotcha," you say triumphantly, slamming the book shut).

But if love loves love, love has no outside; it simply is. One cannot give oneself over to love; one cannot choose to love; love is neither feeling nor emotion; it's impervious to deliberate action, channeling of desire. In this rather Christian space, at least, love is the only social fact.

Love is the social, as connection, relation, attachment.[29]

And the social as love as God has no truck with politics in parliamentary and identitarian forms (though I suppose we find love in unexpected places . . .). Love is not a gathering or assembly. Love's no network. It's amorphous, but its amorphousness differs from Foucault's power and Deleuze's desire. These latter critical concepts insist on their priority as forces—*forces*—that activate the subject.

Love is unenforceable. Love is forceless, vulnerable, trembling, and insecure. Love tears. Love tears.

bell hooks has worked to invigorate a leftist discourse on and of love. She writes, "As long as we refuse to address fully the place of love in struggles for liberation we will not be able to create a culture of conversion where there is a mass turning away from an ethic of domination."[30] I wonder if such cultures of conversion do, in fact, exist in the most dominated of social spaces. The love of history, the amateur attachment to past peoples and places, sidesteps utilitarian efforts to dominate our intellectual lives, our loving imaginations.

Linda's imagination was taken up by forces within Maya studies that I read as structures of epistemic violence. Rendering glyphs intelligible by subjecting them to linguistic structures was a clear reduction—a *reducción*—operative within a colonial register.[31] This space of linguistic and epistemic coloniality was fully saturated with the romance of (space in) the tropics.[32] It attracted an excessive imagination, an embodiment of love in all its excess (because love—*damn it*—insists on excess).

Schele's workshops weren't *mass*. As inspired and inspirational as Linda may have been, she never provoked a "mass turning away from an ethic of domination."[33] But she nevertheless established the grounds for a culture of conversion motivated by love.

Later in hooks's essay "Love as the Practice of Freedom," she says, "Often when Cornel West and I speak with large groups of black folks about the impoverishment of spirit in black life, the lovelessness, sharing that we can collectively recover ourselves in love, the response is overwhelming. Folks want to know how to begin the practice of loving."[34]

This struggle for Black liberation takes form through the intellectual and rhetorical practice of conversion, a practice of transforming souls, giving rise to a spiritual presence that can't be confined to the institution of the church, a soul that centers the social order, love as a collective soul. Ethnographer John Watanabe claims that Maya and US Black communities' respective senses of "soul" have a deep affinity: "Maya souls express an emergent, improvisational, and above all personal engagement with others. Far from blind conformity to some explicit ideal, Maya 'soul' depends on mutual recognition of its possessors' eloquence."[35] *Improvisation.* Liberation can be subtle, improvisational, pervasive. Conversions may happen momentarily; they may even tremble through a sonic escape, as in Fred Moten's poetics of musical fugitivity:

> The themes of culinary enjoyment and musico-political desire have a re-animative, *quickening* function. They bring life and noise, and offer up a bit of anima and aroma, which airs out various venues that had been overwhelmed by a kind of putrefaction, the smell of death that hovers over even those spaces where folks are talking about resistance or hybridity or citizenship or whatever while believing or being driven by a belief that the times we live in or the modes of thinking that are now prevalent are, to use Judith Butler's phrase, "post-liberatory." It's not that what Butler says is not true; or that if she'd said preliberatory that wouldn't have been true as well; it is, rather, that here in this vestibule, where we belatedly await our own invention of, our own coming upon, the liberatory, we operate with an incessant escape that might be said to cohabitate with incessant listening. The taste and smell of music messes up the very idea of the liberatory as well as its before and after.[36]

Listening and liberation, poetics and discovery.

The amateurs' adorations of Schele suggest that her workshops induced an extraordinary escape; she established the crossroads, the intersection, where they might together reimagine social and historical order. Schele's work, then, in its public-mindedness, entailed some self-sacrifice. She didn't sacrifice her immanent form and become the channeling or mediation of the ancient Maya in order to enact the kind of social liberation and transformation advocated by hooks or West, let alone Moten's musical escape. But she did construct an (un)common space where the past—an immaterial form—could become knowable through its material traces and their simulations or mediations, inscriptions that give history temporary coherence, an ephemeral solidity against the coming ruin. Revelatory moments were openings into improvisatory reimaginations of past worlds, always in, and as, the present.

Schele's public epigraphy workshops weren't explicitly grounded in the Christian ethic of love affirmed by hooks, who builds on Martin Luther King Jr., among others. But the ethical substance or content matters less than the form through which a particular emergent community—the world of amateur epigraphers—materializes. Perhaps a community gathered around common historical inscriptions became a Christian community in form if not, exactly, content. And perhaps other scholarly communities are very much the same.

Participants could commune in a kind of charitable—agape—love; workshops suggest the secularized Christian contours of epigraphy's public engagement. Not only were the modes of communion culturally Christian, the ideology of text and language at work had religious determinants as well. The notion that a hieroglyph—or any inscribed form, really—conceals a deeper truth proves consistent not simply with a dichotomization of the world into surface and depth or primary and secondary qualities (or, for that matter, form and content) rooted in foundational early modern texts by the likes of Locke and Kant. It also partakes of the Christian binarization of the world into matter and soul, immanent and transcendent realms. I am left with the weighty but clear feeling that Schele's apolitical assembly assembled around an immanent form of ~~history~~ God. Schele, Christian, yes. *Christian*, meaning Christ-like.

In the Sermon on the Mount, Jesus mentions love twice. The first reference implores followers to love their enemies:

> You have heard that it was said, "Love your neighbor and hate your enemy." But I tell you, love your enemies and pray for those who persecute you, that you may be children of your Father in heaven. He causes his sun to rise on the evil and the good, and sends rain on the righteous and the unrighteous. If you love those who love you, what reward will you get? Are not even the tax collectors doing that? And if you greet only your own people, what are you doing more than others? Do not even pagans do that? Be perfect, therefore, as your heavenly Father is perfect.[37]

A Christian expression of love, agape love or communion, is marked here by a distinctively aporetic construction. Isn't it impossible to love one's enemy? Doesn't the enemy emerge as such through feelings of hatred? To love your enemy is to dissolve the antagonism itself. Once one begins to love one's enemies, the very fact of antagonism transforms into agonism or even friendship, philial love brought on by agapic love. Agape, as such, gives up the conceit or fiction of the self, recognizing being as an improvisation in the crossroads, performed with whatever odds and ends are at hand.

Even tax collectors love those who reciprocate their love. Theirs is a selfish love, love in the idiom of greed. The tax collector loves in return because it's a return on investment; it's a reinvestment that he'll reciprocate indefinitely. But is this love at all? Or does the tax collector (merely) desire? His gift of love is a selfish gift, a gift given to obligate reciprocation, and knowingly so. But what, here, counts as reciprocity?

In 2009 a collective of anthropologists debated the proposition that "the anthropological fixation with reciprocity leaves no room for love."[38] Given that reciprocity has occupied such a central position in anthropological thought over the course of the past century, it's remarkable that we've paid little attention to forms of reciprocal love: erotic, philial, or agapic (to offer only the concept's Christian parsing). If love loves love, love can't be bound and domesticated by the practice and idiom of reciprocity. Love exceeds exchange because love as Love is God.

Jesus remarks that even pagans greet their familiars. The Loving thing to do is to "greet" strangers. "Greeting" is about more than passing phatics; it's a mode of listening and hospitality. Schele and the glyphers, like all of us, haven't always been hospitable. Passionately attached to her shining sense of discovery, Schele sometimes refused to listen to claims that contradicted newfound convictions about the ancient Maya. I maintain this cautious skepticism even if my critiques themselves aren't necessarily the most hospitable; they haven't always clearly invited their subjects to respond. Seeing no alternative, I live with the noninnocence of my positions. Some, I suppose, will take "noninnocence" to mean "guilt."

Forgive me, if you can.

But the obligation to greet—and to love—not simply neighbors but strangers stands. How does one greet, welcome, and love the stranger? How would one love the other if, to take a dictum critiqued by Derrida, "*tout autre est tout autre*"?[39] This untranslatable phrase means, at once, that every other is every other and that every other is absolutely or infinitely other. Seeking to preserve the tautology's semantic duality, David Wills offers the translation "Every other (one) is every (bit) other." If the other is infinitely other, if she, to use Whitman's tired phrase, "contain[s] multitudes,"[40] aren't we faced with the impossibility of greeting, let alone loving? We have no choice but to greet the other and to love him while knowing that both acts always and inevitably fail. *Tout autre est tout autre.* Derrida says that the phrase "trembles,"[41] as one trembles before God, or before the surprise of a musical improvisation that unsettles our understanding of the relational intersection that we inhabit. No: not inhabit. The intersection that we *are*.

And we are coming apart. Martin Hägglund reads Derrida's love as love of ruins, of ruination, of being's finitude. (Human) being is delimited by time, haunted by the coming termination, like the terminations of rulership—and life—recorded in Classic Maya inscriptions. Responding to Derrida's engagement with Walter Benjamin's critique of violence, Hägglund maintains that love thus bears a kind of internal ruination. He quotes Derrida on this point:

One cannot love a monument, a work of architecture, an institution as such except in an experience itself precarious in its fragility: it has not always been there, it will not always be there, it is finite. And for this very reason one loves it as mortal, through its birth and its death, through one's birth and death, through the ghost or the silhouette of its ruin, one's own ruin—which it already is, therefore, or already prefigures.[42]

In the line that precedes—prefigures? haunts?—Hägglund's block of quoted text, Derrida, playing with the idea of writing a treatise on ruins, with or against Benjamin, asks, "What else is there to love, anyway?"[43] For Derrida, then, the object of love is not, exactly, love itself. It is closer to love's mortality. One loves deictically, from the here and now.

This departs from the infinity of agape love, whether we construct that infinity as an exteriority to immanent human experience or as a kind of numinous interiority, the infinity of a subjectivity that recedes into multitudes or haunts us from a dark recess of psychic depths.

One cannot, then, love the infinite; nor can one love the real. Subjectivity is ephemeral; and Nature is always and inevitably under erasure. Nor is this love Badiou's love-of-becoming. It is, instead, an unbecoming love. This love cannot be reduced to a destructive love; it is not love as order's undoing. It is love as the embrace of being's ephemerality. The object of Derrida's love is not Love itself, but the prefiguration of death, a spectral mortality, "the ghost or the silhouette of its ruin; one's own ruin."[44]

Wait! Wait! "One's own ruin." What do we make of this? What would Linda make of this? What have I made of Linda?

What if my love for Linda, for beauty, comes too late? Can I love the dead without having "known" her? Can love *start* with the silhouette or the trace?

What of this haunting feeling of amateurity? My own amateurity, immaturity.

Is (my) love immature?

The first listing for *immature* in the *Oxford English Dictionary* offers, "Esp. of death: occurring before the usual or proper time; untimely, premature. Now somewhat *rare*."[45]

The time is out of joint (again [a redundancy (I suppose)]).[46]

Immature death. The dictionary's most timely example comes from Dönmez-Colin's (2006) *Cinemas of the Other*: "the leader of the popular rock band Kino, whose immature death created a James Dean–like cult."[47]

By academic standards, Linda's was an immature death. Fifty-five, pancreatic cancer. The cult came first. The cult of amateurs assembling around the Amateur herself, around the figure of love whose earthly ephemerality was unclear until it was all too clear, until the horizon closed in. Maybe the cult bade her ruin.

But let us not depart too quickly from Derrida's love as love-of-ruins. What else is there to love? If we love "a monument, a work of architecture, an institution," we love it as "the ghost or the silhouette of its ruin, one's own ruin—which it already is, therefore, or already prefigures."[48] Why must Derrida turn here to architecture and institutions? Love conjures not a subject-in-cobecoming but a ruined dwelling, landscape, or collectivity, the impossibility of an indefinitely enduring *socius*. The silhouette of ruin, of a building in ruins, as a sign of one's inevitable termination. The omens pile up.

Walking ruins metonymically internalizes one's own ruin.

What do we make, then, of the tasks of archaeology and epigraphy? What of this world where an art historian's immature death may be preceded by a cult, if not exactly a James Dean–like cult? What of this amateurity, this love? Isn't the insistence here (my insistence) an insistence on infinitude, on spiritual persistence, transcendence, or at least the open futurity of decipherment? Couldn't decipherment, if it's decipherment at all, still surprise?

Epigraphy, like most knowledge practices, insists on futurity. Schele's imaging practices instate an enduring future. No decipherment, not now. Finitude is yet to come.

Linda's simulation of ancient traces resurrects Pakal.

Archaeology too produces pasts and future pasts in a manner that insists on its own endurance, but it remains captured by the ruins. Unlike the epigrapher or art historian, at home among simulated traces, the archaeologist needs the worldliness—and the imaginative play—of being-in-the-dirt. Archaeologists colloquially distinguish between theorists and "dirt archaeologists," or excavation-obsessed practitioners. And readers of Mary Douglas—alas, more likely to be the theorists—know that dirt is sacred, that dirt is *the* sacred.[49]

For Derrida, such an archaeological ontology demands an impossible and illusory presence. Though it does live well with finitude, decay. The epigrapher locates the real within the virtuality of the trace. Linda's drawings aren't originals; they (should) have no pretense to authenticity. The archaeological encounter with the hieroglyphic text, on the other hand, constructs artifacts as singular, distinct, and—to some extent, at least—original.

Decipherment's spirit is virtualizing. Virtualization mediates the past, cleanses it of dirt, of context, and gives it spectral presence.

Virtualization or mediatization enacts a modality of communal love. To re-vise the past, to bring it into contemporary forms of visualization and imagination reads as a charitable (agape) mode of historical communion.

Agape love is charitable love, communal love. The agape was a Eucharist or "love-feast."

Engaging the past, then, becomes a transtemporal communion, a feast, a fest, an act of hospitable excess. History is a company, like Badiou's theater company, a commons-in-the-making, made through loving gifts.[50] Historical discourse reads as reciprocating the past, as a countergift, and as the enactment of a future past through the loving mediation of specters like Linda's Pakal. And maybe now Pakal's Linda. Or, for that matter, my Linda. Or your me, if you please.

So anthropology need not decide between love and the gift. God, love, and the gift nourish one another.

By nominalizing and instating Pakal, Linda remade herself in his image. The ancient Maya now can't be alienated from Linda's love.

Linda was an amateur, an amateur epigrapher, an amateur Mayanist, a Christian lover of the ancient, of lords like Pakal. Such a spectral love. Perhaps decipherment is itself best comprehended not as a contribution to secular historical knowledge, but to a particularly Christian "historiality."[51] Virtualization is historial, and not simply historical, because it always and inevitably destabilizes the conceit of the original; it mucks up temporality through improvisatory inference.

Here, as always, we're at a crossroads. Can we, at once, embrace Christian love and a Derridean fixation on finitude, love as love of ruins? Or does this aporia threaten to ruin God?

Perhaps, here, we may wayfare down an unexpected path, a temporary appeal to ~~love~~ God—virtualization and resurrection, decipherment, history-as-the-Word—while knowing that decipherment too will become ruins.

The deruination of the ancient will succumb again to the slow and largely imperceptible destruction of time/nature (if it doesn't first succumb to a disworlding apocalypse). In ruins we find the crux of nature and culture, the motor of anthropology's untimely persistence. Ruin, including the coming ruination of decipherment and its Christian reinstatement (and recolonization) of ancient Maya worlds, prefigures our inevitable end.

"Our" end. Who communes here?

Anthropologists ought to anticipate their collective termination, their disciplinary collapse; and I hope that we can do so with a plenarist joy, a refusal to succumb to nihilism. Archaeologists may be ahead of the game here. They recognize how their actions leave material traces that outlast them, constituting emergent-if-ultimately-ephemeral "horizons," patterns of soils or artifacts that help the archaeologist define a particular stratigraphically delimited cultural phase. Make of this Derrida-inspired fragment what you will: "The multiplicity of internal times in an open horizon creates what can be called historiality."[52]

Archaeologists, soiled souls, live within these horizons. They share with geologists a particularly passionate attachment to groundedness. Few scholarly collectives are as resolute in their self-styled secularism as archaeologists. Recent rapprochements in the United States between sectors of the archaeological community and Natives who narrate attachment to ancestral remains in explicitly spiritual terms are particularly remarkable in this respect.[53] But Schele's spiritualism clearly anticipated—prefigured—them.

Dialogue across cultural and epistemic lines helps mark archaeologists' worldliness. Is it possible that the secularism indulged and defended by many archaeologists has its own conceptual horizon? The archaeologist shares with Derrida a love of ruins, a relentless commitment to the finitude of cultural and material formations. Can we have the archaeologists' gritty attachment to the world without the corollary (rather Protestant) reduction of spiritual experience to mere metaphoric symbolicity? Is it possible to ground-truth spiritualism?

Read in Hägglund's atheist frame, Derrida seems to salvage love from its relegation to a domain of abstract, receding transcendent Being. Derrida's love is love of detritus, of rot.

There's a scene in Darren Aronofsky's film *The Fountain* in which the protagonists—one resigned to dying of cancer, and her partner manically trying to find the cure—discuss the Maya wisdom of Palenque tour guide Moises Morales (anglicizing his given name, like Linda in their first encounter, as Moses).[54] Rachel Weisz's character, Izzy, on her deathbed, recounts Morales's recounting of the ostensible Maya belief in corporeal transformation, the body-becoming-soil-becoming-plant-life.

This kind of (no doubt Orientalist) construction of Maya cosmology as a monistic affirmation of worldly oneness could use a sense of humor, or at least an awareness that the world—the cosmos?—has its own sense of humor.[55] Izzy doesn't need to laugh at her impending death because she's committed herself to a more reserved smile. It's damn close to a smirk, an "I know better than you, world" attitude that warms the soul by signaling that one's own body/corpus will become the dirt, dust, and ash of the earth (as the contemporary cosmic guru wearing Carl Sagan's shoes, Neil deGrasse Tyson, doesn't hesitate to remind). Izzy's lover becomes an unwitting antagonist because he hardly recognizes, let alone comprehends and abides, her reconciliation. His love, love against finitude, insists on the permanency of an open future. His science is the Science of Heaven-on-Earth, at times cloying, at times clawing. But one can hardly resist laughing at the well-meaning fool.

In these somber times, we need fools. Especially in overearnest academic spaces.

Some of Moises's real-life friends told me that he was proud of being referenced in the popular film. And, having had a few conversations with Moises before it was made, I have no doubt that the filmmakers' invocation was true to the form of his practiced storytelling and clever invocations of Maya belief.

One afternoon in Palenque I was guiding my father, Dwight, through the Morales family's jungle tourist compound when we ran into Moises. He eagerly shared an artist's photographs of his sun-scorched, veiny arms, camouflaging themselves into the root buttresses of that Maya tree of life, the ceiba.

Moises, an amateur, a lover of Palenque's phantasmic Maya, a lover of Palenque's visitors, died recently. Did his family, friends, and legions of devoted followers plant a ceiba for him? Did they plant a ceiba for Moises on the tourist-trod grounds of Palenque, as they did years before for Linda?

* * *

What are we to make of the amateur epigraphers' love, their passionate attachments to Schele and the ancient Maya that she reanimated? Eagleton tells us that

> love can indeed be rationally investigated, even if it cannot be reduced to reason. Unless you can give some coherent account, one in principle intelligible to others, of what you find lovable about someone, it is hard to see how you can describe what you are feeling as love. Love finally goes beyond reason—someone else may see what you see in your partner while not being in the least in love with him or her—

but it is not antithetical to reason, as writers afraid of being robbed of their brooding inwardness by some bloodless theorist sometimes believe of their art.[56]

Terry here casts writers as beings who are *afraid* of theorists purloining their letters. I tend to see the shamans as less fearful of than indifferent to the anthropologists.

Anyway, Linda wasn't an anthropologist; she sided with the shamans. What if agape love *is* shamanism, as spiritual companionship, mutual nourishment across boundaries (including past/present)?

Feed the gods sustaining, precious substances. Blood, alms—the word in Yucatec is *k'awil*. As Schele puts it,

> The Popol Vuh records that the gods wanted to create beings who could reciprocate their love and care by returning nourishment to their creators. The gods failed several times before finally hitting upon the right formula—human beings made from a mixture of maize dough and water. And that final try was successful beyond their wildest hopes, resulting in beings who were capable of prayer and worship, providing sustenance for their gods by "suckling" them, through bloodletting and sacrifice.[57]

Human existence in this "Maya" mode becomes an act of reciprocation. Why would gods so powerful that they could make humans out of maize and water, or out of ancient inscriptions for that matter, need sustenance? Maize and wax, chicken and blood, bread and wine; prayer and dedication are acts of loving reciprocation, reciprocating acts that ultimately can't, for the life of us, be reciprocal. The humans *suckled* their gods; devotion, then, is mothering; and these children are no Christian gods. Livingston, lover, says, "It was a moving experience—trying to visualize the ceremony."[58] Love, indeed, isn't antithetical to reason; the only good reason's a loving reason, a godly reason, a reason that brings sacrilege full circle, leaving it face-to-face with sacrifice, leaving us to face our own cowardice in Schele's paintings on the wall, to face ourselves as Maya lords facing, in turn, the bound, tortured prisoners molded onto stones lining a Palenque Palace courtyard.

Schele, *as* love, constructed a public of amateurs, pure tures. Tortuous self-love. *Amor, pura tura.*

Schele, *as* love, tricked her public. Her craft was more than craft. As she stood on stage, drawing glyphs writ large on transparencies, she called the crowd to loving response. A ceiba tree herself, a centering subject towering above and spiriting the crowd through drawing, art that was at once so *her* and so *foreign*.

In his "Essay on the Origin of Languages," Rousseau offers, "Love, it is said, was the inventor of drawing. It might also have invented speech, though less happily."[59]

Love invented drawing. So love emerges as an attachment to image, to an image, to someone's image. Doesn't this reduce love to superficialities? Love, skin-deep. If love invented drawing because love loves the skin and folds of bodily surfaces, isn't Derrida right that love is love of ruins? To love another is to love their becoming undone, the intensifying imperfection that betrays their finitude.

Their decrepitude.

"But Schele's love," you may counter, "is love of *soul*, love of the possibility that the ancient Maya might be saved, that their images might take felicitous form as speech once more." But how felicitous can signs even be? The iconic image, the image that partakes of its referent, as a dislocated index, an index driven from its home and cast into the semiotic wild, must adore the world. This adoration has its limits. Icons betray their referents through the imperfection of similitude; even the most careful forgery must fail. The pretense to replication is unbecoming. Linda's drawings of glyphs betray; they're tricky. Love's invention of drawing is tricky. But this betrayal is a loving betrayal. Messy icons may well be loving images. Images are a tricky sort of love. Glyphs tricked Linda's predecessors; they tricked Linda; they trick me. So maybe Rousseau is right that love's invention of speech could not be felicitous, happy.

I'm amateur, immature. I love Linda.

You're Linda, of course.

Ruins and all.

One Linda before Linda was Benjamin Lee Whorf, whose decipherment faltered, in the details at least (and, as the epigraphers of Schele's generation had it, it was all detail). But Whorf also offers a prescient precedent to Lévi-Strauss's insistence that "divine understanding alone can soak up" the inadequation between signifier and signified.[60] In his speculative essay "Language, Mind, and Reality," Whorf lays out a critique of narrowly referentialist ideas of meaning, showing clearly that lexemes, morphemes, or words only mean through the patterned or "systematic, configurative nature of higher mind."[61] He appears to be thinking here along the lines of what Ferdinand de Saussure called *langue* and the structuralists called "deep" or "cognitive" structure.[62]

But is he really? Whorf originally published the essay in a journal of Theosophy, and he draws this proto-structuralist thinking into dialogue with Hindu concepts. There's something quite strange going on here.

For Whorf, as for me, the idea that meaning emerges through cognitive structuration assimilates the meaning- and sense-generating functions of language into the spiritual domain, or, at least, *a* spiritual domain. Whorf anticipates the invocation of divine comprehension at the core of Lévi-Strauss's remarkable conceptualization of the floating signifier. In one passage Whorf sums this up by stating, "We have seen that the higher mind deals in symbols that have no fixed reference to anything, but are like blank checks, to be filled in as required, that stand for 'any value' of a given variable, like the . . . x, y, z, of algebra."[63] But Whorf differs from—even escapes— the theological precepts of Lévi-Straussian structuralism when discussing the realities of science, including science's predication on mathematical tautologies or "truths."

After rendering lexemes' semantic openness equivalent to the arbitrariness of algebraic notations' values, Whorf asserts, "There is a queer Western notion that the ancients who invented algebra made a great discovery, though the human unconscious has been doing the same sort of thing for eons! For the same reason the ancient Mayas or the ancient Hindus, in their staggering cycles upon cycles of astronomical numbers, were simply being human."[64] The meaninglessness, or arbitrariness, of the sign, then, is what makes humans human. Built into the arbitrariness of the sign is the possibility of algebraic reasoning. But what if the floating signifier is another kind of opening altogether? What if it's an opening for God, the gods, divinity, or the repressed transcendent?

There's a relevant passage in Maggie Nelson's memoir, *The Argonauts*, that crests and crashes to shore:

> Many years ago, [Anne] Carson gave a lecture . . . at which she introduced (to me) the concept of leaving a space empty so that God could rush in. I knew a bit about this concept from . . . bonsai. In bonsai you often plant the tree off-center in the pot to make space for the divine. But that night Carson made the concept literary. . . . I went home fastened to the concept of leaving the center empty for God. It was like stumbling into a tarot reading or AA meeting and hearing the one thing that will keep you going, in heart or art, for years.[65]

Whorf's linguistics and Schele's art-epigraphy, as cosmic transmissions of joy, love, and genius, needed empty spaces, openings, gaps not to decipher—

because they're indecipherable—but to allow space for God. Linda was an argonaut too.

Her sphere of exchange crossed the Rio Grande, ensnaring—no: *ensouling*—her Austin home with a colonial North American frontier: the Maya area, where Mexico's scarred, edgy extremity bleeds into a Central—but not *too* central—America.[66] This circuit didn't traffic in the objects of that tome we might now retitle *The Other Argonauts*: Melanesian necklaces, armbands, and surplus yams.[67] It trafficked in the signs of elite Maya lives, ancient hieroglyphs rerouted from native ecologies into alien letters, workbooks, and articles.

Will you join my effort to receive these signals with generosity? I have worked to understand how Linda became a medium of historical transmission, an opening for spiritual prestations in a structuralist circuit. Linda's science was cluttered with Near Art Objects.[68] But it was, nonetheless, a capacious inner and outer space. And she was off-center enough for God to rush in.

That said, Linda's botanical fixation was a centering arborescence, the wooden soul of Maya communities, the ceiba tree, the axis mundi or passage-point from this cosmopolitical muddle to its starry other, Xibalba, the Milky Way.[69] You can't plant a ceiba tree off-center. Sooner or later, it comes of age, breaking through the canopy, standing tall enough that, in aggressive acts of vegetal semiosis, it insists on its towering self, self-assured to the point of cockiness, and interpellates with intemperate wildness.

Linda stayed with the ceiba, including the ceiba planted in her memory at Palenque. Linda, an unknowing transcendental materialist,[70] synthesized with the stars of ancient Maya cosmology. She opened her soul in public workshops and tours to almost anyone who would listen.[71] The next generation of epigraphers, kids whom Linda called the Young Turks,[72] now run the show and boast golden MacArthurs. One called her the last amateur epigrapher. I love this—the *amateur* part—because *amateur* means "lover," and Linda loved the dead recklessly, wildly, a wild pansy, a *pensée sauvage*.[73] But to say she was the *last* amateur is just plain silly.

In workshops, popular books, and a major exhibition, Linda channeled a wild proliferation of historical meanings.[74] She and the other Mayanists, our resident American Orientalists, reduced these meanings to one vexing floating signifier, a trope of modernist critical work par excellence: decipherment.

If William Mazzarella is to be believed, we've returned to a mana moment.[75] And mana may be a sci-aesthetic sign that yins the yang of "decipherment."

In his *Introduction to the Work of Marcel Mauss*, Lévi-Strauss conveys a prophetic warning. The augury cuts through the fog of mana, as anthropology's most-adored sacred impersonal force. Lévi-Strauss sets out to let us in on a tabooed secret. In the works of that avuncular line knotting Durkheim to Mauss, the mana concept came to play a surprising role. To Lévi-Strauss's stated disappointment, mana edges Mauss out of his aspirant scientificity. With the last drops of his well's ink, Mauss dried mana into "the expression of social sentiments which are formed—sometimes inexorably and universally, sometimes fortuitously—with regard to certain things, chosen for the most part in an arbitrary fashion."[76]

Here Lévi-Strauss finds himself irked by Mauss's oeuvre, the work he's introducing. Sentiment, fortuitousness, fated inexorability, arbitrariness. Where's the science here, monsieur Mauss, monsieur Durkheim? A few pages on, the arbitrary and floating sign will land on the slippery shore of a grand cartography sketched to prove the human sciences' potential for rigor and systematicity. But not yet. To get there, he must first circumnavigate a literary and scientific storm, turning mana itself against its sociologist envoys. Mauss's sense of mana doesn't lead to the world, or, at least, to the worlds of Oceania, New Zealand, and the Māori. And if its bearing doesn't point to Austronesian bodies, it certainly has no course for or recourse to Polynesian metaphysics.

Mana is untraceable. And worse, it's a fact rift with sentiment. It doesn't point to a desert island, let alone a shore of meaning. It leaves us without orientation, anxiously fixated on the horizon. Soon we'll be overcome by waves of sentiment induced by the realized inexorability of our salty fate. Lévi-Strauss has to drown sociology to save himself, and to save us with him.

Reflecting on the surfacing of sentiment within this most serious act of scientific nominalization, Lévi-Strauss says, "So we can see that in one case, at least, the notion of *mana* does present those characteristics of a secret power, a mysterious force, which Durkheim and Mauss attributed to it: for such is the role it plays in their own system. *Mana* really is *mana* there."[77]

Who knows what mana might be in Melanesia, in Polynesia? But in Paris, which is to say, in *The Elementary Forms of Religious Life* and in *A General Theory of Magic*, mana works to rescue texts from sinking into the ocean of banality, the banal quasi-Kantian truth that facts, like gods, are real enough because they are social, which is to say, because we say they are.[78]

But mana—and hau—matter because, according to Mauss, they ground certain a priori synthetic judgements.[79] I think that Lévi-Strauss intends for us to read between the lines here, to understand that their status as Kantian a priori synthetics enacted in social reality sublates the premise of oppositionality that haunts the Western tradition from Hegel, at least, if not from the earlier Enlightenment reinvention of the ancient Greeks.

He's warning that if anthropology doesn't set its course for a philosophical demonstration of the givenness of the gift within thought itself, it's surely bound to crash. The shortest distance to such a foundering, for Lévi-Strauss, would be the transformation of ethnography into a field that seeks nothing more than the redescription of social reality in indigenous terms. On this prospect, Lévi-Strauss sounds a pronouncement from the bow. He says: "Then ethnography would dissolve into a verbose phenomenology, a falsely naïve mixture in which the apparent obscurities of indigenous thinking would only be brought to the forefront to cover the confusions of the ethnographer which would otherwise be too obvious."[80] "A verbose phenomenology"! Lévi-Strauss can be eerily on point sometimes.

Linda, my subject, was no verbose phenomenologist. She was a doer, a lover, an amateur. Claude dug it.

By classifying and reclassifying the ceiba and the signs that grew under it, Schele became a savvy scientist of the concrete.[81] For Lévi-Strauss, again, between the signified and the floating signifier there is "a non-fit and overspill which divine understanding alone can soak up."[82] The surfeit of the signifier exists because human language—as opposed to divine speech—suffers from the duality of the sign. The human response to encountering a floating signifier, such as mana or God, is to attach it, provisionally, to a signified. The magic of human communication is its efficaciousness despite the divergent signifieds that speakers attach to an exchanged signifier. The coherency of communication is predicated on semantic gaps or lacunae. Divine understanding, on the other hand, doesn't require floating signifiers, because God understands without the mediation of fallible utterances. In Lévi-Strauss's implicit theology, divine speech amounts to a transmission of meaning that can't fail. Divine speech acts comprise true "performatives" that don't require supplementation by a floating signifier such as mana.

But today, in this mana time, we need such immanent supplementation.[83] And through the crack of Claude's turtle skull floats a hare-y signifier, my signifier, Linda—*linda*, beautiful.

In my reading (at times a willfully forced reading), I want to channel the gut-wrenching fierceness of Nelson's *The Argonauts* to help us hone anthropology's sensitivities to moments when God, mana, or *way* rushes in. Again, Nelson says: "I went home fastened to the concept of leaving the center empty for God. It was like stumbling into a tarot reading or AA meeting and hearing the one thing that will keep you going, in heart or art, for years."[84]

It's almost too close to home, Linda's home. Toward the end of her life, while dying of cancer, Linda ported her experience in AA meetings to God up the ancient Maya site of Palenque.[85] She knew something that I'm slowly learning about leaving the center empty for God. I've followed Linda's posthumous followers into *their* meetings, the Maya Meetings, where Linda once laid on the revelations, channeling the ancient Maya as a spiritual form, a charismatic gift.

Mana, hau, wakan, orenda. Life, spirit, genius, god.

In such terms, in our terms, in the heart of language or the mind, there's an emptiness, a foundering of meaning. But need this emptiness always actuate the despair and critical negativity of those poststructuralists who were all too satisfied to let the sign set?[86]

At the heart of a renewed anthropological structuralism, we could leave some space or wiggle room, an open-enough field, an immanent God, the play of language, voice as theological self-discovery.

The field's been mowed again and again, yams harvested, networks cut away.[87]

But what's that I see sprouting? A wild pansy?[88] Take care. Uproot it slowly. Allow the trowel to be gentle; feel with the roots. Transplant it well, in a nourishing matrix. Off-center, please.

Cultura, colore. That's anthropology's way of saying: make space for our loves and our gods, for our Lindas, to flourish, to grow.

Whorf, another Linda (among several) at the crossroads here, voiced a set of claims that might seem to take us down a different line of flight; he inscribes a dialectical image that may depart from the later work of Lévi-Strauss. Lévi-Strauss distinguishes, at least for didactic purposes, between poetic and scientific thought. Whorf draws no such line. In a sense, Whorf anticipates—or hauntingly prefigures—Derrida's criticism of the bricoleur/engineer opposition: "The odds are that the engineer is a myth of the bricoleur's making."[89] I believe Lévi-Strauss knew this through and through. But he didn't say it quite as bluntly as either his predecessor Whorf or his follower Derrida.

So how does Whorf make the point? After parsing the context-dependent referentialities of words such as *hand* and *electrical*, he turns to semantic vagueness and ambiguity within scientific language:

For science, poetry, and love are alike in being "flights" above and away from the slave-world of literal reference and humdrum prosaic details, attempts to widen the petty narrowness of the personal self's outlook, liftings toward *Arūpa*, toward that world of infinite harmony, sympathy and order, of unchanging truths and eternal things. And while all words are pitiful enough in their mere "letter that killeth," it is certain that scientific terms like "force, average, sex, allergic, biological" are not less pitiful, and in their own way no more certain in reference than "sweet, gorgeous, rapture, enchantment, heart and soul, star dust."

And if you think that anthropology's resident engineer must now be ready to correct, to pivot toward insistence upon the narrower and more literal semantic determinations of scientific language vis-à-vis poetic, you're wrong. Whorf is just beginning. He proceeds: "You have probably heard of 'star dust'—what is it? Is it a multitude of stars, a sparkling powder, the soil of the planet mars, the Milky Way, a state of daydreaming, poetic fancy, pyrophoric iron, a spiral nebula, a suburb of Pittsburgh, or a popular song?" Are you listening yet? Are you here with this scientist expounding the semantic indeterminacy of "star dust"? Do you know where he's taking you? Can you feel it? Can you anticipate what comes next?

Whorf thinks you don't know what star dust is. He says it bluntly: "You don't know, and neither does anybody."

Maybe the closest thing to anyone really knowing and responsively responding to Whorf on the semantic indeterminacy of "star dust" shows up in Simon Critchley's book on David Bowie. Critchley says,

> Art's filthy lesson is inauthenticity all the way down, a series of repetitions and reenactments: fakes that strip away the illusion of reality in which we live and confront us with the reality of illusion. Bowie's world is like a dystopian version of *The Truman Show*, the sick place of the world that is forcefully expressed in . . . ruined, violent cityscapes. . . . To borrow Iggy Pop's idiom from *Lust for Life* . . . Bowie is the passenger who rides through the city's ripped backside, under a bright and hollow sky.[90]

But even Critchley and Bowie don't get there; they don't know what star dust is. Yes, art has—or *is*—a filthy lesson; of course it's "inauthenticity all the way down"; of course it becomes semiotic free fall and intertextual, repetitive play. Floating signifiers rend art with aporetic asignifying voids, enabling its transposability into heterogeneous worlds of embodied feeling. "Meaning," as such, is predicated on meaninglessness, the seemingly endless expanse of space. Critchley's fixation on Bowie's inauthenticity is smart, poetic, and pornographic. Far from original.

"But, your fixation on Linda . . . ," you say. *I know, I know.* Then again, one can't know. And that's the bind of ethnography.

Maybe all that you can know or I can know—maybe all that Schele's and Bowie's cosmic signs can teach us—is Whorf's provocative relativity: "You don't know [what star dust is], and neither does anybody." To be human is to not know what star dust is. Face the oblique and opaque sublimity of it all. And, by "it all," I mean, again and again, the floating signifier, Linda, genius, love, God.

But Whorf is still talking about "star dust." Star dust, why star dust? He's spelling it with two words, distinct from Ziggy's one. But Whorf knows that he doesn't know, that he can't know:

> The word—for it is one LEXATION, not two—has no reference of its own. Some words are like that. As we have seen, reference is the lesser part of meaning, patternment the greater. Science, the quest for truth, is a sort of divine madness like love. And music—is it not in the same category? Music is a quasilanguage based entirely on patternment, without having developed lexation.[91]

Even with a considerable archive of Schele's correspondence at my fingertips, I can't know—can't feel—the worldly ephemerality and everydayness of Linda's being and the nitty-gritty work of those who gathered around her. I don't even know what music Linda liked, if she liked music at all.

She and her disciples shared a narrow attentiveness to scientific lexation, to cutting glyphs up and cutting them out, to stabilizing sign and referent so as to have something—you know, something *important*—to say about the patternments of Maya inscriptions and their corollary cosmology. They were a lot like those ancient Maya and Hindus; "Myths get thought in man unbeknownst to him";[92] their staggeringly detailed work only made them human.

But if Ziggy made the rounds on her record player, I don't know it. Maybe being an ethnographer of the dead isn't all it's cracked up to be. But it did bring me, by the end, to star dust.

I don't know what star dust is. But I know that I love it.

Does love really betray one's finitude? Is love necessarily love of one's becoming-dead-and-gone, one's unbecoming? Is an unbecoming death—and aren't all deaths, in a sense, unbecoming(s)?—merely an entropic movement down C. S. Peirce's hierarchy of signs?[93] When we die—when a "we" such as

Linda dies—we descend from the domain of language-wielding symbolicity into a more evocative indexicality.

Now there's a concept that points toward a semiotic theory of ~~life~~. Whatever death may be, it's not nonbeing. It's only nonsymbolizing.

So the poet John Berger says, "Having lived, the dead can never be inert."[94] But the dead aren't active *in the same form* as the living. The dead relinquish the capacity to produce symbols in new combinations, their Chomskyan "creativity."[95] Their language function, as such, has come undone.

But the dead continue to signify indexically and iconically. What is a memory, if not a lived experience displaced from the domain of attachment—or indexicality—to the domain of the mental image? The mental image amounts to an iconic and symbolic resignification of the remembered act, including memories of the dead. What is a letter, like Livingston's letter, but the indexical trace of a moment of signification, a moment lived and maybe loved?

What are Maya hieroglyphs? To be symbols, to be arbitrary linguistic forms, hieroglyphs must first be understood as indexical traces of and in the world.[96] That's the archaeological sensibility that I'll never give up. And they happen to be indexical traces embedded with iconic representations of worldly fragments. They are semiotically compounded fragments of fragments.

Maya hieroglyphs—like any "texts" of the dead—may retain a trace of symbolic value. They are "language" secondarily or inferentially, because their animated performances no longer exist as such (though they, too, left traces). Perhaps Maya glyphs were spirited beings, life-forms that died with their makers and users.

When Schele respirited ancient Maya glyphs, she did not reendow them with the same metaphysical life that originally animated them. She extended her personhood into those objects as a *spiritual gift*. She drained her symbolic, language-generating, and language-wielding soul into those mute stones.

So Linda made music, or poetry, or love with and out of Maya glyphs. Loving meant making them into language.

Rousseau should only get partial credit for his answer to the question on language and love. When he says that love invented drawing—and, maybe, speech—Rousseau seems to mean *erotic* love. This isn't quite the eros of Badiou's more copular communism, which rechannels its force from control of the loved object to an act of becoming-with. It may be a more objectifying eros, a stabilization and control of the loved being that transformed her indexical presence into a fallible icon, a trace viewable at a distance, enacting a mediated affection.

If we are to take up an erotics, I'd prefer that it be a bit more alive, embodied, sensorial. Susan Sontag advocates, touchingly, feelingly, for such an erotics in "Against Interpretation," her counter to the sensorial alienation and frank dullness produced by modern life and reproduced by theory-driven art criticism.[97] Although she had a place in her heart for Lévi-Strauss, "The Anthropologist as Hero," she certainly wouldn't give cultural criticism a pass here either. "Against Interpretation" casts off any negativity that its title might imply with clarity and poignancy when Sontag concludes with that cutting final line: "In place of a hermeneutics we need an erotics of art."[98]

Imagine what anthropology might have become if Sontag's contemporaries in the field had taken up such an imperative. Lévi-Strauss, perhaps, achieved such an erotics early, in the youthful longing of *Tristes Tropiques*, rift with that escapist romanticism that seems to have arrived, for Anglophone readers at least, a century late.[99] Once the tropics returned Lévi-Strauss to Paris, all his tropes seemed cooked. And, before long, structuralism spoils. But there's just so much mythological work still to do (requiring an elaborate material culture, notecard after notecard for mytheme after mytheme). But Lévi-Strauss did know that myths—which is to say humans—were tricky, were tricksters. Weird tricksters. *Were*-tricksters. And when he points to the surfeit of the signifier, he does so, I believe, with a wink.[100]

The rise of Geertz's symbols-and-meaningism in the United States in the decade after Sontag's "Against Interpretation" helped bury any hope for an erotic anthropology, for a time at least. Geertz's prose was alive, but it was almost theologically hermeneutical. Geertz's love for writing was more philial, or friendly, than erotic or agapic. His interpretative anthropology entails a deep hermeneutics, but it always borders on paranoid reading.[101] Interpretivism didn't binarize the world as starkly as structuralism had, but Geertz couldn't trust reality as it was given in experience. He insisted that the world had to make more sense, that it had to have a deeper layer of meaning that the ethnographer could, by virtue of gritty and determined "being there," eventually approach.[102]

Decipherment and symbolic anthropology came of age in the same era, and decipherment too, in its more pervasive non-*aha* moments, entails a humdrum hermeneutics. It would be easy to write off as an effect of Cold War sensibilities. But I'm insisting, against ever-more-paranoid readings, upon the open creativity and generativity, the devoted religiosity, and the effusive love of Schele's contributions to decipherment.

Not only did Schele's spiritual mediation of the ancient Maya unfold into an agapic communion of amateurs; it also spurred new forms of play, seduction, and erotic enjoyment. Sontag's invocation of eros touches Roland Barthes, with whom she shares a notion that teaching can be a kind of play, writing a kind of seduction, and reading a site of eros, as intimate or romantic love. Although this sensibility entails a determined refusal to impose frames from, for example, psychoanalysis on objects of art, Sontag and Barthes knew well that, psychoanalytically speaking, the generativity of eros opposes thanatos, the death instinct. Schele's decipherments didn't close the book on the ancient Maya; they constructed a material and semiotic field of passionate, loving attachments. Standing in this field, partaking of Schele's spectral joy, I find myself staring skybound, making out the dialectical image of the rabbit on the moon.

Wasn't Schele's transformation of indexically accessed mute stones and images into narrated, collectively imagined lives full of human symbolism and language a subtly erotic act? Her spiritualism was, in the end, a loving generativity, not just against interpretation but against death. It entailed a refusal to allow thanatos to reign, a reanimation that was at once agapic and erotic. Doesn't this also suggest that the distinction between agapic and erotic love is too stark, that all kinds of communion entail forms of joy-producing creativity? We can't all write like Barthes or Sontag, or Haraway for that matter, who has offered what may well be an erotics of science. But even if Schele was no prose-eroticist, she was, nevertheless, doing something, making something, creating something that exceeded the library-bound hermeneuticist's dusty textual criticism or even the liberal interpretive anthropologist's peeling away of the symbolic onion's layers.

Perhaps, in Schele's books, the erotic event—the *aha* moment—which I've described as a religious revelation, must alternate with humdrum historical exposition. The artistic moment is the God-event, the opening of the heavens, the arrival of a divine surfeit-signifier that feels and speaks through us.

Schele must have agreed with Whorf: "Science, the quest for truth, is a sort of divine madness like love."[103] Or, more simply: star dust.

Notes

....

1 For another ethnographic entry into Palenque, see James Clifford, "Palenque Log," *Museum Anthropology* 17, no. 3 (1993).

2 John L. Stephens, *Incidents of Travel in Central America, Chiapas, and Yucatan*, 2 vols. (1841; repr., New York: Dover, 1969); see Fabio Bourbon, *The Lost Cities of the Mayas: The Life, Art, and Discoveries of Frederick Catherwood* (New York: Abbeville, 2000).

3 Linda Schele to "collegues [*sic*], friends, and friendly crazies," March 24, 1974, Linda Schele Papers, private library of David and Elaine Schele, Austin, TX (hereafter cited as Schele Papers).

4 Anthropological attention to the gift tracks to Marcel Mauss's classic manuscript on the subject. Mauss's metaphysics of exchange has inspired a series of anthropological problematics over the course of the past century. I take "the gift" as an anthropological index signifying the priority of the relation, the claim that relations precede and give rise to both subject and society. In the structuralist tradition, exchange has taken form as thought and language, abstract human capacities that amplify the consequences of Mauss's argument that gifts are spiritual extensions of the person that expect or demand reciprocation. Much of the implicit theoretical arc of this book tracks from a view of reciprocity that aligns with contemporary "affect theory," particularly monistic, neo-Spinozian views inspired by Gilles Deleuze and Félix Guattari's vitalism, to a more dialectical and structuralist insistence on the theological character of thought/language itself (in critical engagement with Claude Lévi-Strauss and Jacques Derrida). This book is both an act of reciprocation, as thoughtful as I can make it, and a resolute refusal to close the circuit of exchange. Marcel Mauss, *The Gift* (1925), trans. Jane I. Guyer (Chicago: HAU Books, 2016); Gilles Deleuze and Félix Guattari, *Anti-Oedipus: Capitalism and Schizophrenia* (1972), trans. Robert Hurley, Mark Seem, and Helen R. Lane (Minneapolis: University of Minnesota Press, 1983); Gilles Deleuze and Félix Guattari, *A Thousand Plateaus: Capitalism and Schizophrenia* (1980), trans. Brian Massumi (Minneapolis: University of

Minnesota Press, 1987). For key engagements with Maussian exchange theory, see Claude Lévi-Strauss, *Introduction to the Work of Marcel Mauss* (1950), trans. Felicity Baker (London: Routledge and Kegan Paul, 1987); Nancy D. Munn, *The Fame of Gawa: A Symbolic Study of Value Transformation in a Massim (Papua New Guinea) Society* (Cambridge: Cambridge University Press, 1986); Marilyn Strathern, *The Gender of the Gift: Problems with Women and Problems with Society in Melanesia* (Berkeley: University of California Press, 1988); Annette B. Weiner, *Inalienable Possessions: The Paradox of Keeping-While-Giving* (Berkeley: University of California Press, 1992); Maurice Godelier, *The Enigma of the Gift*, trans. Nora Scott (Chicago: University of Chicago Press, 1999); Jacques Derrida, *Given Time: I. Counterfeit Money*, trans. Peggy Kamuf (Chicago: University of Chicago Press, 1992); Jacques Derrida, *The Gift of Death; and Literature in Secret* (1999; repr., Chicago: University of Chicago Press, 2008).

5 Karl Herbert Mayer, "A Painted Venus Glyph in the Tower at Palenque," *Archaeoastronomy* 6 (1983).

6 Schele to "collegues, friends, and friendly crazies," March 24, 1974.

7 Schele to "collegues, friends, and friendly crazies," March 24, 1974.

8 Schele to "collegues, friends, and friendly crazies," March 24, 1974.

9 Contemporary practitioners of Maya epigraphy have inherited and propagated a concept of "the Maya" as a coherent cultural entity. The cultural designation "Maya" covers speakers of historically related languages who have principally inhabited eastern Mesoamerica, including areas now territorialized as southern Mexico, Belize, Guatemala, and parts of Honduras and El Salvador. In popular publications, scholars claim that a continuous Maya culture has inhabited these territories from approximately 2000 BCE to the present. See, e.g., David Freidel, Linda Schele, and Joy Parker, *Maya Cosmos: Three Thousand Years on the Shaman's Path* (New York: William Morrow, 1993). The contestable notion of a unified "Maya culture" predates the rise of contemporary hieroglyphic studies. See, e.g., John L. Stephens, *Incidents of Travel in Yucatan*, 2 vols. (1843; repr., New York: Dover, 1963); Stephens, *Incidents of Travel in Central America, Chiapas, and Yucatan*, 2 vols. (1841; repr., New York Dover, 1963). Yet epigraphers have helped solidify this singularized epistemic object by treating inscriptions rendered on diverse media throughout the Maya area between the third century BCE and the sixteenth century CE as a single script. In recent years, a small, influential group of hieroglyph experts has abandoned their field's antiquarian and art historical roots in favor of claims that epigraphy is grounded in a linguistic science that permits them privileged access to the literal meanings of Maya hieroglyphs. In so doing, they have come to exercise significant—and, arguably, problematic—control over the definition of the Maya both inside and outside academia. Cf. Stephen D. Houston, "Into the Minds of Ancients: Advances in Maya Glyph Studies," *Journal of World Prehistory* 14, no. 2 (2000). Scholarship that turns a critical eye to the notion of "Maya culture" includes Quetzil Castañeda, *In the Museum of Maya Culture: Touring Chichén Itzá* (Minneapolis: University of Minnesota Press, 1996); Nora C. England, "Mayan Language Revival and Revi-

talization: Linguists and Linguistic Ideologies," *American Anthropologist* 105, no. 4 (2003); Diane M. Nelson, "Maya Hackers and the Cyberspatialized Nation-State: Modernity, Ethnostalgia, and a Lizard Queen in Guatemala," *Cultural Anthropology* 11, no. 3 (1996); Diane M. Nelson, *Reckoning: The Ends of War in Guatemala* (Durham, NC: Duke University Press, 2009); John M. Watanabe, "Unimagining the Maya: Anthropologists, Others, and the Inescapable Hubris of Authorship," *Bulletin of Latin American Research* 14, no. 1 (1995); Richard Wilk, "The Ancient Maya and the Political Present," *Journal of Anthropological Research* 41, no. 3 (1988).

10 My critiques of decipherment have persistently suggested that the translation of Maya hieroglyphic writing into contemporary scripts has been determined by a "modernist" language ideology. For example, elsewhere I have asserted, "The particular language ideology governing decipherment treats hieroglyphs as objects that independently and transparently convey the literal, interior thoughts of ancient Maya subjects." Matthew C. Watson, "Staged Discovery and the Politics of Maya Hieroglyphic Things," *American Anthropologist* 114, no. 2 (2012): 283. By calling attention to the historically situated construction of language as a transparent medium, distinct from art, I hoped to encourage the development of epigraphic methods more sensitive to inscriptions' contexts of use, ideological constructions, and functions within a broader ecology of semiotic and nonsemiotic beings. I continue to believe that ancient Maya scribes, dynasts, and commoners conceived "writing" in terms that differ dramatically from recent constructions, particularly constructions that privilege a conception of writing as a neutral means of recording or conveying "ideas" (let alone a sign of "civilizational" achievement). Although I continue to call attention, here, to epigraphers' adoption of the "modernist" conceit of language as a transparent medium, I am now primarily invested in crafting a distinct critical approach. Rather than treating this transformation of ancient inscriptions into modernist texts as a system of symbolic violence, I am centering—and elegizing— the spiritual joy and genius of decipherment. In so doing, I am working to show how the science of epigraphy was, in practice, a complex nonmodernist field, and how Schele herself employed modernist conceits about language's transparency more strategically than I have tended to acknowledge. This repositioning constitutes an effort to frame my engagement in more deeply ethnographic terms, terms that estrange epigraphy itself, revealing its modernist tendencies as popularizing devices that obscure more complex considerations of hieroglyphs' pragmatic and semiotic functions.

11 Mayanists have positioned two early innovations as foundational events in the shift away from such emphasis of noncalendrical components and toward the emergence of a persuasive argument for hieroglyphs as writing: Yuri Knorozov's identification of phonetic signs; and Tatiana Proskouriakoff's identification of patterns in hieroglyphic dates that indicated the texts' historical content. These events signaled the beginning of the end for a dominant early twentieth-century assumption that the hieroglyphs were largely icons, rebuses, and logographs (or word signs) that served limited purposes for religious acts of divination and lacked a full capacity for

signification, as Sylvanus Morley and J. Eric S. Thompson had maintained. The rise of the "phonetic" and "historical" approaches also led to a shift in interpretations of representational imagery associated with the writing. Mayanists such as Morley and Thompson considered such images representations of religious or cosmological figures and events and worked within an epistemology that distinguished rigidly between "religious" and "historical" figures. By the 1970s, the emerging community of hieroglyph scholars had begun to make claims that the hieroglyphs were "more" than icons, rebuses, and logographs, and in fact comprised texts with signs that combined logographic and phonetic components amounting to a completely syntactic script. See, e.g., Peter Mathews and Linda Schele, "Lords of Palenque—The Glyphic Evidence," in *Primera Mesa Redonda de Palenque: A Conference on the Art, Iconography, and Dynastic History of Palenque*, ed. Merle Greene Robertson (Pebble Beach, CA: Pre-Columbian Art Research Institute, 1974); Linda Schele, *Maya Glyphs: The Verbs* (Austin: University of Texas Press, 1982). In turn, the accompanying images could no longer be considered primarily or entirely mythological. Many such images came to be understood as realist historical representations of elite Mayas. See, e.g., Linda Schele and Mary Miller, *The Blood of Kings: Dynasty and Ritual in Maya Art* (Fort Worth: Kimbell Art Museum, 1986). Internal histories of the field include Michael Coe, *Breaking the Maya Code*, rev. ed. (New York: Thames and Hudson, 1999); Stephen Houston, Oswaldo Chinchilla Mazarieogos, and David Stuart, *The Decipherment of Ancient Maya Writing* (Norman: University of Oklahoma Press, 2001); George E. Stuart, "Quest for Decipherment: A Historical and Biographical Survey of Maya Hieroglyphic Investigation," in *New Theories on the Ancient Maya*, ed. E. C. Danien and R. J. Sharer (Philadelphia: University of Pennsylvania Press, 1992). Classic contributions to hieroglyphic analysis relevant here include Yuri V. Knorozov, "Drevniaia Pis'mennost' Tsentral'noi Ameriki," *Sovietskaya Etnografiya* 3, no. 2 (1952); Yuri V. Knorozov, "The Problem of the Study of the Maya Hieroglyphic Writing," *American Antiquity* 23, no. 3 (1958); Sylvanus Griswold Morley, *The Ancient Maya* (Stanford, CA: Stanford University Press, 1946); J. Eric S. Thompson, *Maya Hieroglyphic Writing: Introduction* (Washington, DC: Carnegie Institution of Washington, 1950).

12 The notion of a "paradigm shift" or "revolution" in scientific thinking derives from Thomas Kuhn's gestalt-oriented history and philosophy of science (HPS). It has proven to have great appeal to scientists themselves, even as its explanatory power within history, sociology, philosophy, and anthropology has faded. The decipherers did not typically conceive of developments in their field in terms congruent with either Kuhn's history and philosophy of science or subsequent events within HPS or science studies. In his popular account of decipherment, *Breaking the Maya Code*, Michael Coe passingly refers to developments in the field as a "revolution," but he cites neither Kuhn nor, in fact, any other relevant literature within HPS or science studies. Despite (or because of?) its weak conceptual foundation and tendency toward a narrow internalism, *Breaking the Maya Code* is now in its third edition. This is all the more evidence that a contagious enthusiasm—I'd say a contagious

magic—marked or even manifested hieroglyphic decipherment. For the notion of scientific paradigms, see Thomas Kuhn, *The Structure of Scientific Revolutions*, 4th ed. (Chicago: University of Chicago Press, 2012). The major popular internal history of the field is Coe, *Maya Code*. The notion of contagious magic derives from James George Frazer, *The Golden Bough: A Study in Magic and Religion* (1922; repr., New York: Macmillan, 1963). For an internal account of decipherment more open to epistemological perspectives (though, in nicely counterparanoid fashion, not mine), see Marc Zender, "Theory and Method in Maya Decipherment," PARI *Journal* 18, no. 2 (2018).

13 Ethnographers have long engaged with archival documents. Among the more important and relevant recent contributions to archive-based ethnographic work include the following: Ann Laura Stoler, *Along the Archival Grain: Epistemic Anxieties and Colonial Common Sense* (Princeton, NJ: Princeton Universtiy Press, 2009); Elizabeth Edwards, *The Camera as Historian: Amateur Photographers and Historical Imagination, 1885–1918* (Durham, NC: Duke University Press, 2012); Sally Engle Merry, "Ethnography in the Archives," in *Practicing Ethnography in Law: New Dialogues, Enduring Methods*, ed. June Starr and Mark Goodale (New York: Palgrave Macmillan, 2002). See also the work on documents as epistemic artifacts: Annelise Riles, ed., *Documents: Artifacts of Modern Knowledge* (Ann Arbor: University of Michigan Press, 2006).

14 Matthew C. Watson, "Assembling the Ancient: Public Science in the Decipherment of Maya Hieroglyphs" (PhD diss., University of Florida, 2010), chap. 6. See also England, "Mayan Language Revival."

15 See, e.g., Sarah Franklin, "Science as Culture, Cultures of Science," *Annual Review of Anthropology* 24 (1995); Gary Lee Downey, Joseph Dumit, and Sarah Williams, "Cyborg Anthropology," *Cultural Anthropology* 10, no. 2 (1995); Emily Martin, "Anthropology and the Cultural Study of Science," *Science, Technology, and Human Values* 23, no. 1 (1998); Sharon Traweek, *Beamtimes and Lifetimes: The World of High Energy Physics* (Cambridge, MA: Harvard University Press, 1988); Kim Fortun, *Advocacy after Bhopal: Environmentalism, Disaster, New Global Orders* (Chicago: University of Chicago Press, 2001); Paul Rabinow, *French DNA: Trouble in Purgatory* (Chicago: University of Chicago Press, 1999). See also systems-oriented, anthropological allies. See, e.g., Donna J. Haraway, "A Cyborg Manifesto: Science, Technology, and Socialist-Feminism in the Late Twentieth Century," in *Simians, Cyborgs, and Women: The Reinvention of Nature* (New York: Routledge, 1991); Donna J. Haraway, *Modest_Witness@Second_Millennium. FemaleMan©_Meets_OncoMouse™: Feminism and Technoscience* (New York: Routledge, 1997); Donna J. Haraway, *Staying with the Trouble: Making Kin in the Chthulucene* (Durham, NC: Duke University Press, 2016); Bruno Latour and Steve Woolgar, *Laboratory Life: The Construction of Scientific Facts* (Princeton, NJ: Princeton University Press, 1986); Bruno Latour, *We Have Never Been Modern* (Cambridge, MA: Harvard University Press, 1993); Bruno Latour, *Politics of Nature: How to Bring the Sciences into Democracy*, trans. Catherine Porter (Cambridge, MA: Harvard University Press, 2004);

Karen Barad, *Meeting the Universe Halfway: Quantum Physics and the Entanglement of Matter and Meaning* (Durham, NC: Duke University Press, 2007). Finally, historians and philosophers of science have, in recent years, engaged closely both with ideas drawn from anthropology—including the gift—and with the history of anthropology itself. See, e.g., Warwick Anderson, *The Collectors of Lost Souls: Turning Kuru Scientists into Whitemen* (Baltimore: Johns Hopkins University Press, 2008); Joanna Radin, *Life on Ice: A History of New Uses for Cold Blood* (Chicago: University of Chicago Press, 2017).

16 There's a faint echo, here, of Haraway, *Modest_Witness@Second_Millennium*.

17 Matthew C. Watson, "Assembling the Ancient" and "Staged Discovery"; Matthew C. Watson, "Mediating the Maya: Hieroglyphic Imaging and Objectivity," *Journal of Social Archaeology* 13, no. 2 (2013); Matthew C. Watson, "Listening in the Pakal Controversy: A Matter of Care in Ancient Maya Studies," *Social Studies of Science* 44, no. 6 (2014).

18 For "lines of flight," see Deleuze and Guattari, *A Thousand Plateaus*. For "spheres of exchange," see Paul Bohannan, "The Impact of Money on an African Subsistence Economy," *Journal of Economic History* 19, no. 4 (1959).

19 Cf. Kathleen Stewart, *Ordinary Affects* (Durham, NC: Duke University Press, 2007).

20 See, e.g., Londa Schiebinger, *Nature's Body: Gender in the Making of Modern Science* (Boston: Beacon, 1993).

21 Cf. Joel Robbins, "Beyond the Suffering Subject: Toward an Anthropology of the Good," *Journal of the Royal Anthropological Institute* 19, no. 3 (2013).

22 The rhetorical practice of ethnographic evocation—as distinct from description—now has a substantive and significant history. Classic discussions include Stephen A. Tyler, "Post-modern Ethnography: From Document of the Occult to Occult Document," in *Writing Culture: The Poetics and Politics of Ethnography*, ed. James Clifford and George E. Marcus (Berkeley: University of California Press, 1986); Marilyn Strathern, *Partial Connections* (Savage, MD: Rowman, 1991).

23 On "systems of attitudes," see Claude Lévi-Strauss, *The Elementary Structures of Kinship* (1949), trans. James Harle Bell and John Richard von Sturmer (Boston: Beacon, 1969). On "structures of feeling," see Raymond Williams, *Marxism and Literature* (Oxford: Oxford University Press, 1977).

24 On the "hyperreal," see Jean Baudrillard, *Simulations*, trans. Paul Foss, Paul Patton, and Philip Batchman (New York: Semiotext(e), 1983); Dipesh Chakrabarty, *Provincializing Europe: Postcolonial Thought and Historical Difference* (Princeton, NJ: Princeton University Press, 2000).

25 I share with anthropologist Sasha Newell a sense that the language of "affect" extends, rather than departs from, long-standing anthropological attention to semiosis. Sasha Newell, "The Affectiveness of Symbols: Materiality, Magicality, and the Limits of the Antisemiotic Turn," *Current Anthropology* 59, no. 1 (2018). Moreover, if we align semiotics of a structuralist variety with dialectical reasoning, such a view may come into generative engagement with contemporary philosophical assessments of Continental theory's reception of Hegelian dialectics and Spinozist monism, espe-

cially views that take these frames as unexpectedly complementary epistemologies. See, e.g., Gregor Moder, *Hegel and Spinoza: Substance and Negativity* (Evanston, IL: Northwestern University Press, 2017).

26 I am indebted in particular to Eve Sedgwick's and Bruno Latour's respective efforts to advocate for modes of thinking and writing beyond critique, as a negative, subtractive, or paranoid discourse and epistemic stance. Eve Kosofsky Sedgwick, *Touching Feeling: Affect, Pedagogy, Performativity* (Durham, NC: Duke University Press, 2003); Bruno Latour, "Why Has Critique Run Out of Steam? From Matters of Fact to Matters of Concern," *Critical Inquiry* 30, no. 2 (2004); see also Elizabeth S. Anker and Rita Felski, eds., *Critique and Postcritique* (Durham, NC: Duke University Press, 2017).

27 On charismatic authority, see Max Weber, *On Charisma and Institution Building* (Chicago: University of Chicago Press, 1968).

28 Though, as I find at times here, optimism can be tricky, even cruel. Cf. Lauren Berlant, *Cruel Optimism* (Durham, NC: Duke University Press, 2011).

29 I mean "supplementing" in a sense loosely inspired by Jacques Derrida's sense of the term. For a preliminary orientation, consider his early discussion in *Of Grammatology*: "The concept of the supplement—which here determines that of the representative image—harbors within itself two significations whose cohabitation is as strange as it is necessary. The supplement adds itself, it is a surplus, a plenitude enriching another plenitude, the *fullest measure* of presence. It cumulates and accumulates presence. It is thus that art, *technè*, image, representation, convention, etc., come as supplements to nature and are rich with this entire cumulating function. . . . But the supplement supplements. It adds only to replace. It intervenes or insinuates itself *in-the-place-of*; if it fills, it is as if one fills a void. If it represents and makes an image, it is by the anterior default of a presence. Compensatory [*suppléant*] and vicarious, the supplement is an adjunct, a subaltern insistence which *takes-(the)-place* [*tient-lieu*]." Jacques Derrida, *Of Grammatology*, trans. Gayatri Chakravorty Spivak (Baltimore: Johns Hopkins University Press, 1974), 144–45.

30 The concept of "speaking nearby" sources from the work of Trinh T. Minh-ha and is exemplified in films by Trinh including *Reassemblage* and *Surname Viet Given Name Nam*. In Trinh's own words, "speaking nearby" amounts to "a speaking that does not objectify, does not point to an object as if it is distant from the speaking subject or absent from the speaking place. A speaking that reflects on itself and can come very close to a subject without, however, seizing or claiming it. A speaking in brief, whose closures are only moments of transition opening up to other possible moments of transition." Nancy N. Chen, "'Speaking Nearby': A Conversation with Trinh T. Minh-ha," *Visual Anthropology Review* 8, no. 1 (1992): 87. The antirepresentationalist political aesthetics of the 1980s–1990s that motivated Trinh's conceptualization of "speaking nearby" have faded in significance. And ethnographers have, once again, become more confident in their efforts to revoice the worlds of their subjects (or objects). Such renewed epistemic confidence is laudable at a historical moment when careful and caring accounts of peoples' worlds could achieve traction within

extra-academic political discourse. Nevertheless, as a writer interested mainly in how we encounter the past, I find the methodological imperative of speaking (as well as writing and thinking) nearby to be of persisting value. Can we truly speak *of* the dead? Or are our engagements with the dead proximate and proximal engagements, forms of affinity or approach, approaches without necessary rapprochements, without requisite representational clarity? My speaking nearby Linda is a trickster method for waiting/hoping—for *esperanza*—with, or alongside, a "dead" being. In the terms of Gilles Deleuze and Félix Guattari, my esperanza has been something of an affirmative becoming-other, but an affirmative becoming-other that's an affirmative becoming-dead or becoming-with-the-dead. In this sense, I may be speaking nearby—and not speaking of, about, or with—the ethnographic form that animates and haunts me here, because I have no choice in the matter. In fact, my esperanza is to feel as close a proximity to Linda as I can. This is a failing esperanza, a work of desperado science. Consult Trinh T. Minh-ha, *Reassemblage* (New York: Women Make Movies, 1982); Trinh T. Minh-ha, *Surname Viet Given Name Nam* (New York: Women Make Movies, 1989); Deleuze and Guattari, *A Thousand Plateaus*. Cf. Sedgwick, *Touching Feeling*, on speaking and writing "beside."

31 This curt characterization may be something of a disservice to the complex epistemic-ethical problem of ethnographic positioning, a matter characterized by the contingencies of research sites and subjects. Regardless, Isabelle Stengers's concept of an "ecology of practices" may be particularly helpful here, because it emphasizes the dynamism of the sciences as situated technologies of becoming and offers the distinctive ethnographic advantage of refusing to position critical, philosophical, or anthropological engagements with sciences as external to the sciences themselves. It amounts to a provocation to take seriously the performative effects of our critical practices. As Stengers puts it, "An ecology of practices does not have any ambition to describe practices 'as they are;' it resists the master word of a progress that would justify their destruction. It aims at the construction of new 'practical identities' for practices, that is, new possibilities for them to be present, or in other words to connect. It thus does not approach practices as they are—physics as we know it, for instance—but as they may become." Isabelle Stengers, "Introductory Notes on an Ecology of Practices," *Cultural Studies Review* 11, no. 1 (2005): 186. See also Isabelle Stengers, "The Cosmopolitical Proposal," in *Making Things Public: Atmospheres of Democracy*, ed. Bruno Latour and Peter Weibel (Cambridge, MA: MIT Press, 2005); Isabelle Stengers, *Cosmopolitics I* (Minneapolis: University of Minnesota Press, 2010); Isabelle Stengers, *Cosmopolitics II* (Minneapolis: University of Minnesota Press, 2011).

32 Clifford and Marcus, *Writing Culture*; George E. Marcus and Michael M. J. Fischer, *Anthropology as Cultural Critique: An Experimental Moment in the Human Sciences*, 2nd ed. (Chicago: University of Chicago Press, 1999); Ruth Behar and Deborah A. Gordon, eds., *Women Writing Culture* (Berkeley: University of California Press, 1995); Orin Starn, ed., *Writing Culture and the Life of Anthropology* (Durham, NC: Duke University Press, 2015).

33 James Clifford, "On Ethnographic Surrealism," *Comparative Studies in Society and History* 23, no. 4 (1981).

34 Marcel Mauss, *A General Theory of Magic* (1950), trans. Robert Brain (London: Routledge, 2001); Mauss, *The Gift*; Georges Bataille, *The Accursed Share: An Essay on General Economy*, vol. 1, *Consumption* (1949), trans. Robert Hurley (New York: Zone Books, 1991).

35 See, e.g., William Mazzarella, *The Mana of Mass Society* (Chicago: University of Chicago Press, 2017); William Mazzarella, "Sense out of Sense: Notes on the Affect/ Ethics Impasse," *Cultural Anthropology* 32, no. 2 (2017); Michael Hardt and Antonio Negri, *Empire* (Cambridge, MA: Harvard University Press, 2000); Michael Hardt and Antonio Negri, *Commonwealth* (Cambridge, MA: Harvard University Press, 2009); Benjamin Noys, *The Persistence of the Negative: A Critique of Contemporary Continental Theory* (Edinburgh: Edinburgh University Press, 2010); Moder, *Hegel and Spinoza*.

36 Walter Benjamin, *The Arcades Project*, trans. Howard Eiland and Kevin McLaughlin (Cambridge, MA: Harvard University Press, 1999); see also Susan Buck-Morss, *The Dialectics of Seeing: Walter Benjamin and the Arcades Project* (Cambridge, MA: MIT Press, 1989).

37 Benjamin, *The Arcades Project*, 462, N2a,3. A different version of this passage also appears in N3,1.

38 Benjamin, quoted in Buck-Morss, *The Dialectics of Seeing*, 219.

39 Fred Moten, *Black and Blur* (Durham, NC: Duke University Press, 2017).

40 Bruno Latour designates such an escape from—or provisional incommensurability with—a given sociomaterial order, or "common world," as a "small transcendence." Latour, *Politics of Nature*, 196.

41 Cf. Hans-Jörg Rheinberger, "Experimental Systems, Graphematic Spaces," in *Inscribing Science: Scientific Texts and the Materiality of Communication*, ed. Timothy Lenoir (Stanford, CA: Stanford University Press, 1998); Kim Fortun, "Ethnography in/of/as Open Systems," *Reviews in Anthropology* 32 (2003).

42 Jacques Derrida, "Hostipitality," in *Acts of Religion*, ed. Gil Anidjar (New York: Routledge, 2002).

43 Anand Pandian and Stuart McLean, eds., *Crumpled Paper Boat* (Durham, NC: Duke University Press, 2017), 3.

44 Pandian and McLean, *Crumpled Paper Boat*, 3.

45 After Jacques Lacan, the notion of an "apparatus of *jouissance*" owes to Jacques-Alain Miller. Jacques-Alain Miller, "The Monologue of *L'Apparole*," *Qui Parle: Critical Humanities and Social Sciences* 9, no. 2 (1996).

46 Kathleen Stewart, *A Space on the Side of the Road: Cultural Poetics in an "Other" America* (Princeton, NJ: Princeton University Press, 1996); Stewart, *Ordinary Affects*; Allen C. Shelton, *Dreamworlds of Alabama* (Minneapolis: University of Minnesota Press, 2007); Allen C. Shelton, *Where the North Sea Touches Alabama* (Chicago: University of Chicago Press, 2013).

47 Stewart, *Ordinary Affects*; Shelton, *Where the North Sea Touches Alabama*.

48 Berlant, *Cruel Optimism*.

49 Shelton, *Where the North Sea Touches Alabama*; see also Shelton, *Dreamworlds of Alabama*.

50 Aníbal Quijano, "Coloniality of Power and Eurocentrism in Latin America," *International Sociology* 15, no. 2 (2000). See also Walter D. Mignolo, "Introduction: Coloniality of Power and De-Colonial Thinking," *Cultural Studies* 21, nos. 2–3 (2007); Walter D. Mignolo, *Local Histories/Global Designs: Coloniality, Subaltern Knowledges, and Border Thinking* (Princeton, NJ: Princeton University Press, 2000); Nelson Maldonado-Torres, "On the Coloniality of Being: Contributions to the Development of a Concept," *Cultural Studies* 21, nos. 2–3 (2007); Alberto Moreiras, "A Storm Blowing from Paradise: Negative Globality and Critical Regionalism," in *The Latin American Subaltern Studies Reader*, ed. Ileana Rodríguez (Durham, NC: Duke University Press, 2001).

51 See, e.g., Florencia E. Mallon, "The Promise and Dilemma of Subaltern Studies: Perspectives from Latin American History," *American Historical Review* 99, no. 5 (1994); John Beverley, *Subalternity and Representation: Arguments in Cultural Theory* (Durham, NC: Duke University Press, 1999). On the coloniality of Latin American knowledge production, see, e.g., Robert D. Aguirre, *Informal Empire: Mexico and Central America in Victorian Culture* (Minneapolis: University of Minnesota Press, 2004); Jorge Cañizares-Esguerra, *Nature, Empire, and Nation: Explorations of the History of Science in the Iberian World* (Stanford, CA: Stanford University Press, 2006); Cori Hayden, *When Nature Goes Public: The Making and Unmaking of Bioprospecting in Mexico* (Princeton, NJ: Princeton University Press, 2004); Peter Redfield, *Space in the Tropics: From Convicts to Rockets in French Guiana* (Berkeley: University of California Press, 2000); Londa Schiebinger, *Plants and Empire: Colonial Bioprospecting in the Atlantic World* (Cambridge, MA: Harvard University Press, 2007); Mauricio Tenorio Trillo, "Stereophonic Scientific Modernisms: Social Science between Mexico and the United States, 1880s–1930s," *Journal of American History* 86, no. 3 (1999).

52 For an engaging feminist reading of the coloniality of power in the Andes, see Florence E. Babb, *Women's Place in the Andes: Engaging Decolonial Feminist Anthropology* (Berkeley: University of California Press, 2018). On the coloniality of history and spiritual being as a cosmopolitical problem, see, e.g., Marisol de la Cadena, *Earth Beings: Ecologies of Practice across Andean Worlds* (Durham, NC: Duke University Press, 2015). Cf. Arturo Escobar, *Designs for the Pluriverse: Radical Interdependence, Autonomy, and the Making of Worlds* (Durham, NC: Duke University Press, 2018).

53 For the case of Mexico, see, e.g., Analisa Taylor, *Indigeneity in the Mexican Cultural Imagination: Thresholds of Belonging* (Tucson: University of Arizona Press, 2009); Florence E. Babb, "Theorizing Gender, Race, and Cultural Tourism in Latin America: A View from Peru and Mexico," *Latin American Perspectives* 39, no. 6 (2012).

54 See, e.g., Arturo Arias, "The Maya Movement, Postcolonialism and Cultural Agency," *Journal of Latin American Cultural Studies* 15, no. 2 (2006); Brian Gollnick, *Reinventing the Lacandón: Subaltern Representations in the Rain Forest of Chiapas* (Tucson:

University of Arizona Press, 2008); Diane M. Nelson, *A Finger in the Wound: Body Politics in Quincentennial Guatemala* (Berkeley: University of California Press, 1999); John M. Watanabe and Edward F. Fischer, eds., *Pluralizing Ethnography: Comparison and Representation in Maya Cultures, Histories, and Identities* (Santa Fe, NM: School for Advanced Research Press, 2004).

55 For a finely nuanced and beautifully rendered reading of the "wake" within the politics of US Blackness, see Christina Sharpe, *In the Wake: On Blackness and Being* (Durham, NC: Duke University Press, 2016).

56 My sense of "ethno-pessimism" here points toward a decolonial indigenous engagement with the field of "Afro-pessimist" thought, particularly in its consideration of Blackness as an ontologically constitutive negation. See, e.g., Hortense J. Spillers, *Black, White, and in Color: Essays on American Literature and Culture* (Chicago: University of Chicago Press, 2003); Calvin L. Warren, *Ontological Terror: Blackness, Nihilism, and Emancipation* (Durham, NC: Duke University Press, 2018).

57 See, e.g., Kay B. Warren, *Indigenous Movements and Their Critics: Pan-Maya Activism in Guatemala* (Princeton, NJ: Princeton University Press, 1998).

58 Benjamin Noys has offered a smart reading of recent trends in French philosophy as appeals to an antidialectical "affirmationism." Affect studies and multispecies anthropology have tended to partake in such an affirmative negation of negation. The pervasive influence of Gilles Deleuze's work today, and the disavowal of more-dialectical thinkers, such as Jacques Derrida, reads as symptomatic. The theoretical arc of this book tracks from a rather chaotic Deleuzian field of generative feeling and contingent connection toward a more sustained neocritical, Derrida-influenced reading of the common religiosity of Schele and Lévi-Strauss. On affirmationism, see Noys, *The Persistence of the Negative*. On contemporary multispecies anthropology's affirmationism, see Matthew C. Watson, "On Multispecies Mythology: A Critique of Animal Anthropology," *Theory, Culture, and Society* 33, no. 5 (2016). See also Gregor Moder's convincing effort to read Hegel and Spinoza as complementary, rather than antithetical, thinkers. Moder, *Hegel and Spinoza*. Moder's philosophical project resonates with my defense of Derridean and subalternist thought as necessary complements or correctives to the affirmationist tendencies of Bruno Latour's "cosmopolitical" efforts to unify science and politics. Matthew C. Watson, "Cosmopolitics and the Subaltern: Problematizing Latour's Idea of the Commons," *Theory, Culture, and Society* 28, no. 3 (2011); Matthew C. Watson, "Derrida, Stengers, Latour, and Subalternist Cosmopolitics," *Theory, Culture, and Society* 31, no. 1 (2014).

59 See, e.g., Quetzil Castañeda, "'We Are Not Indigenous!' The Maya Identity of Yucatan, an Introduction," *Journal of Latin American Anthropology* 9, no. 1 (2004); R. Tripp Evans, *Romancing the Maya: Mexican Antiquity in the American Imagination, 1820–1915* (Austin: University of Texas Press, 2004); Victor D. Montejo, "Becoming Maya? Appropriation of the White Shaman," *Native Americas* 16, no. 1 (1999); Watanabe, "Unimagining the Maya"; Nelson, *A Finger in the Wound*; Matthew Restall, "Maya Ethnogenesis," *Journal of Latin American Anthropology* 9, no. 1 (2004).

60 On the closed corporate community in unromanticized form, see Eric Wolf, "Closed Corporate Peasant Communities in Mesoamerica and Central Java," *Southwest Journal of Anthropology* 13, no. 1 (1957); cf. Evon Vogt, *Zinacantan: A Maya Community in the Highlands of Chiapas* (Cambridge, MA: Harvard University Press, 1969).

61 Andrew Weeks, Simon Martin, and Lori Conley, dirs., *Edgewalker: A Conversation with Linda Schele* (DVD, Austin: Home Life Productions, 1999).

62 Coe, *Maya Code*.

63 Coe, *Maya Code*, 201.

64 Weeks, Martin, and Conley, *Edgewalker*.

65 Coe, *Maya Code*, 202.

66 The case of Schele, here, has some resonance with that of Carlton Gajdusek, as developed in Anderson, *The Collectors of Lost Souls*.

67 Weeks, Martin, and Conley, *Edgewalker*.

68 Coe, *Maya Code*, 202.

69 See, e.g., Freidel, Schele, and Parker, *Maya Cosmos*; Schele and Miller, *Blood of Kings*; Linda Schele and David Freidel, *A Forest of Kings: The Untold Story of the Ancient Maya* (New York: William Morrow and Co., 1990); Linda Schele and Peter Mathews, *The Code of Kings: The Language of Seven Sacred Maya Temples and Tombs* (New York: Scribner, 1998).

70 Weeks, Martin, and Conley, *Edgewalker*; emphasis added.

71 J. Eric S. Thompson, *Maya Hieroglyphs without Tears* (London: British Museum, 1980).

72 Robertson, *Primera Mesa Redonda de Palenque*.

73 Coe, *Maya Code*, 203.

74 Lisa C. Breglia, *Monumental Ambivalence: The Politics of Heritage* (Austin: University of Texas Press, 2006); Lindsay Jones, "Conquests of the Imagination: Maya-Mexican Polarity and the Story of Chichén Itzá," *American Anthropologist* 99, no. 2 (1997).

75 Coe, *Maya Code*, 203.

76 Weeks, Martin, and Conley, *Edgewalker*.

77 Linda Schele, *Maya Glyphs*.

78 See Matthew C. Watson, "Assembling the Ancient" and "Staged Discovery."

79 Wendy Brown, *Edgework: Critical Essays on Knowledge and Politics* (Princeton, NJ: Princeton University Press, 2005).

80 *Oxford English Dictionary*, s.v. "trope," accessed September 26, 2018, https://oed.com/view/Entry/206679.

81 Georg Wilhelm Friedrich Hegel, *Phenomenology of Spirit* (1807), trans. A. V. Miller (Oxford: Clarendon, 1977), 208.

82 Lévi-Strauss, *Introduction to the Work of Marcel Mauss*.

83 Person-centered works of anthropology and history to which this book is indebted include Anderson, *The Collectors of Lost Souls*; João Biehl, *Vita: Life in a Zone of Social Abandonment* (Berkeley: University of California Press, 2005); Dipesh Chakrabarty, *The Calling of History: Sir Jadunath Sarkar and His Empire of Truth*

(Chicago: University of Chicago Press, 2015); Hélène Mialet, *Hawking Incorporated: Stephen Hawking and the Anthropology of the Knowing Subject* (Chicago: University of Chicago Press, 2012).

84 For an important recent walk along this edge, see Stuart McLean, *Fictionalizing Anthropology: Encounters and Fabulations at the Edges of the Human* (Minneapolis: University of Minnesota, 2017).

CHAPTER 1: SACRILEGE

1 Frank Freidel to David Freidel, January 20, 1989, Schele Papers.

2 The book manuscript in question became Schele and Freidel, *Forest of Kings.*

3 Deleuze and Guattari, *A Thousand Plateaus*, 19.

4 Deleuze and Guattari, *A Thousand Plateaus*, 19.

5 Deleuze and Guattari, *A Thousand Plateaus*, 25. "People without history" refers to anthropologist Eric Wolf's classic critique of the concept. Eric Wolf, *Europe and the People without History* (Berkeley: University of California Press, 1982).

6 See, e.g., Frank Freidel, *Franklin D. Roosevelt: A Rendezvous with Destiny* (Boston: Back Bay Books, 1990).

7 Elaine Markson to Linda Schele, June 19, 1989, Schele Papers.

8 Deleuze and Guattari, *A Thousand Plateaus*, 19.

9 Linda Schele, quoted in Andrew Robinson, "Symbolic Victory," *Times Higher Education*, March 17, 1995, http://www.timeshighereducation.co.uk/story.asp?storyCode=97205&sectioncode=26.

10 Michael Taussig, *The Corn Wolf* (Chicago: University of Chicago Press, 2015), 10–11.

11 John Berger, "Twelve Theses on the Economy of the Dead," in *Hold Everything Dear: Dispatches on Survival and Resistance* (1994; repr., New York: Pantheon, 2007).

12 *Oxford English Dictionary*, s.v. "eliminate," accessed June 9, 2012, https://oed.com/view/Entry/60472.

13 Berger, "Twelve Theses," 4.

14 Berger, "Twelve Theses," 4, 5, emphasis in original.

15 See, e.g., Daniel C. Dennett, *The Intentional Stance* (Cambridge, MA: MIT Press, 1987); Paul M. Churchland, "Reduction, Qualia, and the Direct Introspection of Brain States," *Journal of Philosophy* 82, no. 1 (1985).

16 Eugene Thacker, "Darklife: Negation, Nothingness, and the Will-to-Life in Schopenhauer," *Parrhesia: A Journal of Critical Philosophy* 12 (2011): 24.

17 Thacker, "Darklife," 24; Steven Shaviro, "Pansychism and/or Eliminativism," *Pinocchio Theory* (blog), October 4, 2011, http://www.shaviro.com/Blog/?p=1012.

18 Berger, "Twelve Theses," 5.

19 Latour, *We Have Never Been Modern.*

20 Berger, "Twelve Theses," 4.

21 Gillett Griffin to Linda Schele, November 20, 1984, Schele Papers.

22 Elizabeth P. Benson, "The Rabbit Woman," in *Heart of Creation: The Mesoamerican World and the Legacy of Linda Schele*, ed. Andrea Stone (Tuscaloosa: University of Alabama Press, 2002).

23 John Monaghan, "The Person, Destiny, and the Construction of Difference in Mesoamerica," *RES: Anthropology and Aesthetics* 33 (1998).

24 Monaghan, "The Person," 140.

25 Monaghan, "The Person," 140.

26 Monaghan, "The Person," 141.

27 Monaghan, "The Person," 141.

28 Deleuze and Guattari, *A Thousand Plateaus*, 171. On Deleuze and Guattari's critique of Levinas's ethics of the face, see Gavin Rae, "The Political Significance of the Face: Deleuze's Critique of Levinas," *Critical Horizons* 17, nos. 3–4 (2016).

29 Deleuze and Guattari, *A Thousand Plateaus*, 171. Cf. Eduardo Viveiros de Castro's conjugation of Deleuzian and structuralist thought in his engagement with Amazonian Amerindian constructions of the primal state of organismic life as humanity, as distinct from the naturalist evolutionary appeal to a prior animality. Eduardo Viveiros de Castro, *Cannibal Metaphysics: For a Post-structural Anthropology*, trans. Peter Skafish (Minneapolis: Univocal, 2014).

30 Deleuze and Guattari, *A Thousand Plateaus*, 176.

31 Deleuze and Guattari, *A Thousand Plateaus*, 176.

32 David Schele, "Linda Scholastica," in Stone, *Heart of Creation*, 287.

33 David Schele, "Linda Scholastica," 288.

34 Michael Coe, "Ideology of the Maya Tomb," in *Maya Iconography*, ed. Elizabeth P. Benson and Gillett G. Griffin (Princeton, NJ: Princeton University Press, 1988). See Susan D. Gillespie, "Body and Soul among the Maya: Keeping the Spirits in Place," in *The Space and Place of Death*, ed. Helaine Silverman and David B. Small, special issue, *Archeological Papers of the American Anthropological Association* 11, no. 1 (2002).

35 Patricia McAnany, *Living with the Ancestors: Kinship and Kingship in Ancient Maya Society* (Austin: University of Texas Press, 1995).

36 Gillespie, "Body and Soul."

37 J. Eric S. Thompson, *Ethnology of the Mayas of Southern and Central British Honduras*, Field Museum of Natural History Publication 274, Anthropological Series, vol. 17, no. 2 (Chicago: Field Museum of Natural History, 1930); Vogt, *Zinacantan*; Evon Z. Vogt, "Human Souls and Animal Spirits in Zinacantan," in *Échanges et communications: Mélanges offerts à Claude Lévi-Strauss à l'occasion de son 60ème anniversaire*, ed. Jean Pouillon and Pierre Maranda (The Hague: Mouton, 1970); Robert Redfield and Alfonso Villa Rojas, *Chan Kom: A Maya Village* (1934; repr., Chicago: University of Chicago Press, 1971).

38 Gillespie, "Body and Soul."

39 Gillespie, "Body and Soul," 72.

40 Robert S. Carlsen, *The War for the Heart and Soul of a Highland Maya Town* (Austin: University of Texas Press, 1997); Robert S. Carlsen and Martin Prechtel,

"The Flowering of the Dead: An Interpretation of Highland Maya Culture," *Man* 26, no. 1 (1991); Vogt, *Zinacantan*, 373. See also John M. Watanabe, "From Saints to Shibboleths: Image, Structure, and Identity in Maya Religious Syncretism," *American Ethnologist* 17, no. 1 (1990); Gillespie, "Body and Soul."

41 Gillespie, "Body and Soul," 73.

42 Gillespie, "Body and Soul," 73.

43 Berger, "Twelve Theses," 4.

44 Vogt, *Zinacantan*, 371–72.

45 Vogt, *Zinacantan*, 373.

46 Evon Z. Vogt and Catherine C. Vogt, "Lévi-Strauss among the Maya," *Man* 5, no. 3 (1970): 383–84.

47 Jared Diamond to Linda Schele, May 14, 1992, Schele Papers.

48 Jared Diamond, *The Third Chimpanzee: The Evolution and Future of the Human Animal* (New York: HarperCollins, 1992).

49 Jared Diamond, *Guns, Germs, and Steel: The Fates of Human Societies* (New York: W. W. Norton, 1997).

50 Evon Vogt to David Freidel, February 26, 1994, Schele Papers.

51 Freidel, Schele, and Parker, *Maya Cosmos*.

52 Schele and Miller, *Blood of Kings*.

53 Claude Lévi-Strauss to Linda Schele, November 4, 1986, Schele Papers.

54 Nikolai Grube, "Ancient Maya Royal Biographies in a Comparative Perspective," in *Janaab' Pakal of Palenque: Reconstructing the Life and Death of a Maya Ruler*, ed. Vera Tiesler and Andrea Cucina (Tucson: University of Arizona Press, 2006), 158.

55 Eusebio Dávalos and Arturo Romano, "Estudio preliminar de los restos osteológicos encontrados en la Tumba del Templo de las Inscripciones, Palenque (in Alberto Ruz Lhullier, 'Exploraciones en Palenque: 1952')," *Anales del Instituto Nacional de Antropología e Historia, México* 6, no. 1 (1955).

56 Alberto Ruz Lhuillier, "Gerontocracy at Palenque?," in *Social Process in Maya Prehistory: Studies in Honour of Sir Eric Thompson*, ed. Norman Hammond (London: Academic Press, 1977).

57 Mathews and Schele, "Lords of Palenque." For my reading of the age-at-death controversy, see Matthew C. Watson, "Listening in the Pakal Controversy."

58 Ruz Lhuillier, "Gerontocracy at Palenque?," 292–93.

59 Ruz Lhuillier, "Gerontocracy at Palenque?," 291.

60 Heinrich Berlin, *Signos y significados en las inscripciones mayas* (Guatemala City: Instituto Nacional del Patrimonio Cultural de Guatemala, 1977).

61 Joyce Marcus, *Emblem and State in the Classic Maya Lowlands: An Epigraphic Approach to Territorial Organization* (Washington, DC: Dumbarton Oaks Center for Pre-Columbian Studies, 1976).

62 Jane E. Buikstra, George R. Milner, and Jesper L. Boldsen, "Janaab' Pakal: The Age-at-Death Controversy Revisited," in Tiesler and Cucina, *Janaab' Pakal of Palenque*, 59.

63 Buikstra, Milner, and Boldsen, "Age-at-Death Controversy," 59.

64 Allen J. Christenson, "The Sacred Tree of the Ancient Maya," *Journal of Book of Mormon Studies* 6, no. 1 (1997): 14.

65 Sigmund Freud, *Beyond the Pleasure Principle* (New York: W. W. Norton, 1990), 76. Quoted in Michael Taussig, *What Color Is the Sacred?* (Chicago: University of Chicago Press, 2009), 201.

66 Alberto Ruz Lhuillier, *La tumba de Palenque* (Mexico City: Instituto Nacional de Antropología e Historia, 1974).

67 Friedrich Nietzsche, *The Gay Science, with a Prelude in German Rhymes and an Appendix of Songs*, trans. Josefine Nauckhoff and Adrian Del Caro (Cambridge: Cambridge University Press, 2001), 110. Quoted in Taussig, *What Color Is the Sacred?*, 201.

68 Coe, *Maya Code*, 202. On the "philosophy of the happy accident," see the introduction.

69 Char Solomon, *Tatiana Proskouriakoff: Interpreting the Ancient Maya* (Norman: University of Oklahoma Press, 2002).

70 See four works by Tatiana Proskouriakoff: "Historical Implications of a Pattern of Dates at Piedras Negras, Guatemala," *American Antiquity* 25, no. 4 (1960); "The Lords of the Maya Realm," *Expedition Magazine* 4, no. 1 (1961); "Historical Data in the Inscriptions of Yaxchilan (Part I)," *Estudios de Cultura Maya* 3 (1963); and "Historical Data in the Inscriptions of Yaxchilan (Part II)," *Estudios de Cultura Maya* 4 (1964).

71 Rosemary A. Joyce, introduction to Tatiana Proskouriakoff, *Maya History*, ed. Joyce (Austin: University of Texas Press, 1993).

72 Linda Schele and Jeffrey H. Miller, *The Mirror, the Rabbit, and the Bundle: "Accession" Expressions from the Classic Maya Inscriptions*, Studies in Pre-Columbian Art and Archaeology (Washington, DC: Dumbarton Oaks Research Library and Collection, 1983).

73 Linda Schele to "the Group," January 12, 1977, Schele Papers.

74 Tatiana Proskouriakoff to Linda Schele, January 28, 1977, Schele Papers.

75 Coe, *Maya Code*, 202.

76 Solomon, *Tatiana Proskouriakoff*, 28.

77 Linda Schele, in Weeks, Martin, and Conley, *Edgewalker*.

78 Linda Schele, in Weeks, Martin, and Conley, *Edgewalker*.

79 Martin, "Anthropology and the Cultural Study of Science"; Traweek, *Beamtimes and Lifetimes*; Karin Knorr Cetina, *Epistemic Cultures: How the Sciences Make Knowledge* (Cambridge, MA: Harvard University Press, 1999); Mialet, *Hawking Incorporated*.

80 Linda Schele, in Weeks, Martin, and Conley, *Edgewalker*.

81 On "spokespersons," see Latour, *Politics of Nature*.

82 Linda Schele, in Weeks, Martin, and Conley, *Edgewalker*. See also Schele and Mathews, *Code of Kings*, 13. On "art worlds," see Howard S. Becker, *Art Worlds* (Berkeley: University of California Press, 1982).

83 See, e.g., Cecelia Klein, "Mayamania: *The Blood of Kings* in Retrospect," *Art Journal* 47, no. 1 (1988).

84 Andrea J. Stone, introduction to Stone, *Heart of Creation*, 1.

85 Stone, introduction, 1–2.

86 Linda Schele and Peter Mathews to Tatiana Proskouriakoff and Heinrich Berlin, August 1977, Schele Papers.

87 Heinrich Berlin to Linda Schele and Peter Mathews, August 25, 1977, Schele Papers.

88 Stone, *Heart of Creation*.

89 Benson, "The Rabbit Woman," 268.

90 James Riding In, "Repatriation: A Pawnee's Perspective," *American Indian Quarterly* 20, no. 2 (1996): 238.

91 Riding In, "Repatriation," 240.

92 Susan D. Gillespie, "Personhood, Agency, and Mortuary Ritual: A Case Study from the Ancient Maya," *Journal of Anthropological Archaeology* 20, no. 1 (2001): 89. See Diane Z. Chase and Arlen F. Chase, "Maya Multiples: Individuals, Entries, and Tombs in Structure A34 of Caracol, Belize," *Latin American Antiquity* 7, no. 1 (1996). See also Miguel Angel Astor-Aguilera, *The Maya World of Communicating Objects: Quadripartite Crosses, Trees, and Stones* (Albuquerque: University of New Mexico Press, 2010).

93 Benson Saler, "Nagual, Witch and Sorcerer in a Quiché Village," *Ethnology* 3 (1964): 319.

94 On contagious magic, see Frazer, *The Golden Bough*.

95 Saler, "Nagual, Witch and Sorcerer," 319.

CHAPTER 2: ANIMALS

Part of this chapter was previously published as Matthew C. Watson, "The Animal Anthropology of Linda Schele's Spirits," *Cultural Critique* 88 (fall 2014): 125–59.

1 The work of Michel Foucault, Giorgio Agamben, and Roberto Esposito has profoundly shaped how contemporary scholars conceive life as an epistemic and political category. See Michel Foucault, *The Order of Things: An Archaeology of the Human Sciences* (New York: Vintage Books, 1970); Michel Foucault, *The History of Sexuality*, vol. 1, *An Introduction*, trans. Robert Hurley (New York: Vintage Books, 1978); Giorgio Agamben, *Homo Sacer: Sovereign Power and Bare Life*, trans. Daniel Heller-Roazen (Stanford, CA: Stanford University Press, 1998); Roberto Esposito, *Bíos: Biopolitics and Philosophy*, trans. Timothy Campbell (Minneapolis: University of Minnesota Press, 2008). For a careful examination of scholarship on life and an ethnographic account of scientists' attention to the limits of life, see Stefan Helmreich, "What Was Life? Answers from Three Limit Biologies," *Critical Inquiry* 37, no. 4 (2011). On "life itself," see Nikolas S. Rose, *The Politics of Life Itself: Biomedicine, Power, and Subjectivity in the Twenty-First Century* (Princeton, NJ: Princeton University Press, 2006).

2 R. G. Latham, *Man and His Migrations* (London: John Van Voorst, Paternoster Row, 1851), 4.

3 Latham, *Man and His Migrations*, 5.

4 Latham, *Man and His Migrations*.

5 Latham, *Man and His Migrations*, 6. The near quotation within the quotation "Who shows a Newton as he shows an ape" is unattributed in the original. Latham is paraphrasing a line from the second epistle of Alexander Pope, *An Essay on Man* (1734; repr., Indianapolis: Bobbs-Merrill, 1965), 18–19. The original stanza is "Superior beings, when of late they saw / A mortal man unfold all Nature's law; / Admired such wisdom in the earthly shape / And showed a Newton as we show an ape."

6 Clifford Geertz, "Thick Description: Toward an Interpretive Theory of Culture," in *The Interpretation of Cultures* (New York: Basic Books, 1973).

7 Geertz, "Thick Description," 5.

8 I acknowledge that Geertz doesn't say that man is a *spider* suspended in webs of significance. The metaphor's limited to the web. I fill in the gap and assume others do the same. It's hard to think that Geertz was imagining anything other than a spider's web. Then again, with the exception of a passing reference to the Navajo mythological figure Spider Woman, Geertz may have never discussed spiders at all. For mention of Spider Woman, see Clifford Geertz, *Islam Observed: Religious Developments in Morocco and Indonesia* (Chicago: University of Chicago Press, 1968), 3. On the dubious animality of Geertz's spider, see also Adrian Ivakhiv, "Toward a Multicultural Ecology," *Organization and Environment* 15, no. 4 (2002): 396.

9 Under laboratory conditions, Tim Ingold has tried to mate the Geertzian spider with its more-down-to-earth arthropod cousin, Bruno Latour's ANT (actor-network theory). See Tim Ingold, *Being Alive: Essays on Movement, Knowledge, and Description* (New York: Routledge, 2011), 89–94; Bruno Latour, *Reassembling the Social: An Introduction to Actor-Network-Theory* (Oxford: Oxford University Press, 2005). Respecting incest taboos more than we anthropologists do, philosopher Graham Harman's lab offers up another fruitful coupling: "When the centaur of classical metaphysics is mated with the cheetah of actor-network theory, their offspring is not some hellish monstrosity, but a thoroughbred colt able to carry us for half a century and more." Graham Harman, *Prince of Networks: Bruno Latour and Metaphysics* (Melbourne: re.press, 2009), 5.

10 See, e.g., Todd A. Blackledge et al., "Reconstructing Web Evolution and Spider Diversification in the Molecular Era," *Proceedings of the National Academy of the Sciences* 106, no. 3 (2009).

11 See, e.g., Suresh P. Benjamin and Samuel Zschokke, "Untangling the Tangle-Web: Web Construction Behavior of the Comb-Footed Spider *Steatoda triangulosa* and Comments on Phylogenetic Implications (Araneae: Theridiidae)," *Journal of Animal Behavior* 15, no. 6 (2002). The thoroughly tangled vocabulary of "rhizomes," "lines of flight," and "plateaus" comes from Deleuze and Guattari, *A Thousand Plateaus*; see also Gregory Bateson, *Steps to an Ecology of Mind: Collected Essays in Anthropology, Psychiatry, Evolution, and Epistemology* (Chicago: University of Chicago Press, 1972). For an important critique of this vocabulary, see Malini Johar Schuel-

ler, "Analogy and (White) Feminist Theory: Thinking Race and the Color of the Cyborg Body," *Signs: Journal of Women in Culture and Society* 31, no. 1 (2005): 79–80.

12 Richard B. Lee and Irven DeVore, eds., *Man the Hunter* (New York: Aldine, 1968). Cf. Hetty Jo Brumbach and Robert Jarvenpra, "Woman the Hunter: Ethnoarchaeological Lessons from Chipewyan Life-Cycle Dynamics," in *Women in Prehistory*, ed. Cheryl Classen and Rosemary A. Joyce (Philadelphia: University of Pennsylvania Press, 1997).

13 Bonnie Malkin, "Giant Spider Eating Bird Caught on Camera," *Telegraph*, October 22, 2008, http://www.telegraph.co.uk/earth/earthnews/3353693/Giant-spider-eating-a-bird-caught-on-camera.html; Bonnie Malkin, "Bird-Eating Spiders: New Pictures," *Telegraph*, October 30, 2008, http://www.telegraph.co.uk/earth/earthnews/3354097/Bird-eating-spiders-new-pictures.html.

14 Malkin, "Giant Spider."

15 Anthoula Lazaris et al., "Spider Silk Fibers Spun from Soluble Recombinant Silk Produced in Mammalian Cells," *Science* 295, no. 5554 (2002).

16 Lazaris et al., "Spider Silk Fibers," 472.

17 Steve Connor, "A Spider's Web That Could Catch an F-16," *Independent*, January 18, 2002, http://www.independent.co.uk/news/science/a-spiders-web-that-could-catch-an-f16-663700.html.

18 E. B. White, *Charlotte's Web* (New York: Harper, 1952).

19 On the various immunologies circulating through and around biopolitical worlds, see Esposito, *Bíos*; Timothy Campbell, "Bíos, Immunity, Life: The Thought of Roberto Esposito," in Esposito, *Bíos*; Rossella Bonito Oliva, "From the Immune Community to the Communitarian Immunity: On the Recent Reflections of Roberto Esposito," *Diacritics* 36, no. 2 (2006); Donna J. Haraway, "The Biopolitics of Postmodern Bodies: Determinations of Self in Immune System Discourse," *Differences* 1, no. 1 (1989); Jacques Derrida, "Faith and Knowledge: The Two Sources of Religion," in *On Religion*, ed. Jacques Derrida and Gianni Vattimo (Stanford, CA: Stanford University Press, 1998); A. David Napier, *The Age of Immunology: Conceiving a Future in an Alienating World* (Chicago: University of Chicago Press, 2003); Anne Allison and Charles Piot, "Special Issue Section: Immunology," *Cultural Anthropology* 27, no. 1 (2012).

20 Or perhaps we should resign ourselves to the inevitability, or even necessity, of entrapment in our own designs. In *An Anthropology of the Subject*, Roy Wagner finds himself caught in a speculative, even wild, commentary on the Hindu deity Indra. In Wagner's reading (if we can call it that), Indra casts a net that recursively constitutes reality (including Indra himself) as a holographic illusion. Of particular relevance here is Wagner's likening of Indra's self-constituting net to history as a process of convergence rather than temporal, sequential development. See *An Anthropology of the Subject* (Berkeley: University of California Press, 2001). In some ways, as I discuss below, Linda Schele came to converge with the ancient Maya; she invented them as they invented her.

21 Michael Silverstein, "Languages/Cultures Are Dead! Long Live the Linguistic/Cultural," in *Unwrapping the Sacred Bundle: Reflections on the Disciplining of Anthropology*, ed. Daniel A. Segal and Sylvia J. Yanagisako (Durham, NC: Duke University Press, 2005), 103.

22 Immanuel Kant, *Prolegomena to Any Future Metaphysics That Will Be Able to Present Itself as a Science* (1783), trans. and ed. Gary Hatfield (Cambridge: Cambridge University Press, 1997).

23 On "category mistakes," see Gilbert Ryle, *The Concept of Mind* (1949; repr., Chicago: University of Chicago Press, 2000). In many ways, Kim Fortun effectively outlines the possibility of a queered anthropological comparativism; see Fortun, "Ethnography in/of/as Open Systems." Cf. Matei Candea, *Comparison in Anthropology: The Impossible Method* (Cambridge: Cambridge University Press, 2018).

24 Linda Schele to Floyd Lounsbury, Peter Mathews, and David H. Kelley, October 14, 1978, Schele Papers.

25 Schele's drawing is a play on Georg Pencz's mid-sixteenth-century painting *The Hunter Caught by the Hares*. In 1983, five years after Schele circulated this letter and drawing, the painting was exhibited in UT-Austin's Archer M. Huntington Art Gallery. I'm grateful to Spencer Smith for calling my attention to this surprising historical detail.

26 Stephen D. Houston, "The Shifting Now: Aspect, Deixis, and Narrative in Classic Maya Texts," *American Anthropologist* 99, no. 2 (1997): 293.

27 Linda Schele, "Part 2: T757 as *Umul*, 'Rabbit,'" in Schele and Miller, *The Mirror, the Rabbit, and the Bundle*. Although it was not published until 1983, Schele and Miller authored this book in the mid-1970s.

28 Schele, "T757 as *Umul*," 59.

29 On the hieroglyph scholars' communing with the ancestors, cf. McAnany, *Living with the Ancestors*. On mine, cf. Latour, *Reassembling the Social*.

30 In saying that the interpretation "makes me its mouthpiece" and that it "has to show" this, I mean that it presents itself to my consciousness as if it were the most natural thing in the world. The interpretation naturalizes itself, making me its "spokesperson," to use a term from Latour. It is, in other words, the commonsensical interpretation, if not necessarily the best one or the right one. Saying that it's commonsensical is, of course, another way of saying that it's a reflection of the cosmologies that help to make me a thinking being. Here, and not without some reservations, I'm following Claude Lévi-Strauss, *Myth and Meaning: Cracking the Code of Culture* (1978; repr., New York: Schocken, 1995), 3. Lévi-Strauss tells us, "I have written that myths get thought in man unbeknownst to him. That has been much discussed and even criticized by my English-speaking colleagues, because their feeling is that, from an empirical point of view, it is an utterly meaningless sentence. But for me it describes a lived experience, because it says exactly how I perceive my own relationship to my work. That is, my work gets thought in me unbeknown to me." This is a wonderful idea, one of the best anthropological ideas, and it's no doubt very accurate despite the Anglophones' objections. But I do find myself diverging from Lévi-Strauss in

the degree to which I'm willing to cede truth to the ghostly prehensions that pop into my head. On "spokespersons," see, especially, Latour, *Politics of Nature*. On "prehensions," see Alfred North Whitehead, *Process and Reality* (1929; repr., New York: Free Press, 1978).

31 As the last comment in a seventeen-point list of facts presented to justify, thinly, how the Balinese cockfight is "fundamentally a dramatization of status concerns," Geertz writes, "Finally, the Balinese peasants themselves are quite aware of all this and can and, at least to an ethnographer, do state most of it in approximately the same terms I have." Clifford Geertz, "Deep Play: Notes on the Balinese Cockfight," *Daedalus* 101, no. 1 (1972): 20–21.

32 As W. J. T. Mitchell quips, "Pictures want equal rights with language, not to be turned into language." W. J. T. Mitchell, *What Do Pictures Want? The Lives and Loves of Images* (Chicago: University of Chicago Press, 2005), 47. For a plethora of other reasons to love drawings and how they draw us into other worlds, including the surreal worlds of our own pasts, see Michael Taussig, *I Swear I Saw This: Drawings in Fieldwork Notebooks, Namely My Own* (Chicago: University of Chicago Press, 2011).

33 Dennis Tedlock, ed., *Popol Vuh: The Mayan Book of the Dawn of Life* (New York: Simon and Schuster, 1985).

34 Andrea J. Stone, *Images from the Underworld: Naj Tunich and the Tradition of Maya Cave Painting* (Austin: University of Texas Press, 1995). On belief in the coessence (a.k.a. spirit companion, nagual, or *way*), see George Foster, "Nagualism in Mexico and Guatemala," *Acta Americana* 2, nos. 1–2 (1944); Alfonso Villa Rojas, "Kinship and Nagualism in a Tzeltal Community, Southeastern Mexico," *American Anthropologist* 49 (1947); Saler, "Nagual, Witch and Sorcerer"; Vogt, "Human Souls and Animal Spirits"; Gary H. Gossen, "Animal Souls and Human Destiny in Chamula," *Man* 10, no. 3 (1975); Gary H. Gossen, "Animal Souls, Co-essences, and Human Destiny in Mesoamerica," in *Monsters, Tricksters, and Sacred Cows: Animal Tales and American Identities*, ed. Albert James Arnold (Charlottesville: University of Virginia Press, 1996); Stephen Houston and David Stuart, "The *Way* Glyph: Evidence for 'Co-essences' among the Classic Maya," in *Research Reports on Ancient Maya Writing*, ed. George Stuart (Washington DC: Center for Maya Research, 1989); Michael Taussig, "The Disorganization of the 'Organization of Mimesis': The *Subcomandante* Unmasked," in *Defacement: Public Secrecy and the Labor of the Negative* (Stanford, CA: Stanford University Press, 1999). On Maya and Mesoamerican souls more generally, see, for example, Susan D. Gillespie and Rosemary A. Joyce, "Deity Relationships in Mesoamerican Cosmologies: The Case of the Maya God L," *Ancient Mesoamerica* 9, no. 2 (1998); Gillespie, "Body and Soul"; Elsie Clews Parsons, *Mitla: Town of Souls* (Chicago: University of Chicago Press, 1936); John M. Watanabe, *Maya Saints and Souls in a Changing World* (Austin: University of Texas Press, 1992).

35 Barbara Kerr and Justin Kerr, "The *Way* of God L: The Princeton Vase Revisited," *Record of the Art Museum, Princeton University* 64 (2005); Carolyn E. Tate, "Writing

on the Face of the Moon: Women's Products, Archetypes, and Power in Ancient Maya Civilization," in *Manifesting Power: Gender and the Interpretation of Power in Archaeology*, ed. Tracy L. Sweely (London: Routledge).

36 Edward Said, *Orientalism* (New York: Vintage Books, 1978); Philip J. Deloria, *Playing Indian* (New Haven, CT: Yale University Press, 1998).

37 In *In the Museum of Maya Culture*, Quetzil Castañeda questions the imperialist underpinnings of Mayanist archaeologists' and epigraphers' interpretive narratives. Castañeda describes his early longing for an alternative in these terms: "I wanted an unfiltered, pure voice, yet I sensed that the speech of the carved stones, glyphs, and living Maya was the result, and could only be the result, of various forms of ventriloquism." Castañeda, *In the Museum of Maya Culture*, 20. In stark contrast, my ethnographic immersion into the world of Schele's documents has come to suggest that her hieroglyphic readings were practices of sincere, loving attachment, far from ventriloquist acts steeped in ideological projection and cultural appropriation. So here I'm working to develop a (cautiously) postcritical stance that foregrounds Schele's affective experiences of reimagining the ancient Maya world, becoming vulnerable to intractable and powerful institutions governing Maya studies, and feeling recursively transformed by it in the process.

38 Geertz, "Deep Play," 26.

39 On this point, see Stone, *Images from the Underworld*; Barbara MacLeod and Dennis E. Puleston, "Pathways into Darkness: The Search for the Road to Xibalbá," in *Tercera Mesa Redonda de Palenque*, vol. 4, ed. Merle Greene Robertson and Donnan Call Jeffers (Monterey, CA: Pre-Columbian Art Research, 1979); Karen Bassie-Sweet, *From the Mouth of the Dark Cave: Commemorative Sculpture of the Late Classic Maya* (Norman: University of Oklahoma Press, 1991); Karen Bassie-Sweet, *At the Edge of the World: Caves and Late Classic Maya World View* (Norman: University of Oklahoma Press, 1996); Evon Z. Vogt and David Stuart, "Some Notes on Ritual Caves among the Ancient and Modern Maya," in *In the Maw of the Earth Monster: Mesoamerican Ritual Cave Use*, ed. James E. Brady and Keith M. Prufer (Austin: University of Texas Press, 2005).

40 Schele and Freidel, *Forest of Kings*.

41 I'm working here to respect and respond to Schele's extraordinary affective attachment to the world of the ancient Maya as it was rendered present through mediated inscriptions. Part of this attachment emerged through her intimate acts of drawing ancient Maya glyphs. In this sense, Schele's work resembles that of the insect-drawing artist, scientist, and antinuclear activist Cornelia Hesse-Honneger; see Hugh Raffles, *Insectopedia* (New York: Pantheon, 2010), 15–40. Furthermore, as Hesse-Honneger used her art to make scientific and political claims, by the late 1980s Schele lent her epigraphic talents to activists and community leaders involved in Maya cultural activism; see Matthew C. Watson, "Assembling the Ancient."

42 Kerr and Kerr, "The *Way* of God L," 73.

43 On mimesis, see Eric Auerbach, *Mimesis: The Representation of Reality in Western Literature* (Princeton, NJ: Princeton University Press, 1953); Michael Taussig,

Mimesis and Alterity: A Particular History of the Senses (New York: Routledge, 1993); Homi Bhabha, "Of Mimicry and Man: The Ambivalence of Colonial Discourse," *October* no. 28 (1984). Cf. Geertz's section "Of Cocks and Men" in "Deep Play," 5–7. Poor, parasitic mice, always subject to substitution. Mythic and no doubt mimetic accounts of rats and ants and hosting the gods proliferate wildly in Michel Serres, *The Parasite* (1980), trans. Lawrence R. Schehr (Minneapolis: University of Minnesota Press, 2007).

44 Émile Durkheim, *The Elementary Forms of Religious Life* (1912), trans. Carol Cosman (Oxford: Oxford University Press, 2001).

45 On rites of transformation, see Arnold van Gennep, *The Rites of Passage* (1909; repr., London: Routledge, 2010).

46 Tom Gidwitz, "Picture Perfect," *Archaeology* 56, no. 6 (2003): 48.

47 David Lebrun, "Transcript of Filmed Interview: Gillett Griffin," Night Fire Films, interview from March 24, 2005, accessed November 7, 2019, http://www .nightfirefilms.org/breakingthemayacode/interviews/GriffinTRANSCRIPT.pdf.

48 Anna Lowenhaupt Tsing, *The Mushroom at the End of the World: On the Possibility of Life in Capitalist Ruins* (Princeton, NJ: Princeton University Press, 2015); Matei Candea, "'I Fell in Love with Carlos the Meerkat': Engagement and Detachment in Human-Animal Relations," *American Ethnologist* 37, no. 2 (2010); Jake Kosek, "Ecologies of Empire: On the New Uses of the Honeybee," *Cultural Anthropology* 25, no. 4 (2010); Raffles, *Insectopedia*; Debbora Battaglia, "Aeroponic Gardens and Their Magic: Plants/Persons/Ethics in Suspension," *History and Anthropology* 28, no. 3 (2017); Heather Paxson, "Post-Pasteurian Cultures: The Microbiopolitics of Raw-Milk Cheese in the United States," *Cultural Anthropology* 23, no. 1 (2008). In this spirit, though they model diverse epistemological and ethical approaches to animality, see also, e.g., Timothy K. Choy et al., "A New Form of Collaboration in Cultural Anthropology: Matsutake Worlds," *American Ethnologist* 36, no. 2 (2009); Sarah Franklin, *Dolly Mixtures: The Remaking of Genealogy* (Durham, NC: Duke University Press, 2007); Donna J. Haraway, *When Species Meet* (Minneapolis: University of Minnesota Press, 2008); John Hartigan, *Aesop's Anthropology: A Multispecies Approach* (Minneapolis: University of Minnesota Press, 2014); Eleana Kim, "Invasive Others and Significant Others: Strange Kinship and Interspecies Ethics near the Korean Demilitarized Zone," *Social Research: An International Quarterly* 84, no. 1 (2017); Eben Kirksey, ed., *The Multispecies Salon* (Durham, NC: Duke University Press, 2014); Eduardo Kohn, *How Forests Think: Toward an Anthropology beyond the Human* (Berkeley: University of California Press, 2013); Julie Livingston and Jasbir K. Puar, eds., "Interspecies," special issue, *Social Text* 29, no. 1 (2011); Deborah Rose, "Introduction: Writing in the Anthropocene," *Australian Humanities Review* 47 (2009); Heather Anne Swanson, "Methods for Multispecies Anthropology: Thinking with Salmon Otoliths and Scales," *Social Analysis* 61, no. 2 (2017); Thom van Dooren, Eben Kirksey, and Ursula Münster, "Multispecies Studies: Cultivating Arts of Attentiveness," *Environmental Humanities* 8, no. 1 (2016). For critiques of multispecies ethnography see, e.g., Helen Kopnina,

"Beyond Multispecies Ethnography: Engaging with Violence and Animal Rights in Anthropology," *Critique of Anthropology* 37, no. 3 (2017); Alan Smart, "Critical Perspectives on Multispecies Ethnography," *Critique of Anthropology* 34, no. 1 (2014); Matthew C. Watson, "On Multispecies Mythology."

49 Agustín Fuentes, "Naturalcultural Encounters in Bali: Monkeys, Temples, Tourists, and Ethnoprimatology," *Cultural Anthropology* 25, no. 4 (2010).

50 Eben Kirksey and Stefan Helmreich, "The Emergence of Multispecies Ethnography," *Cultural Anthropology* 25, no. 4 (2010).

51 Haraway, "A Cyborg Manifesto," 81.

52 Serres, *The Parasite*.

53 Deleuze and Guattari, *A Thousand Plateaus*; Lynn Margulis and René Fester, eds., *Symbiosis as a Source of Evolutionary Innovation* (Cambridge, MA: MIT Press, 1991).

54 Haraway, *When Species Meet*, 3–4.

55 Kirksey and Helmreich, "The Emergence of Multispecies Ethnography," 566.

56 James Clifford attributes the phrase "deep hanging out" to Renato Rosaldo. James Clifford, *Routes: Travel and Translation in the Late Twentieth Century* (Cambridge, MA: Harvard University Press, 1997), 56.

57 Matei Candea, "Arbitrary Locations: In Defence of the Bounded Field-Site," *Journal of the Royal Anthropological Institute* 13, no. 1 (2007).

58 In *Alien Ocean*, Helmreich seems to part the Red Sea that divides Geertzian interpretivism from Harawayan multispecificity. Stefan Helmreich, *Alien Ocean: Anthropological Voyages in Microbial Seas* (Berkeley: University of California Press, 2009).

59 See, e.g., D. W. Steadman et al., "The Effects of Chemical and Heat Maceration Techniques on the Recovery of Nuclear and Mitochondrial DNA from Bone," *Journal of Forensic Sciences* 51, no. 1 (2006).

60 Contemporary scholars from a wide range of areas are seeking to conceive more ambitious expressions of empathy and more democratic constitutions of and for ontological politics. See, for example, Latour, *Politics of Nature*; Harman, *Prince of Networks*; Levi R. Bryant, *The Democracy of Objects* (Ann Arbor: Open Humanities Press, 2011); Timothy Morton, *The Ecological Thought* (Cambridge, MA: Harvard University Press, 2010); Jane Bennett, *Vibrant Matter: A Political Ecology of Things* (Durham, NC: Duke University Press, 2010); Maria Puig de la Bellacasa, "Matters of Care in Technoscience: Assembling Neglected Things," *Social Studies of Science* 41, no. 1 (2011). Efforts to develop a nonhumanist anthropology that doesn't succumb to biocentrism may also benefit by engagement with archaeologists' and material culture studies scholars' work on stones and landscapes; Christopher Tilley, *The Materiality of Stone: Explorations in Landscape Phenomenology* (New York: Berg, 2004); Tim Ingold, "Toward an Ecology of Materials," *Annual Review of Anthropology* 41 (2012). Finally, as I've argued elsewhere, the nonhumanist historiography formulated by Dipesh Chakrabarty in *Provincializing Europe* opens historical explanation to the agency of spirits in ways that are commensurable with the open ontological politics formulated by Latour and other science studies

scholars. Chakrabarty, *Provincializing Europe*; Matthew C. Watson, "Cosmopolitics and the Subaltern."

61 Dorion Sagan, *Notes from the Holocene* (White River Junction, VT: Chelsea Green, 2007), 21.

62 Helmreich, "What Was Life?," 676. See also Stefan Helmreich and Sophia Roosth, "Life Forms: A Keyword Entry," *Representations* 112, no. 1 (2010).

63 Ludwig Wittgenstein, *Philosophical Investigations* (Oxford: Blackwell, 1967).

64 Geertz, "Thick Description."

65 Helmreich, *Alien Ocean*.

66 Cf. Judith Farquhar, *Appetites: Food and Sex in Post-socialist China* (Durham, NC: Duke University Press, 2002).

67 Schele and Freidel, *Forest of Kings*; Freidel, Schele, and Parker, *Maya Cosmos*.

68 Freidel, Schele, and Parker, *Maya Cosmos*, 60.

69 Freidel, Schele, and Parker, *Maya Cosmos*, 75.

70 Freidel, Schele, and Parker, *Maya Cosmos*, 120.

71 Freidel, Schele, and Parker, *Maya Cosmos*, 120.

72 Freidel, Schele, and Parker, *Maya Cosmos*, 121.

73 Cf. Lorraine Daston and Katharine Park, *Wonders and the Order of Nature, 1150–1750* (New York: Zone Books, 1998).

74 Coe, *Breaking the Maya Code*, 202.

75 The Greek root of "semiotics" signified the medical interpretation of physical, bodily symptoms or signs. *Oxford English Dictionary*, s.v. "semiotics," accessed January 31, 2012, https://oed.com/view/Entry/175724.

76 William Shakespeare, *Hamlet, Prince of Denmark* (Cambridge: Cambridge University Press, 1999), 1.5.166–67.

77 I don't maintain that Schele's quasi-essentialism was politically innocent or should be exempted from critical scrutiny. But, as David Schele's response suggests, the argument for a strong form of Maya cultural continuity resembles strategic essentialism. In fact, at the time that Freidel, Schele, and Parker wrote *Maya Cosmos*, Schele was contributing to pan-Maya nationalism through epigraphy workshops in Guatemala and Yucatán. Thus, her quasi-essentialism (and problematic acceptance of colonial language ideologies) differed from—say—the racism of Erich von Däniken because it contributed new modes of historical consciousness to Mayan-language speakers themselves, rather than denying their ancestors' achievements (among other reasons).

78 Weeks, Martin, and Conley, *Edgewalker*.

79 Haraway, *When Species Meet*, 17.

80 "Alien anthropology" is an insistence that anthropology become open and critically hospitable to any and all beings, especially those that upset and unsettle our assumptions about how the world works. The anthropology of aliens and outer space has become one formative site for reforming contemporary constructions of alterity. Alien anthropology, though, remains an insistence that the alien comes in all forms, including the uncannily familiar. Cf. Debbora Battaglia, ed., *E.T. Culture:*

Anthropology in Outerspaces (Durham, NC: Duke University Press, 2005); Helmreich, *Alien Ocean*; Susan Lepselter, *The Resonance of Unseen Things: Poetics, Power, Captivity and UFOs in the American Uncanny* (Ann Arbor: University of Michigan Press, 2016).

81 Schele, "T757 as *Umul*," 59; cf. Latour, *Reassembling the Social*.

82 S.v. "animal" and "anima," *Oxford English Dictionary*, 2nd ed., accessed January 31, 2012, https://oed.com/view/Entry/273779 and https://oed.com/view/Entry/7734. See also Ivakhiv, "Toward a Multicultural Ecology," 396.

83 On cells as monads that comprise the body, as a society, see Gabriel Tarde, *Monadology and Sociology* (1895), trans. Theo Lorenc (Melbourne: re.press, 2012). On monads, see Gottfried Leibniz, *The Monadology* (1714), trans. George MacDonald Ross (Oxford: Oxford University Press, 1984). Leibniz sought to overcome René Descartes's mind/body dualism with his theory of the monad as a singular cosmic building block. So, I acknowledge that, like secular Cartesians themselves, this sentence is philosophically challenged.

84 Stephen Houston, David Stuart, and Karl Taube, *The Memory of Bones: Body, Being, and Experience among the Classic Maya* (Austin: University of Texas Press, 2006), 147.

85 Weeks, Martin, and Conley, *Edgewalker*.

86 Jacques Derrida, "Plato's Pharmacy," in *Dissemination* (Chicago: University of Chicago Press, 1981); Isabelle Stengers, "Culturing the *Pharmakon*?," in *Cosmopolitics I*.

87 Jacques Derrida, *Specters of Marx: The State of the Debt, the Work of Mourning and the New International*, trans. Peggy Kamuf (New York: Routledge, 1994), 11.

88 Linda Schele, in Weeks, Martin, and Conley, *Edgewalker*.

89 Kirby Dick and Amy Ziering Kofman, dirs., *Derrida* (DVD, Los Angeles: Jane Doe Films, 2002).

90 On Derrida's inattentiveness to real animals and their scientist companions in his exploration of animality and what it meant to meet the gaze of his cat while naked one morning, see Haraway, *When Species Meet*, 20–23.

91 Michael D. Coe, "Linda Schele (1942–1998)," *American Anthropologist* 102, no. 1 (2000); Stone, *Heart of Creation*.

92 Linda Schele, in Weeks, Martin, and Conley, *Edgewalker*.

93 Shakespeare, *Hamlet*, 1.5.183–91.

94 My sense of "strange stranger" here differs from that found in Morton, *The Ecological Thought*. But there are probably some affinities that are worth digging up.

CHAPTER 3: COSMOS

1 *Oxford English Dictionary*, s.v. "plenary," accessed May 25, 2012, https://oed.com /view/Entry/145668.

2 On the planetary, or planetarity, see, e.g., Gayatri Chakravorty Spivak, *Death of a Discipline* (New York: Columbia University Press, 2003); Paul Gilroy, "Planetarity and Cosmopolitics," *British Journal of Sociology* 61, no. 3 (2010).

3 Ruth Benedict's classic portrayal of the Kwakwaka'wakw (or "Kwakiutl") Potlatch as a mode of "Dionysian" competitive gifting exemplifies anthropology's interwar tendency to characterize cultures as value systems differentially configured to promote particular personality types. Her understanding of Kwakwaka'wakw culture was based, almost exclusively, on the teaching and writing of Franz Boas, who worked closely with an indigenous collaborator, George Hunt. See, e.g., Franz Boas, *The Social Organization and Secret Societies of the Kwakiutl Indians* (Washington, DC: Smithsonian Institution, 1897); Ruth Benedict, *Patterns of Culture* (New York: Houghton Mifflin, 1934).

4 Joseph Masco, "'It Is a Strict Law That Bids Us Dance': Cosmologies, Colonialism, Death, and Ritual," *Comparative Studies in Society and History* 37, no. 1 (1995): 43.

5 Masco, "'It Is a Strict Law,'" 49.

6 As a trend in anthropological theory that sought to surpass psychology's and sociology's respective individualizing and collectivizing epistemologies, personality studies, including Ruth Benedict's, exercised a traceable impact on constructions of Maya culture—ancient and modern. See, e.g., Anthony F. C. Wallace, "A Possible Technique for Recognizing Psychological Characteristics of the Ancient Maya from an Analysis of their Art," *American Imago* 7, no. 3 (1950). The construction of Maya cultures as systems affirming particular personality structures has persisted into the present in the works of cosmology- and personhood-oriented anthropologists including John Monaghan, Gary Gossen, Barbara Tedlock, and Dennis Tedlock. See, e.g., Monaghan, "The Person"; Gary H. Gossen, "From Olmecs to Zapatistas: A Once and Future History of Souls," *American Anthropologist* 96, no. 3 (1994); Barbara Tedlock, *Time and the Highland Maya* (Albuquerque: University of New Mexico Press, 1992); Dennis Tedlock, *2000 Years of Mayan Literature* (Berkeley: University of California Press, 2010).

7 Masco, "'It Is a Strict Law.'"

8 I recognize that "soul" here functions as a "floating signifier," traversing disparate cultural logics of self, personhood, interiority, and corporeality. I don't assume that Kwakwaka'wakw, Maya, or "Western" constructions of the "soul" necessary overlap in semantic value or pragmatic function. Nonetheless, anthropology's coherency is predicated on such provisional translations. Translation—linguistic and cultural—remains a method for resisting modernist purifying practices; it is a noninnocent method. The ostensible nontranslatability of certain anthropological key terms becomes integral to my construction of anthropology as a quasi-theological discourse beginning, substantively, in chapter 5. On the "floating signifier," see Lévi-Strauss, *Introduction to the Work of Marcel Mauss.*

9 Strathern, *Partial Connections.*

10 Cf. Anna Tsing, *Friction: An Ethnography of Global Connection* (Princeton, NJ: Princeton University Press, 2005).

11 On science as never pure, see, e.g., Latour, *We Have Never Been Modern*; Steven Shapin, *Never Pure: Historical Studies of Science as If It Was Produced by People with*

Bodies, Situated in Time, Space, Culture, and Society, and Struggling for Credibility and Authority (Baltimore: Johns Hopkins University Press, 2010). Critical studies of secularism, today, are wide-ranging and disunified. One predominant thread has explored how European liberal secularism is predicated on and reproduces Protestant frames and assumptions. See, e.g., Talal Asad, *Formations of the Secular: Christianity, Islam, Modernity* (Stanford, CA: Stanford University Press, 2003); Talal Asad et al., *Is Critique Secular? Blasphemy, Injury and Free Speech* (New York: Fordham University Press, 2013); Abou Farman, "Speculative Matter: Secular Bodies, Minds, and Persons," *Cultural Anthropology* 28, no. 4 (2013); Saba Mahmood, *Religious Difference in a Secular Age: A Minority Report* (Princeton, NJ: Princeton University Press, 2016); Charles Taylor, *A Secular Age* (Cambridge, MA: Harvard University Press, 2007).

12 The respective valorizations of nothingness/nonbeing—nihilism—and fullness/being—plenarism—are theologically opposed. Donald Wayne Viney, *Charles Hartshorne and the Existence of God* (Albany: State University of New York Press, 1985), 148n30. On plenarism (in Merleau-Ponty), see Edward Casey, "Edges of Time, Edges of Memory," in *Time, Memory, Institution: Merleau-Ponty's New Ontology of Self*, ed. David Morris and Kym Maclaren (Athens: Ohio University Press, 2015).

13 On scientific witnessing and listening, see Steven Shapin and Simon Schaffer, *Leviathan and the Air-Pump: Hobbes, Boyle and the Experimental Life* (Princeton, NJ: Princeton University Press, 1985); Haraway, *Modest_Witness@Second_Millennium*; Matthew C. Watson, "Listening in the Pakal Controversy."

14 Louis Althusser's theory of interpellation has been discussed and debated extensively. The classic source is Louis Althusser, "Ideology and Ideological State Apparatuses (Notes towards an Investigation)," in *Lenin and Philosophy and Other Essays* (London: New Left Books, 1971).

15 Durkheim, *Elementary Forms of Religious Life*; Mauss, *The Gift*.

16 Janet Roitman, *Anti-Crisis* (Durham, NC: Duke University Press, 2014), 7.

17 Roitman, *Anti-Crisis*, 9.

18 On the anthropological "otherwise," see Elizabeth A. Povinelli, "Routes/Worlds," *e-flux* 27 (2011), https://www.e-flux.com/journal/27/67991/routes-worlds/; Elizabeth A. Povinelli, "Geontologies of Otherwise," Theorizing the Contemporary, *Cultural Anthropology* website, January 13, 2014, http://www.culanth.org/fieldsights/465-geontologies-of-the-otherwise.

19 On multispecies muddles, see Haraway, *When Species Meet*.

20 Foucault's critique of the construction of "population" is foundational here. Michel Foucault, *Security, Territory, Population: Lectures at the Collège de France, 1977–1978*, trans. Graham Burchell (New York: Palgrave Macmillan, 2007); Michel Foucault, "Governmentality," in *The Foucault Effect: Studies in Governmentality*, ed. Graham Burchell, Colin Gordon, and Peter Miller (Chicago: University of Chicago Press, 1991).

21 See Sedgwick, *Touching Feeling*.

22 Carl Sagan, *Broca's Brain: Reflections on the Romance of Science* (New York: Random House, 1974).

23 Sagan, *Broca's Brain*, 293.

24 Carl Sagan, *The Varieties of Scientific Experience: A Personal View of the Search for God*, ed. Ann Druyan (New York: Penguin, 2006), 47. On Kant's nebular knowledge see, e.g., Stephen Palmquist, "Kant's Cosmogony Re-evaluated," *Studies in History and Philosophy of Science* 18, no. 3 (1987).

25 William James, *The Varieties of Religious Experience: A Study in Human Nature* (New York: Longmans Green, 1936).

26 Sagan, *The Varieties of Scientific Experience*.

27 Ann Druyan, "Editor's Introduction," in Sagan, *The Varieties of Scientific Experience*, xv; Carl Sagan, *Pale Blue Dot: A Vision of the Human Future in Space* (New York: Ballantine Books, 1994).

28 Delia Goetz and Sylvanus Griswold Morley, eds., *Popol Vuh: The Sacred Book of the Ancient Quiché Maya* (Norman: University of Oklahoma Press, 1950), 167–69. Quoted in Carl Sagan, *Cosmos* (New York: Random House, 1980), 3. Sagan (or an editor) appears to have modified the passage slightly, substituting loose English translations of the K'iche' names retained in the Spanish and English (Goetz and Morley) editions. In the English edition cited by Sagan, the first sentence actually reads, "These are the names of the first men who were created and formed: the first man was Balam-Quitzé, the second, Balam-Acab, the third, Mahucutah, and the fourth was Iqui-Balam." Goetz and Morley, *Popol Vuh*, 167.

29 Dorion Sagan, "Truth of My Father," in *Dazzle Gradually: Reflections on the Nature of Nature*, ed. Lynn Margulis and Dorion Sagan (White River Junction, VT: Chelsea Green, 2007).

30 Miriam Sagan, *Map of the Lost* (Albuquerque: University of New Mexico Press, 2008); Miriam Sagan, "Model Solar System," *Miriam's Well: Poetry, Land Art, and Beyond* (blog), July 17, 2014, https://miriamswell.wordpress.com/2014/07/30/model-solar-system/.

31 Miriam Sagan, *Map of the Lost*, 3.

32 Marilyn Strathern, *Kinship, Law and the Unexpected: Relatives Are Always a Surprise* (Cambridge: Cambridge University Press, 2005).

33 On the dialectical image, see Benjamin, *The Arcades Project*.

34 Wilfrid Sellars, *Science, Perception, and Reality* (London: Routledge, 1963); Ray Brassier, *Nihil Unbound: Enlightenment and Extinction* (New York: Palgrave Macmillan, 2007).

35 On the Americas as Turtle Island see, e.g., Leanne Simpson, *Dancing on Our Turtle's Back: Stories of Nishnaabeg Re-creation, Resurgence and a New Emergence* (Chico, CA: AK Press, 2011); Hilary N. Weaver, ed., *Social Issues in Contemporary Native America: Reflections from Turtle Island* (New York: Routledge, 2014).

36 Stephen W. Hawking, *A Brief History of Time: From the Big Bang to Black Holes* (New York: Bantam, 1988), 1; Geertz, "Thick Description," 28–29. On "contact

zones," see Mary Louise Pratt, *Imperial Eyes: Studies in Travel Writing and Trans-culturation* (New York: Routledge, 1992); Haraway, *When Species Meet*.

37 "Meaning," as Debbora Battaglia—channeling Mikhail Bakhtin and reception theory—frequently reminds me, "is made at the point of reception." On sound waves vis-à-vis the cultural experience of hearing, see, e.g., Stefan Helmreich, *Sounding the Limits of Life: Essays in the Anthropology of Biology and Beyond* (Princeton, NJ: Princeton University Press, 2016); Jennifer C. Hsieh, "Noise Governance and the Hearing Subject in Urban Taiwan" (PhD diss., Stanford University, 2017).

38 On language ideology, see, e.g., Michael Silverstein, "Language Structure and Linguistic Ideology," in *The Elements: A Parasession on Linguistic Units and Levels*, ed. P. R. Clyne, W. F. Hanks, and C. L. Hofbauer (Chicago: Chicago Linguistic Society, 1979); Michael Silverstein, "The Uses and Utility of Ideology: Some Reflections," *Pragmatics* 2, no. 3 (1992); Kathryn A. Woolard, "Language Ideology: Issues and Approaches," *Pragmatics* 2, no. 3 (1992); Judith T. Irvine and Susan Gal, "Language Ideology and Linguistic Differentiation," in *Regimes of Language: Ideologies, Politics, and Identities*, ed. P. V. Kroskrity (Santa Fe, NM: School for Advanced Research Press, 2000). The conceit or fantasy of rationality as the definitive condition of collective, public life emerges most forcefully in the work of Jürgen Habermas. Jürgen Habermas, *The Structural Transformation of the Public Sphere: An Inquiry into a Category of Bourgeois Society* (1962), trans. Thomas Burger (Cambridge, MA: MIT Press, 1989). Cf. Foucault's critique of the conceit of intersubjective, discursive neutrality and rationality. Michael Kelly, ed., *Critique and Power: Recasting the Foucault/Habermas Debate* (Cambridge, MA: MIT Press, 1994).

39 On gathering and assembly, see Martin Heidegger, *The Question Concerning Technology and Other Essays*, trans. William Lovitt (New York: Harper and Row, 1977); Bruno Latour, "From Realpolitik to Dingpolitik or How to Make Things Public," in Latour and Weibel, *Making Things Public*.

40 Cf. Michelle Z. Rosaldo, "The Things We Do with Words: Ilongot Speech Acts and Speech Act Theory in Philosophy," *Language in Society* 11 (1982).

41 Among the most falsifiable claims of such scientific rubbish is the philosophical premise of falsificationism itself. Karl Popper, *The Logic of Scientific Discovery* (1934; repr., New York: Routledge, 1959).

42 Cf. Kelly, *Critique and Power*.

43 Benjamin, *The Arcades Project*.

44 The floating signifier sources to Lévi-Strauss, *Introduction to the Work of Marcel Mauss*.

45 On fractality and anthropology, see Roy Wagner, "The Fractal Person," in *Big Men and Great Men: The Personifications of Power*, ed. Maurice Godelier and Marilyn Strathern (Cambridge: Cambridge University Press, 1991); Strathern, *Partial Connections*.

46 Hans-Jörg Rheinberger, *Toward a History of Epistemic Things: Synthesizing Proteins in the Test Tube* (Stanford, CA: Stanford University Press, 1997); Fortun, "Ethnography in/of/as Open Systems."

47 Bruno Latour, *Pandora's Hope: Essays on the Reality of Science Studies* (Cambridge, MA: Harvard University Press, 1999).

48 Derrida, "Hostipitality."

49 Debbora Battaglia and Rafael Antunes Almeida, "'Otherwise Anthropology' Otherwise: The View from Technology," Dispatches, *Cultural Anthropology* website, February 24, 2014, https://culanth.org/fieldsights/493-otherwise-anthropology-otherwise-the-view-from-technology.

50 Chen, "'Speaking Nearby.'"

51 Sara Ahmed, *Queer Phenomenology: Orientations, Objects, Others* (Durham, NC: Duke University Press, 2006).

52 On the trickster as both mythological and critical figure, see Paul Radin, *The Trickster: A Study in American Indian Mythology* (1956; repr., New York: Schocken, 1972); Donna J. Haraway, "Situated Knowledges: The Science Question in Feminism and the Privilege of Partial Perspective," *Feminist Studies* 14, no. 3 (1988); Donna J. Haraway, "Ecce Homo, Ain't (Ar'n't) I a Woman, and Inappropriate/d Others: The Human in a Post-humanist Landscape," in *Feminists Theorize the Political*, ed. Judith Butler and Joan W. Scott (New York: Routledge, 1992); David Turnbull, *Masons, Tricksters and Cartographers: Comparative Studies in the Sociology of Scientific and Indigenous Knowledge* (Amsterdam: Harwood Academic, 2000).

53 Derrida, "Hostipitality."

54 Haraway, "A Cyborg Manifesto," 153.

55 The idea of the "body without organs," in critical theory, traces to Deleuze and Guattari's critique of Artaud. Antonin Artaud, *To Have Done with the Judgment of God* (1947; repr., Santa Rosa, CA: Black Sparrow, 1975); Gilles Deleuze, *The Logic of Sense* (1969), trans. Mark Lester and Charles J. Stivale (New York: Columbia University Press, 1990); Deleuze and Guattari, *Anti-Oedipus*.

56 Jacques Derrida, *The Animal That Therefore I Am* (New York: Fordham University Press, 2008).

57 Brassier, *Nihil Unbound*.

58 I (still) strongly agree with Gayatri Spivak's now-no-doubt-passé, and widely ignored, condemnation of Deleuze and Guattari's rhetorical use of "becoming-woman," articulated most clearly in the final passage of "Can the Subaltern Speak?." See Gayatri Chakravorty Spivak, "Can the Subaltern Speak?," in *Marxism and the Interpretation of Culture*, ed. Cary Nelson and Lawrence Grossberg (Urbana: University of Illinois Press, 1988), 104.

59 Walt Whitman, *Leaves of Grass* (1855; repr., Boston: Small, Maynard and Co., 1907), 78.

60 On accelerationism, see Nick Land, *Fanged Noumena: Collected Writings 1987–2007* (Falmouth: Urbanomic, 2011); Noys, *The Persistence of the Negative*.

61 Deleuze and Guattari, *Anti-Oedipus*; Gilles Deleuze, "Letter to a Harsh Critic," in *Negotiations, 1972–1990*, trans. Martin Joughin (New York: Columbia University Press, 1995), 7–8.

62 Nicholas C. Kawa, "Shit," Theorizing the Contemporary, *Cultural Anthropology* website, April 6, 2016, https://culanth.org/fieldsights/843-shit.

63 Deleuze, "Letter to a Harsh Critic," 8. In their *Anti-Oedipus* chapter "Savages, Barbarians, Civilized Men," Deleuze and Guattari challenge anthropology's privileging of exchange through their radically extended concepts of desire and desiring-production. By way of responding to such a universalized plenarist productivity, anthropologists may want to demand a counterprestation. If we exchange, what will we receive in return? A regime of pure productivity? This French affirmationist disgust for anything that resembles the dialectic, or even simply mutual responsiveness and accountability, reeks of what Nancy Hartsock called "abstract masculinity." Deleuze and Guattari, "Savages, Barbarians, Civilized Men," in *Anti-Oedipus*; Nancy C. M. Hartsock, "The Feminist Standpoint: Developing the Ground for a Specifically Feminist Historical Materialism," in *Feminist Social Thought: A Reader*, ed. Diana Tietjens Meyers (New York: Routledge, 1997). But exchange theorists, including Lévi-Strauss, don't get a pass here either. See, e.g., Gayle Rubin, "The Traffic in Women: Notes on the 'Political Economy' of Sex," in *Toward an Anthropology of Women*, ed. Rayna R. Reiter (New York: Monthly Review Press, 1975).

64 See, e.g., Silvia Federici, *Caliban and the Witch: Women, the Body and Primitive Accumulation* (New York: Autonomedia, 2004).

65 Cf. Matthew C. Watson, "Raging Hallelujah" (review of *Staying with the Trouble: Making Kin in the Chthulucene*, by Donna J. Haraway), *Science as Culture* 26, no. 2 (2017).

66 On spheres of exchange, in the narrow sense employed in economic anthropology, see Bohannan, "The Impact of Money on an African Subsistence Economy"; Paul Sillitoe, "Why Spheres of Exchange?," *Ethnology* 45, no. 1 (2006).

67 Darren Aronofsky, dir., *The Fountain* (Los Angeles: Warner Brothers Pictures, 2006).

68 Freidel, Schele, and Parker, *Maya Cosmos*.

69 Carl Sagan to Linda Schele, 1986 (undated), Schele Papers.

70 Dennis Tedlock, *Popol Vuh*.

71 Carl Sagan to Linda Schele, December 17, 1986, Schele Papers.

72 Carl Sagan, *Billions and Billions: Thoughts on Life and Death at the Brink of the Millennium* (New York: Ballantine Books, 1998), 3–4.

73 Freidel, Schele, and Parker, *Maya Cosmos*, 122. The Itz'at are mythological Maya artists or sages who created the sky.

74 Linda Schele and Khristaan D. Villela, "Creation, Cosmos, and the Imagery of Palenque and Copan," in *Eighth Palenque Round Table, 1993*, ed. Martha J. Macri and Jan McHargue (San Francisco: Pre-Columbian Art Research Institute, 1993), 1.

75 Schele and Villela, "Creation," 17.

76 Schele and Villela, "Creation," 23, 27.

77 Dennis Tedlock, *Popol Vuh*.

78 Schele and Villela, "Creation," 27.

79 For models of paradigm-oriented structural analysis, see Claude Lévi-Strauss, *Structural Anthropology*, trans. Claire Jacobsen and Brooke Grundfest Schoepf (New York: Basic Books, 1963).

80 Ahmed, *Queer Phenomenology*.

81 On "social dramas," see Victor Turner, *Dramas, Fields, and Metaphors: Symbolic Action in Human Society* (Ithaca, NY: Cornell University Press, 1974).

82 Helmreich, *Sounding the Limits*, 76.

83 Miriam Sagan, *Map of the Lost*.

84 Miriam Sagan, *Map of the Lost*, 7.

85 Lew Wallace, *Ben-Hur: A Tale of the Christ* (New York: Harper and Brothers, 1880).

86 Anne M. Moore [Shaw], Christopher R. Moore, and Zachary R. Gross, "History beneath Us: Public Archaeology at the Lew Wallace Study and Museum in Crawfordsville," *Indiana Archaeology* 7, no. 1 (2012).

87 Linda Schele to William Morrow and Company, Inc., October 30, 1989, Schele Papers.

88 Schele and Freidel, *Forest of Kings*.

89 Miriam Sagan, *Map of the Lost*, 8.

90 Cf. Haraway, *When Species Meet*, 7–8.

91 For the Maya case, see Evans, *Romancing the Maya*; Bruce Harvey, "The Archaeological Sublime of Tropical America: Ephraim G. Squier and John L. Stephens," in *American Geographics: U.S. National Narratives and the Representation of the Non-European World, 1830–1865* (Stanford, CA: Stanford University Press, 2001); Juan Castillo Cocom, "'It Was Simply Their Word': Yucatec Maya PRInces in YucaPAN and the Politics of Respect," *Critique of Anthropology* 25, no. 2 (2005); Brian Gollnick, *Reinventing the Lacandón: Subaltern Representations in the Rain Forest of Chiapas* (Tucson: University of Arizona Press, 2008).

92 Dorion Sagan is also a sleight-of-hand magician. For Mauss's and Lévi-Strauss's constructions of language as a magic form, see Mauss, *A General Theory of Magic*; Lévi-Strauss, *Introduction to the Work of Marcel Mauss*.

93 Ilya Prigogine and Isabelle Stengers, *Order out of Chaos: Man's New Dialogue with Nature* (London: Bantam, 1984).

94 Prigogine and Stengers, *Order out of Chaos*, xxviii.

95 C. P. Snow, *The Two Cultures* (1950; repr., Cambridge: Cambridge University Press, 1998).

96 Prigogine and Stengers, *Order out of Chaos*, 12.

97 On "auratic" forms, see Walter Benjamin, "The Work of Art in the Age of Mechanical Reproduction," in *Illuminations*, ed. Hannah Arendt (New York: Schocken, 1968).

98 Schele and Miller, *Blood of Kings*.

99 David Freidel to Linda Schele, September 17, 1985, Schele Papers.

100 Prigogine and Stengers, *Order out of Chaos*.

101 David Freidel to Linda Schele, September 17, 1985.

102 Prigogine and Stengers, *Order out of Chaos*, 22–23.

103 Ilya Prigogine to Linda Schele, January 10, 1989, Schele Papers. A stamp on this letter indicates that Schele replied on February 3, 1990, possibly indicating that Prigogine misdated his early January letter. It is unlikely that Schele would have delayed more than a year in replying to Prigogine.

104 Schele and Miller, *Blood of Kings*.

105 Prigogine and Stengers, *Order out of Chaos*, 23.

106 See, e.g., Bateson, *Steps to an Ecology of Mind*.

107 Douglas Cole, *Franz Boas: The Early Years, 1858–1906* (Seattle: University of Washington Press, 1999).

108 On "reading athwart," see Stefan Helmreich, "Nature/Culture/Seawater," *American Anthropologist* 113, no. 1 (2011); Graham M. Jones, *Magic's Reason: An Anthropology of Analogy* (Chicago: University of Chicago Press, 2017). On truths told slant see, after Emily Dickinson, Margulis and Sagan, *Dazzle Gradually*. Margulis and Sagan preface their book with the Dickinson poem "Tell all the Truth but tell it slant": "Tell all the truth but tell it slant— / Success in Circuit lies / Too bright for our infirm Delight / The Truth's superb surprise // As Lightning to the Children eased / With explanation kind / The Truth must dazzle gradually / Or every man be blind." Emily Dickinson, *The Poems of Emily Dickinson* (Cambridge, MA: Harvard University Press, 1998), poem 1129.

109 Bruno Latour, "Foreword: Stengers's Shibboleth," in *Power and Invention: Situating Science* (Minneapolis: University of Minnesota Press, 1997).

110 Latour, "Foreword: Stengers's Shibboleth," vii.

111 *Oxford English Dictionary*, s.v. "lunatic," accessed May 25, 2012, https://oed.com/view/Entry/111179.

112 Deleuze and Guattari, *Anti-Oedipus*, 5.

113 Deleuze and Guattari, *Anti-Oedipus*, 7.

114 Stengers, "The Cosmopolitical Proposal," 994–95. On Stengers's reading of Alfred North Whitehead, see Isabelle Stengers, *Thinking with Whitehead: A Free and Wild Creation of Concepts*, trans. Michael Chase (Cambridge, MA: Harvard University Press, 2011).

115 See three works by Stengers: "The Cosmopolitical Proposal," *Cosmopolitics I*, and *Cosmopolitics II*.

116 Hegel, *Phenomenology of Spirit*. See Jason Wirth, "Schelling's Contemporary Resurgence: The Dawn after the Night when All Cows Were Black," *Philosophy Compass* 6, no. 9 (2011).

117 Claude Lévi-Strauss, "The Structural Study of Myth," *Journal of American Folklore* 68, no. 270 (1955).

118 Lévi-Strauss, "The Structural Study of Myth," 431, 443.

119 Latour, *Politics of Nature*; Stengers, "The Cosmopolitical Proposal"; Isabelle Stengers, *Another Science Is Possible: A Manifesto for Slow Science* (Cambridge, UK: Polity, 2018).

120 See also Puig de la Bellacasa, "Matters of Care in Technoscience"; Matthew C. Watson, "Cosmopolitics and the Subaltern"; Matthew C. Watson, "Derrida, Stengers, Latour, and Subalternist Cosmopolitics."

121 Lynn Margulis and Dorion Sagan, *Acquiring Genomes: A Theory of the Origins of Species* (New York: Basic Books, 2002), 13.

122 Margulis and Sagan, *Acquiring Genomes*, 11–12.

123 Haraway, *When Species Meet*, 31.

124 Haraway, *When Species Meet*, 32.

125 Jennifer Margulis, "Do You Want to Be Buried or Cremated?," *Jennifer Margulis: Sticking My Neck Out* (blog), February 1, 2012, http://jennifermargulis.net/blog/2012/02/do-you-want-to-be-buried-or-cremated/.

126 Dorion Sagan, "The Human Is More Than Human: Interspecies Communities and the New Facts of Life," in *Cosmic Apprentice: Dispatches from the Edges of Science* (Minneapolis: University of Minnesota Press, 2013).

127 See, e.g., Farman, "Speculative Matter."

128 Dorion Sagan, *Cosmic Apprentice*.

129 Geertz, "Thick Description," 28–29.

130 On Indra's net, see Wagner, *An Anthropology of the Subject*. On the heath (or the wild) and the heathen, see Lou Cornum, "White Magic," *New Inquiry*, February 5, 2018, https://thenewinquiry.com/white-magic/; Federici, *Caliban and the Witch*. For the Zinacantecos studied by Evon Vogt, the wild is *el monte*. Vogt, *Zinacantan*.

CHAPTER 4: BONES

1 Perry Miller Adato, *Georgia O'Keeffe: A Life in Art* (Santa Fe, NM: Georgia O'Keeffe Museum, 2002).

2 Adato, *Georgia O'Keeffe*.

3 Adato, *Georgia O'Keeffe*.

4 Working a bit harder, recent experts on O'Keeffe's work have noted that her osteological era evoked the Transcendentalists' ruminations on death as an experience of regeneration rather than ultimate mortality. See Rita Donagh, "Georgia O'Keeffe in Context," *Oxford Art Journal* 3, no. 1 (1980); Barbara Rose, *American Art since 1900* (New York: Thames and Hudson, 1967); Leital Molad, "American Icons: Georgia O'Keeffe's Skull Paintings," *Studio 360*, September 2, 2011 (originally aired November 12, 2010), Public Radio International and WNYC, https://www.pri.org/stories/2011-09-02/american-icons-georgia-okeeffes-skull-paintings.

5 Hegel, *Phenomenology of Spirit*, 208. The passage in Miller's translation states, "The being of Spirit is a bone." Žižek repeatedly quotes this as "The Spirit is a bone" and does not provide a citation. See, e.g., Slavoj Žižek, *The Sublime Object of Ideology* (London: Verso, 1989), 207–9; Slavoj Žižek, *The Parallax View* (Cambridge, MA: MIT Press, 2006), 33, 84.

6 Hegel, *Phenomenology of Spirit*.

7 Fredric Jameson, "First Impressions" (review of *The Parallax View*, by Slavoj Žižek), *London Review of Books* 28, no. 4 (September 7, 2006).

8 Jameson, "First Impressions."

9 Bruno Latour, "Anthropology at the Time of the Anthropocene: A Personal View of What Is to Be Studied," in *The Anthropology of Sustainability: Beyond Development and Progress*, ed. Marc Brightman and Jerome Lewis (New York: Palgrave Macmillan, 2017), 37.

10 Cf. Bennett, *Vibrant Matter*.

11 Ruth Ozeki, "The Art of Losing: On Writing, Dying, and Mom," *Shambhala Sun* 2 (2008).

12 Ozeki, "The Art of Losing," 73.

13 Ozeki, "The Art of Losing," 72.

14 Ruth Ozeki, dir., *Halving the Bones* (New York: Women Make Movies, 1995).

15 Ozeki, "The Art of Losing," 72.

16 Ozeki, "The Art of Losing," 76.

17 Ozeki, "The Art of Losing," 76.

18 Nancy M. Farriss, "Remembering the Future, Anticipating the Past: History, Time, and Cosmology among the Maya of Yucatan," *Comparative Studies in Society and History* 29, no. 3 (1987).

19 Ruth Ozeki, "The Anthropologists' Kids," in *Mixed: An Anthology of Short Fiction on the Multiracial Experience*, ed. Chandra Prasad (New York: W. W. Norton, 2006), 22.

20 See Michael Coe, *Final Report: An Archaeologist Excavates His Past* (New York: Thames and Hudson, 2006).

21 Ozeki, "The Anthropologists' Kids," 45.

22 Ozeki, *Halving the Bones*.

23 Ozeki, *Halving the Bones*.

24 Ozeki, *Halving the Bones*.

25 Ozeki, *Halving the Bones*.

26 Ozeki, *Halving the Bones*.

27 Ozeki, *Halving the Bones*.

28 Ozeki, *Halving the Bones*.

29 Ozeki, *Halving the Bones*.

30 Ozeki, *Halving the Bones*.

31 Ozeki, *Halving the Bones*.

32 Ozeki, *Halving the Bones*.

33 Linda Schele, "Mira, Omicron Ceti" (MFA thesis, University of Cincinnati, 1968).

34 Cf. Battaglia, "Aeroponic Gardens."

35 Floyd Lounsbury to Linda Schele, February 13, 1974, Schele Papers.

36 Floyd Lounsbury to Colleagues, March 18, 1974, Schele Papers.

37 Linda Schele to "collegues, friends, and friendly crazies," March 24, 1974, Schele Papers.

38 See the opening pages of the introduction for a discussion of this letter.

39   See chapter 2.

40   Bataille, *The Accursed Share*, vol. 1.

41   See, e.g., Mauss, *A General Theory of Magic*.

42   Matthew C. Watson, "Staged Discovery."

43   Mathews and Schele, "Lords of Palenque."

44   On paranoid reading, see Sedgwick, *Touching Feeling*.

45   Schele and Miller, *Blood of Kings*.

46   Quoted in Anthony J. Bertino, *Forensic Science: Fundamentals and Investigations* (Mason, OH: Cengage Learning, 2012), 377.

47   Taussig, *What Color Is the Sacred?*

48   Taussig, *What Color Is the Sacred?*, 81.

49   See Mauss, *The Gift*.

50   So, maybe I *can't* forgive Linda after all.

51   Taussig, *The Corn Wolf*.

52   James C. Scott, *Domination and the Arts of Resistance: Hidden Transcripts* (New Haven, CT: Yale University Press, 1990).

53   Frank Cancian, *Change and Uncertainty in a Peasant Economy: The Maya Corn Farmers of Zinacantan* (Stanford, CA: Stanford University Press, 1972), 65.

54   See, e.g., Vera Tiesler, Andrea Cucina, and Arturo Romano Pacheco, "Who Was the Red Queen? Identity of the Female Maya Dignitary from the Sarcophagus Tomb of Temple XIII, Palenque, Mexico," *HOMO—Journal of Comparative Human Biology* 55, nos. 1–2 (2004).

55   George B. Wood and Franklin Bache, *The Dispensatory of the United States of America*, 8th ed. (Philadelphia: Grigg, Elliot, and Co., 1849), 170–71.

56   Brian Stross, "Palenque: The Name," *International Journal of American Linguistics* 51, no. 4 (1985).

57   Alphonso Lingis, *Excesses: Eros and Culture* (Albany: State University of New York Press, 1983).

58   Lingis, *Excesses*, 23; emphasis in original.

59   Cf. Miguel Covarrubias, *The Eagle, the Jaguar, and the Serpent: Indian Art of the Americas* (New York: Alfred A. Knopf, 1954); Miguel Covarrubias, *Indian Art of Mexico and Central America* (New York: Alfred A. Knopf, 1957).

60   Through archive research at the Rockefeller Estate, Elaine Day Schele tracked down Rosa Covarrubias's role in advocating for Nelson Rockefeller's support of Ruz Lhuillier's excavations. Rockefeller is also acknowledged in Ruz Lhuillier's site reports from 1949, 1950, and 1951. He apparently withdrew his support in late 1951 and reinstated it in 1954 (after the Pakal discovery). Both decisions followed from Rosa's requests. So, although Rockefeller did not directly fund the 1952 season, his support was integral to Ruz Lhuillier's excavations of the era. See Elaine Schele, Exploring Lakamha', September 4, 2010, gispalenque.blogspot.com.

61   Miguel Covarrubias, *Island of Bali* (New York: Alfred A. Knopf, 1937), 11.

62   Mabel Dodge Luhan, *Lorenzo in Taos* (London: Martin Secker, 1933).

63 On Hopper and the Luhan home, see Lois Palken Rudnick, *Utopian Vistas: The Mabel Dodge Luhan House and the American Counterculture* (Albuquerque: University of New Mexico Press, 1996); Noel King, "'At Least a Witness to Myself': On Watching *The American Dreamer* after Learning of the Death of Dennis Hopper," *Studies in Documentary Film* 4, no. 2 (2010).

64 Adato, *Georgia O'Keeffe*.

65 Linda Schele, in Weeks, Martin, and Conley, *Edgewalker*.

66 Cf. Moten, *Black and Blur*; Benjamin, *The Arcades Project*.

CHAPTER 5: GENIUS

1 Lebrun, "Transcript of Filmed Interview."

2 Stone, introduction, 6.

3 Anthony Aveni, "Reaching for the Stars: Linda Schele's Contributions to Maya Astronomy," in Stone, *Heart of Creation*, 20.

4 Aveni, "Reaching for the Stars," 20.

5 Aveni, "Reaching for the Stars," 20.

6 Aveni, "Reaching for the Stars," 20.

7 Dumbarton Oaks Archives, "David Stuart," *75th Anniversary Blog* (2017), posted July 19, 2018, https://www.doaks.org/research/library-archives/dumbarton-oaks-archives/historical-records/75th-anniversary/blog/david-stuart.

8 Judith (Jack) Halberstam, *Female Masculinity* (Durham, NC: Duke University Press, 1998).

9 Linda Schele, "Notebook for the Maya Hieroglyphic Writing Workshop at Texas" (Institute of Latin American Studies, University of Texas at Austin, 1980).

10 David Bowie, "Space Oddity," on *Space Oddity* (Philips Records, 1969, LP).

11 Matthew C. Watson, "Staged Discovery."

12 Dumbarton Oaks Archive, "David Stuart."

13 Margaret Atwood, *Negotiating with the Dead: A Writer on Writing* (New York: Anchor, 2002), 100.

14 For critiques of the psychological category of "hysteria," see, e.g., Charles Bernheimer and Claire Kahane, eds., *In Dora's Case: Freud, Hysteria, Feminism*, 2nd ed. (New York: Columbia University Press, 1990); Frida Gorbach, "Hysteria and History: A Meditation on Mexico," *Social Text* 25, no. 3 (2007).

15 *Oxford English Dictionary*, s.v. "genius," accessed July 19, 2018, https://oed.com/view/Entry/77607.

16 *Oxford English Dictionary*, s.v. "genius," accessed July 19, 2018, https://oed.com/view/Entry/77607.

17 Claude Lévi-Strauss, *The Savage Mind* (Chicago: University of Chicago Press, 1966).

18 Stone, introduction, 6–7.

19 On Spanish colonial bishops' *reducción*—or linguistic standardization and construction of a prestige variety—of Yucatec Mayan through writing and socialization

practices, see William F. Hanks, *Converting Words: Maya in the Age of the Cross* (Berkeley: University of California Press, 2010).

20 On "mythistory," see William H. McNeill, *Mythistory and Other Essays* (Chicago: University of Chicago Press, 1986); Prudence M. Rice, *Maya Calendar Origins: Monuments, Mythistory, and the Materialization of Time* (Austin: University of Texas Press, 2007).

21 This refers to Lévi-Strauss's radical affirmation of the creativity—wildness or savagery—of all thought, captured in his punning title, *La pensée sauvage*, which designates both wild, undomesticated thinking and the wild pansy. The title's English translation sadly threatens to redomesticate. Lévi-Strauss, *The Savage Mind*.

22 Jacques Derrida, "Structure, Sign, and Play in the Discourse of the Human Sciences," in *Writing and Difference* (London: Routledge, 1978), 285.

23 Latour, *We Have Never Been Modern*. But for a reading of Latour's and Derrida's complementarity, see Matthew C. Watson, "Derrida, Stengers, Latour, and Subalternist Cosmopolitics."

24 Bruno Latour, *Science in Action: How to Follow Scientists and Engineers through Society* (Cambridge, MA: Harvard University Press, 1987).

25 Cf. Anker and Felski, *Critique and Postcritique*.

26 Derrida, "Structure, Sign, and Play," 285; Linda Schele, *Maya Glyphs*.

27 Shelton, *Where the North Sea Touches Alabama*, 33.

28 See chapter 2.

29 Jacques Derrida, *The Post Card: From Socrates to Freud and Beyond*, trans. Alan Bass (Chicago: University of Chicago Press, 1987), 12–13. The gaps before and after the opening sentences are "incinerations" that Derrida deploys to conceal or distort such letters' senses; this is a technique for evoking the limits of linguistic sense in communicative exchange.

30 Monaghan, "The Person."

31 Derrida, *The Post Card*; J. Hillis Miller, "Derrida's Destinerrance," *MLN* 121, no. 4 (2006).

32 On coincident discovery of the *way* glyph, see Matthew C. Watson, "Assembling the Ancient."

33 Mary Douglas, *Purity and Danger: An Analysis of Concepts of Pollution and Taboo* (1966; repr., New York: Routledge, 2002).

34 Claude Lévi-Strauss, *We Are All Cannibals and Other Essays*, trans. Jane Marie Todd (New York: Columbia University Press, 2016).

35 Claude Lévi-Strauss to Linda Schele, November 4, 1986, Schele Papers.

36 Lévi-Strauss, *Introduction to the Work of Marcel Mauss*.

37 Mauss, *A General Theory of Magic*.

38 Lévi-Strauss, *Introduction to the Work of Marcel Mauss*, 61.

39 Ferdinand de Saussure, *Course in General Linguistics* (1959), trans. Wade Baskin (New York: Columbia University Press, 2011).

40 On "transduction," see Michael Silverstein, "Translation, Transduction, Transformation: Skating 'Glossando' on Thin Semiotic Ice," in *Translating Cultures: Perspectives on*

Translation and Anthropology, ed. Paula G. Rubel and Abraham Rosman (Oxford: Berg, 2003).

41 Lévi-Strauss, *Introduction to the Work of Marcel Mauss*, 62.

42 Lévi-Strauss, *Introduction to the Work of Marcel Mauss*, 63.

43 Lévi-Strauss, *Introduction to the Work of Marcel Mauss*, 63.

44 Lévi-Strauss, *Introduction to the Work of Marcel Mauss*, 64.

45 See, e.g., Derrida, "Structure, Sign, and Play." Anthropological work that attends closely to the cultural function or significance of the floating signifier is far-ranging. James Siegel's work on Indonesian constructions of witchcraft and the logic of the gift merits particular attention here for its conceptual rigor and ambitiousness. See, e.g., James Siegel, *Naming the Witch* (Stanford, CA: Stanford University Press, 2006); James Siegel, "False Beggars: Marcel Mauss, *The Gift*, and Its Commentators," *diacritics* 41, no. 2 (2013). See also, e.g., Emiko Ohnuki-Tierney, "The Power of Absence: Zero Signifiers and Their Transgressions," *L'Homme* 130 (April–June 1994); James D. Faubion, "From the Ethical to the Themitical (and Back): Groundwork for an Anthropology of Ethics," in *Ordinary Ethics*, ed. Michael Lambek (New York: Fordham University Press, 2011); Martin Holbraad, "The Power of Powder: Multiplicity and Motion in the Divinatory Cosmology of Cuban Ifá (or *Mana*, Again)," in *Thinking through Things: Theorising Artefacts Ethnographically*, ed. Amiria Henare, Martin Holbraad, and Sari Wastell (New York: Routledge, 2007); Toomas Gross, "Letting the Air Out: *Aire* as an Empty Signifier in Oaxacan Understandings of Illness," *Culture, Medicine, and Psychiatry* 40, no. 4 (2016).

46 Charles Sanders Peirce, *Collected Papers of Charles Sanders Peirce* (Cambridge, MA: Harvard University Press, 1931).

47 In their mediation and proliferation by poststructuralists, particularly Derrida, views of the human condition as a linguistic experience became, by the 1970s, a kind of omnipresent theoretical common sense. Consider, for example, the formative power of such framing questions as that offered by Judith Butler in *Excitable Speech*: "Is our vulnerability to language a consequence of our being constituted within its terms?" Judith Butler, *Excitable Speech: A Politics of the Performative* (New York: Routledge, 1997), 2.

48 Lévi-Strauss, *Introduction to the Work of Marcel Mauss*, 62.

49 John L. Austin, *How to Do Things with Words* (London: Oxford University Press, 1962).

50 See, e.g., Butler, *Excitable Speech*; Shoshana Felman, *The Scandal of the Speaking Body: Don Juan with J. L. Austin, or Seduction in Two Languages* (Stanford, CA: Stanford University Press, 2003); Sedgwick, *Touching Feeling*; Michael Silverstein, "Cultural Prerequisites to Grammatical Analysis," in *Georgetown University Round Table on Languages and Linguistics*, ed. Muriel Saville-Troike (Washington, DC: Georgetown University Press, 1977); Kira Hall, "Performativity," *Journal of Linguistic Anthropology* 9, nos. 1–2 (2000); Constantine V. Nakassis, "Brand, Citationality, Performativity," *American Anthropologist* 114, no. 4 (2012).

51 Rosaldo, "The Things We Do with Words."

52 Within the terms of the anthropology of religion, it closely aligns with the forms of nineteenth-century naturalism that Durkheim challenges, alongside animism, in establishing the groundwork for building a narrowly sociological theory of religion. Durkheim, *Elementary Forms*.

53 Mauss, *The Gift*.

54 Edward B. Tylor, *Primitive Culture: Researches into the Development of Mythology, Philosophy, Religion, Language, Art, and Custom* (London: John Murray, 1871).

55 See, e.g., Clifford Geertz, "Religion as a Cultural System," in *The Interpretation of Cultures* (New York: Basic Books, 1973); Talal Asad, *Genealogies of Religion: Discipline and Reasons of Power in Christianity and Islam* (Baltimore: Johns Hopkins University Press, 1993); Saba Mahmood, *Politics of Piety: The Islamic Revival and the Feminist Subject* (Princeton, NJ: Princeton University Press, 2005).

56 Derrida, "Structure, Sign, and Play," 285.

57 Slavoj Žižek, *Less Than Nothing: Hegel and the Shadow of Dialectical Materialism* (London: Verso, 2012), 584–85.

58 Lévi-Strauss, *Introduction to the Work of Marcel Mauss*, 63.

59 Lévi-Strauss, *Introduction to the Work of Marcel Mauss*, 63.

60 Derek Bickerton has claimed that "true language, via the emergence of syntax, was a catastrophic event, occurring within the first few generations of *H. sapiens sapiens*." Derek Bickerton, *Language and Human Behavior* (Seattle: University of Washington Press, 1995), 69; quoted in Michael C. Corballis, "Mirror Neurons and the Evolution of Language," *Brain and Language* 112, no. 1 (2010): 31. Might we say that language, today, remains a catastrophe?

61 Lévi-Strauss, *Introduction to the Work of Marcel Mauss*, 59. Although this assertion is extraordinary in its assumptions and implications, it also fixates, in a manner symptomatic of the limits of Lévi-Strauss's semiotic thinking, on symbolization as an absolute break from indexical and iconic signification. Such an extrication of the symbolic from the broader semiotic field merits criticism from positions attuned to more variegated fields of semiosis, including "biosemiotic" positions that regard biology itself as a sign-system that generally privileges indexicality and iconicity. See, e.g., Terrence W. Deacon, *Incomplete Nature: How Mind Emerged from Matter* (New York: W. W. Norton, 2011); Kohn, *How Forests Think*.

62 Lévi-Strauss, *Introduction to the Work of Marcel Mauss*, 63.

63 Bronislaw Malinowski, *Magic, Science and Religion and Other Essays* (Glencoe, IL: Free Press, 1948); Mauss, *A General Theory of Magic*.

64 See four works by Isabelle Stengers: "The Cosmopolitical Proposal," *Cosmopolitics I*, *Cosmopolitics II*, and *Another Science Is Possible*.

65 Lévi-Strauss, *Introduction to the Work of Marcel Mauss*, 63.

66 See, e.g., Holbraad, "The Power of Powder," 197.

67 Lévi-Strauss, *Introduction to the Work of Marcel Mauss*, 49.

68 Žižek, *Less Than Nothing*, 585.

69 This reading of Lévi-Strauss further suggests that Deleuze and Guattari's disavowal of exchange theory may hinge on a misunderstanding of Lévi-Strauss's construction of exchange, a misunderstanding that presumes exchange to be dialectical movement rather than an ontologically prior relationality, the irruptive singularity of language/thought itself. Deleuze and Félix Guattari, "Savages, Barbarians, Civilized Men."

70 Houston and Stuart, "The *Way* Glyph." See also Matthew C. Watson, "Assembling the Ancient."

71 See, e.g., Freidel, Schele, and Parker, *Maya Cosmos.*

72 Franz Boas, *The Mind of Primitive Man* (New York: Macmillan, 1911).

73 Asad, *Formations of the Secular.*

74 Asad, *Formations of the Secular*, 38; Michel de Certeau, *The Mystic Fable*, vol. 1: *The Sixteenth and Seventeenth Centuries* (Chicago: University of Chicago Press, 1992), 123.

75 For a critical discussion of the "crossed-out God," see, e.g., Latour, *We Have Never Been Modern.*

76 I take the language of scientific witnessing from Shapin and Schaffer, *Leviathan and the Air-Pump*; Haraway, *Modest_Witness@Second_Millennium.* See also Matthew C. Watson, "Staged Discovery."

77 Cf. Rheinberger, *Toward a History of Epistemic Things.*

78 On the linguistic production of a zone of indistinction, see Agamben, *Homo Sacer*, 25.

79 I use the term *reduction* deliberately. Not only does the language ideology of the epigraphers construct glyphs as "text" functionally consistent with post-Gutenberg writing, it seems largely consistent with the language ideology that governed the Spanish colonial *reducción*—in its religious, spatial, *and linguistic* dimensions—as described compellingly in Hanks, *Converting Words.*

80 See the controversy over the concept of "shamanism," e.g., Cecelia F. Klein et al., "The Role of Shamanism in Mesoamerican Art," *Current Anthropology* 43, no. 3 (2002).

81 Schele and Miller, *The Mirror, the Rabbit, and the Bundle.*

82 What the scholars colloquially refer to as the "Vienna dictionary" is the *Bocabulario de maya than por su abecedario*, an anonymous 1670 Spanish to Yucatec Mayan dictionary.

83 "The Motul" is an anonymous Yucatec Mayan to Spanish dictionary produced in 1600.

84 Linda Schele to Floyd Lounsbury, January 1975, Schele Papers.

85 Compare the later work of Alfredo López Austin, *The Rabbit on the Face of the Moon: Mythology in the Mesoamerican Tradition* (Salt Lake City: University of Utah Press, 1996).

86 Clifford Geertz, *Works and Lives: The Anthropologist as Author* (Stanford, CA: Stanford University Press, 1988).

87 See, e.g., Anthony Aveni, *Empires of Time: Calendars, Clocks, and Cultures* (New York: Basic Books, 1989).

88 On "text-artifacts," see Paul Ricoeur, *Hermeneutics and the Human Sciences*, trans. John B. Thompson (Cambridge: Cambridge University Press, 1981); Michael Silverstein and Greg Urban, "The Natural History of Discourse," in *Natural Histories of Discourse*, ed. Michael Silverstein and Greg Urban (Chicago: University of Chicago Press, 1996).

89 See, e.g., Edward Casey, "How to Get from Space to Place in a Fairly Short Stretch of Time," in *Senses of Place*, ed. Steven Feld and Keith Basso (Santa Fe, NM: School for Advanced Research Press, 1996).

90 Cf. James F. Weiner, *The Empty Place: Poetry, Space, and Being among the Foi of Papua New Guinea* (Bloomington: Indiana University Press, 1991).

91 On "chronotopes," see Mikhail Bakhtin, *The Dialogic Imagination: Four Essays*, trans. Caryl Emerson and Michael Holquist (Austin: University of Texas Press, 1981).

92 On linguistic "context of situation," see Bronislaw Malinowski, *Argonauts of the Western Pacific* (1928; repr., New York: E. P. Dutton, 1961).

93 The term *epi-ontology* sources to the work of Debbora Battaglia. See, e.g., Debbora Battaglia, "Cosmos as Commons: An Activation of Cosmic Diplomacy," *e-flux* 58 (2014), https://www.e-flux.com/journal/58/61180/cosmos-as-commons-an -activation-of-cosmic-diplomacy/.

94 See chapter 2.

95 Lévi-Strauss, "The Structural Study of Myth."

96 Cf. Ralph Bulmer, "Why Is the Cassowary Not a Bird? A Problem of Zoological Taxonomy among the Karam of the New Guinea Highlands," *Man* 2, no. 1 (1967).

97 Lévi-Strauss, *The Savage Mind*, 3.

98 Lévi-Strauss, *The Savage Mind*, 9.

99 Lévi-Strauss, *The Savage Mind*, 9.

100 Lévi-Strauss, *The Savage Mind*, 10.

101 Lévi-Strauss, *The Savage Mind*, 10.

102 See, e.g., Geoffrey C. Bowker and Susan Leigh Star, *Sorting Things Out: Classification and Its Consequences* (Cambridge, MA: MIT Press, 1999).

103 Bruno Latour, "Irreductions," in *The Pasteurization of France* (Cambridge, MA: Harvard University Press, 1988).

104 This is not to say that Linnaean taxonomies are innocent, politically or otherwise. It is, instead, an argument that we need to carefully consider all kinds of categorization as situated cultural practices, including, perhaps especially, scientific categorizations. On the politics of Linnaean taxonomy, see Schiebinger, *Nature's Body*.

105 Certeau, *The Mystic Fable*, 1:123. See also the discussion of this passage in John Montag SJ, "Revelation: The False Legacy of Suárez," in *Radical Orthodoxy: A New Theology* ed. John Milbank, Catherine Pickstock, and Graham Ward (London: Routledge, 2002), 50–51.

106 On posts of all kinds, see Derrida, *The Post Card*.

1 Terry Eagleton, "Anti-humanism" (review of *D. H. Lawrence and "Difference": Postcoloniality and the Poetry of the Present*, by Amit Chaudhuri), *London Review of Books* 26, no. 3 (2004).

2 Julio Cortázar, *Hopscotch* (London: Harvill, 1967), 376.

3 Taussig, *The Corn Wolf*, 7.

4 Lévi-Strauss, *Myth and Meaning*.

5 Cortázar, *Hopscotch*.

6 Lévi-Strauss, *Myth and Meaning*, 3–4.

7 Cf. Derrida, *The Post Card*.

8 Dwight Watson, "Intersection of Time," *Cha: An Asian Literary Journal* 28 (2015).

9 Matthew C. Watson, "Staged Discovery," "Mediating the Maya," and "Listening in the Pakal Controversy."

10 What if my critique of decipherment issued less from the suggestion of a kind of colonial violence, and more from a sense that the innocent or not-so-innocent subject's encounter with glyphs produces new forms of value, even a new regime of historical value? What kinds of "encounter value" are entailed in decipherment? I owe this cuing to the question of encounter value to a host of illuminating conversations with Debbora Battaglia. On encounter value, see, e.g., Haraway, *When Species Meet*; Maan Barua, "Lively Commodities and Encounter Value," *Environment and Planning D: Society and Space* 34, no. 4 (2016).

11 Taussig, *The Corn Wolf*, 4.

12 Cortázar, *Hopscotch*, 200.

13 Shapin and Schaffer, *Leviathan and the Air-Pump*; Haraway, *Modest_Witness@ Second_Millennium*.

14 Cf. Alain Badiou and Nicolas Truong, *In Praise of Love*, trans. Peter Bush (New York: New Press, 2012).

15 Joyce Livingston to Linda Schele, February 25, 1994, Schele Papers.

16 Freidel, Schele, and Parker, *Maya Cosmos*.

17 Freidel, Schele, and Parker, *Maya Cosmos*, 393–97.

18 See, e.g., Vera Tiesler and Andrea Cucina, eds., *New Perspectives on Human Sacrifice and Ritual Body Treatments in Ancient Maya Society* (New York: Springer, 2007).

19 Derrida, *Given Time*.

20 Kyle Cashulin, "Joyce Livingston, Inverness Artist and Traveler," *Point Reyes (CA) Light*, July 29, 2010, http://www.ptreyeslight.com/article/joyce-livingston-inverness-artist-and-traveler.

21 Livingston to Schele, February 25, 1994.

22 Livingston to Schele, February 25, 1994.

23 Livingston to Schele, February 25, 1994.

24 Cf. Haraway, *When Species Meet*.

25 Badiou and Truong, *In Praise of Love*, 89–90.

26 Badiou and Truong, *In Praise of Love*, 90.

27 Badiou and Truong, *In Praise of Love*, 57.

28 Cf. Berlant, *Cruel Optimism*.

29 This idea has a history within French sociology. The nineteenth-century psychological sociologist Gabriel Tarde, for example, linked love and the social. Tarde's imitation-oriented conceptualization of love as the social may even owe a debt to Auguste Comte, who argued (against Kant) that the social preceded the ego and who positioned feelings as integral to human sociality. This differs considerably from the more Spinozist-Deleuzian inclinations of contemporary affect theory. Comte did not necessarily celebrate humans as feelers; he thought, rather, that we needed to cultivate a positive sociology that would, through thought, bring order to feeling and action. Tarde was more inclined to a romanticist celebration or affirmation of love as the substance or force of the social. Gabriel Tarde, *Social Laws: An Outline of Sociology* (1899; repr., Kitchener, Ontario: Batoche Books, 2000). See also Matthew C. Watson, "Imitation and Society: How Boasian Anthropology Reassembled the Social," *Anthropological Theory* 17, no. 2 (2017).

30 bell hooks, *Outlaw Culture: Resisting Representations* (New York: Routledge, 1994), 243.

31 Latour, "Irreductions"; Hanks, *Converting Words*.

32 Evans, *Romancing the Maya*; cf. Peter Redfield, *Space in the Tropics*.

33 hooks, *Outlaw Culture*, 243.

34 hooks, *Outlaw Culture*, 248.

35 Watanabe, "Unimagining the Maya," 35.

36 Moten, *Black and Blur*, 29. The phrase "post-liberatory" is from Judith Butler, *The Psychic Life of Power: Theories in Subjection* (Stanford, CA: Stanford University Press, 1997), 17–18.

37 Michael D. Coogan, ed., *New Oxford Annotated Bible: New Revised Standard Version* (New York: Oxford University Press, 2001), Matthew 5:43–48.

38 Soumhya Venkatesan et al., "The Anthropological Fixation with Reciprocity Leaves No Room for Love: 2009 Meeting of the Group for Debates in Anthropological Theory," *Critique of Anthropology* 31, no. 3 (2011).

39 Derrida, *The Gift of Death*.

40 Whitman, *Leaves of Grass*, 78.

41 Derrida, "Force of Law: The 'Mystical Foundation of Authority,'" trans. Mary Quaintance, in Anidjar, *Acts of Religion*.

42 Derrida, "Force of Law," 278, quoted in Martin Hägglund, *Radical Atheism: Derrida and the Time of Life* (Stanford, CA: Stanford University Press, 2008), 111.

43 Derrida, "Force of Law," 278.

44 Derrida, "Force of Law," 278.

45 *Oxford English Dictionary*, s.v. "immature," accessed September 4, 2016, https://oed.com/view/Entry/91822.

46 Shakespeare, *Hamlet*, 1.5.189.

47 Gönül Dönmez-Colin, *Cinemas of the Other: A Personal Journey with Film-Makers from the Middle East and Central Asia* (Portland, OR: Intellect, 2006), 172.

48 Derrida, "Force of Law," 278.

49 Douglas, *Purity and Danger*.

50 Indeed, the communal character of Schele and her colleagues' decipherment-work marked a clear break from scholars of preceding generations, such as Thompson and Proskouriakoff.

51 Hans-Jörg Rheinberger takes the concept of "historiality"—a form of history that doesn't succumb to the violence of claims to originality—from Derrida and links it to Prigogine and Stengers's notion of operator-time. On historiality: "The multiplicity of internal times in an open horizon creates what can be called historiality: It escapes the classical notions of linear causation, retroaction, influence, and dominance, as well as that of a purely stochastic process. . . . It is only the trace that will remain which creates, through its action, the origin of its nonorigin." Hans-Jörg Rheinberger, "Experimental Systems: Historiality, Narration, and Deconstruction," *Science in Context* 7, no. 1 (1994): 69; Derrida, *Of Grammatology*; Prigogine and Stengers, *Order out of Chaos*.

52 Rheinberger, "Experimental Systems," 69.

53 See, e.g., Chip Colwell-Chanthaphonh and T. J. Ferguson, eds., *Collaboration in Archaeological Practice: Engaging Descendant Communities* (Lanham, MD: AltaMira, 2008).

54 Aronofsky, *The Fountain*.

55 Cf. Isabelle Stengers, "Another Look: Relearning to Laugh," *Hypatia: A Journal of Feminist Philosophy* 15, no. 4 (2000); Isabelle Stengers, *The Invention of Modern Science* (Minneapolis: University of Minnesota Press, 2000); Martin Savransky, "The Humor of the Problematic: Thinking with Stengers," *SubStance* 47, no. 1 (2018). "Orientalism," of course, references Edward Said's famous critique of the field: Said, *Orientalism*.

56 Eagleton, "Anti-humanism."

57 Freidel, Schele, and Parker, *Maya Cosmos*, 194–95.

58 Livingston to Schele, February 25, 1994.

59 Jean-Jacques Rousseau, "Essay on the Origin of Languages," in *Essay on the Origin of Languages and Writings Related to Music* (1761), ed. John T. Scott, *The Collected Writings of Rousseau* (Hanover, NH: University Press of New England, 1998), 290.

60 Lévi-Strauss, *Introduction to the Work of Marcel Mauss*, 62.

61 Benjamin Lee Whorf, "Language, Mind, and Reality," in *Language, Thought, and Reality: Selected Writings of Benjamin Lee Whorf*, ed. John B. Carroll (1942; repr., Cambridge, MA: MIT Press, 1956), 258.

62 Saussure, *Course in General Linguistics*.

63 Whorf, "Language, Mind, and Reality," 258.

64 Whorf, "Language, Mind, and Reality," 258–59.

65 Maggie Nelson, *The Argonauts* (Minneapolis: Graywolf, 2015), 49.

66 On Maya ensoulment, see, e.g., Gillespie, "Body and Soul."

67   Malinowski, *Argonauts of the Western Pacific*.

68   Cf. Valerie A. Olson, "Political Ecology in the Extreme: Asteroid Activism and the Making of an Environmental Solar System," *Anthropological Quarterly* 85, no. 4 (2012).

69   See, e.g., Schele and Freidel, *Forest of Kings*.

70   Cf. Lévi-Strauss, *The Savage Mind*.

71   This framing smooths over a range of ethical, epistemological, and aesthetic complexities that marked decipherment, including Schele's role in excluding scholars who dissented from her collective's rather normative claims. Cf. Matthew C. Watson, "Staged Discovery" and "Listening in the Pakal Controversy."

72   Michael Coe and David Lebrun, "Interview with Linda Schele" (2005), *Breaking the Maya Code Interview Archives*, accessed November 12, 2019, http://www .nightfirefilms.org/breakingthemayacode/interview.archives.htm.

73   Lévi-Strauss, *The Savage Mind*.

74   Linda Schele, *Maya Glyphs*; Schele and Miller, *Blood of Kings*; Schele and Freidel, *Forest of Kings*; Schele and Mathews, *Code of Kings*.

75   Mazzarella, *The Mana of Mass Society*.

76   Lévi-Strauss, *Introduction to the Work of Marcel Mauss*, 56.

77   Lévi-Strauss, *Introduction to the Work of Marcel Mauss*, 57.

78   Durkheim, *Elementary Forms*; Mauss, *A General Theory of Magic*.

79   Immanuel Kant, *Critique of Pure Reason* (1781), trans. Paul Guyer and Allen W. Wood (Cambridge: Cambridge University Press, 1998).

80   Lévi-Strauss, *Introduction to the Work of Marcel Mauss*, 58.

81   Lévi-Strauss, *The Savage Mind*.

82   Lévi-Strauss, *Introduction to the Work of Marcel Mauss*, 62.

83   Mazzarella, *The Mana of Mass Society*.

84   Maggie Nelson, *The Argonauts*, 49.

85   See chapter 2.

86   Cf. François Dosse, *History of Structuralism: The Sign Sets, 1967–Present*, trans. Deborah Glassman (Minneapolis: University of Minnesota Press, 1997).

87   Cf. Battaglia, "Aeroponic Gardens"; Marilyn Strathern, "Cutting the Network," *Journal of the Royal Anthropological Institute* 2, no. 3 (1996).

88   Lévi-Strauss, *The Savage Mind*.

89   Derrida, "Structure, Sign, and Play," 285.

90   Simon Critchley, *Bowie* (New York: OR Books, 2016), 26–27.

91   Whorf, "Language, Mind, and Reality," 261.

92   Lévi-Strauss, *Myth and Meaning*, 3.

93   Peirce, *Collected Papers*.

94   Berger, "Twelve Theses," 20.

95   See, e.g., Noam Chomsky, *Topics in the Theory of Generative Grammar* (The Hague: Mouton, 1966).

96   Cf. Kohn, *How Forests Think*.

97   Susan Sontag, *Against Interpretation* (New York: Dell, 1964).

98   Sontag, *Against Interpretation*, 14.

99   Claude Lévi-Strauss, *Tristes Tropiques* (1955), trans. John Weightman and Doreen Weightman (New York: Penguin, 1973).

100 Lévi-Strauss, *Introduction to the Work of Marcel Mauss*, 62.

101 Sedgwick, *Touching Feeling*.

102 Geertz, *Works and Lives*.

103 Whorf, "Language, Mind, and Reality," 261.

Bibliography

Adato, Perry Miller. *Georgia O'Keeffe: A Life in Art*. Santa Fe, NM: Georgia O'Keeffe Museum, 2002.

Agamben, Giorgio. *Homo Sacer: Sovereign Power and Bare Life*. Translated by Daniel Heller-Roazen. Stanford, CA: Stanford University Press, 1998.

Aguirre, Robert D. *Informal Empire: Mexico and Central America in Victorian Culture*. Minneapolis: University of Minnesota Press, 2004.

Ahmed, Sara. *Queer Phenomenology: Orientations, Objects, Others*. Durham, NC: Duke University Press, 2006.

Allison, Anne, and Charles Piot. "Special Issue Section: Immunology." *Cultural Anthropology* 27, no. 1 (2012): 118–80.

Althusser, Louis. "Ideology and Ideological State Apparatuses (Notes towards an Investigation)." In *Lenin and Philosophy and Other Essays*, 121–73. London: New Left Books, 1971.

Anderson, Warwick. *The Collectors of Lost Souls: Turning Kuru Scientists into Whitemen*. Baltimore: Johns Hopkins University Press, 2008.

Anker, Elizabeth S., and Rita Felski, eds. *Critique and Postcritique*. Durham, NC: Duke University Press, 2017.

Arias, Arturo. "The Maya Movement, Postcolonialism and Cultural Agency." *Journal of Latin American Cultural Studies* 15, no. 2 (2006): 251–62.

Aronofsky, Darren, dir. *The Fountain*. Burbank, CA: Warner Brothers Pictures, 2006.

Artaud, Antonin. *To Have Done with the Judgment of God*. 1947. Reprint, Santa Rosa, CA: Black Sparrow, 1975.

Asad, Talal. *Formations of the Secular: Christianity, Islam, Modernity*. Stanford, CA: Stanford University Press, 2003.

Asad, Talal. *Genealogies of Religion: Discipline and Reasons of Power in Christianity and Islam*. Baltimore: Johns Hopkins University Press, 1993.

Asad, Talal, Wendy Brown, Judith Butler, and Saba Mahmood. *Is Critique Secular? Blasphemy, Injury, and Free Speech*. New York: Fordham University Press, 2013.

Astor-Aguilera, Miguel Angel. *The Maya World of Communicating Objects: Quadripartite Crosses, Trees, and Stones*. Albuquerque: University of New Mexico Press, 2010.

Atwood, Margaret. *Negotiating with the Dead: A Writer on Writing*. New York: Anchor, 2002.

Auerbach, Eric. *Mimesis: The Representation of Reality in Western Literature*. Translated by Willard R. Trask. Princeton, NJ: Princeton University Press, 1953. First published 1946.

Austin, John L. *How to Do Things with Words*. London: Oxford University Press, 1962.

Aveni, Anthony. *Empires of Time: Calendars, Clocks, and Cultures*. New York: Basic Books, 1989.

Aveni, Anthony. "Reaching for the Stars: Linda Schele's Contributions to Maya Astronomy." In *Heart of Creation: The Mesoamerican World and the Legacy of Linda Schele*, edited by Andrea Stone, 13–20. Tuscaloosa: University of Alabama Press, 2002.

Babb, Florence E. "Theorizing Gender, Race, and Cultural Tourism in Latin America: A View from Peru and Mexico." *Latin American Perspectives* 39, no. 6 (2012): 36–50.

Babb, Florence E. *Women's Place in the Andes: Engaging Decolonial Feminist Anthropology*. Berkeley: University of California Press, 2018.

Badiou, Alain, and Nicolas Truong. *In Praise of Love*. Translated by Peter Bush. New York: New Press, 2012.

Bakhtin, Mikhail. *The Dialogic Imagination: Four Essays*. Translated by Caryl Emerson and Michael Holquist. Austin: University of Texas Press, 1981.

Barad, Karen. *Meeting the Universe Halfway: Quantum Physics and the Entanglement of Matter and Meaning*. Durham, NC: Duke University Press, 2007.

Barua, Maan. "Lively Commodities and Encounter Value." *Environment and Planning D: Society and Space* 34, no. 4 (2016): 725–44.

Bassie-Sweet, Karen. *At the Edge of the World: Caves and Late Classic Maya World View*. Norman: University of Oklahoma Press, 1996.

Bassie-Sweet, Karen. *From the Mouth of the Dark Cave: Commemorative Sculpture of the Late Classic Maya*. Norman: University of Oklahoma Press, 1991.

Bataille, Georges. *The Accursed Share: An Essay on General Economy*. Vol. 1, *Consumption*. Translated by Robert Hurley. New York: Zone Books, 1991. First published 1949.

Bateson, Gregory. *Steps to an Ecology of Mind: Collected Essays in Anthropology, Psychiatry, Evolution, and Epistemology*. Chicago: University of Chicago Press, 1972.

Battaglia, Debbora. "Aeroponic Gardens and Their Magic: Plants/Persons/Ethics in Suspension." *History and Anthropology* 28, no. 3 (2017): 263–92.

Battaglia, Debbora. "Cosmos as Commons: An Activation of Cosmic Diplomacy." *e-flux* 58 (2014). https://www.e-flux.com/journal/58/61180/cosmos-as-commons-an-activation-of-cosmic-diplomacy/.

Battaglia, Debbora, ed. *E.T. Culture: Anthropology in Outerspaces*. Durham, NC: Duke University Press, 2005.

Battaglia, Debbora, and Rafael Antunes Almeida. "'Otherwise Anthropology' Otherwise: The View from Technology." Dispatches, *Cultural Anthropology* website,

February 24, 2014. https://culanth.org/fieldsights/493-otherwise-anthropology -otherwise-the-view-from-technology.

Baudrillard, Jean. *Simulations*. Translated by Paul Foss, Paul Patton, and Philip Batchman. New York: Semiotext(e), 1983.

Becker, Howard S. *Art Worlds*. Berkeley: University of California Press, 1982.

Behar, Ruth, and Deborah A. Gordon, eds. *Women Writing Culture*. Berkeley: University of California Press, 1995.

Benedict, Ruth. *Patterns of Culture*. New York: Houghton Mifflin, 1934.

Benjamin, Suresh P., and Samuel Zschokke. "Untangling the Tangle-Web: Web Construction Behavior of the Comb-Footed Spider *Steatoda triangulosa* and Comments on Phylogenetic Implications (Araneae: Theridiidae)." *Journal of Animal Behavior* 15, no. 6 (2002): 791–809.

Benjamin, Walter. *The Arcades Project*. Translated by Howard Eiland and Kevin McLaughlin. Cambridge, MA: Harvard University Press, 1999.

Benjamin, Walter. "The Work of Art in the Age of Mechanical Reproduction." In *Illuminations*, edited by Hannah Arendt, 217–51. New York: Schocken, 1968.

Bennett, Jane. *Vibrant Matter: A Political Ecology of Things*. Durham, NC: Duke University Press, 2010.

Benson, Elizabeth P. "The Rabbit Woman." In *Heart of Creation: The Mesoamerican World and the Legacy of Linda Schele*, edited by Andrea Stone, 266–68. Tuscaloosa: University of Alabama Press, 2002.

Berger, John. "Twelve Theses on the Economy of the Dead." In *Hold Everything Dear: Dispatches on Survival and Resistance*, 3–5. 1994. Reprint, New York: Pantheon, 2007.

Berlant, Lauren. *Cruel Optimism*. Durham, NC: Duke University Press, 2011.

Berlin, Heinrich. *Signos y significados en las inscripciones mayas*. Guatemala City: Instituto Nacional del Patrimonio Cultural de Guatemala, 1977.

Bernheimer, Charles, and Claire Kahane, eds. *In Dora's Case: Freud, Hysteria, Feminism*. 2nd ed. New York: Columbia University Press, 1990.

Bertino, Anthony J. *Forensic Science: Fundamentals and Investigations*. Mason, OH: Cengage Learning, 2012.

Beverley, John. *Subalternity and Representation: Arguments in Cultural Theory*. Durham, NC: Duke University Press, 1999.

Bhabha, Homi. "Of Mimicry and Man: The Ambivalence of Colonial Discourse." *October*, no. 28 (1984): 125–33.

Bickerton, Derek. *Language and Human Behavior*. Seattle: University of Washington Press, 1995.

Biehl, João. *Vita: Life in a Zone of Social Abandonment*. Berkeley: University of California Press, 2005.

Blackledge, Todd A., Nikolaj Scharff, Jonathan A. Coddington, Tamas Szüts, John W. Wenzel, Cheryl Y. Hayashi, and Ingi Agnarsson. "Reconstructing Web Evolution and Spider Diversification in the Molecular Era." *Proceedings of the National Academy of the Sciences* 106, no. 3 (2009): 5229–34.

Boas, Franz. *The Mind of Primitive Man*. New York: Macmillan, 1911.

Boas, Franz. *The Social Organization and Secret Societies of the Kwakiutl Indians*. Washington, DC: Smithsonian Institution, 1897.

Bohannan, Paul. "The Impact of Money on an African Subsistence Economy." *Journal of Economic History* 19, no. 4 (1959): 491–93.

Bonito Oliva, Rossella. "From the Immune Community to the Communitarian Immunity: On the Recent Reflections of Roberto Esposito." *Diacritics* 36, no. 2 (2006): 70–82.

Bourbon, Fabio. *The Lost Cities of the Mayas: The Life, Art, and Discoveries of Frederick Catherwood*. New York: Abbeville, 2000.

Bowie, David. "Space Oddity." On *Space Oddity*. RCA Victor LSP 4813, 1969, LP.

Bowker, Geoffrey C., and Susan Leigh Star. *Sorting Things Out: Classification and Its Consequences*. Cambridge, MA: MIT Press, 1999.

Brassier, Ray. *Nihil Unbound: Enlightenment and Extinction*. New York: Palgrave Macmillan, 2007.

Breglia, Lisa C. *Monumental Ambivalence: The Politics of Heritage*. Austin: University of Texas Press, 2006.

Brown, Wendy. *Edgework: Critical Essays on Knowledge and Politics*. Princeton, NJ: Princeton University Press, 2005.

Brumbach, Hetty Jo, and Robert Jarvenpra. "Woman the Hunter: Ethnoarchaeological Lessons from Chipewyan Life-Cycle Dynamics." In *Women in Prehistory*, edited by Cheryl Classen and Rosemary A. Joyce, 17–32. Philadelphia: University of Pennsylvania Press, 1997.

Bryant, Levi R. *The Democracy of Objects*. Ann Arbor: Open Humanities Press, 2011.

Buck-Morss, Susan. *The Dialectics of Seeing: Walter Benjamin and the Arcades Project*. Cambridge, MA: MIT Press, 1989.

Buikstra, Jane E., George R. Milner, and Jesper L. Boldsen. "Janaab' Pakal: The Age-at-Death Controversy Revisited." In *Janaab' Pakal of Palenque: Reconstructing the Life and Death of a Maya Ruler*, edited by Vera Tiesler and Andrea Cucina, 48–59. Tucson: University of Arizona Press, 2006.

Bulmer, Ralph. "Why Is the Cassowary Not a Bird? A Problem of Zoological Taxonomy among the Karam of the New Guinea Highlands." *Man* 2, no. 1 (1967): 5–25.

Butler, Judith. *Excitable Speech: A Politics of the Performative*. New York: Routledge, 1997.

Butler, Judith. *The Psychic Life of Power: Theories in Subjection*. Stanford, CA: Stanford University Press, 1997.

Campbell, Timothy. "Bíos, Immunity, Life: The Thought of Roberto Esposito." In Roberto Esposito, *Bíos: Biopolitics and Philosophy*, vii–xlii. Minneapolis: University of Minnesota Press, 2008.

Cancian, Frank. *Change and Uncertainty in a Peasant Economy: The Maya Corn Farmers of Zinacantan*. Stanford, CA: Stanford University Press, 1972.

Candea, Matei. "Arbitrary Locations: In Defence of the Bounded Field-Site." *Journal of the Royal Anthropological Institute* 13, no. 1 (2007): 167–84.

Candea, Matei. *Comparison in Anthropology: The Impossible Method*. Cambridge: Cambridge University Press, 2018.

Candea, Matei. "'I Fell in Love with Carlos the Meerkat': Engagement and Detachment in Human-Animal Relations." *American Ethnologist* 37, no. 2 (2010): 241–58.

Cañizares-Esguerra, Jorge. *Nature, Empire, and Nation: Explorations of the History of Science in the Iberian World*. Stanford, CA: Stanford University Press, 2006.

Carlsen, Robert S. *The War for the Heart and Soul of a Highland Maya Town*. Austin: University of Texas Press, 1997.

Carlsen, Robert S., and Martin Prechtel. "The Flowering of the Dead: An Interpretation of Highland Maya Culture." *Man* 26, no. 1 (1991): 23–42.

Casey, Edward. "Edges of Time, Edges of Memory." In *Time, Memory, Institution: Merleau-Ponty's New Ontology of Self*, edited by David Morris and Kym Maclaren, 254–74. Athens: Ohio University Press, 2015.

Casey, Edward. "How to Get from Space to Place in a Fairly Short Stretch of Time." In *Senses of Place*, edited by Steven Feld and Keith Basso, 13–52. Santa Fe: School for Advanced Research Press, 1996.

Cashulin, Kyle. "Joyce Livingston, Inverness Artist and Traveler." *Point Reyes (CA) Light*, July 29, 2010. http://www.ptreyeslight.com/article/joyce-livingston -inverness-artist-and-traveler.

Castañeda, Quetzil. *In the Museum of Maya Culture: Touring Chichén Itzá*. Minneapolis: University of Minnesota Press, 1996.

Castañeda, Quetzil. "'We Are Not Indigenous!' The Maya Identity of Yucatan, an Introduction." *Journal of Latin American Anthropology* 9, no. 1 (2004): 36–63.

Castillo Cocom, Juan. "'It Was Simply Their Word': Yucatec Maya PRInces in Yuca-PAN and the Politics of Respect." *Critique of Anthropology* 25, no. 2 (June 2005): 131–55.

Certeau, Michel de. *The Mystic Fable*. Vol. 1, *The Sixteenth and Seventeenth Centuries*. Chicago: University of Chicago Press, 1992.

Chakrabarty, Dipesh. *The Calling of History: Sir Jadunath Sarkar and His Empire of Truth*. Chicago: University of Chicago Press, 2015.

Chakrabarty, Dipesh. *Provincializing Europe: Postcolonial Thought and Historical Difference*. Princeton, NJ: Princeton University Press, 2000.

Chase, Diane Z., and Arlen F. Chase. "Maya Multiples: Individuals, Entries, and Tombs in Structure a34 of Caracol, Belize." *Latin American Antiquity* 7, no. 1 (1996): 61–79.

Chen, Nancy N. "'Speaking Nearby': A Conversation with Trinh T. Minh-ha." *Visual Anthropology Review* 8, no. 1 (1992): 82–91.

Chomsky, Noam. *Topics in the Theory of Generative Grammar*. The Hague: Mouton, 1966.

Choy, Timothy K., Lieba Faier, Michael J. Hathaway, Miyako Inoue, Shiho Satsuka, and Anna Tsing. "A New Form of Collaboration in Cultural Anthropology: Matsutake Worlds." *American Ethnologist* 36, no. 2 (2009): 380–403.

Christenson, Allen J. "The Sacred Tree of the Ancient Maya." *Journal of Book of Mormon Studies* 6, no. 1 (1997): 1–23.

Churchland, Paul M. "Reduction, Qualia, and the Direct Introspection of Brain States." *Journal of Philosophy* 82, no. 1 (1985): 8–28.

Clifford, James. "On Ethnographic Surrealism." *Comparative Studies in Society and History* 23, no. 4 (1981): 539–64.

Clifford, James. "Palenque Log." *Museum Anthropology* 17, no. 3 (1993): 58–66.

Clifford, James. *Routes: Travel and Translation in the Late Twentieth Century.* Cambridge, MA: Harvard University Press, 1997.

Clifford, James, and George E. Marcus, eds. *Writing Culture: The Poetics and Politics of Ethnography.* Berkeley: University of California Press, 1986.

Coe, Michael. *Breaking the Maya Code.* Rev. ed. New York: Thames and Hudson, 1999.

Coe, Michael. *Final Report: An Archaeologist Excavates His Past.* New York: Thames and Hudson, 2006.

Coe, Michael. "Ideology of the Maya Tomb." In *Maya Iconography,* edited by Elizabeth P. Benson and Gillett G. Griffin, 222–35. Princeton, NJ: Princeton University Press, 1988.

Coe, Michael D. "Linda Schele (1942–1998)." *American Anthropologist* 102, no. 1 (2000): 133–35.

Coe, Michael, and David Lebrun. "Interview with Linda Schele." 2005. *Breaking the Maya Code Interview Archives,* http://www.nightfirefilms.org/breakingthe mayacode/interview.archives.htm.

Cole, Douglas. *Franz Boas: The Early Years, 1858–1906.* Seattle: University of Washington Press, 1999.

Colwell-Chanthaphonh, Chip, and T. J. Ferguson, eds. *Collaboration in Archaeological Practice: Engaging Descendant Communities.* Lanham, MD: AltaMira, 2008.

Connor, Steve. "A Spider's Web That Could Catch an F-16." *Independent,* January 18, 2002. http://www.independent.co.uk/news/science/a-spiders-web-that-could -catch-an-f16-663700.html.

Coogan, Michael D., ed. *New Oxford Annotated Bible: New Revised Standard Version.* New York: Oxford University Press, 2001.

Corballis, Michael C. "Mirror Neurons and the Evolution of Language." *Brain and Language* 112, no. 1 (2010): 25–35.

Cornum, Lou. "White Magic." *New Inquiry,* February 5, 2018. https://thenewinquiry .com/white-magic/.

Cortázar, Julio. *Hopscotch.* London: Harvill, 1967.

Covarrubias, Miguel. *The Eagle, the Jaguar, and the Serpent: Indian Art of the Americas.* New York: Alfred A. Knopf, 1954.

Covarrubias, Miguel. *Indian Art of Mexico and Central America.* New York: Alfred A. Knopf, 1957.

Covarrubias, Miguel. *Island of Bali.* New York: Alfred A. Knopf, 1937.

Critchley, Simon. *Bowie.* New York: OR Books, 2016.

Daston, Lorraine, and Katharine Park. *Wonders and the Order of Nature, 1150–1750.* New York: Zone Books, 1998.

Dávalos, Eusebio, and Arturo Romano. "Estudio preliminar de los restos osteológicos encontrados en la Tumba del Templo de las Inscripciones, Palenque (in Alberto Ruz Lhullier, 'Exploraciones en Palenque: 1952')." *Anales del Instituto Nacional de Antropología e Historia, México* 6, no. 1 (1955): 107–10.

Deacon, Terrence W. *Incomplete Nature: How Mind Emerged from Matter.* New York: W. W. Norton, 2011.

de la Cadena, Marisol. *Earth Beings: Ecologies of Practice across Andean Worlds.* Durham, NC: Duke University Press, 2015.

Deleuze, Gilles. "Letter to a Harsh Critic." In *Negotiations, 1972–1990*, translated by Martin Joughin, 3–12. New York: Columbia University Press, 1995.

Deleuze, Gilles. *The Logic of Sense.* Translated by Mark Lester and Charles J. Stivale. New York: Columbia University Press, 1990. First published 1969.

Deleuze, Gilles, and Félix Guattari. *Anti-Oedipus: Capitalism and Schizophrenia.* Translated by Robert Hurley, Mark Seem, and Helen R. Lane. Minneapolis: University of Minnesota Press, 1983. First published 1972.

Deleuze, Gilles, and Félix Guattari. "Savages, Barbarians, Civilized Men." Translated by Robert Hurley and Mark Seem. In *Anti-Oedipus: Capitalism and Schizophrenia*, 139–271. Minneapolis: University of Minnesota Press, 1983. First published 1972.

Deleuze, Gilles, and Félix Guattari. *A Thousand Plateaus: Capitalism and Schizophrenia.* Translated by Brian Massumi. Minneapolis: University of Minnesota Press, 1987. First published 1980.

Deloria, Philip J. *Playing Indian.* New Haven, CT: Yale University Press, 1998.

Dennett, Daniel C. *The Intentional Stance.* Cambridge, MA: MIT Press, 1987.

Derrida, Jacques. *The Animal That Therefore I Am.* Translated by David Wills. New York: Fordham University Press, 2008.

Derrida, Jacques. "Faith and Knowledge: The Two Sources of 'Religion' at the Limits of Reason Alone." Translated by Samuel Weber. In *Religion*, edited by Jacques Derrida and Gianni Vattimo, 1–78. Stanford, CA: Stanford University Press, 1998.

Derrida, Jacques. "Force of Law: The 'Mystical Foundation of Authority.'" Translated by Mary Quaintance. In *Acts of Religion*, edited by Gil Anidjar, 230–98. New York: Routledge, 2002.

Derrida, Jacques. *The Gift of Death; and Literature in Secret.* Translated by David Wills. 1999. Reprint, Chicago: University of Chicago Press, 2008.

Derrida, Jacques. *Given Time: I. Counterfeit Money.* Translated by Peggy Kamuf. Chicago: University of Chicago Press, 1992.

Derrida, Jacques. "Hostipitality." In *Acts of Religion*, edited by Gil Anidjar, 358–420. New York: Routledge, 2002.

Derrida, Jacques. *Of Grammatology.* Translated by Gayatri Chakravorty Spivak. Baltimore: Johns Hopkins University Press, 1974.

Derrida, Jacques. "Plato's Pharmacy." In *Dissemination*, 67–186. Translated by Barbara Johnson. Chicago: University of Chicago Press, 1981.

Derrida, Jacques. *The Post Card: From Socrates to Freud and Beyond*. Translated by Alan Bass. Chicago: University of Chicago Press, 1987.

Derrida, Jacques. *Specters of Marx: The State of the Debt, the Work of Mourning and the New International*. Translated by Peggy Kamuf. New York: Routledge, 1994.

Derrida, Jacques. "Structure, Sign, and Play in the Discourse of the Human Sciences." In *Writing and Difference*, translated by Alan Bass, 278–93. London: Routledge, 1978.

Diamond, Jared. *Guns, Germs, and Steel: The Fates of Human Societies*. New York: W. W. Norton, 1997.

Diamond, Jared. *The Third Chimpanzee: The Evolution and Future of the Human Animal*. New York: HarperCollins, 1992.

Dick, Kirby, and Amy Ziering Kofman, dirs. *Derrida*. Los Angeles: Jane Doe Films, 2002.

Dickinson, Emily. *The Poems of Emily Dickinson*. Cambridge, MA: Harvard University Press, 1998.

Donagh, Rita. "Georgia O'Keeffe in Context." *Oxford Art Journal* 3, no. 1 (1980): 44–50.

Dönmez-Colin, Gönül. *Cinemas of the Other: A Personal Journey with Film-Makers from the Middle East and Central Asia*. Portland, OR: Intellect, 2006.

Dosse, François. *History of Structuralism: The Sign Sets, 1967–Present*. Translated by Deborah Glassman. Minneapolis: University of Minnesota Press, 1997.

Douglas, Mary. *Purity and Danger: An Analysis of Concepts of Pollution and Taboo*. 1966. Reprint, New York: Routledge, 2002.

Downey, Gary Lee, Joseph Dumit, and Sarah Williams. "Cyborg Anthropology." *Cultural Anthropology* 10, no. 2 (1995): 264–69.

Druyan, Ann. "Editor's Introduction." In Carl Sagan, *The Varieties of Scientific Experience: A Personal View of the Search for God*, ix–xvi. New York: Penguin, 2006.

Dumbarton Oaks Archives. "David Stuart." *75th Anniversary Blog*, September 26, 2017. https://www.doaks.org/research/library-archives/dumbarton-oaks-archives/historical-records/75th-anniversary/blog/david-stuart.

Durkheim, Émile. *The Elementary Forms of Religious Life*. Translated by Carol Cosman. Oxford: Oxford University Press, 2001. First published 1912.

Eagleton, Terry. "Anti-humanism." Review of *D. H. Lawrence and "Difference": Post-coloniality and the Poetry of the Present*, by Amit Chaudhuri. *London Review of Books* 26, no. 3 (2004): 16–18.

Edwards, Elizabeth. *The Camera as Historian: Amateur Photographers and Historical Imagination, 1885–1918*. Durham, NC: Duke University Press, 2012.

England, Nora C. "Mayan Language Revival and Revitalization: Linguists and Linguistic Ideologies." *American Anthropologist* 105, no. 4 (2003): 733–43.

Escobar, Arturo. *Designs for the Pluriverse: Radical Interdependence, Autonomy, and the Making of Worlds*. Durham, NC: Duke University Press, 2018.

Esposito, Roberto. *Bíos: Biopolitics and Philosophy*. Translated by Timothy Campbell. Minneapolis: University of Minnesota Press, 2008.

Evans, R. Tripp. *Romancing the Maya: Mexican Antiquity in the American Imagination, 1820–1915*. Austin: University of Texas Press, 2004.

Farman, Abou. "Speculative Matter: Secular Bodies, Minds, and Persons." *Cultural Anthropology* 28, no. 4 (2013): 737–59.

Farquhar, Judith. *Appetites: Food and Sex in Post-socialist China*. Durham, NC: Duke University Press, 2002.

Farriss, Nancy M. "Remembering the Future, Anticipating the Past: History, Time, and Cosmology among the Maya of Yucatan." *Comparative Studies in Society and History* 29, no. 3 (1987): 566–93.

Faubion, James D. "From the Ethical to the Themitical (and Back): Groundwork for an Anthropology of Ethics." In *Ordinary Ethics*, edited by Michael Lambek, 84–101. New York: Fordham University Press, 2011.

Federici, Silvia. *Caliban and the Witch: Women, the Body and Primitive Accumulation*. New York: Autonomedia, 2004.

Felman, Shoshana. *The Scandal of the Speaking Body: Don Juan with J. L. Austin, or Seduction in Two Languages*. Stanford, CA: Stanford University Press, 2003.

Fortun, Kim. *Advocacy after Bhopal: Environmentalism, Disaster, New Global Orders*. Chicago: University of Chicago Press, 2001.

Fortun, Kim. "Ethnography in/of/as Open Systems." *Reviews in Anthropology* 32, no. 2 (2003): 171–90.

Foster, George. "Nagualism in Mexico and Guatemala." *Acta Americana* 2, nos. 1–2 (1944): 85–103.

Foucault, Michel. "Governmentality." In *The Foucault Effect: Studies in Governmentality*, edited by Graham Burchell, Colin Gordon, and Peter Miller, 87–104. Chicago: University of Chicago Press, 1991.

Foucault, Michel. *The History of Sexuality*. Vol. 1, *An Introduction*. Translated by Robert Hurley. New York: Vintage Books, 1978.

Foucault, Michel. *The Order of Things: An Archaeology of the Human Sciences*. New York: Vintage Books, 1970.

Foucault, Michel. *Security, Territory, Population: Lectures at the Collège de France, 1977–1978*. Translated by Graham Burchell. New York: Palgrave Macmillan, 2007.

Franklin, Sarah. *Dolly Mixtures: The Remaking of Genealogy*. Durham, NC: Duke University Press, 2007.

Franklin, Sarah. "Science as Culture, Cultures of Science." *Annual Review of Anthropology* 24 (1995): 163–84.

Frazer, James George. *The Golden Bough: A Study in Magic and Religion*. 1922. Reprint, New York: Macmillan, 1963.

Freidel, David, Linda Schele, and Joy Parker. *Maya Cosmos: Three Thousand Years on the Shaman's Path*. New York: William Morrow, 1993.

Freidel, Frank. *Franklin D. Roosevelt: A Rendezvous with Destiny*. Boston: Back Bay Books, 1990.

Freud, Sigmund. *Beyond the Pleasure Principle*. New York: W. W. Norton, 1990. First
　published 1920.
Fuentes, Agustín. "Naturalcultural Encounters in Bali: Monkeys, Temples, Tourists,
　and Ethnoprimatology." *Cultural Anthropology* 25, no. 4 (2010): 600–624.
Geertz, Clifford. "Deep Play: Notes on the Balinese Cockfight." *Daedalus* 101, no. 1
　(1972): 1–37.
Geertz, Clifford. *Islam Observed: Religious Developments in Morocco and Indonesia*.
　Chicago: University of Chicago Press, 1968.
Geertz, Clifford. "Religion as a Cultural System." In *The Interpretation of Cultures*,
　88–125. New York: Basic Books, 1973.
Geertz, Clifford. "Thick Description: Toward an Interpretive Theory of Culture."
　In *The Interpretation of Cultures*, 3–30. New York: Basic Books, 1973.
Geertz, Clifford. *Works and Lives: The Anthropologist as Author*. Stanford, CA: Stan-
　ford University Press, 1988.
Gidwitz, Tom. "Picture Perfect." *Archaeology* 56, no. 6 (2003): 42–49.
Gillespie, Susan D. "Body and Soul among the Maya: Keeping the Spirits in Place." In
　"The Space and Place of Death," edited by Helaine Silverman and David B. Small,
　special issue, *Archeological Papers of the American Anthropological Association* 11, no. 1
　(2002): 67–78.
Gillespie, Susan D. "Personhood, Agency, and Mortuary Ritual: A Case Study from
　the Ancient Maya." *Journal of Anthropological Archaeology* 20, no. 1 (2001):
　73–112.
Gillespie, Susan D., and Rosemary A. Joyce. "Deity Relationships in Mesoamerican
　Cosmologies: The Case of the Maya God L." *Ancient Mesoamerica* 9, no. 2
　(1998): 279–96.
Gilroy, Paul. "Planetarity and Cosmopolitics." *British Journal of Sociology* 61, no. 3
　(2010): 620–26.
Godelier, Maurice. *The Enigma of the Gift*. Translated by Nora Scott. Chicago: University
　of Chicago Press, 1999.
Goetz, Delia, and Sylvanus Griswold Morley, eds. *Popol Vuh: The Sacred Book of the
　Ancient Quiché Maya*. Norman: University of Oklahoma Press, 1950.
Gollnick, Brian. *Reinventing the Lacandón: Subaltern Representations in the Rain
　Forest of Chiapas*. Tucson: University of Arizona Press, 2008.
Gorbach, Frida. "Hysteria and History: A Meditation on Mexico." *Social Text* 25, no. 3
　(2007): 85–101.
Gossen, Gary H. "Animal Souls and Human Destiny in Chamula." *Man* 10, no. 3
　(1975): 448–61.
Gossen, Gary H. "Animal Souls, Co-essences, and Human Destiny in Mesoamerica."
　In *Monsters, Tricksters, and Sacred Cows: Animal Tales and American Identities*,
　edited by Albert James Arnold, 80–107. Charlottesville: University of Virginia
　Press, 1996.
Gossen, Gary H. "From Olmecs to Zapatistas: A Once and Future History of Souls."
　American Anthropologist 96, no. 3 (1994): 553–70.

Gross, Toomas. "Letting the Air Out: *Aire* as an Empty Signifier in Oaxacan Understandings of Illness." *Culture, Medicine, and Psychiatry* 40, no. 4 (2016): 707–25.

Grube, Nikolai. "Ancient Maya Royal Biographies in a Comparative Perspective." In *Janaab' Pakal of Palenque: Reconstructing the Life and Death of a Maya Ruler*, edited by Vera Tiesler and Andrea Cucina, 146–66. Tucson: University of Arizona Press, 2006.

Habermas, Jürgen. *The Structural Transformation of the Public Sphere: An Inquiry into a Category of Bourgeois Society*. Translated by Thomas Burger. Cambridge, MA: MIT Press, 1989. First published 1962.

Hägglund, Martin. *Radical Atheism: Derrida and the Time of Life*. Stanford, CA: Stanford University Press, 2008.

Halberstam, Judith [Jack]. *Female Masculinity*. Durham, NC: Duke University Press, 1998.

Hall, Kira. "Performativity." *Journal of Linguistic Anthropology* 9, nos. 1–2 (2000): 184–87.

Hanks, William F. *Converting Words: Maya in the Age of the Cross*. Berkeley: University of California Press, 2010.

Haraway, Donna J. "The Biopolitics of Postmodern Bodies: Determinations of Self in Immune System Discourse." *Differences* 1, no. 1 (1989): 3–43.

Haraway, Donna J. "A Cyborg Manifesto: Science, Technology, and Socialist-Feminism in the Late Twentieth Century." In *Simians, Cyborgs, and Women: The Reinvention of Nature*, 149–81. New York: Routledge, 1991.

Haraway, Donna J. "Ecce Homo, Ain't (Ar'n't) I a Woman, and Inappropriate/d Others: The Human in a Post-humanist Landscape." In *Feminists Theorize the Political*, edited by Judith Butler and Joan W. Scott, 86–100. New York: Routledge, 1992.

Haraway, Donna J. *Modest_Witness@Second_Millennium. FemaleMan©_Meets_OncoMouse™: Feminism and Technoscience*. New York: Routledge, 1997.

Haraway, Donna J. "Situated Knowledges: The Science Question in Feminism and the Privilege of Partial Perspective." *Feminist Studies* 14, no. 3 (1988): 575–99.

Haraway, Donna J. *Staying with the Trouble: Making Kin in the Chthulucene*. Durham, NC: Duke University Press, 2016.

Haraway, Donna J. *When Species Meet*. Minneapolis: University of Minnesota Press, 2008.

Hardt, Michael, and Antonio Negri. *Commonwealth*. Cambridge, MA: Harvard University Press, 2009.

Hardt, Michael, and Antonio Negri. *Empire*. Cambridge, MA: Harvard University Press, 2000.

Harman, Graham. *Prince of Networks: Bruno Latour and Metaphysics*. Melbourne: re.press, 2009.

Hartigan, John. *Aesop's Anthropology: A Multispecies Approach*. Minneapolis: University of Minnesota Press, 2014.

Hartsock, Nancy C. M. "The Feminist Standpoint: Developing the Ground for a Specifically Feminist Historical Materialism." In *Feminist Social Thought: A Reader*, edited by Diana Tietjens Meyers, 461–83. New York: Routledge, 1997.

Harvey, Bruce. "The Archaeological Sublime of Tropical America: Ephraim G. Squier and John L. Stephens." In *American Geographics: U.S. National Narratives and the Representation of the Non-European World, 1830–1865*, 150–93. Stanford, CA: Stanford University Press, 2001.

Hawking, Stephen W. *A Brief History of Time: From the Big Bang to Black Holes.* New York: Bantam, 1988.

Hayden, Cori. *When Nature Goes Public: The Making and Unmaking of Bioprospecting in Mexico.* Princeton, NJ: Princeton University Press, 2004.

Hegel, Georg Wilhelm Friedrich. *Phenomenology of Spirit.* Translated by A. V. Miller. Oxford: Clarendon, 1977. First published 1807.

Heidegger, Martin. *The Question Concerning Technology and Other Essays.* Translated by William Lovitt. New York: Harper and Row, 1977.

Helmreich, Stefan. *Alien Ocean: Anthropological Voyages in Microbial Seas.* Berkeley: University of California Press, 2009.

Helmreich, Stefan. "Nature/Culture/Seawater." *American Anthropologist* 113, no. 1 (2011): 132–44.

Helmreich, Stefan. *Sounding the Limits of Life: Essays in the Anthropology of Biology and Beyond.* Princeton, NJ: Princeton University Press, 2016.

Helmreich, Stefan. "What Was Life? Answers from Three Limit Biologies." *Critical Inquiry* 37, no. 4 (2011): 671–96.

Helmreich, Stefan, and Sophia Roosth. "Life Forms: A Keyword Entry." *Representations* 112, no. 1 (2010): 27–53.

Holbraad, Martin. "The Power of Powder: Multiplicity and Motion in the Divinatory Cosmology of Cuban Ifá (Or *Mana*, Again)." In *Thinking through Things: Theorising Artefacts Ethnographically*, edited by Amiria Henare, Martin Holbraad, and Sari Wastell, 189–224. New York: Routledge, 2007.

hooks, bell. *Outlaw Culture: Resisting Representations.* New York: Routledge, 1994.

Houston, Stephen D. "Into the Minds of Ancients: Advances in Maya Glyph Studies." *Journal of World Prehistory* 14, no. 2 (2000): 121–201.

Houston, Stephen D. "The Shifting Now: Aspect, Deixis, and Narrative in Classic Maya Texts." *American Anthropologist* 99, no. 2 (1997): 291–305.

Houston, Stephen, Oswaldo Chinchilla Mazarieogos, and David Stuart. *The Decipherment of Ancient Maya Writing.* Norman: University of Oklahoma Press, 2001.

Houston, Stephen, and David Stuart. "The *Way* Glyph: Evidence for 'Co-essences' among the Classic Maya." In *Research Reports on Ancient Maya Writing*, edited by George Stuart. Washington, DC: Center for Maya Research, 1989.

Houston, Stephen, David Stuart, and Karl Taube. *The Memory of Bones: Body, Being, and Experience among the Classic Maya.* Austin: University of Texas Press, 2006.

Hsieh, Jennifer C. "Noise Governance and the Hearing Subject in Urban Taiwan." PhD diss., Stanford University, 2017.

Ingold, Tim. *Being Alive: Essays on Movement, Knowledge, and Description*. New York: Routledge, 2011.

Ingold, Tim. "Toward an Ecology of Materials." *Annual Review of Anthropology* 41 (2012): 427–42.

Irvine, Judith T., and Susan Gal. "Language Ideology and Linguistic Differentiation." In *Regimes of Language: Ideologies, Politics, and Identities*, edited by P. V. Kroskrity, 35–83. Santa Fe, NM: School for Advanced Research Press, 2000.

Ivakhiv, Adrian. "Toward a Multicultural Ecology." *Organization and Environment* 15, no. 4 (2002): 389–409.

James, William. *The Varieties of Religious Experience: A Study in Human Nature*. New York: Longmans Green and Co., 1936.

Jameson, Fredric. "First Impressions." Review of *The Parallax View*, by Slavoj Žižek. *London Review of Books* 28, no. 17 (September 7, 2006): 7–8.

Jones, Graham M. *Magic's Reason: An Anthropology of Analogy*. Chicago: University of Chicago Press, 2017.

Jones, Lindsay. "Conquests of the Imagination: Maya-Mexican Polarity and the Story of Chichén Itzá." *American Anthropologist* 99, no. 2 (1997): 275–90.

Joyce, Rosemary A. "Introduction." In Tatiana Proskouriakoff, *Maya History*, edited by Rosemary A. Joyce, xvii–xxv. Austin: University of Texas Press, 1993.

Kant, Immanuel. *Critique of Pure Reason*. Translated by Paul Guyer and Allen W. Wood. Cambridge: Cambridge University Press, 1998. First published 1781.

Kant, Immanuel. *Prolegomena to Any Future Metaphysics That Will Be Able to Present Itself as a Science*. Translated and edited by Gary Hatfield. Cambridge: Cambridge University Press, 1997. First published 1783.

Kawa, Nicholas C. "Shit." Theorizing the Contemporary, *Cultural Anthropology* website, April 6, 2016. https://culanth.org/fieldsights/843-shit.

Kelly, Michael, ed. *Critique and Power: Recasting the Foucault/Habermas Debate*. Cambridge, MA: MIT Press, 1994.

Kerr, Barbara, and Justin Kerr. "The *Way* of God L: The Princeton Vase Revisited." *Record of the Art Museum, Princeton University* 64 (2005): 71–79.

Kim, Eleana. "Invasive Others and Significant Others: Strange Kinship and Interspecies Ethics near the Korean Demilitarized Zone." *Social Research: An International Quarterly* 84, no. 1 (2017): 203–20.

King, Noel. "'At Least a Witness to Myself': On Watching *The American Dreamer* after Learning of the Death of Dennis Hopper." *Studies in Documentary Film* 4, no. 2 (2010): 109–18.

Kirksey, Eben, ed. *The Multispecies Salon*. Durham, NC: Duke University Press, 2014.

Kirksey, Eben, and Stefan Helmreich. "The Emergence of Multispecies Ethnography." *Cultural Anthropology* 25, no. 4 (2010): 545–76.

Klein, Cecilia. "Mayamania: *The Blood of Kings* in Retrospect." *Art Journal* 47, no. 1 (1988): 42–46.

Klein, Cecelia F., Eulogio Guzmán, Elisa C. Mandell, and Maya Stanfield-Mazzi. "The Role of Shamanism in Mesoamerican Art." *Current Anthropology* 43, no. 3 (2002): 383–419.

Knorozov, Yuri V. "Drevniaia Pis'mennost' Tsentral'noi Ameriki." *Sovietskaya Etnografiya* 3, no. 2 (1952): 100–118.

Knorozov, Yuri V. "The Problem of the Study of the Maya Hieroglyphic Writing." *American Antiquity* 23, no. 3 (1958): 284–91.

Knorr Cetina, Karin. *Epistemic Cultures: How the Sciences Make Knowledge.* Cambridge, MA: Harvard University Press, 1999.

Kohn, Eduardo. *How Forests Think: Toward an Anthropology beyond the Human.* Berkeley: University of California Press, 2013.

Kopnina, Helen. "Beyond Multispecies Ethnography: Engaging with Violence and Animal Rights in Anthropology." *Critique of Anthropology* 37, no. 3 (2017): 333–57.

Kosek, Jake. "Ecologies of Empire: On the New Uses of the Honeybee." *Cultural Anthropology* 25, no. 4 (2010): 241–58.

Kuhn, Thomas. *The Structure of Scientific Revolutions.* 4th ed. Chicago: University of Chicago Press, 2012. First published 1962.

Land, Nick. *Fanged Noumena: Collected Writings 1987–2007.* Falmouth, UK: Urbanomic, 2011.

Latham, R. G. *Man and His Migrations.* London: John Van Voorst, Paternoster Row, 1851.

Latour, Bruno. "Anthropology at the Time of the Anthropocene: A Personal View of What Is to Be Studied." In *The Anthropology of Sustainability: Beyond Development and Progress,* edited by Marc Brightman and Jerome Lewis, 35–50. New York: Palgrave Macmillan, 2017.

Latour, Bruno. "Foreword: Stengers's Shibboleth." Translated by Paul Bains. In Isabelle Stengers, *Power and Invention: Situating Science,* vii–xx. Minneapolis: University of Minnesota Press, 1997.

Latour, Bruno. "From Realpolitik to Dingpolitik or How to Make Things Public." In *Making Things Public: Atmospheres of Democracy,* edited by Bruno Latour and Peter Weibel, 14–41. Cambridge, MA: MIT Press, 2005.

Latour, Bruno. "Irreductions." In *The Pasteurization of France,* 153–238. Cambridge, MA: Harvard University Press, 1988.

Latour, Bruno. *Pandora's Hope: Essays on the Reality of Science Studies.* Cambridge, MA: Harvard University Press, 1999.

Latour, Bruno. *Politics of Nature: How to Bring the Sciences into Democracy.* Translated by Catherine Porter. Cambridge, MA: Harvard University Press, 2004.

Latour, Bruno. *Reassembling the Social: An Introduction to Actor-Network-Theory.* Oxford: Oxford University Press, 2005.

Latour, Bruno. *Science in Action: How to Follow Scientists and Engineers through Society.* Cambridge, MA: Harvard University Press, 1987.

Latour, Bruno. *We Have Never Been Modern.* Cambridge, MA: Harvard University Press, 1993.

Latour, Bruno. "Why Has Critique Run Out of Steam? From Matters of Fact to Matters of Concern." *Critical Inquiry* 30, no. 2 (2004): 225–48.

Latour, Bruno, and Steve Woolgar. *Laboratory Life: The Construction of Scientific Facts*. Princeton, NJ: Princeton University Press, 1986.

Lazaris, Anthoula, Steven Arcidiacono, Yue Huang, Jiang-Feng Zhou, François Duguay, Nathalie Chretien, Elizabeth A. Welsh, Jason W. Soares, and Costas N. Karatzas. "Spider Silk Fibers Spun from Soluble Recombinant Silk Produced in Mammalian Cells." *Science* 295, no. 5554 (2002): 472–76.

Lebrun, David. "Transcript of Filmed Interview: Gillett Griffin." Night Fire Films, interview from March 24, 2005, accessed November 7, 2019. http://www .nightfirefilms.org/breakingthemayacode/interviews/GriffinTRANSCRIPT .pdf.

Lee, Richard B., and Irven DeVore, eds. *Man the Hunter*. New York: Aldine, 1968.

Leibniz, Gottfried. *The Monadology*. Translated by George MacDonald Ross. Oxford: Oxford University Press, 1984. First published 1714.

Lepselter, Susan. *The Resonance of Unseen Things: Poetics, Power, Captivity and UFOs in the American Uncanny*. Ann Arbor: University of Michigan Press, 2016.

Lévi-Strauss, Claude. *The Elementary Structures of Kinship*. Translated by James Harle Bell and John Richard von Sturmer. Boston: Beacon, 1969. First published 1949.

Lévi-Strauss, Claude. *Introduction to the Work of Marcel Mauss*. Translated by Felicity Baker. London: Routledge and Kegan Paul, 1987. First published 1950.

Lévi-Strauss, Claude. *Myth and Meaning: Cracking the Code of Culture*. 1978. Reprint, New York: Schocken, 1995.

Lévi-Strauss, Claude. *The Savage Mind*. Chicago: University of Chicago Press, 1966.

Lévi-Strauss, Claude. *Structural Anthropology*. Translated by Claire Jacobsen and Brooke Grundfest Schoepf. New York: Basic Books, 1963.

Lévi-Strauss, Claude. "The Structural Study of Myth." *Journal of American Folklore* 68, no. 270 (1955): 428–44.

Lévi-Strauss, Claude. *Tristes Tropiques*. Translated by John Weightman and Doreen Weightman. New York: Penguin, 1973. First published 1955.

Lévi-Strauss, Claude. *We Are All Cannibals and Other Essays*. Translated by Jane Marie Todd. New York: Columbia University Press, 2016.

Lingis, Alphonso. *Excesses: Eros and Culture*. Albany: State University of New York Press, 1983.

Livingston, Julie, and Jasbir K. Puar, eds. "Interspecies" (special issue). *Social Text* 29, no. 1 (2011).

López Austin, Alfredo. *The Rabbit on the Face of the Moon: Mythology in the Mesoamerican Tradition*. Salt Lake City: University of Utah Press, 1996.

Luhan, Mabel Dodge. *Lorenzo in Taos*. London: Martin Secker, 1933.

MacLeod, Barbara, and Dennis E. Puleston. "Pathways into Darkness: The Search for the Road to Xibalbá." In *Tercera Mesa Redonda de Palenque*, edited by Merle Greene Robertson and Donnan Call Jeffers, 71–77. Monterey, CA: Pre-Columbian Art Research, 1979.

Mahmood, Saba. *Politics of Piety: The Islamic Revival and the Feminist Subject*. Princeton, NJ: Princeton University Press, 2005.

Mahmood, Saba. *Religious Difference in a Secular Age: A Minority Report*. Princeton, NJ: Princeton University Press, 2016.

Maldonado-Torres, Nelson. "On the Coloniality of Being: Contributions to the Development of a Concept." *Cultural Studies* 21, nos. 2–3 (2007): 240–70.

Malinowski, Bronislaw. *Argonauts of the Western Pacific*. 1928. Reprint, New York: E. P. Dutton, 1961.

Malinowski, Bronislaw. *Magic, Science and Religion and Other Essays*. Glencoe, IL: Free Press, 1948.

Malkin, Bonnie. "Bird-Eating Spiders: New Pictures." *Telegraph*, October 30, 2008. http://www.telegraph.co.uk/earth/earthnews/3354097/Bird-eating-spiders-new-pictures.html.

Malkin, Bonnie. "Giant Spider Eating Bird Caught on Camera." *Telegraph*, October 22, 2008. http://www.telegraph.co.uk/earth/earthnews/3353693/Giant-spider-eating-a-bird-caught-on-camera.html.

Mallon, Florencia E. "The Promise and Dilemma of Subaltern Studies: Perspectives from Latin American History." *American Historical Review* 99, no. 5 (1994): 1491–1515.

Marcus, George E., and Michael M. J. Fischer. *Anthropology as Cultural Critique: An Experimental Moment in the Human Sciences*. 2nd ed. Chicago: University of Chicago Press, 1999.

Marcus, Joyce. *Emblem and State in the Classic Maya Lowlands: An Epigraphic Approach to Territorial Organization*. Washington, DC: Dumbarton Oaks Center for Pre-Columbian Studies, 1976.

Margulis, Lynn, and René Fester, eds. *Symbiosis as a Source of Evolutionary Innovation*. Cambridge, MA: MIT Press, 1991.

Margulis, Lynn, and Dorion Sagan. *Acquiring Genomes: A Theory of the Origins of Species*. New York: Basic Books, 2002.

Margulis, Lynn, and Dorion Sagan. *Dazzle Gradually: Reflections on the Nature of Nature*. White River Junction, VT: Chelsea Green, 2007.

Martin, Emily. "Anthropology and the Cultural Study of Science." *Science, Technology and Human Values* 23, no. 1 (1998): 24–44.

Masco, Joseph. "'It Is a Strict Law That Bids Us Dance': Cosmologies, Colonialism, Death, and Ritual." *Comparative Studies in Society and History* 37, no. 1 (1995): 41–75.

Mathews, Peter, and Linda Schele. "Lords of Palenque—The Glyphic Evidence." In *Primera Mesa Redonda de Palenque: A Conference on the Art, Iconography, and Dynastic History of Palenque*, edited by Merle Greene Robertson, 63–75. Pebble Beach, CA: Pre-Columbian Art Research Institute, 1974.

Mauss, Marcel. *A General Theory of Magic*. Translated by Robert Brain. London: Routledge, 2001. First published 1950.

Mauss, Marcel. *The Gift*. Translated by Jane I. Guyer. Chicago: HAU Books, 2016. First published 1925.

Mayer, Karl Herbert. "A Painted Venus Glyph in the Tower at Palenque." *Archaeoastronomy* 6 (1983): 96–98.

Mazzarella, William. *The Mana of Mass Society*. Chicago: University of Chicago Press, 2017.

Mazzarella, William. "Sense out of Sense: Notes on the Affect/Ethics Impasse." *Cultural Anthropology* 32, no. 2 (2017): 199–208.

McAnany, Patricia. *Living with the Ancestors: Kinship and Kingship in Ancient Maya Society*. Austin: University of Texas Press, 1995.

McLean, Stuart. *Fictionalizing Anthropology: Encounters and Fabulations at the Edges of the Human*. Minneapolis: University of Minnesota, 2017.

McNeill, William H. *Mythistory and Other Essays*. Chicago: University of Chicago Press, 1986.

Merry, Sally Engle. "Ethnography in the Archives." In *Practicing Ethnography in Law: New Dialogues, Enduring Methods*, edited by June Starr and Mark Goodale, 128–42. New York: Palgrave Macmillan, 2002.

Mialet, Hélène. *Hawking Incorporated: Stephen Hawking and the Anthropology of the Knowing Subject*. Chicago: University of Chicago Press, 2012.

Mignolo, Walter D. "Introduction: Coloniality of Power and De-Colonial Thinking." *Cultural Studies* 21, nos. 2–3 (2007): 155–67.

Mignolo, Walter D. *Local Histories/Global Designs: Coloniality, Subaltern Knowledges, and Border Thinking*. Princeton, NJ: Princeton University Press, 2000.

Miller, Jacques-Alain. "The Monologue of L'Apparole." *Qui Parle: Critical Humanities and Social Sciences* 9, no. 2 (1996): 160–82.

Miller, J. Hillis. "Derrida's Destinerrance." *MLN* 121, no. 4 (2006): 893–910.

Trinh T. Minh-ha, dir. *Reassemblage: From the Firelight to the Screen*. New York: Women Make Movies, 1983.

Trinh T. Minh-ha, dir. *Surname Viet Given Name Nam*. New York: Women Make Movies, 1989.

Mitchell, W. J. T. *What Do Pictures Want? The Lives and Loves of Images*. Chicago: University of Chicago Press, 2005.

Moder, Gregor. *Hegel and Spinoza: Substance and Negativity*. Evanston, IL: Northwestern University Press, 2017.

Molad, Leital. "American Icons: Georgia O'Keeffe's Skull Paintings." *Studio 360*, September 2, 2011 (originally aired November 12, 2010), Public Radio International and WNYC. https://www.pri.org/stories/2011-09-02/american-icons -georgia-okeeffes-skull-paintings.

Monaghan, John. "The Person, Destiny, and the Construction of Difference in Mesoamerica." *RES: Anthropology and Aesthetics* 33 (1998): 137–46.

Montag, John, S.J. "Revelation: The False Legacy of Suárez." In *Radical Orthodoxy: A New Theology*, edited by John Milbank, Catherine Pickstock, and Graham Ward, 38–63. London: Routledge, 2002.

Montejo, Victor D. "Becoming Maya? Appropriation of the White Shaman." *Native Americas* 16, no. 1 (1999): 58–60.

Moore [Shaw], Anne M., Christopher R. Moore, and Zachary R. Gross. "History beneath Us: Public Archaeology at the Lew Wallace Study and Museum in Crawfordsville." *Indiana Archaeology* 7, no. 1 (2012): 166–70.

Moreiras, Alberto. "A Storm Blowing from Paradise: Negative Globality and Critical Regionalism." In *The Latin American Subaltern Studies Reader*, edited by Ileana Rodríguez, 81–107. Durham, NC: Duke University Press, 2001.

Morley, Sylvanus Griswold. *The Ancient Maya*. Stanford, CA: Stanford University Press, 1946.

Morton, Timothy. *The Ecological Thought*. Cambridge, MA: Harvard University Press, 2010.

Moten, Fred. *Black and Blur*. Durham, NC: Duke University Press, 2017.

Munn, Nancy D. *The Fame of Gawa: A Symbolic Study of Value Transformation in a Massim (Papua New Guinea) Society*. Cambridge: Cambridge University Press, 1986.

Nakassis, Constantine V. "Brand, Citationality, Performativity." *American Anthropologist* 114, no. 4 (2012): 624–38.

Napier, A. David. *The Age of Immunology: Conceiving a Future in an Alienating World*. Chicago: University of Chicago Press, 2003.

Nelson, Diane M. *A Finger in the Wound: Body Politics in Quincentennial Guatemala*. Berkeley: University of California Press, 1999.

Nelson, Diane M. "Maya Hackers and the Cyberspatialized Nation-State: Modernity, Ethnostalgia, and a Lizard Queen in Guatemala." *Cultural Anthropology* 11, no. 3 (1996): 287–308.

Nelson, Diane M. *Reckoning: The Ends of War in Guatemala*. Durham, NC: Duke University Press, 2009.

Nelson, Maggie. *The Argonauts*. Minneapolis: Graywolf, 2015.

Newell, Sasha. "The Affectiveness of Symbols: Materiality, Magicality, and the Limits of the Antisemiotic Turn." *Current Anthropology* 59, no. 1 (2018): 1–22.

Nietzsche, Friedrich. *The Gay Science, with a Prelude in German Rhymes and an Appendix of Songs*. Translated by Josefine Nauckhoff and Adrian Del Caro. Cambridge: Cambridge University Press, 2001.

Noys, Benjamin. *The Persistence of the Negative: A Critique of Contemporary Continental Theory*. Edinburgh: Edinburgh University Press, 2010.

Ohnuki-Tierney, Emiko. "The Power of Absence: Zero Signifiers and Their Transgressions." *L'Homme* 130 (1994): 59–76.

Olson, Valerie A. "Political Ecology in the Extreme: Asteroid Activism and the Making of an Environmental Solar System." *Anthropological Quarterly* 85, no. 4 (2012): 1027–44.

Ozeki, Ruth. "The Anthropologists' Kids." In *Mixed: An Anthology of Short Fiction on the Multiracial Experience*, edited by Chandra Prasad, 21–45. New York: W. W. Norton, 2006.

Ozeki, Ruth. "The Art of Losing: On Writing, Dying, and Mom." *Shambhala Sun* 2 (2008): 68–76.

Ozeki, Ruth, dir. *Halving the Bones*. New York: Women Make Movies, 1995.

Palmquist, Stephen. "Kant's Cosmogony Re-evaluated." *Studies in History and Philosophy of Science* 18, no. 3 (1987): 255–69.

Pandian, Anand, and Stuart McLean, eds. *Crumpled Paper Boat*. Durham, NC: Duke University Press, 2017.

Parsons, Elsie Clews. *Mitla: Town of Souls*. Chicago: University of Chicago Press, 1936.

Paxson, Heather. "Post-Pasteurian Cultures: The Microbiopolitics of Raw-Milk Cheese in the United States." *Cultural Anthropology* 23, no. 1 (2008): 15–47.

Peirce, Charles Sanders. *Collected Papers of Charles Sanders Peirce*. Cambridge, MA: Harvard University Press, 1931.

Pope, Alexander. *An Essay on Man*. 1734. Reprint, Indianapolis: Bobbs-Merrill, 1965.

Popper, Karl. *The Logic of Scientific Discovery*. 1934. Reprint, New York: Routledge, 1959.

Povinelli, Elizabeth A. "Geontologies of the Otherwise." Theorizing the Contemporary, *Cultural Anthropology* website, January 13, 2014. http://www.culanth .org/fieldsights/465-geontologies-of-the-otherwise.

Povinelli, Elizabeth A. "Routes/Worlds." *e-flux* 27 (2011). https://www.e-flux.com /journal/27/67991/routes-worlds/.

Pratt, Mary Louise. *Imperial Eyes: Studies in Travel Writing and Transculturation*. New York: Routledge, 1992.

Prigogine, Ilya, and Isabelle Stengers. *Order out of Chaos: Man's New Dialogue with Nature*. London: Bantam, 1984.

Proskouriakoff, Tatiana. "Historical Data in the Inscriptions of Yaxchilan (Part I)." *Estudios de Cultura Maya* 3 (1963): 149–67.

Proskouriakoff, Tatiana. "Historical Data in the Inscriptions of Yaxchilan (Part II)." *Estudios de Cultura Maya* 4 (1964): 177–201.

Proskouriakoff, Tatiana. "Historical Implications of a Pattern of Dates at Piedras Negras, Guatemala." *American Antiquity* 25, no. 4 (1960): 454–75.

Proskouriakoff, Tatiana. "The Lords of the Maya Realm." *Expedition Magazine* 4, no. 1 (1961): 14–21.

Puig de la Bellacasa, Maria. "Matters of Care in Technoscience: Assembling Neglected Things." *Social Studies of Science* 41, no. 1 (2011): 85–106.

Quijano, Aníbal. "Coloniality of Power and Eurocentrism in Latin America." *International Sociology* 15, no. 2 (2000): 215–32.

Rabinow, Paul. *French DNA: Trouble in Purgatory*. Chicago: University of Chicago Press, 1999.

Radin, Joanna. *Life on Ice: A History of New Uses for Cold Blood*. Chicago: University of Chicago Press, 2017.

Radin, Paul. *The Trickster: A Study in American Indian Mythology*. 1956. Reprint, New York: Schocken, 1972.

Rae, Gavin. "The Political Significance of the Face: Deleuze's Critique of Levinas." *Critical Horizons* 17, nos. 3–4 (2016): 279–303.

Raffles, Hugh. *Insectopedia*. New York: Pantheon, 2010.

Redfield, Peter. *Space in the Tropics: From Convicts to Rockets in French Guiana*. Berkeley: University of California Press, 2000.

Redfield, Robert, and Alfonso Villa Rojas. *Chan Kom: A Maya Village*. 1934. Reprint, Chicago: University of Chicago Press, 1971.

Restall, Matthew. "Maya Ethnogenesis." *Journal of Latin American Anthropology* 9, no. 1 (2004): 64–89.

Rheinberger, Hans-Jörg. "Experimental Systems, Graphematic Spaces." In *Inscribing Science: Scientific Texts and the Materiality of Communication*, edited by Timothy Lenoir, 285–303. Stanford, CA: Stanford University Press, 1998.

Rheinberger, Hans-Jörg. "Experimental Systems: Historiality, Narration, and Deconstruction." *Science in Context* 7, no. 1 (1994): 65–81.

Rheinberger, Hans-Jörg. *Toward a History of Epistemic Things: Synthesizing Proteins in the Test Tube*. Stanford, CA: Stanford University Press, 1997.

Rice, Prudence M. *Maya Calendar Origins: Monuments, Mythistory, and the Materialization of Time*. Austin: University of Texas Press, 2007.

Ricoeur, Paul. *Hermeneutics and the Human Sciences*. Translated by John B. Thompson. Cambridge: Cambridge University Press, 1981.

Riding In, James. "Repatriation: A Pawnee's Perspective." *American Indian Quarterly* 20, no. 2 (1996): 238–50.

Riles, Annelise, ed. *Documents: Artifacts of Modern Knowledge*. Ann Arbor: University of Michigan Press, 2006.

Robbins, Joel. "Beyond the Suffering Subject: Toward an Anthropology of the Good." *Journal of the Royal Anthropological Institute* 19, no. 3 (2013): 447–62.

Robertson, Merle Greene, ed. *Primera Mesa Redonda de Palenque: A Conference on the Art, Iconography, and Dynastic History of Palenque*. San Francisco: Pre-Columbian Art Research Institute, 1974.

Robinson, Andrew. "Symbolic Victory." *Times Higher Education*, March 17, 1995. http://www.timeshighereducation.co.uk/story.asp?storyCode=97205& sectioncode=26.

Roitman, Janet. *Anti-Crisis*. Durham, NC: Duke University Press, 2014.

Rosaldo, Michelle Z. "The Things We Do with Words: Ilongot Speech Acts and Speech Act Theory in Philosophy." *Language in Society* 11 (1982): 203–37.

Rose, Barbara. *American Art since 1900*. New York: Thames and Hudson, 1967.

Rose, Deborah. "Introduction: Writing in the Anthropocene." *Australian Humanities Review* 47 (2009): 87.

Rose, Nikolas S. *The Politics of Life Itself: Biomedicine, Power, and Subjectivity in the Twenty-First Century*. Princeton, NJ: Princeton University Press, 2006.

Rousseau, Jean-Jacques. "Essay on the Origin of Languages." Translated by John T. Scott. In *Essay on the Origin of Languages and Writings Related to Music*, edited by John T. Scott, 289–332. Hanover, NH: University Press of New England, 1998. First published 1761.

Rubin, Gayle. "The Traffic in Women: Notes on the 'Political Economy' of Sex." In *Toward an Anthropology of Women*, edited by Rayna R. Reiter, 157–210. New York: Monthly Review Press, 1975.

Rudnick, Lois Palken. *Utopian Vistas: The Mabel Dodge Luhan House and the American Counterculture.* Albuquerque: University of New Mexico Press, 1996.

Ruz Lhuillier, Alberto. "Gerontocracy at Palenque?" In *Social Process in Maya Prehistory: Studies in Honour of Sir Eric Thompson*, edited by Norman Hammond, 287–95. London: Academic Press, 1977.

Ruz Lhuillier, Alberto. *La tumba de Palenque.* Mexico City: Instituto Nacional de Antropología e Historia, 1974.

Ryle, Gilbert. *The Concept of Mind.* 1949. Reprint, Chicago: University of Chicago Press, 2000.

Sagan, Carl. *Billions and Billions: Thoughts on Life and Death at the Brink of the Millennium.* New York: Ballantine Books, 1998.

Sagan, Carl. *Broca's Brain: Reflections on the Romance of Science.* New York: Random House, 1974.

Sagan, Carl. *Cosmos.* New York: Random House, 1980.

Sagan, Carl. *Pale Blue Dot: A Vision of the Human Future in Space.* New York: Ballantine Books, 1994.

Sagan, Carl. *The Varieties of Scientific Experience: A Personal View of the Search for God.* Edited by Ann Druyan. New York: Penguin, 2006.

Sagan, Dorion. *Cosmic Apprentice: Dispatches from the Edges of Science.* Minneapolis: University of Minnesota Press, 2013.

Sagan, Dorion. "The Human Is More Than Human: Interspecies Communities and the New Facts of Life." In *Cosmic Apprentice: Dispatches from the Edges of Science*, 17–32. Minneapolis: University of Minnesota Press, 2013.

Sagan, Dorion. *Notes from the Holocene.* White River Junction, VT: Chelsea Green, 2007.

Sagan, Dorion. "Truth of My Father." In *Dazzle Gradually: Reflections on the Nature of Nature*, edited by Lynn Margulis and Dorion Sagan, 8–15. White River Junction, VT: Chelsea Green, 2007.

Sagan, Miriam. *Map of the Lost.* Albuquerque: University of New Mexico Press, 2008.

Sagan, Miriam. "Model Solar System." In *Miriam's Well: Poetry, Land Art, and Beyond* (blog), July 30, 2014. https://miriamswell.wordpress.com/2014/07/30/model -solar-system/.

Said, Edward. *Orientalism.* New York: Vintage Books, 1978.

Saler, Benson. "Nagual, Witch and Sorcerer in a Quiché Village." *Ethnology* 3 (1964): 305–28.

Saussure, Ferdinand de. *Course in General Linguistics.* Translated by Wade Baskin. New York: Columbia University Press, 2011. First published 1959.

Savransky, Martin. "The Humor of the Problematic: Thinking with Stengers." *SubStance* 47, no. 1 (2018): 29–46.

Schele, David. "Linda Scholastica." In *Heart of Creation: The Mesoamerican World and the Legacy of Linda Schele*, edited by Andrea Stone, 287–89. Tuscaloosa: University of Alabama Press, 2002.

Schele, Elaine. "The Pursuasive Powers of Rosa Covarrubias." In *Exploring Lakamha'* (blog), September 4, 2010. http://gispalenque.blogspot.com/2010/09/pursuasive-powers-of-rosa-covarruibas.html.

Schele, Linda. *Maya Glyphs: The Verbs*. Austin: University of Texas Press, 1982.

Schele, Linda. "Mira, Omicron Ceti." MFA thesis, University of Cincinnati, 1968.

Schele, Linda. "Notebook for the Maya Hieroglyphic Writing Workshop at Texas." Institute of Latin American Studies, University of Texas at Austin, 1980.

Schele, Linda. "Part 2: T757 as *Umul*, 'Rabbit.'" In *The Mirror, the Rabbit, and the Bundle: "Accession" Expressions from the Classic Maya Inscriptions*, 23–60. Washington, DC: Dumbarton Oaks Research Library and Collection, 1983.

Schele, Linda, and David Freidel. *A Forest of Kings: The Untold Story of the Ancient Maya*. New York: William Morrow, 1990.

Schele, Linda, and Peter Mathews. *The Code of Kings: The Language of Seven Sacred Maya Temples and Tombs*. New York: Scribner, 1998.

Schele, Linda, and Jeffrey H. Miller. *The Mirror, the Rabbit, and the Bundle: "Accession" Expressions from the Classic Maya Inscriptions*. Studies in Pre-Columbian Art and Archaeology. Washington, DC: Dumbarton Oaks Research Library and Collection, 1983.

Schele, Linda, and Mary Miller. *The Blood of Kings: Dynasty and Ritual in Maya Art*. Fort Worth: Kimbell Art Museum, 1986.

Schele, Linda, and Khristaan D. Villela. "Creation, Cosmos, and the Imagery of Palenque and Copan." In *Eighth Palenque Round Table, 1993*, edited by Martha J. Macri and Jan McHargue, 15–30. San Francisco: Pre-Columbian Art Research Institute, 1993.

Schiebinger, Londa. *Nature's Body: Gender in the Making of Modern Science*. Boston: Beacon, 1993.

Schiebinger, Londa. *Plants and Empire: Colonial Bioprospecting in the Atlantic World*. Cambridge, MA: Harvard University Press, 2007.

Schueller, Malini Johar. "Analogy and (White) Feminist Theory: Thinking Race and the Color of the Cyborg Body." *Signs: Journal of Women in Culture and Society* 31, no. 1 (2005): 63–92.

Scott, James C. *Domination and the Arts of Resistance: Hidden Transcripts*. New Haven, CT: Yale University Press, 1990.

Sedgwick, Eve Kosofsky. *Touching Feeling: Affect, Pedagogy, Performativity*. Durham, NC: Duke University Press, 2003.

Sellars, Wilfrid. *Science, Perception, and Reality*. London: Routledge, 1963.

Serres, Michel. *The Parasite*. Translated by Lawrence R. Schehr. Minneapolis: University of Minnesota Press, 2007. First published 1980.

Shakespeare, William. *Hamlet, Prince of Denmark*. Cambridge: Cambridge University Press, 1999.

Shapin, Steven. *Never Pure: Historical Studies of Science as If It Was Produced by People with Bodies, Situated in Time, Space, Culture, and Society, and Struggling for Credibility and Authority*. Baltimore: Johns Hopkins University Press, 2010.

Shapin, Steven, and Simon Schaffer. *Leviathan and the Air-Pump: Hobbes, Boyle, and the Experimental Life*. Princeton, NJ: Princeton University Press, 1985.

Sharpe, Christina. *In the Wake: On Blackness and Being*. Durham, NC: Duke University Press, 2016.

Shaviro, Steven. "Panpsychism and/or Eliminativism." *Pinocchio Theory* (blog), October 4, 2011. http://www.shaviro.com/Blog/?p=1012.

Shelton, Allen C. *Dreamworlds of Alabama*. Minneapolis: University of Minnesota Press, 2007.

Shelton, Allen C. *Where the North Sea Touches Alabama*. Chicago: University of Chicago Press, 2013.

Siegel, James. "False Beggars: Marcel Mauss, *The Gift*, and Its Commentators." *diacritics* 41, no. 2 (2013): 60–79.

Siegel, James. *Naming the Witch*. Stanford, CA: Stanford University Press, 2006.

Sillitoe, Paul. "Why Spheres of Exchange?" *Ethnology* 45, no. 1 (2006): 1–23.

Silverstein, Michael. "Cultural Prerequisites to Grammatical Analysis." In *Georgetown University Round Table on Languages and Linguistics*, edited by Muriel Saville-Troike, 139–51. Washington, DC: Georgetown University Press, 1977.

Silverstein, Michael. "Languages/Cultures Are Dead! Long Live the Linguistic/Cultural." In *Unwrapping the Sacred Bundle: Reflections on the Disciplining of Anthropology*, edited by Daniel A. Segal and Sylvia J. Yanagisako, 99–125. Durham, NC: Duke University Press, 2005.

Silverstein, Michael. "Language Structure and Linguistic Ideology." In *The Elements: A Parasession on Linguistic Units and Levels*, edited by P. R. Clyne, W. F. Hanks, and C. L. Hofbauer, 193–247. Chicago: Chicago Linguistic Society, 1979.

Silverstein, Michael. "Translation, Transduction, Transformation: Skating 'Glossando' on Thin Semiotic Ice." In *Translating Cultures: Perpectives on Translation and Anthropology*, edited by Paula G. Rubel and Abraham Rosman, 75–105. Oxford: Berg, 2003.

Silverstein, Michael. "The Uses and Utility of Ideology: Some Reflections." *Pragmatics* 2, no. 3 (1992): 311–23.

Silverstein, Michael, and Greg Urban. "The Natural History of Discourse." In *Natural Histories of Discourse*, edited by Michael Silverstein and Greg Urban, 1–17. Chicago: University of Chicago Press, 1996.

Simpson, Leanne. *Dancing on Our Turtle's Back: Stories of Nishnaabeg Re-creation, Resurgence and a New Emergence*. Chico, CA: AK Press, 2011.

Smart, Alan. "Critical Perspectives on Multispecies Ethnography." *Critique of Anthropology* 34, no. 1 (2014): 3–7.

Snow, C. P. *The Two Cultures*. 1959. Reprint, Cambridge: Cambridge University Press, 1998.

Solomon, Char. *Tatiana Proskouriakoff: Interpreting the Ancient Maya*. Norman: University of Oklahoma Press, 2002.

Sontag, Susan. *Against Interpretation*. New York: Dell, 1964.

Spillers, Hortense J. *Black, White, and in Color: Essays on American Literature and Culture*. Chicago: University of Chicago Press, 2003.

Spivak, Gayatri Chakravorty. "Can the Subaltern Speak?" In *Marxism and the Interpretation of Culture*, edited by Cary Nelson and Lawrence Grossberg, 271–313. Urbana: University of Illinois Press, 1988.

Spivak, Gayatri Chakravorty. *Death of a Discipline*. New York: Columbia University Press, 2003.

Starn, Orin, ed. *Writing Culture and the Life of Anthropology*. Durham, NC: Duke University Press, 2015.

Steadman, D. W., L. L. DiAntonio, K. E. Sheridan, and S. P. Tammariello. "The Effects of Chemical and Heat Maceration Techniques on the Recovery of Nuclear and Mitochondrial DNA from Bone." *Journal of Forensic Sciences* 51, no. 1 (2006): 11–17.

Stengers, Isabelle. "Another Look: Relearning to Laugh." *Hypatia: A Journal of Feminist Philosophy* 15, no. 4 (2000): 41–54.

Stengers, Isabelle. *Another Science Is Possible: A Manifesto for Slow Science*. Cambridge, UK: Polity, 2018.

Stengers, Isabelle. "The Cosmopolitical Proposal." In *Making Things Public: Atmospheres of Democracy*, edited by Bruno Latour and Peter Weibel, 994–1003. Cambridge, MA: MIT Press, 2005.

Stengers, Isabelle. *Cosmopolitics I*. Minneapolis: University of Minnesota Press, 2010.

Stengers, Isabelle. *Cosmopolitics II*. Minneapolis: University of Minnesota Press, 2011.

Stengers, Isabelle. "Culturing the *Pharmakon*?" In *Cosmopolitics I*, 28–41. Minneapolis: University of Minnesota Press, 2010.

Stengers, Isabelle. "Introductory Notes on an Ecology of Practices." *Cultural Studies Review* 11, no. 1 (2005): 183–96.

Stengers, Isabelle. *The Invention of Modern Science*. Minneapolis: University of Minnesota Press, 2000.

Stengers, Isabelle. *Thinking with Whitehead: A Free and Wild Creation of Concepts*. Translated by Michael Chase. Cambridge, MA: Harvard University Press, 2011.

Stephens, John L. *Incidents of Travel in Central America, Chiapas, and Yucatan*. 2 vols. 1841. Reprint, New York: Dover, 1969.

Stephens, John L. *Incidents of Travel in Yucatan*. 2 vols. 1843. Reprint, New York: Dover, 1963.

Stewart, Kathleen. *Ordinary Affects*. Durham, NC: Duke University Press, 2007.

Stewart, Kathleen. *A Space on the Side of the Road: Cultural Poetics in an "Other" America*. Princeton, NJ: Princeton University Press, 1996.

Stoler, Ann Laura. *Along the Archival Grain: Epistemic Anxieties and Colonial Common Sense*. Princeton, NJ: Princeton Universtiy Press, 2009.

Stone, Andrea J., ed. *Heart of Creation: The Mesoamerican World and the Legacy of Linda Schele*. Tuscaloosa: University of Alabama Press, 2002.

Stone, Andrea J. *Images from the Underworld: Naj Tunich and the Tradition of Maya Cave Painting*. Austin: University of Texas Press, 1995.

Stone, Andrea J. "Introduction." In *Heart of Creation: The Mesoamerican World and the Legacy of Linda Schele*, edited by Andrea J. Stone, 1–12. Tuscaloosa: University of Alabama Press, 2002.

Strathern, Marilyn. "Cutting the Network." *Journal of the Royal Anthropological Institute* 2, no. 3 (1996): 517–35.

Strathern, Marilyn. *The Gender of the Gift: Problems with Women and Problems with Society in Melanesia*. Berkeley: University of California Press, 1988.

Strathern, Marilyn. *Kinship, Law and the Unexpected: Relatives Are Always a Surprise*. Cambridge: Cambridge University Press, 2005.

Strathern, Marilyn. *Partial Connections*. Savage, MD: Rowman, 1991.

Stross, Brian. "Palenque: The Name." *International Journal of American Linguistics* 51, no. 4 (1985): 592–94.

Stuart, George E. "Quest for Decipherment: A Historical and Biographical Survey of Maya Hieroglyphic Investigation." In *New Theories on the Ancient Maya*, edited by E. C. Danien and R. J. Sharer, 1–63. Philadelphia: University of Pennsylvania Press, 1992.

Swanson, Heather Anne. "Methods for Multispecies Anthropology: Thinking with Salmon Otoliths and Scales." *Social Analysis* 61, no. 2 (2017): 81–99.

Tarde, Gabriel. *Monadology and Sociology*. Translated by Theo Lorenc. Melbourne: re.press, 2012. First published 1895.

Tarde, Gabriel. *Social Laws: An Outline of Sociology*. 1899. Reprint, Kitchener, Ontario: Batoche Books, 2000.

Tate, Carolyn E. "Writing on the Face of the Moon: Women's Products, Archetypes, and Power in Ancient Maya Civilization." In *Manifesting Power: Gender and the Interpretation of Power in Archaeology*, edited by Tracy L. Sweely, 81–102. London: Routledge, 1999.

Taussig, Michael. *The Corn Wolf*. Chicago: University of Chicago Press, 2015.

Taussig, Michael. "The Disorganization of the 'Organization of Mimesis': The Subcomandante Unmasked." In *Defacement: Public Secrecy and the Labor of the Negative*, 236–48. Stanford, CA: Stanford University Press, 1999.

Taussig, Michael. *I Swear I Saw This: Drawings in Fieldwork Notebooks, Namely My Own*. Chicago: University of Chicago Press, 2011.

Taussig, Michael. *Mimesis and Alterity: A Particular History of the Senses*. New York: Routledge, 1993.

Taussig, Michael. *What Color Is the Sacred?* Chicago: University of Chicago Press, 2009.

Taylor, Analisa. *Indigeneity in the Mexican Cultural Imagination: Thresholds of Belonging*. Tucson: University of Arizona Press, 2009.

Taylor, Charles. *A Secular Age*. Cambridge, MA: Harvard University Press, 2007.

Tedlock, Barbara. *Time and the Highland Maya*. Albuquerque: University of New Mexico Press, 1992.

Tedlock, Dennis, ed. *Popol Vuh: The Mayan Book of the Dawn of Life*. New York: Simon and Schuster, 1985.

Tedlock, Dennis. *2000 Years of Mayan Literature*. Berkeley: University of California Press, 2010.

Tenorio Trillo, Mauricio. "Stereophonic Scientific Modernisms: Social Science between Mexico and the United States, 1880s–1930s." *Journal of American History* 86, no. 3 (1999): 1156–87.

Thacker, Eugene. "Darklife: Negation, Nothingness, and the Will-to-Life in Schopenhauer." *Parrhesia: A Journal of Critical Philosophy* 12 (2011): 12–27.

Thompson, J. Eric S. *Ethnology of the Mayas of Southern and Central British Honduras*. Field Museum of Natural History Publication 274, Anthropological Series, vol. 17, no. 2. Chicago: Field Museum of Natural History, 1930.

Thompson, J. Eric S. *Maya Hieroglyphic Writing: Introduction*. Washington, DC: Carnegie Institution of Washington, 1950.

Thompson, J. Eric S. *Maya Hieroglyphs without Tears*. London: British Museum, 1980.

Tiesler, Vera, and Andrea Cucina, eds. *New Perspectives on Human Sacrifice and Ritual Body Treatments in Ancient Maya Society*. New York: Springer, 2007.

Tiesler, Vera, Andrea Cucina, and Arturo Romano Pacheco. "Who Was the Red Queen? Identity of the Female Maya Dignitary from the Sarcophagus Tomb of Temple XIII, Palenque, Mexico." *HOMO—Journal of Comparative Human Biology* 55, nos. 1–2 (2004): 65–76.

Tilley, Christopher. *The Materiality of Stone: Explorations in Landscape Phenomenology*. New York: Berg, 2004.

Traweek, Sharon. *Beamtimes and Lifetimes: The World of High Energy Physics*. Cambridge, MA: Harvard University Press, 1988.

Tsing, Anna. *Friction: An Ethnography of Global Connection*. Princeton, NJ: Princeton University Press, 2005.

Tsing, Anna Lowenhaupt. *The Mushroom at the End of the World: On the Possibility of Life in Capitalist Ruins*. Princeton, NJ: Princeton University Press, 2015.

Turnbull, David. *Masons, Tricksters and Cartographers: Comparative Studies in the Sociology of Scientific and Indigenous Knowledge*. Amsterdam: Harwood Academic, 2000.

Turner, Victor. *Dramas, Fields, and Metaphors: Symbolic Action in Human Society*. Ithaca, NY: Cornell University Press, 1974.

Tyler, Stephen A. "Post-modern Ethnography: From Document of the Occult to Occult Document." In *Writing Culture: The Poetics and Politics of Ethnography*, edited by James Clifford and George E. Marcus, 122–40. Berkeley: University of California Press, 1986.

Tylor, Edward B. *Primitive Culture: Researches into the Development of Mythology, Philosophy, Religion, Language, Art, and Custom*. London: John Murray, 1871.

van Dooren, Thom, Eben Kirksey, and Ursula Münster. "Multispecies Studies: Cultivating Arts of Attentiveness." *Environmental Humanities* 8, no. 1 (2016): 1–23.

Van Gennep, Arnold. *The Rites of Passage.* 1909. Reprint, London: Routledge, 2010.

Venkatesan, Soumhya, Jeanette Edwards, Rane Willerslev, Elizabeth Povinelli, and Perveez Mody. "The Anthropological Fixation with Reciprocity Leaves No Room for Love: 2009 Meeting of the Group for Debates in Anthropological Theory." *Critique of Anthropology* 31, no. 3 (2011): 210–50.

Villa Rojas, Alfonso. "Kinship and Nagualism in a Tzeltal Community, Southeastern Mexico." *American Anthropologist* 49 (1947): 578–87.

Viney, Donald Wayne. *Charles Hartshorne and the Existence of God.* Albany: State University of New York Press, 1985.

Viveiros de Castro, Eduardo. *Cannibal Metaphysics: For a Post-structural Anthropology.* Translated by Peter Skafish. Minneapolis: Univocal, 2014.

Vogt, Evon Z. "Human Souls and Animal Spirits in Zinacantan." In *Échanges et communications: Mélanges offerts à Claude Lévi-Strauss à l'occasion de son 60ème anniversaire,* edited by Jean Pouillon and Pierre Maranda, 1148–67. The Hague: Mouton, 1970.

Vogt, Evon Z. *Zinacantan: A Maya Community in the Highlands of Chiapas.* Cambridge, MA: Harvard University Press, 1969.

Vogt, Evon Z., and David Stuart. "Some Notes on Ritual Caves among the Ancient and Modern Maya." In *In the Maw of the Earth Monster: Mesoamerican Ritual Cave Use,* edited by James E. Brady and Keith M. Prufer, 155–85. Austin: University of Texas Press, 2005.

Vogt, Evon Z., and Catherine C. Vogt. "Lévi-Strauss among the Maya." *Man* 5, no. 3 (1970): 379–92.

Wagner, Roy. *An Anthropology of the Subject.* Berkeley: University of California Press, 2001.

Wagner, Roy. "The Fractal Person." In *Big Men and Great Men: The Personifications of Power,* edited by Maurice Godelier and Marilyn Strathern, 159–73. Cambridge: Cambridge University Press, 1991.

Wallace, Anthony F. C. "A Possible Technique for Recognizing Psychological Characteristics of the Ancient Maya from an Analysis of Their Art." *American Imago* 7, no. 3 (1950): 239–58.

Wallace, Lew. *Ben-Hur: A Tale of the Christ.* New York: Harper and Brothers, 1880.

Warren, Calvin L. *Ontological Terror: Blackness, Nihilism, and Emancipation.* Durham, NC: Duke University Press, 2018.

Warren, Kay B. *Indigenous Movements and Their Critics: Pan-Maya Activism in Guatemala.* Princeton, NJ: Princeton University Press, 1998.

Watanabe, John M. "From Saints to Shibboleths: Image, Structure, and Identity in Maya Religious Syncretism." *American Ethnologist* 17, no. 1 (1990): 131–50.

Watanabe, John M. *Maya Saints and Souls in a Changing World.* Austin: University of Texas Press, 1992.

Watanabe, John M. "Unimagining the Maya: Anthropologists, Others, and the Inescapable Hubris of Authorship." *Bulletin of Latin American Research* 14, no. 1 (1995): 25–45.

Watanabe, John M., and Edward F. Fischer, eds. *Pluralizing Ethnography: Comparison and Representation in Maya Cultures, Histories, and Identities*. Santa Fe, NM: School for Advanced Research Press, 2004.

Watson, Dwight. "Intersection of Time." *Cha: An Asian Literary Journal* 28 (2015): https://www.asiancha.com/content/view/2136/508/.

Watson, Matthew C. "Assembling the Ancient: Public Science in the Decipherment of Maya Hieroglyphs." PhD diss., University of Florida, 2010.

Watson, Matthew C. "Cosmopolitics and the Subaltern: Problematizing Latour's Idea of the Commons." *Theory, Culture, and Society* 28, no. 3 (2011): 55–79.

Watson, Matthew C. "Derrida, Stengers, Latour, and Subalternist Cosmopolitics." *Theory, Culture, and Society* 31, no. 1 (2014): 75–98.

Watson, Matthew C. "Imitation and Society: How Boasian Anthropology Reassembled the Social." *Anthropological Theory* 17, no. 2 (2017): 135–38.

Watson, Matthew C. "Listening in the Pakal Controversy: A Matter of Care in Ancient Maya Studies." *Social Studies of Science* 44, no. 6 (2014): 930–54.

Watson, Matthew C. "Mediating the Maya: Hieroglyphic Imaging and Objectivity." *Journal of Social Archaeology* 13, no. 2 (2013): 177–96.

Watson, Matthew C. "On Multispecies Mythology: A Critique of Animal Anthropology." *Theory, Culture, and Society* 33, no. 5 (2016): 159–72.

Watson, Matthew C. "Raging Hallelujah." Review of *Staying with the Trouble: Making Kin in the Chthulucene*, by Donna J. Haraway. *Science as Culture* 26, no. 2 (2017): 271–75.

Watson, Matthew C. "Staged Discovery and the Politics of Maya Hieroglyphic Things." *American Anthropologist* 114, no. 2 (2012): 282–96.

Weaver, Hilary N., ed. *Social Issues in Contemporary Native America: Reflections from Turtle Island*. New York: Routledge, 2014.

Weber, Max. *On Charisma and Institution Building*. Chicago: University of Chicago Press, 1968.

Weeks, Andrew, Simon Martin, and Lori Conley, dirs. *Edgewalker: A Conversation with Linda Schele*. DVD. Austin: Home Life Productions, 1999.

Weiner, Annette B. *Inalienable Possessions: The Paradox of Keeping-While-Giving*. Berkeley: University of California Press, 1992.

Weiner, James F. *The Empty Place: Poetry, Space, and Being among the Foi of Papua New Guinea*. Bloomington: Indiana University Press, 1991.

White, E. B. *Charlotte's Web*. New York: Harper and Brothers, 1952.

Whitehead, Alfred North. *Process and Reality*. 1929. Reprint, New York: Free Press, 1978.

Whitman, Walt. *Leaves of Grass*. 1855. Reprint, Boston: Small, Maynard and Co., 1907.

Whorf, Benjamin Lee. "Language, Mind, and Reality." In *Language, Thought, and Reality: Selected Writings of Benjamin Lee Whorf*, edited by John B. Carroll, 246–70. 1942. Reprint, Cambridge, MA: MIT Press, 1956.

Wilk, Richard. "The Ancient Maya and the Political Present." *Journal of Anthropological Research* 41, no. 3 (1988): 307–26.

Williams, Raymond. *Marxism and Literature*. Oxford: Oxford University Press, 1977.

Wirth, Jason. "Schelling's Contemporary Resurgence: The Dawn after the Night when All Cows Were Black." *Philosophy Compass* 6, no. 9 (2011): 585–98.

Wittgenstein, Ludwig. *Philosophical Investigations*. Oxford: Blackwell, 1967.

Wolf, Eric. "Closed Corporate Peasant Communities in Mesoamerica and Central Java." *Southwest Journal of Anthropology* 13 (1957): 1–18.

Wolf, Eric. *Europe and the People without History*. Berkeley: University of California Press, 1982.

Wood, George B., and Franklin Bache. *The Dispensatory of the United States of America*. 8th ed. Philadelphia: Grigg, Elliot, and Co., 1849.

Woolard, Kathryn A. "Language Ideology: Issues and Approaches." *Pragmatics* 2, no. 3 (1992): 235–49.

Zender, Marc. "Theory and Method in Maya Decipherment." *PARI Journal* 18, no. 2 (2018): 1–48.

Žižek, Slavoj. *Less Than Nothing: Hegel and the Shadow of Dialectical Materialism*. London: Verso, 2012.

Žižek, Slavoj. *The Parallax View*. Cambridge, MA: MIT Press, 2006.

Žižek, Slavoj. *The Sublime Object of Ideology*. London: Verso, 1989.

Index

....

Ben-Hur: A Tale of the Christ (Wallace), 83
Benjamin, Walter, 10–11
Berger, John, 27–28, 171
Berlant, Lauren, 13
Berlin, Heinrich, 40–41, 109
Bible, the, 132
Bickerton, Derek, 215n60
biocentrism, 55
Black liberation, 153
Blood of Kings, The (Schele and Miller),
    34, 77, 86–87, 109
Boas, Franz, 88
bodies-without-organs, 73, 205n55
bones: and body modifications, 111–12;
    and dialectical circles, 113–14; and fe-
    maleness, 113; in Maya corn production,
    110; and Maya writing, 109; and Geor-
    gia O'Keeffe's paintings, 96, 97, 209n4;
    and Schele's paintings, 104–6; "Spirit
    is a bone" passage, 97–98, 113–14; and
    vitality, 113. *See also* Ozeki, Ruth
Bone-Spirits, 110–11
Boone, Elizabeth, 118
Bowie, David, 20, 169–70
Brassier, Ray, 80
Breaking the Maya Code (Coe), 15–16, 18,
    178n12
Buikstra, Jane, 35
Butler, Judith, 214n47

Cancian, Frank, 110
Castañeda, Quetzil, 196n37
categorization, human, 141–42, 217n104
Catherwood, Frederick, 1, 2
ceiba trees: as axis mundi, 128, 149,
    165; and Schele, 111, 149, 162, 165,
    167; Moses Morales and, 161; and
    Pakal, 36
Certeau, Michel de, 142–43
Chakrabarty, Dipesh, 198n60
chapter overviews, 20–22
Chichén Itzá, 18
Clifford, James, 10
Coe, Michael: and the CIA, 101; on happy
    accident philosophy, 16, 36; on Maya

burial practices, 31; and Schele, 18. *See
    also Breaking the Maya Code* (Coe)
colonialism: anthropology of religion,
    127–28; and decipherment, 13, 153; and
    Maya epigraphy, 5, 13–14; and Maya
    peoples, 14, 85
color, 110
commons, the, 148, 150–51, 159, 171
Comte, Auguste, 219n29
contagious magic, 178n12
conversion and love, 153–54
Copán, 79
Corn, Wanda, 96
Corn Palace, South Dakota, 110, 122
Cortázar, Julio, 145–46, 148
cosmopolitics, 90–91
Covarrubias, Miguel, 112
Covarrubias, Rosa, 112, 211n60
Cracking the Maya Code (documentary),
    53, 116, 118
crises, 65–66
Critchley, Simon, 169–70
critical theory, 74–75, 145
culture: anthropology of, 54, 198n56,
    201n3; definitional attempts, 128–29;
    and floating signifiers, 128–29, 133; Clif-
    ford Geertz on, 44; and science, 5; and
    truth claims, 128

Danien, Elin, 40–41
dead, the, 27–28, 31, 171
death, 31, 36, 59, 157, 170–71
decipherment: as Christian historiality,
    159; and colonialism, 13, 153; common-
    sensical, 194n30; and cosmology, 82;
    critiques of, 5, 177n10; cultural logics
    of, 131–32; and encounter value, 218n10;
    gold metaphor, 147; hermeneutic limits,
    136; as historical communion, 159; as
    knowledge production, 9, 21, 56, 66, 138;
    language ideology of, 124; Claude Lévi-
    Strauss and, 22; and modernism, 8–9, 12,
    177n10; and mythologization of Amer-
    ica, 147; optimism of, 9; and the past,
    knowability of, 66; Quiriguá, 78–80,

82; and rabbit sketch, 48; as reparative project, 67–68; Schele's influence on, 8; Schele's joy in, 7; Schele's popularization of, 65, 67, 71, 108, 139; and structuralism, 8–9, 91, 141; and symbolic anthropology, 172; and text-image dichotomies, 48; and thermodynamics, 86–87; transformations in, 4; and triumphalism, 7; and virtualization, 159. *See also* Schele, Linda, decipherment practices; Schele, Linda, decipherments of

decolonization, 14

deep hanging out, 54, 198n56

Deleuze, Gilles: on American books, 25–26; *Anti-Oedipus*, 75, 206n63; on books, 75; and exchange theory, 216n29; on faces, 29–30; Donna Haraway on, 92; idiot figures, 89–90; influence of, 184n58; influences on, 10; on power, 153; and schizophrenia, 89; vitalism of, 74

Derrida, Jacques: and affirmationism, 185n58; *arrivant* concept, 12; on bricoleurs *versus* engineers, 120–21, 128, 168; and floating signifier concept, 125; Claude Lévi-Strauss, readings of, 125, 127; love and ruins, 156–58, 160, 163; Marcel Mauss's influence on, 10; *The Post Card*, 122, 213n29; on scholars and reality, 61; on supplements, 181n29; and the tortoise and the hare, 73; *"tout autre est tout autre,"* 156

destiny, 29

DeVore, Irven, 44

dialectical images, 10–12, 70, 72

Diamond, Jared, 32–33

Dickinson, Emily, 208n108

disciplinarity, 74

discovery: affects of, 7–8, 85–86; coincident, 123; effects of, 66; feelings of, 85; naiveté of, 7

dissipative structures, 85

Douglas, Mary, 158

Druyan, Ann, 69

Dumbarton Oaks, 116–18

Durkheim, Émile, 65, 127, 166

Eagleton, Terry, 145, 161–62

Earle, Duncan, 40

Edgewalker: A Conversation with Linda Schele (Weeks, Martin, and Conley), 15, 58–59

edgewalking: as attachment, 95; the biogenetic and the spiritual, 95; in ethnography, 22, 58; Dorion Sagan's, 94; Schele's, 8–9, 14–15, 20, 113, 119, 136; secular-spiritual knowledges, 65; and thermodynamics, 85

El Dorado, 147–48

elimination, 27–28

empathy, 55, 198n60

empty centers, 168

enclosures, 74–75

epigraphic methodology, Tatiana Proskouriakoff's, 36, 38. *See also* Proskouriakoff, Tatiana: epigraphic methodology

epigraphy: *versus* archaeology, 5; and colonialism, 13–14; and constellations, 80, 82; and cosmogenesis, 80, 82; cultural boundaries of, 176n9; and elites, 66; enthusiasm for, 178n12; and floating signifiers, 133; futurity, insistence on, 158; and historical reasoning, 12; as historical resource, 7; language ideologies of, 124, 177n10, 216n79; and linguistic science, 176n9; and modernism, 12, 177n10; populating the past, 66–67; Tatiana Proskouriakoff's methodology, 36, 38; as science, 7; and the sky, 82; transformation in, 4–5. *See also* decipherment

erotics, 172

ethnography: and ecologies of practices, 182n31; edgewalking in, 22, 58; experimental, 14, 22–23; Claude Lévi-Strauss on, 167; literary, 12–13; and multispecific anthropology, 54; speaking nearby, 9–10, 14, 181n30; writing, 12–14

ethno-pessimism, 14, 185n56

excess and ritual, 108

exchange, 75–76, 165, 206n63

exchange protensions, 72, 75–76, 80, 82

exchange theory, 206n63, 219n29

faces, 29–30
Feynman, Richard, 93–94
floating signifiers: overview of, 124; and
anthropology, 132–33; and art, 169; in
cognition, 129–30; communication, as
enabling, 125–26; and culture, 128–29,
133; dialectical images, 72; and epigraphy, 133; hieroglyphs as, 165; in human
communication, 167; influences on, 130;
and mana, 126–27, 215n52; and mythopoesis, 132; and Schele's genius, 139, 140;
and science, 72, 133; *versus* scientific
experimentation, 132; secular readings
of, 126; and semantics, 126–27; and
the social, 130, 133; theological aspects,
124–25, 127–28, 164, 167; Benjamin Lee
Whorf's anticipation of, 163–64
Forest of Kings, A (Schele and Freidel), 51,
56, 83–85, 147
Foucault, Michel, 10, 153
Fountain, The (Aronofsky), 76, 160–61
Frazer, James, 127, 178n12
Freidel, David: and Frank Freidel, 25; and
Schele, 59, 86–89; and thermodynam-
ics, 86–87; and Evon Vogt, 33–34.
See also A Forest of Kings (Schele and
Freidel); *Maya Cosmos* (Freidel, Schele,
and Parker)

Geertz, Clifford: on Balinese cockfights,
50, 195n31; on culture, 44; human life,
views on, 53; interpretivism of, 172;
presence and textual hermeneutics, 136;
and the sublime, 94; "turtles all the
way down" story, 94; web metaphors,
44–45, 55, 192n8; writing, love for,
172
genes, 11, 72, 74
genius, 116, 119–20, 131–32. *See also* Schele,
Linda, genius of
Georgia O'Keeffe Museum, 96, 112
Gifford Lecturers, 68
gifts, 127, 159, 167, 175n4, 201n3
Gillespie, Susan, 31
greetings, 156

Griffin, Gillett: Schele correspondence,
28, 51, *52, 60*; on Schele's genius, 53, 115;
seventieth birthday party, 41
Guattari, Félix: on American books,
25–26; *Anti-Oedipus*, 75, 206n63; and
exchange theory, 216n29; on faces,
29–30; Donna Haraway on, 92; and
schizophrenia, 89

Hägglund, Martin, 156–57, 160
happy accidents, 16, 36
Haraway, Donna, 54, 59, 92, 173
hares, 70, 73
Harman, Graham, 192n9
Hartstock, Nancy, 206n63
hau, 126–27, 133, 167
*Heart of Creation: The Mesoamerican
World and the Legacy of Linda Schele*
(Stone), 41
Hegel, Georg Wilhelm Friedrich, 90–91,
97–98, 113
Helmreich, Stefan, 54–56, 82, 198n58
hieroglyphs: as dialectical images, 72; as
knowledge producers, 56–57; as originals, 158; trickiness of, 163
hieroglyphs, Maya: and color, 110; and
constellations, 79–80; crescents and
spheres in, 47; as floating signifiers, 165;
historical content, 36; *ik'*, 59; rabbits
and moons, 134–37, 140; in Schele's
drawings, *46*, 47–48; Schele's respiriting
of, 171; semiotics of, 124, 171; *way*, 131;
ya, 47
historiality, 159, 220n51
historical inference, 138
historiography, nonhumanist, 198n60
history: affect of, 66; *versus* anthropology,
43, 192n5; as commons, 159; ideologies
of, 66; love of, 153; people without, 26,
187n5
hooks, bell, 153–54
Hopscotch (Cortázar), 146, 148
human condition as linguistic experience,
125, 214n47
human exceptionalism, 53, 55

human remains, tampering with, 42
humans: borders of, 54; finitude of, 93–94; Clifford Geertz on, 44; reflexivity of, 94; and spiders, 44; studying, means of, 43
human truths, 84–85, 88–89

icons, 163
idiot figures, 89–90
ik' sign, 59
images: dialectical, 10–12, 70, 72; iconic, 163; and love, 163; mental, 171
imagination and the cosmos, 93–94
improvisation, 11
Ingold, Tim, 192n9
interpretivism, 172
Introduction to the Work of Marcel Mauss (Lévi-Strauss): on dialectical thinking, 130–31; language origins, 129, 215n61; mana, 123–24, 126–27, 166; and religion, 128; signification surpluses, 124; Slavoj Žižek on, 129–31. *See also* floating signifiers
Itzam-Yeh, 36

James, William, 68
Jameson, Fredric, 98
jouissance, 12, 183n45
Joyce, Rosemary, 36

Keim, Patrick, 121–22
Kelley, Dave, 45–48
Kerr, Justin, 51
k'ex, 31–32
Kirksey, Eben, 54
Knorozov, Yuri, 177n11
knowledge production: academic *versus* genius, 120; cultural and historical, 15, 131; and decipherment, 9, 21, 56, 66, 138; everyday, breaks from, 7, 10; linguistic, 4; performative, 152
Koselleck, Reinhart, 65
Kroeber, Alfred, 88
Kuhn, Thomas, 178n12
Kwakwaka'wakw people, 64, 201n3, 201n8

language: and affect, 85; and anthropology of religion, 215n52; as catastrophe, 215n60; and the human condition, 125, 214n47; Claude Lévi-Strauss on, 85, 127, 129, 215n61; Marcel Mauss on, 85, 127; modernist ideologies of, 71; origins of, 129, 215n61; poetic *versus* scientific, 168–69; and sign duality, 167. *See also* floating signifiers
language ideologies, 124, 126, 143, 177n10, 216n79
La nouvelle alliance (Prigogine and Stengers). *See Order out of Chaos* (Prigogine and Stengers)
Latham, Robert Gordon, 43, 53, 192n5
Latour, Bruno: on anthropology, 98; cosmopolitics, 91; on critique, 181n26; and engineers, 121; and G. W. F. Hegel, 90; on modernity, 28; and Isabelle Stengers's *Power and Invention*, 89
Lee, Richard, 44
Lévi-Strauss, Claude: and Americanist anthropology, 132; on categorization, 141–42; cut-and-paste method, 91; decipherment, appreciation of, 22; engineers *versus* bricoleurs, 120; erotics of, 172; on ethnography, 167; and exchange theory, 216n29; on language, 85, 127; life and death of, 34; Marcel Mauss's influence on, 10; on myth, 194n30; and mythopoesis, 132, 146; poetic-scientific thought distinction, 168; and Schele, 34, 61, 123; semiotic thinking of, 215n61; and structuralism, 141; substitution method, 91; on thought, 120, 213n21; *Tristes Tropiques*, 172. *See also Introduction to the Work of Marcel Mauss* (Lévi-Strauss)
life, 27–28, 53, 55–56
Lingis, Alphonso, 111
Livingston, Joyce, 148–50, 162
Lounsbury, Floyd: and the CIA, 101; death of, 99–100, 111; linguistic anthropology of, 100; and Ruth Ozeki, 21, 99–100, 107; wife, Masako, 99, 101–4, 107

Lounsbury, Floyd, and Schele: collaborations with, 18, 20, 59, 100; correspondence, 45–48, 107, 134–37; first meeting, 18, 107

love: agapic, 155, 157, 159, 162, 173; in anthropology, 156; Alain Badiou on, 150–51, 157; and the commons, 148, 150–51, 171; and conversion, 153–54; Jacques Derrida's conception of, 156–58, 160, 163; *versus* desire, 152; and drawing, 163, 171–72; and ephemerality, 157, 163, 170; erotic, 171–73; and force, 153; and gifts, 159; and greetings, 156; of history, 153; and images, 163; and liberation, 153–54; object of, 151; politics of, 151–53; and reason, 162; reciprocal, 156, 162; Jean-Jacques Rousseau on, 163; and ruins, 157–59; of Schele's amateurs, 161–62; of Schele's followers, 148–49; in the Sermon on the Mount, 155–56; as social, 152, 219n29; and strangers, 156; and theater companies, 151

Luhan, Mabel Dodge, 112–13

lunatics, 89

Malinowski, Bronislaw, 109, 130, 141

mana: Émile Durkheim's use of, 166; and floating signifiers, 126–27, 215n52; functions of, 166; Claude Lévi-Strauss on, 123–24, 126–27, 166; Marcel Mauss on, 166–67; as untraceable, 166; Slavoj Žižek on, 129–31

Map of the Lost (Sagan), 83–84

Margulis, Lynn, 65, 67, 92–93, 208n108

Markson, Elaine, 26

Masco, Joe, 64

Mathews, Peter: Festschrift proposal, 40–41; and Pakal's sarcophagus, 3, 35; photographs of, *6*; rabbit letterhead, 50; and Schele, 18, 20, 45–58, 59, 107

Mauss, Marcel: on gifts, 175n4; influence of, 130; interests of, 10; on language, 85, 127; on mana, 166–67. *See also Introduction to the Work of Marcel Mauss* (Lévi-Strauss)

Maya burial practices, 31, 41–42

Maya calendar, 29

Maya cosmogenesis, 48, 50, 69, 78–80, 203n28

Maya cosmology: animal spirit companions, 32; caves, 51; death, 36; destinations in, 122; in *The Fountain*, 160; the Itz'at, 206n73; reciprocation in, 162; Schele and, 7, 78; souls in, 31. *See also Popol Vuh* cosmogony

Maya Cosmos (Freidel, Schele, and Parker): dedication of, 33; discovery in, 79; essentialism of, 58, 199n77; hieroglyphs as knowledge producers, 56–57; Joyce Livingston in, 149; on mythology, 56; popularity of, 76; style of, 108; triumphalism of, 147; wonder in, 57

Maya culture: body modifications, 111–12; calendar system, 100; destiny in, 29; houses, 31; people categories, 29; *reducción* of, 120, 212n19. *See also* Palenque

"Maya Glyphs: The Verbs" (Schele), 19

Maya inscriptions, 4, 109, 111–12, 177n11. *See also* hieroglyphs, Maya

Maya kings, 34. *See also* Pakal

Maya Meetings, 148, 168

Mayanists, 51, 53, 165

Mayan languages: contemporary speakers, 5, 20, 84; and epigraphy, 5, 84–85, 120; Tatiana Proskouriakoff's knowledge of, 38; *reducción* of, 120; Schele's knowledge of, 19–20, 135, 142–43; *vinik* (person), 29

Maya peoples: and colonialism, 14, 85; definitions of, 176n9; as fantasy, 139; humanization of, 84–85; life expectancy of, 34; peasants, 110; writing, conceptions of, 177n10; writing, invention of, 147

Maya rebels, 33

Maya studies, 14, 75, 139, 143, 148, 201n6

Mazzarella, William, 165

McLean, Stuart, 12

meaning, 165, 204n37

Milky Way, the. *See* Xibalba

Miller, Jacques-Alain, 183n45
Miller, Jeff, 134
Trinh T. Minh-ha, 9–10, 72, 181n30
Mirror, the Rabbit, and the Bundle,
   The (Schele and Miller), 134–35
modernism, 8–9, 12, 80, 82, 177n10
modernist ideologies, 71, 73
monads, 59, 200n83
Monaghan, John, 29
monkeys, 48–50
Morales, Moises, 17, 106, 160–61
Moten, Fred, 11, 154
Motul dictionary, 134, 216n83
mythic power, 147
mythopoesis and mythological analysis,
   132–33, 146
myths: creation, 48, 50, 69, 80, 203n28;
   Claude Lévi-Strauss on, 194n30; *Maya*
   Cosmos on, 56; structuralist view of,
   141–42. *See also* Maya cosmology

names and souls, 31
Naranjo rabbit stela, 134
nearby, the, 72–73
Nelson, Maggie, 164, 167–68
Newell, Sasha, 180n25
Nietzsche, Friedrich, 36
nihilism, 66–67, 74, 133, 202n12
Noys, Benjamin, 185n58

O'Keeffe, Georgia, 96, *97*, 112–13, 209n4
ontologies, vitalist, 74
Order out of Chaos (Prigogine and
   Stengers), 86–88
Ozeki, Ruth: "The Anthropologists' Kids,"
   100–1; grandfather, 101–2; grandmother's bones, 98–99, 102–4; *Halving*
   the Bones documentary, 99, 101–4;
   and Floyd Lounsbury, 21, 99–100, 107;
   mother, Masako, 99, 101–4

Pakal: age at death controversy, 35, 109;
   as dialectical image, 11; naming of, 66;
   and/as Schele, 139–40, 159; and Schele's
   method, 136, 138–40

Pakal's sarcophagus: analyses of, 3, 35;
   central motif, 36, *37*, 75; discovery of, 35;
   as exchange protension, 75–76; fame of,
   3; and Quiriguá, 80; skyband, 75–76
Palenque: overview of, 1; as astronomical
   observatory, 3; Bone-Spirits, 111; drawings of, *2*; dynastic lineage decipherment, 36, 38, 107; ethnographic entries
   into, 1–3; excavation and reconstruction, 112; figures at, *81*; name meanings, 111; painting techniques, 110; and
   Quiriguá decipherment, 79–80; rodent
   bone glyphs, 134–35; and Venus, 2–3;
   workshops at, *6*, 18, *19*, 139, 150. *See also*
   Schele, Linda, and Palenque
Pandian, Anand, 12
paradigm shifts, 178n12
Paris Codex, 79
Parker, Joy, 56
partial connections methodology, 64
people without history, 26, 187n5
personality studies, 201n3, 201n6
phenomenology, 72–73, 138, 143, 167
play, 173
plenary consciousness, 70–71, 74
plenary events, 63–64
Popol Vuh cosmogony: Carl Sagan's use
   of, 69; creation myths, 48, 50, 69, 80,
   203n28; publication, mass-market,
   76–77
potlatches, 63–64, 201n3
power, coloniality of, 13–14
Prigogine, Ilya: dissipative structures, 85;
   A Forest of Kings blurb, 83–85; mentioned, 21, 88; *Order out of Chaos*,
   86–87; Schele correspondence, 87;
   success of, 86
Princeton Vase, *49*, 50
Proskouriakoff, Tatiana: about, 36;
   epigraphic methodology, 36, 38; and
   Festschrift proposal, 40–41; and hieroglyphic dates, 177n11; and Schele, 38

Quijano, Aníbal, 13
Quiriguá decipherment, 79–80, 82

and hospitality, 156; the past, production of, 152; photographs of, *6*; private
documents of, 24–25; and Tatiana
Proskouriakoff, 38; public engagement,
108–9, 115–16; quasi-essentialism of,
199n77; in Quintana Roo, 78, 89–91;
and Robert Rands, 17; and Merle
Greene Robertson, 17, 106; and Carl
Sagan, 8, 76–78, 123; science, views on,
39; as scientist, 167; self-construction,
131; shrine for, 31; sphere of exchange,
165; as spiritual figure, 8; spiritualism of,
160; and *Star Trek*, 26–27, 106, 108; and
David Stuart, 20, 116–18; as teacher, 116,
118; as technophile, 33; unknowability
of, 170; workshops of, 18, 20, 108, 139,
148, 153–55, 165. *See also* Lounsbury,
Floyd, and Schele; rabbits and Schele
Schele, Linda, and art: aesthetics, 122; and
decipherment, 57; *Mira, Omicron Ceti*,
104–6; paintings of, 17, 24–25, 39, 57;
relationship to, 17; societies emphasiz-
ing, theory of, 38–39; talent at, 48;
teaching, 17, 38
Schele, Linda, decipherment practices:
aha moments, 4, 12, 51, 56, 91, 173; as
archaeological phenomenology, 143;
and art, 57; colonial assumptions in, 5,
14; as discovery, 16, 79; enthusiasm for,
108, 149; entry into, 19–20; as erotic,
173; ethical issues, 221n71; as experimental, 136, 143; and fantasy, 139, 141; gaps,
need for, 164–65; and happy accidents,
16; and historical inferences, 138–39;
and historical meanings, 165; influences on, 10; and love, 134, 173; as Maya
scribe, 51; Palenque dynastic sequence,
18; Tatiana Proskouriakoff's method,
36, 38; as scientific lexation, 170; and
scientism, 51; as sincere attachment,
196n37; site focus, 120; site-situated,
135–38; spiritualism in, 8–9; and structuralism, 91–92; workshops, 20, 108
Schele, Linda, decipherments of: grammatical, 147; and rabbits, 48; rabbits

and the moon, 134–41; stela at Quiriguá, 78–80, 82; *way* glyph, 131
Schele, Linda, drawings by: of hieroglyph-
ics, *4*, 158, 162–63, 196n41; and Maya
cultural activism, 196n41; monkey
scribe on ceramic, *49*; Palenque figures,
81; rabbits, *46*, 47–48, 50–51, 194n25;
reproduction permissions, 116
Schele, Linda, genius of: Anthony Aveni
on, 115–16; bricoleur *versus* engineer,
121; characterizations of, 123; decipherment methods, 137–40; as engagement
with the past, 139; and gender, 116, 119;
Gillett Griffin on, 53, 115; nature of,
142; Andrea Stone on, 115, 120; total
conquest strategy, 115, 120; unconven-
tionality of, 118
Schele, Linda, and Palenque: attachment
to, 17; goals for, 39; insights into, 115; inspiration of, 2; Round Table meetings,
6, 18, *19*; royalty and history, 39; solstice
description, 3; and spirituality, 59, 61;
workshops, 18
science: *versus* art, 39; and culture, 5; definitions of, 39; and dialectical images, 11;
effects of, 72; and floating signifiers, 72,
133; as mystification, 28; Schele and, 39,
51, 167, 170; structuralist views of, 142;
versus systematic symbolism, 124
scientific objects, 11–12
Scott, James, 110
secular and spiritual knowledges, 65
secularism, 65, 69, 126, 201n11
Sedgwick, Eve, 181n26
Sellars, Wilfrid, 70
semiotics: and affect, 180n25; arbitrariness
of signs, 164; of death, 170–71; etymology of, 199n75; Claude Lévi-Strauss's,
215n61; of sacred speech, 132; structural,
180n25. *See also* floating signifiers
Senior Large Mountain, 32
shamanism, 162
Shelton, Allen, 12–13, 121–22
Silverstein, Michael, 45
Smith, William Robertson, 127

Snow, Clyde, 109
social realism, 127
Sontag, Susan, 172–73
soul, 153–54, 201n8
souls, 31–32, 64–65, 68
speaking nearby, 9–10, 14, 181n30
speech act theory, 125–26
spider webs, 44–45
Spivak, Gayatri, 205n58
star dust, 169–70, 173
Star Trek, 26–27, 106, 108
Stengers, Isabelle: cosmopolitics, 90–91, 130; and Deleuzian philosophy, 89–90; dissipative structures, 85; ecology of practices concept, 182n31; and G. W. F. Hegel, 91; *Order out of Chaos* (Prigogine and Stengers), 86–87; *Power and Invention*, 89
Stewart, Kathleen, 12–13
Stone, Andrea, 40, 115, 120
structuralism: anthropological, 168; and cosmopolitics, 91; cut-and-paste method, 91; and decipherment, 8–9, 91, 141; deep structures, 163; *versus* interpretivism, 172; and language, 141; paradigmatic substitution, 141; and spaces, 168; views of science, 142
Stuart, David, 20, 116–18
supplements, 181n29
symbiogenesis, 92, 94
symbiosis, 92

Tablet of the Ninety-Six Glyphs, 136, 141
talent *versus* genius, 120
Tarde, Gabriel, 219n29
Taussig, Michael: on anthropological writing, 145–46; color history book, 109–10; on fiction and nonfiction, 26–27; on mythic power, 147
Tedlock, Dennis, 76–77, 80
Temple of the Foliated Cross, 80, *81*
temporal imaginaries, 66
text-image dichotomies, 48
texts, narrative senses of, 91

Thacker, Eugene, 27
theater companies, 150
theorists *versus* writers, 145, 161–62
thermodynamics, 85–87
Tikal, 109
Toniná, 110
tortoise and the hare, 73–74
trickster figures, 73
Truong, Nicolas, 150
truth: and anthropology, 128; human, 84–85, 88–89; modernist ideologies of, 71; told slant, 89, 208n108
Turtle Island, 70
turtles, 68, 70–73, 94
Tylor, Edward Burnett, 127
Tzotzil Mayas, 32

unbecomings, 170–71
University of Texas–Austin: decipherment workshops at, 5, 20, 108, 110, 118, 148; Maya Meetings, 148, 168; Schele archive, 120, 122; Schele at, 19, 84, 86

Vienna dictionary, 134, 216n82
Villela, Khristaan D., 78–80
vinik, 29
virtualization, 159
Viveiros de Castro, Eduardo, 188n29
Vogt, Evon, 32–34

Wagner, Roy, 193n20
Wallace, Lew, 83
waste, 75
Watanabe, John, 153–54
Watson, Dwight, 147
webs, 44–45, 55–56, 122, 192n8, 193n20
Whorf, Benjamin Lee, 163–64, 168–70, 173
Willey, Gordon, 25
Wills, David, 156
Wolf, Eric, 187n5
wonder, 57, 106
workshops: amateurs at, 148, 154; decipherment, 5, 20, 108, 110, 118, 148; at

Palenque, 18; Schele's, 20, 108, 139, 148, 153–55, 165

writers *versus* theorists, 145, 161–62

writing: anthropological, 145–46; body modifications as, 111; ethnography, 12–14; as everything, 145; and mortality, 100; and theory, 145

Xibalba: and ceiba trees, 165; and dawning, 80; and death, 109; in *The Fountain*, 76; on Pakal's sarcophagus, 36, *37*

Žižek, Slavoj: on Claude Lévi-Strauss, 129–31; and "Spirit is a bone" passage, 97–98, 209n5

9 781478 008439 *